THE CONCISE
HISTORY
ENCYCLOPEDIA

KINGFISHER
Kingfisher Publications Plc
New Penderel House
283-288 High Holborn
London WC1V 7HZ
www.kingfisherpub.com

First published as *The Kingfisher History Encyclopedia*
by Kingfisher Publications Plc in 1999
Reprinted in a revised format by Kingfisher Publications Plc 2001

2 4 6 8 10 9 7 5 3 1

ITR/0701/SF/UNV(RNB)/157MA

A CIP catalogue record for this book is available from
the British Library.

ISBN 0 7534 0641 1

Printed in China

This edition produced in 2001 by PAGE*One*,
Cairn House, Elgiva Lane, Chesham, Bucks HP5 2JD

PROJECT TEAM
Project Director and Art Editor Julian Holland
Editorial team Julian Holland, Norman Brooke
Designers Julian Holland, Nigel White/RWS Studio
Picture Research Anne-Marie Ehrlich, Josie Bradbury
Maps Jeffrey Farrow

FOR KINGFISHER
Managing Editor Miranda Smith
Art Director Mike Davis
DTP Co-ordinator Nicky Studdart
Artwork Research Katie Puckett
Production Manager Oonagh Phelan

CONTRIBUTORS
Teresa Chris, Neil Grant, Ken Hills, Julian Holland, Palden Jenkins,
Elizabeth Longley, Fiona Macdonald, Hazel Martell,
Mike McGuire, Theodore Rowland-Entwhistle

THE CONCISE
HISTORY
ENCYCLOPEDIA

KING*f*ISHER

CONTENTS

INTRODUCTION

O ften, fact is stranger than fiction. *The Concise History Encyclopedia* is packed full of fascinating facts and real-life stories about the people, places and events of the past that have shaped the colourful but still turbulent world that we know today. The causes and effects of the actions and events are explained in full, giving a vivid picture of how leaders, tyrants, artists and scientists who lived hundreds of years ago have left a legacy which still impinges on people's lives at the beginning of the 21st century.

Use *The Concise History Encyclopedia* to discover past events and find out how people have lived their lives over the last 40,000 years – from Stone Age cave-dwellers to the Anglo-Saxons, from the Aztecs and Incas of Central America to the Manchus in China, and from the American Revolutionary War to United Nations peace-keeping.

This user-friendly encyclopedia contains many features to help you look things up easily, or simply to have fun just browsing through. The in-depth coverage of each period of history also makes the encyclopedia perfect for all your project work and homework assignments.

The clear, informative text is accompanied by key date boxes, colourful photographs and superb illustrations and maps. At-a-glance world maps at the beginning of each chapter tell you quickly the major events that happened during a particular time period. These are arranged according to continent or area of the world.

Whether you use *The Concise History Encyclopedia* for schoolwork or just to dip into at random, it will add considerably to your understanding of the past, and will stimulate you to explore further the lives of our ancestors.

◀ Manmade structures tell us a great deal about the past. One of the largest and most famous is the Great Wall of China. Its construction was ordered by the first Qin emperor, Shi Huangdi, around 221BC, to keep out invaders from the north. Stretching for 6,400km, the wall was built by joining together shorter walls that had been built earlier. The wall has been rebuilt many times. Most of the wall that can be seen today was constructed during the Ming Dynasty (1368–1644).

THE ANCIENT WORLD

40,000 – 500BC

This is the earliest history of humanity, as it
evolved from cave-dwellers to village-dwelling
farmers to populations in towns, up to and
including the first advanced civilizations. It was
around 40,000BC that humans first built their
own homes, made music, and painted pictures on
the walls of caves. It was not until around 8000BC
that the first farming and trading villages were
built, and another 5,000 years – or 250 generations –
had passed before important civilizations
appeared in Egypt and Mesopotamia.

▲ The first peoples lived in caves and made fire by using a bow
to spin a stick against another piece of wood and create sparks.

◄ The Ancient Egyptians believed in life after death. They worshipped
many gods, including Osiris, the god of the dead, whose image is
seen here in a painting on the tomb of Horemheb.

THE WORLD AT A GLANCE 40,000–500BC

Though there is fossil evidence that the earliest humans evolved at least 130,000 years ago on the continent of Africa, their lives were extremely simple compared with ours. By 40,000BC, humans had learned how to use fire to keep themselves warm, cook food and scare away wild animals. From being hunters and gatherers of wild fruit, berries and seeds, they slowly found out how to grow crops and keep domestic animals. About 8000BC, life became more complex as farming villages developed in the Middle East. It was much later that other parts of the world developed in this way. During the next 3,000 years, important basic activities such as building, tilling the land, pottery-making, copper-working, sewing and animal breeding were introduced.

It was not until 3000BC that the first towns were built, beside rivers in Egypt, Mesopotamia and China. By 2600BC, large constructions such as the pyramids of Egypt, the stone circles of eastern Europe, and the first temples of Peru were built. Around the same time, the people of the kingdom of Kush in east Africa were learning to work metal and Chinese astronomers first observed an eclipse of the Sun. Civilization had come into being.

NORTH AMERICA

In ancient times, North Americans hunted animals and foraged for food on a vast continent which had no towns or civilization. However, these peoples, while living off the land, still had their histories and beliefs, their medicines, tools and simple homes. The first moves toward civilization were made around 700BC by the Adena people in the woodlands of what is now Ohio. They built temple mounds, lived in large villages and made items from copper.

NORTH AMERICA

CENTRAL AND SOUTH AMERICA

CENTRAL AND SOUTH AMERICA

Farming was established in Central America (Mexico) before 3000BC, and by 2000BC, the Peruvians of the Andes mountains had also developed farming communities. The growing population lived in permanent villages and over hundreds of years these gradually grew larger and became towns. By 2600BC, large temples had been built on the coast of Peru – around the same time as the earliest stone circles of eastern Europe and the pyramids of Ancient Egypt began to appear. At the same time, the Olmec civilization emerged in Mexico. By 500BC, the Maya of Mexico were also building pyramids.

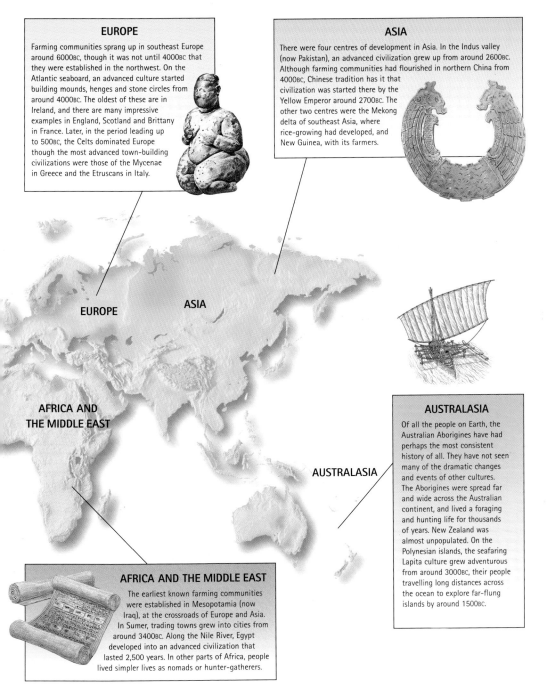

EUROPE

Farming communities sprang up in southeast Europe around 6000BC, though it was not until 4000BC that they were established in the northwest. On the Atlantic seaboard, an advanced culture started building mounds, henges and stone circles from around 4000BC. The oldest of these are in Ireland, and there are many impressive examples in England, Scotland and Brittany in France. Later, in the period leading up to 500BC, the Celts dominated Europe though the most advanced town-building civilizations were those of the Mycenae in Greece and the Etruscans in Italy.

ASIA

There were four centres of development in Asia. In the Indus valley (now Pakistan), an advanced civilization grew up from around 2600BC. Although farming communities had flourished in northern China from 4000BC, Chinese tradition has it that civilization was started there by the Yellow Emperor around 2700BC. The other two centres were the Mekong delta of southeast Asia, where rice-growing had developed, and New Guinea, with its farmers.

EUROPE   ASIA

AFRICA AND
THE MIDDLE EAST

AUSTRALASIA

AUSTRALASIA

Of all the people on Earth, the Australian Aborigines have had perhaps the most consistent history of all. They have not seen many of the dramatic changes and events of other cultures. The Aborigines were spread far and wide across the Australian continent, and lived a foraging and hunting life for thousands of years. New Zealand was almost unpopulated. On the Polynesian islands, the seafaring Lapita culture grew adventurous from around 3000BC, their people travelling long distances across the ocean to explore far-flung islands by around 1500BC.

AFRICA AND THE MIDDLE EAST

The earliest known farming communities were established in Mesopotamia (now Iraq), at the crossroads of Europe and Asia. In Sumer, trading towns grew into cities from around 3400BC. Along the Nile River, Egypt developed into an advanced civilization that lasted 2,500 years. In other parts of Africa, people lived simpler lives as nomads or hunter-gatherers.

THE FIRST HUMANS 40,000–10,000BC

The earliest human-like creatures evolved over a period of several million years. Our closest true human ancestors have developed only within the last 50,000 years.

The first peoples used flints of different shapes for making scrapers, knives, arrowheads and borers.

The earliest hominids (human-like creatures) were the *Australopithecines*. Many of their bones have been found in East Africa. They walked upright and made simple tools from pebbles. They were probably not true humans because their brains were very small in comparison.

PROTO-HUMANS

Homo habilis (handy human) appeared about two million years ago. This hominid had more skills, and lived alongside the last of the Australopithecines. The most advanced of the early humans was *Homo erectus* (upright human), and remains have been found in Africa and Asia. By learning to use fire to cook and keep warm, they were able to move from place to place.

This shelter, discovered in the Ukraine, was made of wood covered with animals skins or turf, weighed down with mammoth bones. It was built to survive harsh winters.

NEANDERTHALS

About 200,000 years ago, *Homo sapiens* (wise human) developed from *Homo erectus*. At the same time another human type, the *Neanderthal*, adapted to the colder climates of the last Ice Age, spreading through the continent of Europe and the Middle East. The Neanderthals developed many different simple stone tools, though their language was limited. They did not survive into modern times – the last known Neanderthals died out in Spain around 28,000 years ago.

THE ICE AGE

The last Ice Age, at its height around 16,000BC, had a major influence on how early people developed. It was the most recent of several ice ages that have occurred over the last 2.3 million years. With much water locked up in ice, the sea level was about 90m lower than today. As a result there was dry land between Siberia and Alaska, between Australia and New Guinea, and between Britain and Europe. This allowed people to migrate.

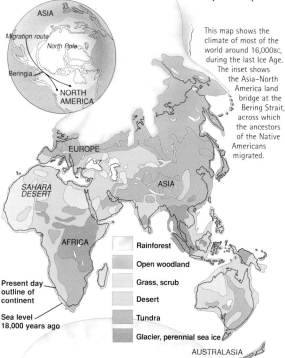

ASIA

Migration route
North Pole

Beringia

NORTH AMERICA

EUROPE

SAHARA DESERT

ASIA

AFRICA

This map shows the climate of most of the world around 16,000BC, during the last Ice Age. The inset shows the Asia–North America land bridge at the Bering Strait, across which the ancestors of the Native Americans migrated.

Present day outline of continent

Sea level 18,000 years ago

Rainforest

Open woodland

Grass, scrub

Desert

Tundra

Glacier, perennial sea ice

AUSTRALASIA

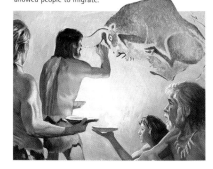

In places such as Lascaux in southwest France, Ice Age people made cave paintings, possibly to honour the spirits of the animals they hunted for food and clothing.

▲ This is a tented encampment in eastern Europe about 25,000 years ago. Using this camp as their base, the hunters gathered their food, using skins for clothes and shelter, and bones for tools and ornaments. This way of life demanded teamwork and co-operation between the hunters.

CRO-MAGNONS

The humans of today are probably descended from the Cro-Magnons, a group of hunter-gatherers who appear to have entered Europe from the Middle East and eventually replaced the Neanderthals. These people gathered fruits, berries and roots and hunted wild animals. They lived in simple caves and shelters. Around 40,000 years ago, they had developed mentally to become more like modern humans, with more ideas and a larger vocabulary. They began creating artworks, including cave paintings in France, Spain and the Sahara desert. They made jewellery, figurines, clothes, shelters, tools and hunting weapons.

◄ Using a bow to spin a stick against a piece of wood, heat was built up by friction to create fire. This could take 10–20 minutes.

The Cro-Magnons made their jewellery from stones, bones, ivory, shells and teeth. It was often buried in their graves.

Cave-dwelling hunters tackled very large animals such as mammoths, but also hunted a variety of smaller animals, including hares and deer.

ANCIENT EGYPT 4000 – 2000BC

Ancient Egypt was surrounded by deserts, yet it was green and fertile because of the Nile River. It flooded every year, depositing rich silty soil along its banks.

The Egyptians loved to wear lucky charms. Their favourites were carved stone scarabs. The scarab beetle was sacred to the Sun god, Re.

The Egyptians irrigated and cultivated land alongside the Nile and used the river for transport. They grew wheat and barley for bread and beer, and flax for making linen clothes, and raised cattle as beasts of burden. Egyptians had a highly developed religion and advanced medical, astronomical and engineering knowledge.

THE PHARAOHS

For most of their long history, Egyptians were united in one kingdom. At the head of society was the pharaoh (god-king), assisted by his ministers and administrators. When a pharaoh died, he was buried with his belongings in a tomb decorated with pictures and hieroglyphics (sacred picture-writing). His body was preserved with oils and salts, and then mummified – wrapped in airtight cloth bindings – ready for an afterlife journey to the stars. As the pharaoh was seen as Egypt's representative to the gods, his welfare in the afterlife mattered to everyone in Egyptian society.

Papyrus is a stiff paper made from papyrus reeds. The Egyptians glued sheets of it together to make scrolls. Administrative and religious hieroglyphic writing was inscribed on them by hand.

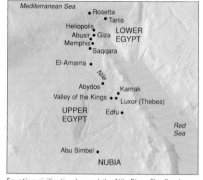

Egyptian civilization hugged the Nile River. The flood plains of the delta were rich and highly populated, though cities stretched a long way up the Nile. River-boat transport was important to traders.

EGYPTIAN SOCIETY

Most people in Egypt were farmers. They gave part of their annual produce to the local temple as taxes. Very few people could read and write, and schooling was only given to boys. Those boys who could write were called scribes. It was they who went on to become the priests and administrators who ran the country for the pharaoh. But at the heart of Egyptian life was communication with the gods.

PYRAMIDS

From around 2630BC Egyptians built many pyramids, the most famous being the Great Pyramid at Giza. No one knows exactly why the shape was chosen – the scale and dimensions suggest astronomical, mathematical and spiritual purposes. By building such great monuments, the pharaohs sought to please the gods and to leave a significant, permanent mark on history. Some of the long stone blocks above the king's chamber weighed 60 tonnes, and around 2.3 million of them were used.

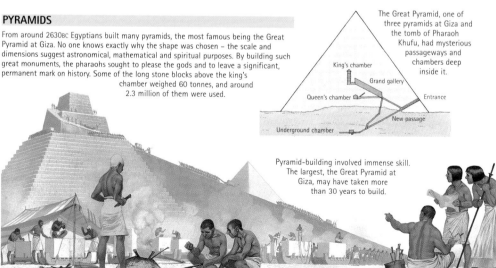

The Great Pyramid, one of three pyramids at Giza and the tomb of Pharaoh Khufu, had mysterious passageways and chambers deep inside it.

King's chamber

Grand gallery

Queen's chamber

Entrance

New passage

Underground chamber

Pyramid-building involved immense skill. The largest, the Great Pyramid at Giza, may have taken more than 30 years to build.

The funeral rites of Egyptian pharaohs were elaborate. Here a pharaoh's procession reaches Abusir on the Nile River in 2500BC. The procession enters the Valley Temple, and the embalmed body is carried up a causeway to the pyramid.

EGYPTIAN GODS

Horus was the sky-god, and his spirit entered the living pharaoh. His eyes were the Sun and the Moon.

Ptah, the creator god, invented the arts. He was the local god of the capital, Memphis.

Hathor, the goddess of love and beauty, once raised the Sun up to heaven on her horns.

Isis, sister and wife of Osiris, was the mother of Horus. She had great magical powers.

Re-Horakhty, the Sun god and Horus joined together, is shown with the Sun on a hawk's head.

Osiris was the god of the dead. In his realm in the west, souls were judged for their worthiness.

Towards this end, the Egyptians created remarkable works of stone carving. They built enormous pyramids and temples. Tall obelisks were cut from one block of stone. No effort or expense was spared to honour the gods – or the pharaoh, who was their living link with humanity. The Egyptians developed a way to preserve the body of their god-king, and many building projects were undertaken to provide him with a tomb for his eternal protection. In time, everyone who could afford it would have their preserved bodies placed in tombs, with treasures for the afterlife and sacred scrolls to guide them to it.

THE MIDDLE KINGDOM

After the time of the first pharaohs and the pyramid builders, there was a decline that lasted for more than 100 years. With no strong ruler, the people believed that the gods had abandoned them. Then, around 2040, Mentuhotep became pharaoh, brought order and restored Egypt's standing in the world. This period was called the Middle Kingdom.

The pharaohs reorganized the country and again built pyramids, although not as large as those at Giza. Some of Egypt's finest art and literature was produced during the Middle Kingdom.

Egypt was isolated from the rest of the world at this time. Ancient Egyptians were not great travellers, sailors or conquerors. But great Middle Kingdom rulers such as Amenemhat I and Senwosret III expanded Egypt's boundaries. They built forts to protect the country, and created a strong army. They even invaded countries such as Nubia to take control of gold reserves.

KEY DATES	
3300	Growth of towns in lower Nile valley and development of hieroglyphics
3000	Upper and Lower Egypt united
2920	The first pharaohs reign
2575	Old Kingdom, capital Memphis – high point of Egyptian civilization
2550	The Great Pyramid is completed
2040	Middle Kingdom – expansion and development
1550	New Kingdom – Egypt at its largest and wealthiest

THE INDUS VALLEY 4000–1800BC

The early peoples of the Indian subcontinent lived on the banks of the Ganges and Indus rivers. The first civilization sprang up in the Indus valley, now in Pakistan.

The two largest cities in the Indus valley around 2000BC were Mohenjo-daro and Harappa, each with around 40,000 people. They were amongst the world's largest cities at the time. At the centre of each lay an artificial mound which served as a citadel (stronghold). On this mound stood a large granary which, to the population, served as a kind of central bank. These forgotten cities were discovered only in the 1920s.

Seals like this were attached to bales of merchandise. They have been found not only in Mohenjo-daro but as far away as Sumer.

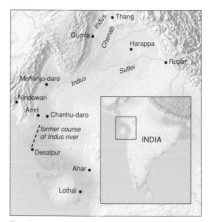

The climate was wetter in the Indus valley than today. The rivers were used not only for transport and trade but also for irrigation of the flat lands of the valley.

CITY LAYOUT

Around the citadel the city buildings were arranged in a grid pattern – administration buildings, markets, workshops, storage areas, houses and temples. Each house was built around a courtyard, and had rooms, a toilet and a well.

Buildings were made from mud bricks baked in wood-fired ovens. The citadel at Mohenjo-daro had a bathhouse, as well as private and public baths and meeting-places.

Brick-lined shafts like this are found in the courtyards of Mohenjo-daro. They may have been wells or used for cool storage of grains or oil.

These ruins are all that remain of the 4,000-year-old city of Mohenjo-daro.

FARMERS AND CRAFTSMEN

Among other crops, the farmers of the Indus valley grew barley, wheat, cotton, melons and dates. Elephants and water buffalo were tamed to work in the fields. The area had many skilled potters who used wheels for throwing pots – a new technology at the time. Harappans used stone tools and made knives, weapons, bowls and figures in bronze. They had an advanced system of waste-disposal that included the building of covered drains and the installation of rubbish chutes.

THE END OF A CIVILIZATION

No one knows who the people of the Indus valley were or where they came from. We do not understand their writing either. The area had similarities to Sumer, but there were also major differences. The city dwellers traded with the cities of Sumer. They also traded with the tribespeople of India and central Asia. The Indus valley civilization lasted 800 years, but came to an end about 3,700 years ago. No one knows why it ended, but there are various possible causes: river flooding; disease; a breakdown in trade, the economy or civil order; or immigration and takeover by the Aryans who moved into India from Central Asia. All trace of the cities lay buried under sand until they were rediscovered in the 1920s.

These are the excavated remains of the Great Bath at Mohenjo-daro. The people appear to have placed great importance on hygiene and access to water. They may have used the baths for sports and ceremonies as well.

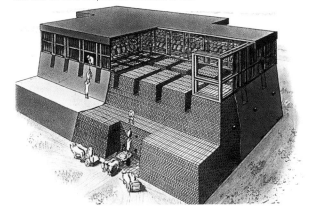

▲ The storehouses at the centre of the cities were very valuable to the inhabitants – they may have had religious as well as practical significance, since grain may have been regarded as sacred.

◄ An artist's impression shows Mohenjo-daro at the height of its prosperity. Unlike Sumerian cities, it was built on a grid pattern, suggesting planning and orderly government. The bathhouse had its own indoor well, and what was probably a granary had a sophisticated storage and ventilation system.

Bathhouse

City granary

ANCIENT CRETE 3000–1450BC

The earliest European civilization began on the island of Crete about 4,500 years ago. It is called the Minoan civilization after the legendary King Minos.

S tories say that Minos built a labyrinth (maze) in which he kept a Minotaur, a creature with the head of a bull and the body of a man. The Minoan civilization was at its height from 2200 to 1450BC. The Minoans owed their prosperity to their abilities as seafarers and traders.

Crete was well placed for trading with and influencing other areas. In the end this was the Minoans' undoing, since the Mycenaeans envied their civilization and eventually invaded.

MINOAN CITIES

The Minoans built several large cities connected by paved roads, each of them a small city-state. At the heart of each city was a palace with a water supply, decorations, windows and stone seats. Minoan craftsmen were renowned as potters and builders. They also made very beautiful silver and gold jewellery. The capital, Knossos, had the grandest palace. It had splendid royal apartments, rooms for religious ceremonies, workshops and a school.

Minoans were expert shipbuilders. They travelled round the Aegean and to Egypt in boats like this, carrying their pottery and other craftworks far and wide.

The internal walls of the palace were plastered and decorated with large, magnificently painted pictures.

DOWNFALL OF A CIVILIZATION

Advanced Minoan civilization came to a sudden and mysterious end in about 1450BC. A volcanic eruption on the nearby island of Thera had already been a major disaster, overwhelming much of Crete. The end came when Knossos was invaded by the Mycenaeans who greatly admired the Minoans and took their ideas to the European mainland. In Crete lay the roots of the later Greek classical civilization.

This figure was found at Knossus. It combines the snake cult of Crete and worship of the mother goddess. The figure is wearing the typical clothing of a Minoan woman.

The royal palace at Knossos was several storeys high and built from wood, stone and clay. The royal apartments lay round a central courtyard. The public rooms were upstairs.

The walls of the state rooms at Knossos were elaborately decorated. The wall painting shows the sport of bull leaping. The bull was a sacred symbol of power, and the ability to vault over its horns symbolized the mastering of its strength.

THE MYCENEANS 2000–1200BC

Mycenae was a city in the southern peninsula of Greece. It was the centre of the first Greek civilization, which developed after that of the Minoans in Crete.

The Mycenaeans (known as Achaeans) migrated to Greece from the Balkans around 2000BC. Mycenaean civilization began as a series of hillside villages occupied by people speaking an ancient form of the Greek language. By about 1650BC, many villages had grown into fortified towns, with rich palaces and luxurious goods that rivalled those made by the highly skilled Minoan craftsmen. Mycenae was made up of about 20 city-states.

This gold mask was found in a grave at Mycenae by archaeologist Heinrich Schliemann. He thought it was Agamemnon's mask, though modern scholars think it belonged to a man who lived 300 years earlier.

The ruins of the Lion Gate at Mycenae, the main entrance to the city, built around 1300BC. It was one of the only ways through the walls, which were built of great stones and easy to defend.

MYCENAEAN TOMBS

Before they built fortresses and cities the Mycenaeans buried their leaders in elaborate 'beehive tombs'. These were built of large stone blocks, shaped to form a great dome. One tomb at Mycenae, the Treasury of Atreus, has a doorway nearly 6m high, that opens into a chamber 13m high and 14m wide. It was once lined with bronze plates. The richness of these tombs shows that a great deal of money and effort was spent on royalty and the aristocracy. One king had as many as 400 bronzesmiths and hundreds of slaves.

This beautiful gold goblet from Mycenae clearly demonstrates the skill of the local craftsmen. It shows men hunting bulls, a common theme at that time.

Wealthy Mycenaeans valued highly the gold that they imported from Egypt. Skilled craftsmen made gold cups, masks, flowers and jewellery; even their swords and armour were inlaid with gold.

EXPANSION AND DOWNFALL

Around 1450BC the Mycenaeans conquered Crete and began to establish colonies around the Aegean Sea and on the islands of Rhodes and Cyprus. They traded throughout the Mediterranean area, particularly with Phoenicia, Egypt and Italy. However, around 1200BC, Mycenae fell to invading wandering raiders, called the Sea Peoples. Many Mycenaeans were forced to flee to other countries.

This reconstruction shows the city of Mycenae as it probably looked at the height of its power. The royal palace on the hilltop was built on several levels.

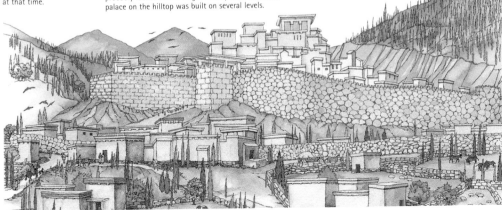

SHANG DYNASTY 1766–1122BC

The earliest civilizations in China from around 3200BC grew up on the banks of the three largest rivers: the Huang He, Chang Jiang and Xi Jiang.

Shang civilization was based around the Huang He River in the north, though it also influenced central China. Later, the Zhou dynasty extended control over a larger area.

Like the people of Sumer, Egypt and the Indus valley, Chinese farmers relied on the country's rivers for transport and water to grow their crops – paddy-fields needed floods in springtime to help the rice grow. But the Chinese also faced two dangers: major floods and devastating raids by tribes from the north and west.

This piece of bronze Shang money was cast in the shape of a spade. It may have been made to slot into a case or sheath where several coins would have been kept.

EARLY CULTURES

The first small towns appeared around 3000BC, during the Longshan period, around the Huang He (Yellow River) in the north. According to tradition, Huangdi, the Yellow Emperor, was the first emperor from around 2700BC. The first dynasty was that of the Xia (Hsia), who ruled for four centuries from 2200BC. Yu, its founder, is credited with taming the rivers by building dykes (banks) to stop floods, and also irrigation channels.

TANG AND THE SHANG

The earliest dynasty we have evidence for was the Shang, founded by Emperor Tang. The Shang ruled north China for more than 600 years. They lived in a string of cities along the Huang He, with the capital at Anyang. The city had many large palaces and temples, built mainly of carved wood. The Zhou dynasty replaced the Shang in 1122BC.

The Shang people grew millet, wheat and rice, and also mulberries for feeding silkworms, from which they produced silk. They kept cattle, pigs, sheep, dogs and chickens, and hunted deer and wild boar. The Shang used horses to draw ploughs, carriages and chariots. To begin with, they used precious cowrie shells as money, later switching to bronze. They were skilled in working bronze and jade, making highly decorated practical and religious objects.

▼ Tradition says that silk was discovered by Empress Xiling Ji around 2690BC. She was the wife of the legendary Yellow Emperor, Huangdi, who was reputed to have brought civilization, medicine and writing to China. The empress found that silkworms fed on mulberry leaves, so she had mulberry groves planted. Silk was spun into a fine textile which was so valued that it was even used as a form of money. Silk manufacture remained a closely kept secret by the Chinese for about 3,000 years.

This is an oracle bone from the 1300s BC. Large numbers of these have been found, engraved with early Chinese pictograms (picture-writing). These were used by diviners to predict the future.

KEY DATES

3000	The first Chinese towns appear, during the Longshan culture
2700	Huangdi, the 'Yellow Emperor', becomes emperor
2200	Period of Xia dynasty – Yu is the emperor
1766	Foundation of the Shang dynasty by Emperor Tang
1400	Peak of the Shang period
1122	Zhou dynasty displaces the Shang

CHINESE WRITING

Around 1600BC, the Shang developed the earliest forms of Chinese calligraphy – a pictorial writing in which each letter represents a whole word. The Chinese script we know today evolved from Shang writing. The Shang worshipped their ancestors, who were seen as wise guides for their way of life, and they used oracles to help them make decisions.

BRONZE

Bronze is a mixture of copper and tin which, when polished, looks like gold. The Shang became strong through their bronze-working, since it was a hard metal with many uses in tools, household items and weapons. Bronze was also used for adornments, artistic and religious items. It was cast in clay moulds carved with patterns. Across the world, bronze represented a technological breakthrough.

▼ This bronze Shang wine vessel was called a *pou*. It would have been used to store large amounts of wine. The high quality and intricate design show that Shang bronze-casting was highly developed. The Shang used other vessels, called *yue*, to offer wine as part of a ceremony. These vessels would have had a long pouring spout.

▲ The ancient Chinese cooked sacrificial food in large bronze decorated vessels like this one. It had long legs so it could stand over a fire.

Shang warriors fought in cumbersome armour made of bamboo and wood, padded with cloth. Early Chinese were warlike, and tribes used to fight long feuds. Centralized states such as the Shang developed to stop the feuding between warlords.

THE HITTITES 1600–1200BC

Around 1650BC, a number of small city states were united through warfare. The result was the rich and powerful Hittite kingdom.

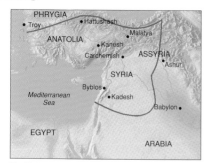

The Hittite territories at their peak around 1300BC. They later fought with the Egyptians, Assyrians and Phrygians, and their empire disappeared in less than a century.

This Hittite stela (carved standing stone) from Anatolia (Turkey) shows a woman doing her spinning, while she speaks to a scribe who is poised with clay tablet and pen.

The Hittites were made up of several tribes and they spoke as many as six languages between them. One was the language of the Hatti, the original occupants of Anatolia. The Hittites were the first known workers of iron – a metal tougher than bronze.

THE HITTITE EMPIRE

For many years the Hittites controlled the supply of iron. This warlike people used chariots, and this gave them a great military advantage. Significantly, the chief god of their 1,000 gods was a storm-god. In 1595BC, they sacked Babylonia, plummeting it into a 'dark age', though they then withdrew again to Anatolia. Gradually, they conquered Anatolia, Syria and the Levant (Lebanon), challenging the hold the Assyrians and Egyptians had on the area.

◀ The Hittites carved many works of art on boulders, shaping only part of the rock and leaving the rest in its natural form. This sphinx-like gateway once guarded a Hittite settlement located at Alaca, in what is now modern Turkey.

The Hittites adopted civilized skills such as writing from other peoples. They also introduced the horse into the Middle East from China. The men were dominant in society, and they were rich and well travelled. The Hittites reached their peak around 1300BC. However, more people were moving into the region, and this led to their downfall. The Hittite kingdom survived many threats but was finally occupied by the Phrygians who came from the Balkans to the north. The Hittites were never heard of again, but they had had a lasting impact on their neighbours.

▲ This Hittite rock-carved relief at Yazilikaya shows the protector-god Sharruma with the goddess Ishtar in the background. The relief was carved around 1250BC.

BABYLON 1900–700BC

Ur's domination of Mesopotamia was followed by many invasions. Around 1894BC the Babylonians replaced their rulers with a dynasty that lasted 300 years.

A local boundary stone from Babylon is carved with prayers that ask the gods to protect the owner's land.

The Babylonians began to dominate southern Mesopotamia under their sixth ruler, Hammurabi the Great (1780–50BC). He was a highly efficient ruler, famous for the code of laws that he laid down, and he gave the region stability after turbulent times.

Babylon became the central power of Mesopotamia. The armies of Babylonia were well-disciplined, and they conquered the city-states of Isin, Elam and Uruk, and the strong kingdom of Mari. But Mesopotamia had no clear boundaries, making it vulnerable to attack. Trade and culture thrived for 150 years, but then the Hittites sacked Babylon in 1595BC.

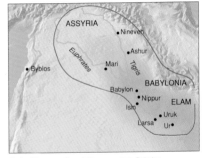

Under Hammurabi and his successors, Babylon controlled the whole of Mesopotamia. However, it became vulnerable to invasion from the north and west.

Its cities continued for 100 years under different foreign rulers. Then, for 500 years, Babylon was overshadowed by Assyria before its next rise to greatness.

EARLY SCIENCE

The mathematicians of Babylonia devised a system of counting based on the number 60, from which we get the number of minutes in an hour and the degrees (60 x 6) in a circle. Babylonian scholars developed early sciences and astrology from the knowledge they gained from the Sumerians.

▲ Hammurabi was famous for his detailed code of laws. Well known to us today is 'An eye for an eye, and a tooth for a tooth', prescribing punishments for personal crimes. The laws brought all of Babylon under a uniform legal system. They protected the weak from the strong, and regulated business and land ownership.

▶ This stela shows Hammurabi talking with the god of justice Shamash. Underneath are inscribed the laws that Hammurabi codified, for all to see. In this way, people were shown that the laws were given to Hammurabi by the gods.

Skilled archers helped Babylon to defend itself against the Assyrians and many other invaders – Kassites, Aramaeans, Elamites and Hittites. Its wealth, and its location at the meeting-place of roads from Asia to the Mediterranean, was envied by jealous neighbours.

THE ASSYRIANS 1900–612BC

While Babylonia ruled southern Mesopotamia, the warlike Assyrians dominated the north. Their kingdom lay in the valley of the upper Tigris River.

Assurbanipal was the last great ruler of Assyria. A ruthless soldier, he was also a patron of the arts, building the great library at Nineveh and vast gardens stocked with plants from all over the known world.

K̲ing Adadnirari I, the country's first powerful ruler (1770-50BC), enlarged the Assyrian lands and took the boastful title 'King of Everything'. He and his successors were fierce dictators who did not allow individual states to be independent. Assyria grew rich through the activities of its trading families, who sold textiles and metals far and wide.

COLLAPSE AND REBIRTH

As Assyria grew in size, rebellions by its conquered subjects increased. Eventually, Assyria fell to the Hurrians (relatives of the Hittites). The Hurrians dominated Assyria for over 250 years. As their overlordship dwindled, Assyria grew in strength again. Its next period of greatness

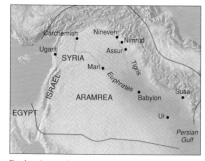

The Assyrian empire grew and shrank in phases. It reached its greatest extent at the end, around 650, covering the whole of the Fertile Crescent. When Assurbanipal died, Egypt and Babylon broke away and the empire collapsed.

lasted for 300 years. It reached its height under King Tiglathpileser I, who led brutal campaigns of conquest on neighbouring lands every year. Assyria grew to dominate the whole region, including Babylon.

ASSURBANIPAL'S PALACE

The Assyrian king was an absolute ruler with a very active involvement in all matters of state. In his magnificent palace, Assurbanipal, surrounded by his advisors, heard the cases presented by the people. The palace was large, with extensive gardens. As a patron of learning, the king had many historic records from Babylon and Sumer written down, as well as texts on mathematics, chemistry and astronomy. Literary texts such as the *Epic of Gilgamesh* and the story of the Flood, from Akkadian times, were recorded. All of these were destroyed by invaders after Assurbanipal's death, though many records survived.

The Assyrian king meets his courtiers and administrators.

The Assyrians believed that the winged lion from Assurbanipal's palace could ward off evil.

Here, Assyrian workers bring in materials for the building of a new palace, supervized by their king. Oarsmen in hide-covered boats tow a raft along the Tigris.

ASSYRIA FLOURISHES

From about 1076BC, Assyria and Babylonia were overrun by Aramaean tribes from Syria. But 150 years later, Ashurdan II and his successors reconquered the Assyrian empire. The capital was moved to Nineveh, and buildings were erected and irrigation schemes established. Assyrian kings expanded their lands to control all trade routes and suppress troublesome neighbours. The Assyrian Empire reached its greatest extent under Tiglathpileser III (745–727BC), when it included the lands of Babylon, Syria, Palestine, Cyprus, northern Arabia and Egypt.

ASSYRIAN LIFE

The Assyrians were great builders and built magnificent cities with temples and palaces. The men wore long coat-like garments and were bearded. Women wore a sleeved tunic and a shawl over their shoulders. It was not unknown for men to sell their wives and children into slavery to pay off debts.

KEY DATES	
2500	Assyrians settle the upper Tigris valley
1900	Growth of Old Assyria
1680	Assyria falls to the Hurrians (until 1400)
1300-1200	Assyrian expansion
1076	Assyria falls to the Aramaeans (until 934)
730-630	Assyrian expansion at its greatest
612	Fall of Assyria to the Babylonians and Medes

THE FINAL CHAPTER

The last and greatest ruler of Assyria was King Assurbanipal. He was a scholarly king and during his reign he created a huge library in Nineveh, his capital. The ancient records of Sumer and Akkad were preserved on clay tablets, together with literature and histories, mathematics and astronomy from ancient times. When Assurbanipal died in 627BC the Assyrian empire fell to the Babylonians and Medes.

Ishtar was the goddess of war to the Assyrians. To the Babylonians she was the mother goddess.

The Assyrians were experts at siege warfare. Their battering-rams could knock holes in city walls, and scaling ladders and mobile towers helped the men climb over. The soldiers protected themselves with large shields.

THE HEBREWS 1800–587BC

The Hebrews first settled in Palestine about 4,000 years ago. They came to Palestine from Ur, although no one knows exactly where they came from before then.

Their name meant 'the people from the other side' of the Euphrates River. Their story is told in the *Bible*. According to the Old Testament, the leader of the first Hebrews was Abraham, a shepherd who lived in Ur. Abraham travelled with his family first to Syria and then to Canaan (now Palestine), where they finally settled.

Solomon (965–928BC) was one of the wiser kings of history and he carried out his royal duties fairly. His rule brought order and peace and Jerusalem became one of the richest cities of the period.

EARLY YEARS

Abraham's grandson, Jacob (also called Israel), had twelve sons who are said to have started the twelve tribes of Israel, which were named after them. After Abraham's death, when famine struck Canaan, Jacob led his people to safety in Egypt. Later, they became slaves of the Egyptians until Moses led them out of Egypt and took them back to Canaan around 1200BC. There, led by Joshua, they fought the Philistines (Palestinians) for the right to settle and establish the land of Israel. Tradition has it that they used the sound of trumpets to bring down the walls of the city of Jericho.

After Solomon's death, Israel shrank and split into two different states, Israel and Judah – this weakened them against outside attack and led to their downfall.

THE FIRST STATE OF ISRAEL

From 1020BC the Israelites began to prosper under a succession of kings, Saul, David and Solomon. Saul was the first king of the Hebrews, and made them into a nation. David united all the tribes of Israel into one state, extending the Israelite territories and establishing Jerusalem as the capital city. King Solomon set in motion many grand building works, including several cities and the famous temple at Jerusalem. He was a peace-loving and wise king.

SOLOMON'S TEMPLE

Solomon built an impressive temple in Jerusalem, at great expense, to house the Israelites' holy treasure, the Ark of the Covenant, which contained Moses' Ten Commandments. The Temple became the focus of Jewish culture. It is said that Solomon's temple had walls inlaid with precious jewels, and that it was designed in accordance with mathematical principles learned from the Egyptians.

The Judaean desert, often mentioned in the Bible, is a landscape of astounding beauty. It was probably greener in ancient times because of a milder climate.

According to the Bible, Solomon used his wisdom well. It is said that two women came before him with a child, each claiming to be its mother. Solomon suggested that he cut the child in two, so each mother could have half. One mother broke down in tears and gave up her claim. Solomon recognized her as the true mother, and gave her the child. His reign marked the peak of Israel's history. After he died, his people argued and divided into two nations, called Israel and Judah.

TROUBLES AND DISPERSION

After a rebellion by the Israelites the Assyrians captured Israel in 721BC, and then Judah in 683. The Jews scattered in various directions, and many were carried away to Assyria as slaves. Nebuchadnezzar of Babylon crushed a Jewish rebellion in 587 and most of the Jews were taken to Babylon. During that exile, much of the Old Testament of the Bible was written down. This was the beginning of the *diaspora*, the dispersion of the Jews, which lasted into the twentieth century.

▲ This copy of a wall-painting from Beni Hassan in Middle Egypt shows a group of Semitic, or Asiatic, people – possibly Hebrew – entering Egypt to trade.

◄ A Jewish man blows on a *shofar*, a ram's horn fitted with a reed to amplify the sound it makes. It is possible these were used to bring down the walls of Jericho – or at least to frighten the inhabitants into opening the gates. The shofar is one of the world's oldest musical instruments, and it is blown on Jewish holy days. The woven prayer-shawl is called a *tallith*.

KEY DATES
c1800 Abraham and the Hebrews move to Canaan
c1200 Moses and Joshua take the Jews to Canaan
c1020 Saul becomes king of the Hebrews
c1000 David becomes king of the Hebrews
965–928 Solomon, king of Israel, reigns
721 Assyrians invade Israel, dispersing many Jews
587 Babylonians destroy Jerusalem and deport most of the Jews to Babylon

AFRICA 6000–200BC

Although the earliest of human remains have been found in Africa, not much was known until recently of the continent's history before 1500BC, except for Egypt.

▲ These are Masai women of recent times, from what is now Kenya. They are dressed in traditional ceremonial clothes.

▼ These ancient rock paintings of warriors from Oum Echna in the Sahara, date from before 3500BC when the Sahara was habitable grassland.

Today the Sahara forms a great desert barrier between northern and central Africa, but in about 6000BC that barrier did not exist. Rock and cave drawings and paintings show that the climate was much wetter, and that more people were able to live in the Sahara. The land began to dry up after around 3500BC, but desert trade towns and routes remained open, providing a link between northern and central Africa.

NUBIA AND KUSH

Egyptian culture spread up the Nile to Nubia (now Sudan), populated by black people. The kingdom of Kush grew out of Nubia from 2000BC onward. Kush was valuable to Egypt as a trading partner and a source of gold. Egypt conquered Kush in 1500BC, to secure gold deposits there but in 750BC was itself conquered by the Kushites, who founded the 25th dynasty of pharaohs. Kush never had a Bronze Age, but went straight from using stone to using iron. The capital was moved from Napata, its religious centre, to Meroë, because Meroë was surrounded

Africa, a vast continent, has many different environments in which diverse cultures have grown up. North Africa was dominated by Egyptian and Mediterranean cultures, though south of the Sahara Desert people lived without being affected directly by them.

by rich iron ore deposits. This meant that Kush became an important centre of iron-working, supplying Egypt, Babylon, Arabia and Ethiopia. Meroë imitated Egypt, and it preserved many Egyptian traditions for the future at a time when Egypt itself was going through cultural changes. Ethiopia was also an important, though self-contained, area of culture with religious traditions of its own.

These ruined pyramids are at Meroë, east of today's Khartoum. The kingdom of Meroë developed from the earlier Nubia, a kingdom once influenced by Egypt.

CENTRAL AND SOUTHERN AFRICA

Around the Niger River lived farming tribes, with a few trading towns. Downstream, the Nok nation of Nigeria became iron-working and village-dwelling craftspeople. To the east there were the nomadic shepherds and village-dwelling people of Chad. Across central Africa, Bantu peoples were moving south from Nigeria, taking iron-working and farming with them. Southern Africa was occupied by shepherds as well as hunter-gatherers known as the Khoisan.

KEY DATES	
3000	Desertification of the Sahara begins
2750	Farming begins in western Africa
700	Nubian kingdom of Kush flourishes
600	Growth of Nok culture, Nigeria and Meroë
200	Jenne-jeno, the first African city, is established

▲ A wall painting in the tomb of Sobekhotep shows foreigners bringing tribute to the pharaoh. Here a group of African peoples bring gifts prized by the Egyptians: from Nubia, gold in large rings, logs of ebony and fly whisks made from giraffes' tails, fruit, a small monkey and, finally, a baboon.

▶ Rock paintings and relief carvings are found across much of the Sahara. This cattle-herding scene was painted on a rock in the Tasili area in the central Sahara. The artist has even recorded the patterns of the individual cows.

AMERICA 1500–350BC

The first Americans arrived in North America overland from Asia in the Ice Age when the sea level was lower. Over thousands of years they populated South America.

A Folsom point, a type of arrowhead found at Folsom in North America, dating from 9000BC.

Many early Americans remained hunters, fishers and food gatherers, but in two separate areas new civilizations developed – Central America (Mexico) and Equador–Peru.

THE OLMECS OF MEXICO

In Central America some 9,000 years ago the native Americans settled down and grew crops of maize, beans and pumpkins. Small villages sprang up in which the people made pottery and wove cloth. Out of this culture, around 1500BC, the first American civilization was born. The city-dwelling Olmecs built their capital at La Venta, in western Mexico. The Olmecs built large earth and stone pyramids as centres for religious worship, and they produced huge sculptures and fine jade carvings. Many of their sculptures mix human and jaguar-like features. The Olmecs also had their own kind of writing and a sophisticated calendar system. Their neighbours, the Zapotecs and Maya, developed their own advanced city civilizations.

This fine stone bowl is an example of the Chavín people's skilled craftsmanship in stone carvings. It was the work of a sculptor living in Peru 2,500 years ago.

CIVILIZATION IN THE ANDES

The first fishing and farming villages in South America were in northern Peru. About 2,800 years ago a more advanced culture appeared, called the Chavín. The Chavín people made pottery, wove cloth on looms, built in stone and made elaborate carvings. The largest building in their capital was three storeys high. Inside was a maze of rooms, corridors and stairs.

KEY DATES	
2600	Ceremonial centres built in Peru
2200	Farming villages founded in Mexico
1200	Olmec towns and ceremonial centres built
850	Chavin culture grows
600	Earliest Maya temple-pyramids built
350	Decline of the Olmecs

▲ This is one of eight heads carved from basalt by the Olmecs; some are 3m tall. They may represent early rulers or gods and each wears a different head covering.

▶ Dating from around 1200BC, this Olmec "altar" was probably a throne. The carved figure of an Olmec ruler sits in the niche underneath.

ARYAN INDIA 1500–500BC

About 3,500 years ago the Aryans, a band of tough warriors and shepherds, fled south across the Hindu Kush mountains to settle in the Indian subcontinent.

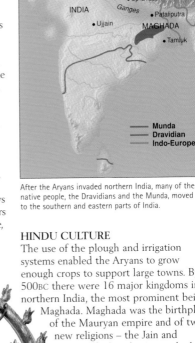

After the Aryans invaded northern India, many of the native people, the Dravidians and the Munda, moved to the southern and eastern parts of India.

Gautama Siddhartha Buddha (c.563–483BC) was a prince who lived 2,500 years ago. One day he saw the suffering of the people and left his family to search for truth. He later attained enlightenment, becoming known as Buddha. He taught a kinder faith that respected all living beings.

A natural disaster, maybe drought or disease, or a civil war made the Aryans flee from their homelands in southern Russia. They spread out to Anatolia and Persia as well as India. They lived in tribal villages, probably in wooden houses, unlike the brick cities of the Indus valley people.

THE ARYANS IN INDIA

Aryans counted their wealth in cattle and sheep. They were not as advanced as the Indian peoples, but they were tougher. They were warriors and gamblers, beef-eaters and wine drinkers and loved music, dancing and chariot racing. Gradually, they settled down and adopted many of the ways of the native Indians, becoming crop-growers and iron-workers. Among the crops was rice, unknown to the Aryans but already grown in the Indus valley.

HINDU CULTURE

The use of the plough and irrigation systems enabled the Aryans to grow enough crops to support large towns. By 500BC there were 16 major kingdoms in northern India, the most prominent being Maghada. Maghada was the birthplace of the Mauryan empire and of two new religions – the Jain and Buddhist faiths. The Aryans had no form of writing. Like many ancient peoples, they passed on their history and religious beliefs by word of mouth. These traditions, called the *Vedas* – the *Books of Knowledge* – were written down much later. The oldest of these is the *Rig-Veda*, a collection of more than 1,000 hymns, composed in their language, Sanskrit. Most of what we know about the Aryans' daily lives in ancient times comes from the *Vedas*, the ancient 'old testament' of the Hindus. Unlike other faiths, Hinduism was not started by one teacher – its beliefs accumulated gradually over time.

▲ The Aryans introduced the caste system, headed by the educated Brahmin priests who ruled the country. The Kshatriyas were warriors, and the Vaisyas were traders and farmers. The darker-skinned native Dravidians were servants and workers. It was impossible to change caste or marry outside a particular caste.

◀ One of the chief Hindu deities is Shiva, the transformer, who is both a creator and destroyer, the lord of change. He is depicted dancing in a halo of flames.

THE FOUNDING OF ROME 753–509BC

According to tradition the city of Rome was founded in 753BC by local tribespeople who had established their camps on Rome's seven hills.

Legends say that early Rome was ruled by local kings, of whom Romulus was the first. The citizens were Sabines and Latins, who united to form one town, thinking of themselves as Romans. They were influenced by their neighbours to the north, the Etruscans, and traders from Greece and Carthage, who brought in new ideas about culture and society.

According to legend Rome was founded by twin brothers, Romulus and Remus, grandsons of King Numitor. The king's wicked brother Amulius put the babies in a basket to float down the Tiber River to their deaths. However, they were rescued and suckled by a she-wolf. They founded Rome, but quarrelled and Remus was killed. Romulus became the first king of Rome.

In its early days, Rome was surrounded by Etruscans, Samnites and others. Greeks and Phoenicians also had colonies in and around Italy. As Rome expanded, the Romans had to overcome these older societies.

ETRUSCANS

The Etruscans, whose kingdom was called Etruria, lived in a group of city-states which emerged around 800BC. They were farmers, metalworkers, seafarers and traders and liked music, games and gambling. They were greatly influenced by the Greeks, adopting the Greek alphabet, wearing himaton (robes) and believing in Greek gods. Many of their ways were passed to the Romans, who eventually took Greek-style culture to its ultimate expression.

Legend has it that seven successive kings ruled Rome for 240 years. Kings did not have complete power – they had to contend with an assembly of nobles, who grew more influential as time passed.

KINGS OF ROME

The kings of Rome wore togas with purple borders. In processions the kings were preceded by standard-bearers who carried a *fasces* (a bundle of rods and an axe blade), a symbol of power representing the king's right to rule over everyone else.

This sarcophagus of an Etruscan husband and wife was made around 510BC. Women had more status in Etruscan society than they did among Greeks or Romans, where they were kept in the background.

An assembly had a say in electing the king and what he could do, especially in war. The kings formed armies to defend Rome. There were arguments between the kings and the patricians (the leading families). The kings represented the old ways, and urban Rome was changing. The new élite of patricians eventually overthrew the monarchy in 509BC, and declared Rome a republic. It was the first republic in the history of the world. The Romans did not plan to become a great imperial power – at first they wanted simply to protect themselves and fight off their interfering neighbours. However, within 500 years, Rome was to become the centre of the Western world, taking over from the Greeks.

KEY DATES

800	The Etruscan civilization emerges
753	Traditional date for the founding of Rome
509	Foundation of the Roman Republic
400	Decline of Etruria

The Etruscans left little writing, though their paintings were vivid. This one from a tomb shows lyre and flute players.

▲ A *fasces* was a symbol of power in Rome. The wooden rods symbolized punishment and the axe represented life and death.

◀ This decorated Etruscan tomb at Tarquinia, from around 500BC, shows the influence of Greek art on the Etruscans. It was called the Tomb of the Augurs (diviners or soothsayers).

BABYLON REVIVED 626–539BC

Tribespeople from the west, called Chaldeans, migrated into Assyria and Babylonia from about 1100BC. Several Chaldeans served as kings under their Assyrian overlords.

Nebuchadnezzar reigned for 43 years and his reign was marked by many military campaigns. Twice he subdued revolts in Judah, and when Phoenicia rebelled, he besieged its chief port, Tyre, for thirteen years.

I n 626BC, a Chaldean king called Nabopolassar took power, declared Babylonia independent and threw off the Assyrian yoke. Nabopolassar then crushed the Assyrians in 612BC. His son Nebuchadnezzar drove the Egyptians back into Egypt and took Syria.

NEBUCHADNEZZAR

Nebuchadnezzar was one of the most famous kings of Babylonia. He came to power in about 605BC. His story is told in the Bible, in the *Book of Daniel*. He invaded many of the former Assyrian lands and the deserts west of Babylon. Among other conquests, Nebuchadnezzar captured Jerusalem and forced thousands of Jews to live in Babylon as prisoners because they had been rebellious. He made Babylon the master of all the lands within the Fertile Crescent.

BABYLON

Nebuchadnezzar devoted most of his time to making Babylon still more beautiful, a capital of the world. He had huge walls built around the city, and he named the main gate after the

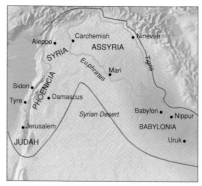

The map shows Nebuchadnezzar's Babylonian empire at its fullest extent, controlling the whole of the lands known as the Fertile Crescent.

goddess Ishtar. He also built the Hanging Gardens – stepped gardens overlooking the city. He built a large bridge over the Euphrates River, and an enormous ziggurat, the Temple of Marduk or Bel (the 'tower of Babel'). Nebuchadnezzar built himself a fine palace and he also improved the other cities. He encouraged the worship of the old god Marduk, seeking to revive Babylon's and Sumer's former greatness. Nebuchadnezzar ruled for more than 40 years but in his later years he is believed to have gone mad.

▲ Flanked by lions and owls, the goddess Ishtar wears a crown of lunar horns. Ishtar was the chief goddess of the Babylonians.

▶ Babylon was a seafaring nation, situated on the Euphrates River. Great reed boats were built that travelled as far as India and east Africa. It was also the focus of land-routes from Asia to the West.

THE CITY OF BABYLON

The Greek historian, Herodotus, described Babylon as the most splendid city in the world. It was already ancient when Nebuchadnezzar rebuilt it with new temples, palaces, roads, walls, gates and a bridge across the Euphrates. The Temple of Marduk, or Bel, a Sumerian-style ziggurat, was very tall and became known as the Tower of Babel. The Greeks regarded the Hanging Gardens as one of the wonders of the world. Babylon was a metropolis with markets and workshops selling and making everything imaginable. It supplied Greeks, Indians, Persians and Egyptians with all kinds of goods.

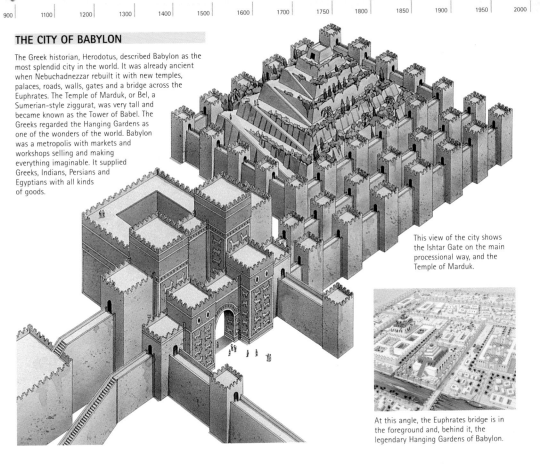

This view of the city shows the Ishtar Gate on the main processional way, and the Temple of Marduk.

At this angle, the Euphrates bridge is in the foreground and, behind it, the legendary Hanging Gardens of Babylon.

DECLINE AND FALL

The great Babylonian empire survived for only six years after Nebuchadnezzar died. His son, Awil-Marduk (given the name of 'Evil Merodach' in the Bible), reigned for three years before being assassinated. Two other kings, one of them a child, reigned for a period of only three more years.

Then a Syrian prince, Nabu-Na'id, seized power in Babylon, and tried to persuade the people to worship his own god, Sin,

rather than Marduk. He made Belsharusur (Belshazzar) co-ruler.

Meanwhile, in Persia, a new young king, Cyrus II, had risen to power after taking the throne in 557BC. He had ambitions to take over Mesopotamia and found a Persian empire. In pursuit of this goal, he invaded Babylonia and captured the city of Babylon in 539BC. Nabu-Na'id was deposed and his son killed by the invading forces. Cyrus the Great, as he became known, freed the rebellious Jews who had been made captive in 586BC by the young Nebuchadnezzar.

Babylonia was then ruled by the Persians for more than two relatively peaceful and stable centuries, until the time of another youthful king, Alexander the Great, who defeated the Persians and captured Babylon in 331BC, making it his capital.

KEY DATES
853 Assyria assumes control of Babylon
626 Babylonians rebel against the Assyrians
612 Nineveh (Assyria) sacked by the Babylonians and the Medes
604 Nebuchadnezzar becomes king – Babylon's peak
539 Babylon conquered by Cyrus the Great of Persia

THE PERSIAN EMPIRE 559–331BC

Iran used to be known as Persia. Its people comprised two groups, the Medes and the Persians, who migrated to Persia from central Asia about 2,800 years ago.

This frieze was carved in low relief on a thin stone at the palace of Apadana, Persepolis. These works of art covered the walls and stairways of the palace.

Darius I (548–486BC) was a great general who extended the empire east and west, reorganizing it into 20 provinces. He built good roads as well as a new royal capital at Persepolis. From Lydia in Anatolia he introduced gold and silver money to Persia. Darius called himself *Shahanshah*, king of kings.

A t first the Medes were very powerful. Then, nearly 2,550 years ago, Cyrus, the ruler of the Persians, rebelled against the Medes and seized control. Cyrus the Great made Persia the centre of a mighty new empire. His capital was at Ecbatana on the Silk Road, now buried under the modern city of Hamadan.

CONQUERING KINGS

Cyrus commanded an army of cavalry and skilled archers. Taking advantage of the weaknesses of his neighbours, he conquered an empire extending from the Mediterranean to Afghanistan. His son Cambyses invaded Egypt. The Persians gained the support of their subjects by ruling fairly. Darius I eventually extended the empire into India and Greece. He reorganized the empire, appointing *satraps* (governors) to each province. They paid him taxes in cereals, silver and agricultural produce.

UNITING THE ANCIENT WORLD

Darius built roads and market towns to reach all the parts of his huge empire, and encouraged trade by introducing a standard coinage. The Persians controlled the western end of the Silk Road from China, and all trade from India to the Mediterranean. This wealthy cosmopolitan empire linked most of the ancient civilizations of the time. However, it relied on the strength of its rulers. Eventually, the Greeks brought the empire down and took it over.

▶ The tomb of Darius was built at Pasargadae in Iran. After his death, the high point of the Persian empire had passed and it went into a steady decline.

▲ This is a foot-soldier of the Persian army. The army was successful because of its clever use of strategy. It covered tremendous distances during its campaigns.

RELIGIOUS TEACHING

In religion the Persians followed the teachings of a Persian prophet named Zarathustra – in Greek, Zoroaster. Zoroaster had adapted the ancient Persian tribal religion, which the Persians had brought with them from central Asia. They worshipped one god, Ahura Mazda, who they believed was locked in divine battle with Ahriman (representing sleep) and Satan (representing evil).

Although Zoroastrianism did not become a world religion, it later influenced many other faiths including Christianity. This influence can be clearly seen in the biblical *Book of Revelations*.

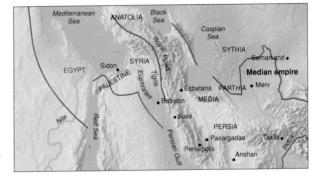

This map shows the Persian empire at its greatest extent under Darius. Susa became its administrative centre and Persepolis was its centre of state. The Royal Road was built to speed up communications.

KEY DATES

c850–750 The Medes and Persians migrate into Iran
c600 Zoroaster reforms the ancient Persian religion
559–525 Cyrus the Great creates the Persian empire
521–486 Darius expands empire to its high point
480 Greeks halt Persian expansion at Salamis
331 Fall of Persia to Alexander the Great

An impression from a cylinder seal, with cuneiform writing on the left, shows Darius I hunting a lion from a chariot with a bow and arrow. The winged figure is an image of the god Ahura Mazda, the chief god of the Persians.

Darius built himself a grand palace in his new capital city of Persepolis. The staircase of the palace was carved with this procession of dignitaries in ceremonial attire.

THE CLASSICAL WORLD

499BC – AD500

This was the great age of ancient Greece and Rome. These two extraordinary civilizations were responsible for shaping much of the world we live in today. By about the 1st century BC, the ancient world was dominated by four empires. The Roman empire was the most powerful, stretching from Europe to north Africa. In the Far East, the Han dynasty controlled almost all of what is now China, and the Middle East was ruled by the Sassanids. In India, the Gupta family held power. But, by about AD450, these four empires had collapsed.

▲ Sages and philosophers traditionally influenced Chinese society, but they came under attack during the modernizing Qin period.

◄ The Temple of Olympian Zeus in Athens, Greece, was begun in the 6th century BC but not completed until the 2nd century BC.

THE WORLD AT A GLANCE 499BC – AD500

The classical civilizations which thrived during this period set many trends and patterns for later times. Discoveries by the Greeks form the foundation of the modern knowledge of biology, mathematics, physics, literature, philosophy and politics. Alexander the Great spread Hellenistic (Greek) ideas into much of Asia. Later, by AD100, the Romans took Hellenistic culture further afield into Europe and north Africa. Further east, the Han dynasty controlled large areas of China, and the Guptas spread classical Hindu culture throughout much of India.

In these empires, life was mainly secure and peaceful, with strong governments and armies. But they soon came under attack from tribes of nomads called barbarians, and the cost of fighting these was high. By about AD450 the great empires had collapsed. At about the same time the city of Teotihuacán in Central America was at its height. Its neighbours, the Mayan people, built great cities and roads, and dominated Central America until the 15th century.

NORTH AMERICA

North American tribes were spread thinly across the continent. They generally lived quite simple lives, hunting, gathering and farming in a wide variety of environments. But in the Ohio area the Hopewell culture built towns and ceremonial mounds, marking the rise of the first civilization north of Mexico. Around AD500, the Anasazi culture began to develop in Utah, Arizona and New Mexico.

NORTH AMERICA

CENTRAL AND SOUTH AMERICA

CENTRAL AND SOUTH AMERICA

In Mexico and in Peru, a number of civilizations grew up. They had their greatest periods between AD1 and AD600. In Mexico, the great trading city of Teotihuacán, with its pyramids and palaces led the way. The Maya were beginning a civilization that would develop writing and astronomy. Quite separately, in Peru, the city of Tiahuanaco grew, high in the Andes mountains, near Lake Titicaca. On the Peruvian coast, the Chavin, Nazca and Moche cultures also began to establish themselves.

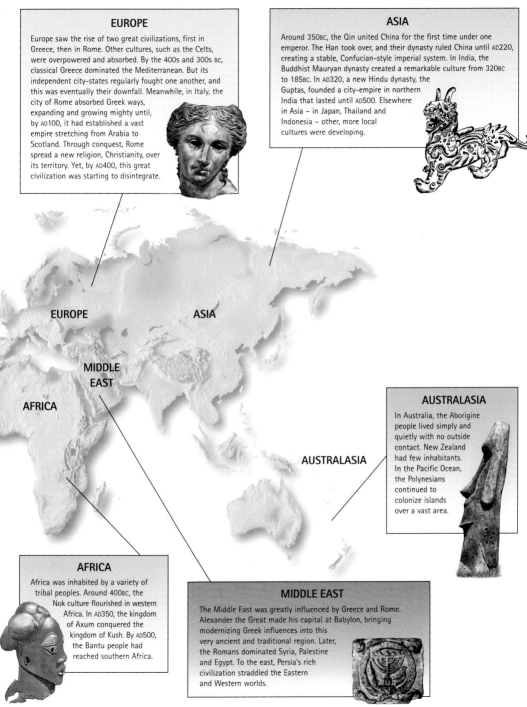

EUROPE

Europe saw the rise of two great civilizations, first in Greece, then in Rome. Other cultures, such as the Celts, were overpowered and absorbed. By the 400s and 300s BC, classical Greece dominated the Mediterranean. But its independent city-states regularly fought one another, and this was eventually their downfall. Meanwhile, in Italy, the city of Rome absorbed Greek ways, expanding and growing mighty until, by AD100, it had established a vast empire stretching from Arabia to Scotland. Through conquest, Rome spread a new religion, Christianity, over its territory. Yet, by AD400, this great civilization was starting to disintegrate.

ASIA

Around 350BC, the Qin united China for the first time under one emperor. The Han took over, and their dynasty ruled China until AD220, creating a stable, Confucian-style imperial system. In India, the Buddhist Mauryan dynasty created a remarkable culture from 320BC to 185BC. In AD320, a new Hindu dynasty, the Guptas, founded a city-empire in northern India that lasted until AD500. Elsewhere in Asia – in Japan, Thailand and Indonesia – other, more local cultures were developing.

EUROPE

ASIA

MIDDLE
EAST

AFRICA

AUSTRALASIA

AUSTRALASIA

In Australia, the Aborigine people lived simply and quietly with no outside contact. New Zealand had few inhabitants. In the Pacific Ocean, the Polynesians continued to colonize islands over a vast area.

AFRICA

Africa was inhabited by a variety of tribal peoples. Around 400BC, the Nok culture flourished in western Africa. In AD350, the kingdom of Axum conquered the kingdom of Kush. By AD500, the Bantu people had reached southern Africa.

MIDDLE EAST

The Middle East was greatly influenced by Greece and Rome. Alexander the Great made his capital at Babylon, bringing modernizing Greek influences into this very ancient and traditional region. Later, the Romans dominated Syria, Palestine and Egypt. To the east, Persia's rich civilization straddled the Eastern and Western worlds.

41

CLASSICAL GREECE 600–337BC

Ancient Greece was made up of independent city-states, each with its own laws and customs. Here, the Greeks created a new society with new ideas.

Athens led the way in the development of richly painted pottery.

Each city-state or *polis* grew up on the plains, and the mountains around them provided natural limits and defences. Citizens built high, strong walls around their cities, and an *acropolis* (fort) was erected on a high place inside the walls. At the heart of each city was an *agora*, a large open space used for meetings and markets.

The Aegean Sea was well placed for the founding of a maritime civilization, with cities dotted along both coastlines, and easy access to the Mediterranean Sea.

CITIES AND COLONIES

The two most important city-states were Athens and Sparta. There were many other cities too, such as Corinth, Chalcis, Miletos, Smyrna and Eretria, each with their own way of life, customs and forms of government. The city-states expanded to build colonies northwards on the Black Sea, in Cyrenaica on the coast of north Africa (Libya), Sicily, southern Italy, and even as far away as the southern coasts of France and Spain. Greek city-states were very competitive with each other.

GREEK CULTURE

The Greeks created a new society with new ideas. They fought hard for their freedom, especially against the Persians who threatened Greece. Being traders, sailors and adventurers, the Greeks influenced many faraway cultures. Philosophers, doctors and scientists taught a new way of thinking based on observation and discussion. Old rural traditions died off as the cities grew to dominate the countryside. New art, architecture and sciences were created.

A Greek colonizing expedition, around 500BC, with traders drawing up their ships on the beach to start business. The newly built walled city contained a marketplace, temples, law courts and council chambers as well as houses, workshops and defences.

◄ At the battle of Salamis, c.480BC, 380 Greek ships, called *triremes*, faced a Persian force of 1,200 ships. The more mobile triremes drove the Persians into a confused huddle. Persian defeats on land and at sea led them to withdraw from Greece.

EDUCATION

The sons of freemen were sent to school, while girls were taught weaving and household skills by their mothers. Starting at the age of six or seven, the boys learned reading, writing, dancing, music and athletics. They wrote on wax tablets, using a stick called a *stylus*.

◀ Greek schoolchildren study a number of subjects in a class with their tutors.

▼ This painting shows a schoolboy being tested by one of his tutors.

DISUNITY BETWEEN CITY-STATES

Athens, Sparta and other city-states united to fight off Persian invasions for 60 years, and triumphed at the battles of Marathon and Salamis around 480BC. However, from 431BC they spent more than 25 years fighting each other in the Peloponnesian War because Sparta feared the growth of Athenian power. The independent Greek cities therefore never became united as one country. This disunity eventually resulted in an invasion around 330BC by Philip II of Macedon, father of Alexander the Great.

KEY DATES

800s	The first city-states founded in Greece
594	Reform of the Athenian constitution
540s	Persians conquer Ionia (eastern Aegean)
480	Persian invasion ends
431–404	Peloponnesian Wars, Athens against Sparta
404	Athens falls to Sparta
371	Sparta declines – Thebes now main city-state
337	Philip of Macedon invades Greece

A silver four drachma 'owl' piece was the most common coin in the ancient Greek world. Issued in Athens, one side carried a picture of Athena, goddess of wisdom and patron and protector of Athens. The other side carried the picture of an owl, symbol of Athena, carrying an olive branch.

Greek philosophers have made a great impact on history, and their works are still studied today. The free-thinking atmosphere in Athens stimulated much enquiry and discussion on many different subjects. Herodotus and Thucydides were famous Greek historians, and Plato, Socrates and Aristotle were philosophers and scientists.

43

CHINA: THE QIN DYNASTY 221–206BC

The warlike Qin tribes of western China conquered their neighbours from 350BC onwards. By 221BC they had built the empire from which China takes its name.

King Zheng of Qin (pronounced *Chin*) united most of China in just ten years, ending the Warring States period. Zheng changed his name to Shi Huangdi (meaning 'First Emperor') and founded the first imperial dynasty of China.

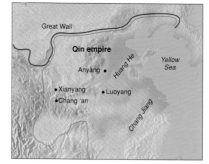

For the first time, China was united. The Qin built the Great Wall to protect it from tribes from the north. The Qin capital was Xianyang on the upper Yellow River, the area where the Qin originated.

The ancient Chinese were great inventors. They invented the wheelbarrow which they used to carry both goods and people in the 2nd century BC – Europe only adopted it 1,000 years later.

IMPERIAL CHINA

Shi Huangdi reorganized the government, bringing everything under central control. He standardized all weights and measures, Chinese writing and even the width of wagon wheels, made laws and institutions in the Qin tradition, and introduced a single currency. He was a ruthless modernizer, abolishing the powers of the feudal aristocracy and sending out administrators to run the regions. He built roads and canals, and improved farming by introducing irrigation and drainage schemes. In order to protect China from barbarians, Shi Huangdi began the lengthy construction of the Great Wall, much of which still exists today. He established imperial traditions which remained quite consistent through different dynastic periods over 2,000 years. In 221BC, Shi Huangdi destroyed many traditional literary works, including those of Confucius, and even executed 400 scholars, to ensure modernization.

THE MANDATE OF HEAVEN

Shi Huangdi was a warrior who used cavalry rather than chariots. He was used to being obeyed, and some of his actions made him very unpopular. Yet he commanded respect and achieved results, and he used his power to make changes quickly and to unite China. He also had principles. He believed that the emperor had been given the 'mandate of heaven' by the gods, and that he must earn the support of the gods by governing well. This principle meant that the emperor could also be deposed if he misgoverned the country.

Sages and philosophers traditionally influenced Chinese society and government and also played a religious role. As preservers of knowledge, they came under attack during the modernizing Qin period.

Life was bustling in a typical Qin town of a few thousand people, with its market, buildings and defences.

KEY DATES

- **350s** Qin becomes a militaristic state
- **315** Qin becomes the leading state in China
- **256** Qin annexes the state of Zhou (Luoyang)
- **230** King Qin Zheng begins to unify China by force
- **221** Qin dynasty unites the country for the first time in one empire
- **214** To protect China from Hun raids, construction of the Great Wall begins
- **212** Shi Hunagdi has all historical documents burnt, books are banned, and Chinese script standardized
- **209–202** Civil war between competing warlords
- **202** Founding of the Han dynasty (to AD9) by Liu Bang

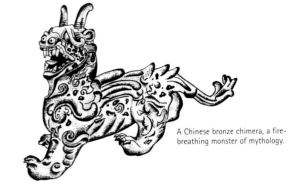

A Chinese bronze chimera, a fire-breathing monster of mythology.

THE QIN LEGACY

Shi Huangdi died in 210BC. Four years later the Qin dynasty was overthrown because the changes and laws they made were too harsh. A civil war broke out. However, the idea of a united empire had become fixed in the minds of the people. An ordinary man, named Liu Bang, who had become a Qin official, founded a new dynasty and, as a result, gained popular support. The Han dynasty was to rule for 400 years, on the basis that Shi Huangdi had established.

Shi Huangdi's tomb housed his body and possessions for use in the afterlife. It also contained 7,000 larger-than-life terracotta soldiers. Each face was realistic and may have represented the actual face of a specific soldier.

THE GREAT WALL OF CHINA

The Qin used large numbers of forced labourers to build much of the Great Wall. It was 2,250km long and built from packed earth and rubble. Stone, bricks and mortar were added later. The scale of this operation shows how important it was to the Chinese to keep out the raiding tribes of the north. These tribes preyed on Chinese security and prosperity, and China suffered greatly in loss and disruption before the wall was built and the raiders beaten off.

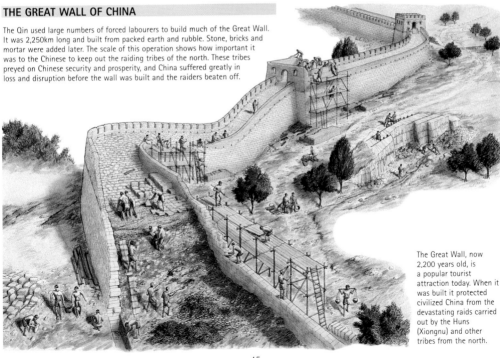

The Great Wall, now 2,200 years old, is a popular tourist attraction today. When it was built it protected civilized China from the devastating raids carried out by the Huns (Xiongnu) and other tribes from the north.

45

AFRICA 500BC – AD500

Most of Africa was unaffected by outside influences. In western Africa, new nations were being formed, and migrations were changing southern Africa.

The introduction of the camel to the Sahara brought big changes around 100BC. Trade caravans were able to cross the desert carrying gold, ivory, gums, spices and slaves. Trading towns became established in west Africa: Jenne-jeno, Niani, Yelwa and Nok were on rivers or at the edges of deserts and rainforests. These towns were the capitals of the first budding African states. North-south trade passed through Meroë and Axum, bypassing the Sahara into regions now known as Chad, Rwanda and Kenya.

This terracotta head from Nok is a fine example of sculpture that flourished from 400BC to AD200.

AXUM

Meroë collapsed in 350BC, and Axum, on the Red Sea coast of Ethiopia, grew rich exporting ivory, precious stones and perfumes to Arabia, Greece and Rome, reaching its peak in AD350. Around that time its king, Ezana, adopted Christianity. Cities and great monoliths were built. Axum thrived until AD1000.

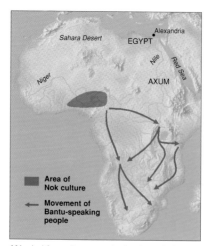

Area of Nok culture

Movement of Bantu-speaking people

Africa had four main centres of cultural growth: Axum (Ethiopia), the Berber north African coast, negro west Africa and the developing Bantu areas further south.

BANTU EXPANSION

Farming Bantu-speaking people from Nigeria gradually migrated south and east, and by AD500 they had occupied central and southern Africa, leaving the rainforests to the pygmies and the Kalahari desert to the Khoisan bushmen. On Africa's east coast the Bantu had started to trade with Greeks and Romans.

Greek trading missions on the east African coast bought medicinal herbs, aromatic gums, jewels and gold from the Bantu-speaking tribespeople of the hinterlands.

The leaders of Axum were very religious. They built tall monoliths like this at places of spiritual or strategic importance.

To smelt iron, iron ore was put into an earthen furnace. Bellows were then used to raise its temperature to extract metal from the ore.

JUDEA 600BC – AD135

Since their 60-year exile in Babylon from 597BC, the Jews, with their different religious beliefs, had grown more and more separate from their near-eastern neighbours.

The Jews worshipped one god, Yahweh, built synagogues and observed strict religious laws. On returning from exile in Babylon in 538BC, they emphasized the Jewish law and beliefs, setting themselves apart from non-Jews, or Gentiles. Palestine was under Greek rule and many Jews fought to stop their influence destroying Jewish traditions.

ROMAN PALESTINE

After Greek rule, Judea was independent for nearly 80 years before being conquered by Rome. The Romans appointed Herod as king of Judea in 37BC. Jewish people were free to travel

The *menorah*, a Jewish ceremonial candlestick, was shaped by Moses to signify the seven days of Creation. One stood in the Temple at Jerusalem.

and trade, and many left to settle elsewhere. When Pontius Pilate became Judea's Roman governor in AD26, life became hard for the Jews. They loathed the Romans and their taxes. After much rebelliousness, the Romans forced the Jews to leave Judea in AD135.

The Western Wall in Jerusalem is at the site of the Temple which was destroyed by the Romans in AD70.

The ancient fortress of Masada is where besieged Jewish rebels committed suicide in AD132 rather than surrender to the Romans.

THE ROMAN REPUBLIC 509–27BC

Rome was by now run by patricians (the ruling class). They expanded Rome's interests, first in Italy and later throughout the Mediterranean.

There followed a struggle between the patricians and *plebeians* (ordinary people), which led to the writing of a legal code and to plebeian influence in government. This formed the backbone of the Republic. Seeking protection from attack, the Romans entered a series of wars which, by 270BC, gave them control of most of Italy. Rome soon clashed with Carthage over trade in the Mediterranean. The Punic Wars that followed lasted 60 years. During this period the Carthaginian emperor, Hannibal, led his army across the Alps to invade Italy. Following a series of victories by Hannibal the brilliant Roman general, Scipio, set off to Africa to attack Carthage. This forced Hannibal to return home, and Scipio finally defeated the Carthaginians. The Romans soon established new cities, building order and prosperity and giving conquered peoples a form of Roman

Jars like this *amphora* were used to store and transport olive oil and wine throughout the Roman Empire.

The Colosseum in Rome, an enormous stadium, was used for gladiatorial contests, sports and the gory killings of animals, captured enemies and slaves.

The central square or *forum* of a Roman town was where people met each other, announcements were made, markets were held, and where the town hall, treasury and the law courts were located.

citizenship if they cooperated. By 44BC the Romans ruled Spain, France, Europe south of the Danube, Anatolia and northern Africa. They dominated the Mediterranean – in less than 200 years, the Romans became the controlling force in the West.

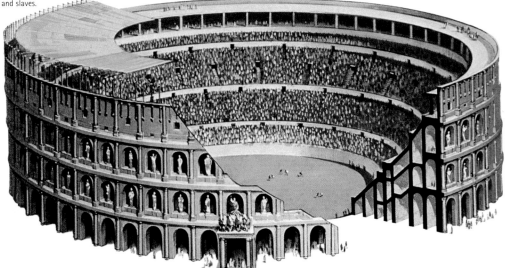

THE END OF THE REPUBLIC

In 100BC, friction grew between the patricians and plebeians. The army was opened up to landless citizens, who were rewarded for their services with land and status in the colonies. Power struggles between generals ended in civil war, and in 44BC, Julius Caesar became dictator for life. Alarmed Republicans assassinated him, and soon after the Republic broke up.

Vital to the growing empire was the system of roads built to speed up trade, postal services and troop movements. On the right, a water-carrying aqueduct is being built over a road.

THE PUNIC WARS

Expanding their influence, the Romans came up against the Phoenicians in Carthage. The Punic Wars (264–241 and 218–202BC) began over a fight for Sicily, but grew to threaten the great cities of Rome and Carthage. The Carthaginian general, Hannibal, nearly won, after invading Italy from the Alps. The Roman general, Scipio Africanus, avoided a head-on battle, attacking Spain in 206 and then Carthage itself in 202BC. The Phoenicians lost everything, and the Romans now dominated the Mediterranean Sea and its trade.

Hannibal's army marched from Spain, over the Alps and into Italy. It was so formidable that the Romans avoided taking it on. They attacked Carthage instead, forcing Hannibal to rush back to defend it.

The Carthaginians used African elephants to frighten the Roman troops. When they crossed the Alps, most of the elephants died.

Hannibal was a brilliant strategist and a modest man who carried out manoeuvres no one believed could work. The Romans beat him only by matching his strategy.

THE ROMAN EMPIRE 27BC–AD475

After Julius Caesar's death in 44BC, Romans preferred dictatorship to chaos. Octavian, his successor, gradually took control. He became the first emperor.

Octavian was Caesar's nephew. He was an able politician, getting himself elected as consul (president) year after year. He called himself *princeps* ('first citizen'), not king. Renamed Augustus ('imposing one'), he reorganized the government and empire and imposed peace. Under him, trade extended as far as east Africa, India and China, and the empire's towns, roads and territories grew ever larger.

Julius Caesar was a ruthless and ambitious general and politician who conquered the Celts of Gaul and later became Rome's first dictator for life, an appointment that angered Republicans and led to Caesar's murder.

Heavily armed Roman legionnaires: a *centurion* (officer) with a *ballista* (catapult), a legionary (soldier) and a standard-bearer.

ROMAN EMPERORS

Emperors relied more on the army than on the Roman people for support. Patricians no longer had great power. Many had moved to rich country estates and the far provinces. Most of the Roman emperors chose their successors, though some unpopular or controversial ones were deposed by soldiers. In AD68–69, four emperors were deposed in one year. From AD100, Rome was ruled by strong emperors – Trajan, Hadrian,

The Roman Empire dominated the whole of the Western world, and united it into one efficient economic system under a single government.

Antoninus and Marcus Aurelius – though most of them were not actually Romans. By AD117, the empire had grown too large and Rome's soldiers could no longer be paid with booty, slaves and land taken in conquest. The burden on Rome grew.

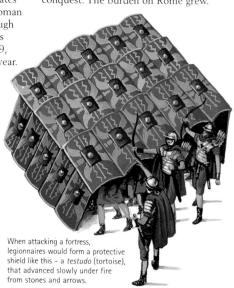

When attacking a fortress, legionnaires would form a protective shield like this – a *testudo* (tortoise), that advanced slowly under fire from stones and arrows.

THE ROMAN ARMY

Soldiers joined the army to gain rewards of promotion, land or power – especially if they were not Romans. This meant that soldiers dominated the empire and its colonies, becoming land-owners and the ruling class. The army was very international, often hiring barbarians as mercenaries. Legions fought in such far-flung places as Scotland, Morocco and Arabia. Roads, forts and border walls were built to maintain security.

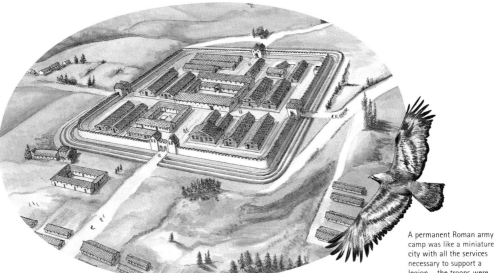

A permanent Roman army camp was like a miniature city with all the services necessary to support a legion – the troops were, after all, far from their homes in other parts of the empire. These military bases were located in the areas which were most in need of permanent protection.

THE ROMAN EMPIRE

The final conquests, in the century following Augustus, had been in Britain, Syria, Palestine and Egypt. The Jews and British had been difficult to beat, and the Parthians impossible. However, most of the conquered peoples adapted. People in Gaul, North Africa, Syria, Britain and Hungary adopted Roman ways and thought of themselves as Roman citizens. Running a huge empire was difficult, and it was united by business, not religious or ethnic ties. Provincial peoples were allowed to get on with their lives, as long as they obeyed the rules set by the Romans.

The Appian Way, a major road from Rome to the southeast coast, was built in 312BC. For the first time, soldiers, traders and travellers travel to these places quickly.

KEY DATES

509BC	Roman republic founded
496	Romans defeat Latins at Battle of Lake Regillus
493	Roman–Latin alliance forms the Latin League, which fights the Etruscans
390	Rome sacked by Celts
306	Romans defeat Etruscans
300s	Romans expand to dominate Italy
264–202	Punic Wars and the fall of Carthage
146	Rome takes Greece
50s	Caesar conquers France
49–31	Civil war between competing generals
27BC	Octavian: end of republic, growth of empire
AD160	Plague and crisis cut population and trade
212	Roman citizenship granted to all inhabitants of the empire
286	Diocletian divides and reorganizes the empire
324	Founding of Constantinople
370	Barbarian attacks on the empire
410	The Visigoths sack Rome - rapid decline of the city results
476	Fall of the last emperor, Romulus Augustus

THE CELTS 500BC–AD43

The Celts were a loose grouping of tribes living in southern Germany from around 1500BC. By Roman times the Celts dominated much of Europe.

This Celtic bronze shield was made around AD100. Set with precious stones, it was more likely to have been made for ceremonial use than for use in battle.

Around 500BC, the Celts were the dominant European power. They had expanded from a heartland in what is now southern Germany. They were not a nation but more a confederation of individual tribes with a shared culture. Their influence eventually stretched from Spain to Britain, Germany and northern Italy and as far as central Anatolia.

CELTIC LIFE

The Celts were tribal farmers who gathered around their chiefs' *oppidae* or strongholds. These were often hill-forts, and some of them later became villages or towns. Most Celts were homesteaders and small farmers, living in a variety of tribes. Sometimes these tribes divided, with one group moving to another place, so that certain tribes might be spread through different areas. The Celts were bound together by the Druids, who were learned priests, lawmakers, bards and wise men. They also had gifted artists, musicians and metalworkers. Their jewellery, pottery, weapons and drinking vessels were often decorated with intricate designs and geometrical shapes. The Celts traded with Rome, Greece and other countries, but they were not much influenced by these civilizations.

This bull's head appeared on a huge bronze ceremonial cauldron found at Gundestrup in Denmark. Animal figures like this, and geometric designs were a popular feature on pieces of elegant Celtic metalwork.

POWER AND LAW

Each Celt was a free person with individual rights. Druidic justice was famous, and bonds of loyalty within each tribe were strong. The chiefs were elected by tribespeople, and the high kings by the chiefs. Both could be deposed if they did not do a good job.

▲ Vertcingetorix was a Gaulish chief who organized a successful rebellion against Julius Caesar's invasion of Gaul in 52BC, but he was later forced to surrender.

▶ A Celtic chief and members of his tribe feast in their timbered hall while listening to the poetic songs of a bard. Laws, history, stories, news and religious teachings were communicated by the druidic bard.

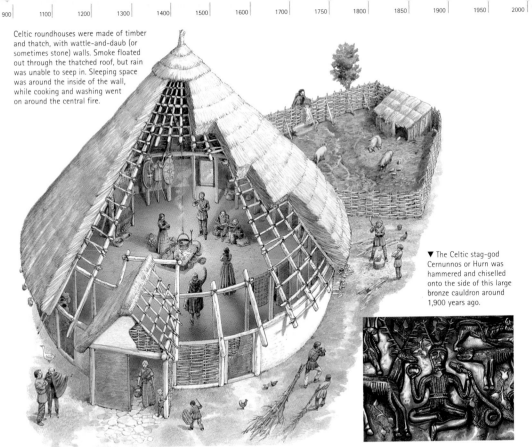

Celtic roundhouses were made of timber and thatch, with wattle-and-daub (or sometimes stone) walls. Smoke floated out through the thatched roof, but rain was unable to seep in. Sleeping space was around the inside of the wall, while cooking and washing went on around the central fire.

▼ The Celtic stag-god Cernunnos or Hurn was hammered and chiselled onto the side of this large bronze cauldron around 1,900 years ago.

CELTIC WARRIORS

Known as fierce warriors (the women fought too), the Celts used iron to make their weapons and tools. In 390BC they sacked Rome and in 280BC they raided Greece and Anatolia, seeking booty. Sometimes they even fought amongst themselves. The Romans exploited this when conquering Gaul (France) and Britain. The British Celtic leader, Caradoc (Caractacus), was betrayed by other Celts. Disunited, the British warriors lost their independence in AD43–80. The Celts came to accept Roman rule and later fought with the Romans against Germanic barbarians. The Celts were also the first European Christians. After the fall of Rome, Celtic ways in Europe survived only in Ireland, Cornwall, Brittany and parts of Wales and Scotland.

Boudicca was the queen of the Iceni of the East of England. She headed a rebellion against the occupying Romans in Britain in AD60 in which 70,000 Romans were killed. However, the rebellion was eventually crushed, and Boudicca committed suicide.

CHINA: THE HAN DYNASTY 202BC–AD220

The Han was the first long-lasting dynasty of united imperial China. Han China enjoyed stability and greatness and was a fine example of civilization.

For four centuries from 202BC to AD220, China was ruled by emperors of the Han dynasty. They were more lenient and stable than the Qin, and practised fair Confucian principles of law and administration.

THE EARLY HAN

The dynasty was founded by Liu Bang, a commoner who was popular because he relaxed the harsh laws, cut taxes and favoured the people. The capital was Chang'an which, after 100 years, became the world's largest city.

It was at the end of the Silk Road along which China traded with Persia and Rome. Han China saw itself as the 'Middle Kingdom', the centre of the world. There was a great flowering of culture, wealth and learning. At this time, Han China was as large and developed as the extensive Roman empire. The Han developed a system of administration by highly educated officials called mandarins. People who wanted to work as public officials had to take an examination on the writings of Confucius.

This bronze model of a prosperous man in his carriage was found in the tomb of the Han official, General Wuw. It was probably made around AD100.

THE MARTIAL EMPEROR

Wu Di, the 'Martial Emperor', reigned for 55 years from 141BC. He added part of central Asia, Korea and much of southern China to his empire. At great expense, he beat back the Xiongnu (Huns) of Mongolia, who often raided China. He improved the mandarin administration, built schools, canals, cities and buildings and encouraged foreign contact. Buddhism was introduced to China during this high point in the country's long history.

▲ A ceramic horse and rider made in Han China around 80BC. Stirrups were not introduced into China until around AD300.

▼ Chinese soldiers of the Han period engage in battle. Lacking stirrups, the horsemen on both sides were easily knocked to the ground during fighting at close quarters.

The emperor's many representatives were always treated with great respect. The speedy transport of officials from one place to another was helped by staging-posts where fresh horses were provided.

◄ The Han emperor Kuang-Wu who declared himself ruler from AD57.

WANG MANG

During the following century, the Han grew weak, while the nobles grew ever stronger. A courtier, Wang Mang, rebelled, took power and ruled from AD9–23. He introduced many changes and reforms, favouring the people against landowners and nobles, and reforming land rights and the judicial system. Eventually the nobles overthrew Wang Mang, and the Han dynasty was restored.

THE LATER HAN

The Han produced exquisite objects of wood, lacquer and silk. They also replaced many of the writings that had been destroyed by the Qin. Chinese inventors were far ahead of the rest of the world. Their invention of paper took centuries to reach the West. Many of the cities they built were elegant and large. However, the population had grown, and rebellions among landless and poor peasants became frequent. Barbarians again attacked the borders, and warlords took over the army. The last Han emperor gave up his throne in AD220 and the empire fell apart.

City streets in Han China were crowded. The muddy roads were full of carts, chariots and traders. Craftsmen, letter writers, storytellers and astrologers also plied their trade noisily in the open air.

55

CHRISTIANITY AD27–337

Around the time that Jesus of Nazareth was born
there were many faiths and sects in the Roman empire.
Within 400 years, Christianity became dominant.

The Jewish people believed that a Messiah (saviour) would be born to lead them. At the time that Jesus of Nazareth was born, Judea was suffering under Roman rule. In about AD27, at the age of 30, Jesus began teaching, and it is said that he performed many miracles, such as healing. The Jewish authorities accused him of blasphemy and he was tried before the Roman governor, Pontius Pilate. He was crucified, but his followers reported meeting him after his death.

The Chi-Rho symbol was the original symbol of the Christians. The cross was emphasized later, after the time of Constantine.

A CHURCH IS BORN

This 'resurrection' formed the basis of a new faith, breaking with old Jewish traditions and founded by Jesus' closest disciples, the apostles. It gradually spread among both exiled Jews and non-Jews throughout the Roman world. Early followers – especially Paul – taught that Christianity was open to anyone who chose to be baptized. By AD300, it had spread to Egypt, Axum, Syria, Armenia, Anatolia, Greece, Rome, France, and as far as Britain and India.

The Dead Sea Scrolls were written by the Essenes around Jesus' time and hidden away from the Romans in a cave at Qumran near the Dead Sea, to be discovered in 1947.

Christians kept their faith quietly, because the Roman authorities often persecuted them, and caused many of them to go into hiding. Many died a painful death in the arena. In Egypt, a group of Christians withdrew to the desert to live as hermits. They were the first Christian monks.

A painting of Jesus as he was portrayed in the first centuries after his death.

JESUS OF NAZARETH

Jesus was born in Bethlehem, in Judea. When he was about 12 years of age, in discussions with learned rabbis at the temple, Jesus showed himself to be special. Then nothing is known about his life until he was around 30 years of age, when he began a public life of teaching. Jesus attracted large crowds. He used parables – stories that taught lessons by example. Love and respect for others was at the heart of his teaching. Three years after he began his mission, the Romans put him to death.

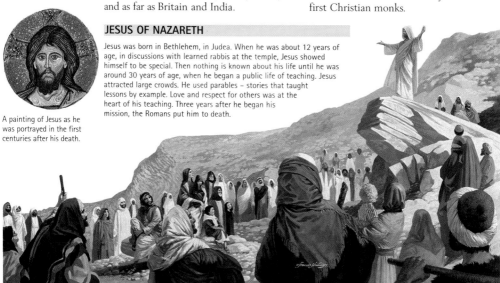

KEY DATES

3BC	Probable year of the birth of Jesus of Nazareth, at Bethlehem
30	Approximate date of the crucifixion of Jesus Christ
45–64	The missions of Paul to Greece, Anatolia and Rome
70–100	The Christian Gospels are written
180	Foundation of early Church institutions
249–311	Periodic persecutions of Christians in the Roman empire
269	St Anthony establishes Christian monasticism in Egypt
313	Emperor Constantine recognizes the Christian church
325	Church doctrine formalized
337	Constantine is baptized on his deathbed

STATE RELIGION

Religious persecution in the Roman empire was halted when Emperor Constantine recognized Christianity in AD313. Later it became the official state religion. Constantine called the first council of all bishops, urging them to resolve their differences and write down one doctrine – the Nicene Creed. Politically, he saw the Church as a way of bringing new life to his flagging empire. His actions defined Christianity, greatly affecting Europe and, eventually, most of the rest of the world. It also meant that the ideas of some of the teachers were outlawed as 'heresies', and this led to the disappearance of many aspects of the faith. It also led to death or exile for those who disagreed with the doctrine. The Gnostic (Egyptian), Celtic and Nestorian churches were examples of branches that eventually died out – although the Nestorians journeyed to Persia and as far as China to avoid this.

In the 4th century AD, an Egyptian Christian, Anthony, travelled to the Sinai desert and began the monastic tradition. St Catherine's monastery, at the base of Mt Sinai, is one of the oldest monasteries in the area.

▲ Constantine changed the church from a sect into a powerful institution.

◀ Legend has it that Constantine adopted the Christian symbol by painting it on his soldiers' shields before a crucial battle outside Rome in AD312 – a battle he won.

THE GUPTA DYNASTY AD240–510

The Guptas became emperors of northern India in AD320 and remained in power for 200 years. The stage was set for them by a people called the Kushans.

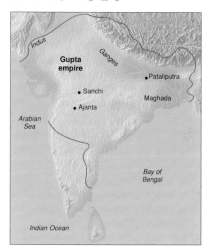

The Guptas ruled most of India and brought about its golden age. Their capital, Pataliputra, was one of the largest cities in the world at that time.

The Kushans were Greek-influenced Asian nomads in Bactria (now Tajikistan). They founded a kingdom there in AD25, and then moved north into Turkestan and south into Afghanistan and India, dominating northern India by 100. Their greatest king was Kanishka (100-130), a Buddhist who supported social tolerance and the arts. Controlling most of the land trade across Asia, the wealthy Kushans gave stability to trade in that area. Around 240, however, Shapur of Persia took much of their land and they never recovered.

The Guptas were minor princes who lived in Maghada. Chandragupta I married a Maghada princess and became king in 320. He began the Gupta tradition of patronage of arts and religions and helped to develop Indian society.

Krishna is one of the ten incarnations of the god Vishnu. He is associated with love and wisdom, and is featured in the *Mahabharata* and *Bhagavad Gita*, two great Hindu holy books.

THE GUPTA MAHARAJAHS

Chandragupta's son Samudragupta continued in his father's footsteps. Ruling from 335 for 45 years, he expanded Gupta rule by force and diplomacy across northern India and into southeastern India. His own son Chandragupta II (380-414) took Gupta India to its high point, one of the greatest times of Indian history. Skandagupta (455-467) beat off an invasion of India by Huns from central Asia. However, the Gupta empire had been ruled through a loose arrangement of local *rajahs* (kings) under the Gupta *maharajah* (emperor), and after Skandagupta died, many local kingdoms broke away. By 510 the Guptas had been beaten by another wave of Hun invaders, and India broke up into *rajputs* (small kingdoms). An alliance of these rajputs beat off the Huns again in 528. India remained divided for 650 years, except for a period when Sri Harsha, a religious rajah of Kanauj (606-647), succeeded in uniting northern India for 40 years.

These large, seated stone buddhas are in Cave 17 of the vast complex at Ajanta. Each of the images is shown with different *mudras*, the symbolic hand gestures still used in Indian dancing.

AJANTA CAVES

The Ajanta caves were rediscovered by a group of British officers on a tiger hunt in 1819. The 29 caves near Bombay were carved out by Buddhist monks between 200BC and AD650, using hammers and chisels. They were built as a monastic retreat, and the walls were covered with fine paintings that depict stories from the life of the Buddha. There were also many sculptures. The caves mark the peak of the religious culture of India, in which yoga and meditation were fully developed. Not far away, at Ellora, other caves contain art from the Hindu, Buddhist and Jain religious traditions which, during the tolerant Gupta period, thrived happily alongside one another.

▲ The elaborately carved Chaitya Hall in the Ajanta caves complex was used as a temple and a hall for meditation and philosophical debates.

◀ A wall-painting from Ajanta shows musicians and dancers entertaining the royal household. Actors, magicians, acrobats and wrestlers would also have taken part in this entertainment.

GUPTA CULTURE

The Gupta maharajahs succeeded one another as good and strong rulers. Copying Asoka, they set up monuments inscribed with religious texts all over India. They built new villages and towns, putting Hindu *brahmins* (priests) in charge. Agriculture and trade flourished. Indians migrated as far as Indonesia, and Buddhism spread to China. Both Hindu and Buddhist culture developed. The Hindu sacred epics, the *Mahabarata* and the *Ramayana*, were written at this time. Kalidasa, India's great poet and dramatist, wrote about love, adventure and the beauty of nature. The Buddhist university at Nalanda had an impressive 30,000 students. This was India's golden age, its classical era of music, dance, sculpture, art and literature.

In the Buddhist Wheel of Life, the eight main spokes represent the eight different states of being that Buddhists identify in the cycle of reincarnation of souls – only one of which is waking daily life.

KEY DATES

AD75–100 The Kushan invasion of India
100–130 Kanishka – the peak of the Kushan period
320–335 Rule by Chandragupta I (founder of the Gupta empire)
335–380 Rule by Samudragupta (conquers northern and eastern India)
380–414 Rule by Chandragupta II (Gupta empire at its peak)
470s Decline of the Gupta empire
505 Gupta empire ends

THE DECLINE OF ROME AD200–476

In AD165, a plague swept through the Roman empire and dramatically reduced the population. Rome's subsequent decline lasted for three hundred years.

The plague laid waste for two years and was followed from 180 by the rule of the mad emperor Commodus, uprisings in Africa and Britain, and a succession of quickly toppled and inadequate emperors. The government at home was falling apart, and Rome was in chaos.

PROVINCIAL CHANGES

Power shifted to the provinces where the people wanted to keep their Roman status. The Parthians in the east and the British in the north created trouble, and a new force was appearing – the barbarians. Marcomanni, Goths, Franks, Alemanni and Vandals were pressing in, and in 260–272, the Romans had to abandon Hungary and Bavaria to them. Parts of the empire such as Gaul, Britain and Syria, were becoming separate and the Roman economy was also declining.

From 250 to 550 the Romans were constantly battling with Germanic and Asiatic barbarians, who sought either to join the empire, to raid it for booty or bring it down.

The emperor Diocletian created a *tetrarchy* (rule of four) to administer the two halves of the empire. The tetrarchy consisted of two emperors helped by two lieutenants.

THE EMPIRE DIVIDES

In 284, the emperor Diocletian decided that the empire was too large for one man to rule and divided it into two, the Greek-speaking east and the Latin-speaking west. He appointed a co-emperor called Maximilian to rule the western half. The army was reorganized and enlarged to 500,000 men, and taxes were changed to pay for it. Provinces were re-organized to make them more governable. Romanitas was promoted by emphasizing the emperor's divine authority.

The vast empire grew too large and complex to rule, so Diocletian divided it. This meant that the rich east was not inclined to help the embattled west, and the west ground to a halt. High taxation levels meant that many Romans cared little – it was cheaper to live without the empire.

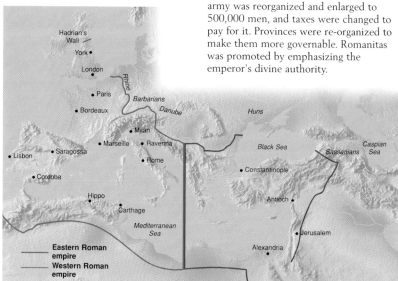

Hadrian's Wall
York
London
Paris
Bordeaux
Barbarians
Rhine
Danube
Huns
Milan
Marseille
Ravenna
Black Sea
Caspian Sea
Sassanians
Lisbon
Saragossa
Rome
Cordoba
Constantinople
Hippo
Antioch
Carthage
Mediterranean Sea
Jerusalem
Alexandria

— Eastern Roman empire
— Western Roman empire

CONSTANTINE

Constantine saw himself as the saviour of the Roman empire. He decided to use the growing strength of Christianity to build a new culture in the empire. Calling bishops to a number of councils, he obliged them to settle church doctrine and become organized. He favoured the Christians, who he considered to be less corrupt and self-seeking than the Romans. However, he was not Christian himself until he converted on his deathbed. He was the last strong emperor of the Roman empire. However, by moving the capital to Constantinople and founding the Byzantine empire, he also weakened the west and hastened Rome's eventual downfall. The Roman Catholic church continued to be a cultural and religious force in the west long after Rome fell.

Constantine ruled as emperor from 312 to 337.

▲ Constantine's arch in Rome was built to bring back a spirit of victory and supremacy to Rome after a century of many disappointments. However, Rome's real achievements at the time were not as great as the arch was meant to suggest.

◄ A detail from the arch of Constantine shows Roman soldiers besieging the town of Verona in 312. This battle was part of Constantine's war against his co-emperor Maxentius. The arch was dedicated in 315.

THE END OF THE EMPIRE

Emperor Constantine tried to revive the empire. He favoured and promoted Christians, built churches and held church councils, making Christianity a state religion. In 330 he moved the capital to Byzantium, calling it Constantinople. This city became as grand as Rome, while the west grew weaker and poorer. The western half of the empire, under attack by the barbarians, collapsed after Rome was sacked in 410 and 455. The last emperor was deposed by the Goths in 476. Following this, the western empire was replaced by a number of Germanic kingdoms. The empire in the east, known as the Byzantine empire, lasted until 1453. Though many Roman ways were adopted by the barbarians, the Roman empire was at an end.

KEY DATES

165–167 Plague sweeps through the Roman empire
167–180 The Marcomanni Wars against the first barbarians
250 Emperor worship made compulsory under Decius
250–270 Barbarians attack the empire from the north
276 Emperor Tacitus killed by his troops
286 Diocletian divides the empire in two halves and rules eastern empire; Maximilian rules western
324 Constantinople founded as the new imperial capital
370 Arrival of Huns in Europe: Germans seek refuge in empire
378–415 The Visigoths rebel and ravage the empire
406 Roman withdrawal from Britain, Gaul and Iberia
410 The Visigoths sack Rome
441 The Huns defeat the Romans
476 Death of the last Roman emperor

Emperor Justinian continued the fight against the barbarians. This gold coin was minted in 535 to celebrate his general Belisarius' defeat of the Vandals.

THE BARBARIANS AD1–450

The term barbarian means 'outsider' – and Romans thought them to be uncivilized. They lived in small farming communities and were ferocious warriors.

An ornate bronze brooch, commonly used by barbarians to fasten their cloaks, is an example of the fine craftsmanship of these people. This piece of jewellery was made around 400 in a style that was fashionable in Denmark and later in Saxon England.

The Germans living in south Sweden and north Germany, moved south and pushed the Celts west. The Romans tried to control the Germans and were seriously beaten by them in AD9. The Romans traded with some friendly German tribes, and recruited some into the Roman army. Some tribes, such as the Franks, Alemanni and Goths raided the empire in 260–270, and the Romans had to make peace and settle them.

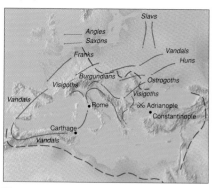

This map shows the complex movements of the main barbarian tribes around 370-450, as they travelled to, and occupied different parts of the western Roman empire.

THE HUNS

The Huns (Xiongnu) had been evicted from Mongolia by the Chinese. They swept into Europe, settling in Hungary around 370. The German tribes panicked, pushing into the empire for safety. The Romans settled many of them, though the Vandals in Greece rebelled, and by 410 they sacked Rome itself. From 440–450, the Huns ravaged Greece, Germany and Gaul, destroying everything. An alliance of Romans and Germans defeated them, but now the empire was in decline. After Attila the Hun attacked northern Italy, the western empire finally collapsed.

THE NEW EUROPEANS

As Rome collapsed, barbarians settled in Germany, Italy, Spain, Britain and France, gradually adopting many Roman customs. By 800, the Frankish king Charlemagne ruled an empire spanning Germany and France. The Visigoths settled in Spain and the Vandals took Carthage. The Huns retreated to Romania and the Ukraine. The Lombards settled in Italy and founded a strong kingdom under King Odoacer. The Burgundians settled in eastern France, and the Saxons and Jutes took England.

A scene based on a Roman tomb carving from around 200, shows Roman soldiers in a fierce battle with German barbarians.

This relief from the obelisk of Theodosius was erected in Constantinople in 390. The stone carvings show the Emperor receiving the submission of the barbarian peoples. Theodosius was the last emperor of a united Roman empire (379–395), and an enthusiastic Christian. He was of barbarian blood, born of Germans who had joined the Roman empire.

▼ This painting shows Attila the Hun marching on Paris during his army's invasion of Gaul in 452.

ATTILA THE HUN

Attila became king of the Huns (Xiongnu) in 433. He set up a new Hun homeland in Hungary after they had massacred, looted and taken slaves through eastern Europe (433–441). The Huns devastated the Balkans and Greece (447–450), forcing the Romans to pay gold to save Constantinople. The Huns later invaded Gaul and northern Italy, but they were beaten by a combined Roman and Visigoth army. In 453, Attila took a German wife and died suddenly in bed, possibly from poisoning. Attila was a military genius and a great Hun leader. When he died, the Huns migrated eastwards to the Ukraine, and ceased to be the fighting force they had once been.

◄ Attila the Hun was highly respected, mainly because no one could beat him and his soldiers. When he died, the Huns fell.

KEY DATES

70BC	Germans migrate to Gaul, beating the Celts
56	Julius Caesar sends the Germans out of Gaul
AD9	Germans rebel against the Romans
200	Germans form a confederation
260	Barbarians move into the Roman empire
367	Scots, Picts and Saxons attack Roman Britain
451–454	Huns devastate Gaul and northern Italy

JAPAN 300BC–AD794

Japan is one of the oldest nations in the world. People were living there from around 30,000BC. Classical Japan took shape from around 300BC.

In ancient times, Japan was occupied by the Ainu people. The Ainu were unique, and not related to any other tribe. Today's Japanese people moved onto the islands in prehistoric times, from Korea and Manchuria on the mainland. They forced the Ainu onto the northernmost island, Hokkaido.

The Ainu, or Ezo, did not look like modern-day Japanese – they had lighter complexions and much more hair, like these two tribal elders. The Ainu had no written language and, because they were looked down on by the Japanese, there are few records of their history.

THE YAYOI

Around 300BC, the Yayoi were beginning the rise that would make them Japan's predominant tribe. They introduced bronze and iron and also rice and barley from Korea and China. They shaped Japanese culture and the Shinto religion, in which nature spirits (*kani*) and tribal ancestors were worshipped. Tradition says that Jimmu, the legendary first emperor (*tenno*), great-grandson of Amreratsu, 'Goddess of the Sun', appeared in 660BC. In fact, if he existed at all, it was probably several hundred years after this.

A painted scroll from the 4th century AD shows a Yamato court lady being dressed by her servant. The boxes are for cosmetics.

Japan is made up of four main islands, and the biggest, Honshu, has always been the dominant one. In early times, the indigenous Ainu people were squeezed out of Honshu north onto the island of Hokkaido.

THE YAMATO

Around AD167, an elderly priestess called Himiko, of the Yamato tribe, became ruler. She used her religious influence to unite about 30 of the Japanese tribes. Himiko sent ambassadors to China, and from that time Chinese culture, and later, Buddhism, influenced the Japanese. The Yamato increased in power during the 3rd century AD. Today's Japanese emperors can trace their ancestry to the Yamato, who claimed descent from the Sun goddess. During this period, until 646, much of Japan was united as one state that included southern Korea. With the establishment of Buddhism during the 6th century, Shinto was threatened. Around 600, Prince Shotoku reformed the Yamato state, centralizing it in the Chinese style and reducing the power of the tribal lords. Temples and towns were built, and there was great cultural development. The 8th century saw Japan's golden age. Rivalry between Shinto and Buddhism was also resolved by merging both into a common Japanese religious culture.

THE SHINTO RELIGION

Shinto is the ancient nature religion of Japan. Its mythology was written down in the 8th century in the *Kojiki* and the *Nihongi*. Shinto worshippers believed in the power of natural energies and spirits or *kami*. Shinto priests sought to please the spirits, attracting their support and protection. In Shinto, it is believed that all life was born from a cosmic egg, formed in the primordial chaos. The egg separated and became the gods (*kamis*), and the marriage of two *kamis* brought the Earth into being, with Japan as their special home. The Sun goddess also came from this marriage, and the emperor was seen to descend from her. Many influences entered Shinto from Buddhism, and both religions coexisted throughout Japanese history, although there were periods of rivalry.

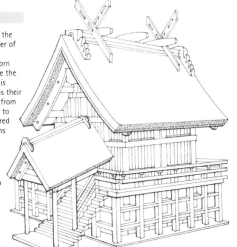

► This is a reconstruction of a Shinto shrine at Izumo. The Shinto priests held ceremonies of renewal and purification there at special times of the year to appeal to the *kami* to send them bumper crops, and give the people good health and fertility.

▲ Shinto priests were originally tribal shamans. In later times their traditions, dress and temples became more formal, in response to the challenge from Buddhism.

► This is the main gate of the Shinto Kasuga shrine at Heian. These gates not only served the usual purpose as an entrance, they also marked the energy lines along which the spirits travelled to reach the temple, which was carefully placed in a special location.

THE NARA PERIOD

A permanent capital was established at Nara around 710. Increasingly, the emperor became a ceremonial figure, serving as the representative of the gods. Government was controlled by officials and monks and there were greater political struggles. In 794, the emperor moved the capital to Heian (Kyoto), where a new phase of Japanese history began. Japan had developed from a tribal land to become a strong state. However, little has been recorded about the life of ordinary people, since records were only kept about the imperial court and temples.

KEY DATES

300BC	Beginning of the Yayoi culture
AD239	Queen Himiko sends an embassy to China
300	The Yamato period – farming, towns, ironworking
366	The Japanese invade southern Korea (until 562)
552	Full introduction of Buddhism
593–622	Prince Shotoku creates a Chinese-style centralized state
646	Yamato period ends
710	Nara becomes the permanent capital (the Nara period)
794	Emperor Kammu moves his court to Heian (Kyoto)

In Shinto, small clay figures were used as totems to bring good fortune to places or to the souls of the dead in the afterlife.

THE MAYA 300BC–AD800

The Maya lived in what is now southern Mexico and Guatemala. They created a civilization that was at its peak while the Roman empire was crumbling.

The Mayan heartlands moved from the south in early times to the centre around Tikal. After AD800 most Maya lived in the north of Yucatán.

The engraved figures found in Mayan ruins often show richly dressed people such as this priest with his ornate headdress.

The Maya existed as far back as 2000BC. Over the centuries, by draining marshy land and building irrigation systems, they became successful farmers, able to support a large population. In the early phase, from 300BC to AD300, they built many cities in Guatemala, Belize and southern Yucatán, each with its own character and artistic style. Their cities had temple pyramids, a fortified palace, marketplaces, workshops and living-quarters.

MAYA CLASS SYSTEM

The Maya had a class system: the nobles, priests, rulers, officials and their servants lived in the cities and the ordinary people worked the land, visiting the cities for markets and religious festivals. There was an alphabet of 800 hieroglyphs, and the Maya studied advanced mathematics, astronomy and calendar systems. As in ancient Greece, each city was an independent city-state, and there was feuding between them, usually to exact tribute and take prisoners. Around AD230, a violent volcanic eruption blew apart Mount Ilopango in the south, and covered a large area with ash. The southern cities had to be abandoned, and this marked the end of the 'pre-classic' period of Maya civilization.

THE CLASSIC PERIOD

Between 300 and 800, Mayan civilization reached its peak. Many new cities were built in Yucatán. The dominant city was Tikal, although Palenque, Yaxchilán, Copán and Calakmul were also important.

▲ The Maya wrote in hieroglyphs (picture writing), which are found carved on the huge stone monuments and written in books made of bark paper.

◀ The Maya played a ball game which may have had religious importance to them as a kind of oracle. In vast courts they bounced a solid rubber ball back and forth using their hips, thighs and elbows, aiming for a hoop in the side wall.

The Maya were skilled craftspeople, making stone sculptures, jade carvings, decorated pottery, paintings, advanced tools and objects of gold and copper. They built roads and shipping lanes to encourage trade. Their mathematical system counted in 20s, and used three symbols: a bar for 'five', a dot for 'one' and a shell for 'zero'.

HUMAN SACRIFICE

The Maya practised blood sacrifice. They viewed this life and the afterlife as equal worlds, so killing people for religious purposes, to please the gods and ancestors and to bring fertility and prosperity, was a natural thing to do. In later times, ambitious building projects meant that peasants had to supply ever more food and labour, and hostage-taking wars to capture sacrifice victims drastically cut the population. The agricultural system collapsed, and with it the cities. By 950, most central Mayan cities lay in ruins – though a later phase followed. The Maya still live in the uplands of central America.

These were the four kinds of people at the top of the Mayan social pyramid. From right to left are an official, a warrior, a noble and a priest.

MAYAN CITIES

In the early days of Mayan city-building, the largest city was El Mirador, founded in 150BC, which had a population of 80,000 people by AD100. It was abandoned around AD150. Tikal, ruled by its king Stormy Sky, later became the largest city, with some 100,000 people around AD450. Most cities were impressive and planned in grids. They were built around the ceremonial centres, and often oriented to astronomical events such as the rising and setting points of the Sun. The religious basis of the Mayan cities and their use of pyramids resembled that of the ancient Egyptians 2,000 years earlier.

Mayan cities were carefully laid out, with many sacred shrines and temples covering many hectares of land, with large open spaces, platforms and meeting-places.

EARLY MIDDLE AGES

501–1100

This period used to be called the Dark Ages because historians thought that civilization ended when the Roman empire fell. Many people now call these years the Early Middle Ages because they mark the start of the period that separates ancient and modern history. The former Roman empire split into two: the western part peopled by farmers, skilled metal-workers and ship-builders; the eastern part became the Byzantine empire. The Chinese and Arabs still led the way in science and technology. Buddhist and Christian religions were spread through trade, while Islam was spread through military conquest.

▲ The Carolingian Renaissance inspired this 9th-century ivory carving of St Gregory and other scholars at work.

◄ This 10th-century Mayan stone carving was found in the ruins of the city of Chichen-Itza on the Yucatan Peninsula of Mexico.

THE WORLD AT A GLANCE 501–1100

After the fall of the Roman empire, new countries and peoples emerged in Europe. The lives of these people were governed by the Christian Church and a rigid social system, later called feudalism.

Between Europe and the Far East there was a huge area containing many different people who all shared the same religion, Islam. Farther north, Slav countries such as Russia and Bulgaria were also forming.

China was still culturally and scientifically far in advance of the rest of the world. Its influence spread all over Asia, and to Japan where there was a great flowering of the arts.

In North America, the first towns were being built and the Toltec civilization developed in Mexico. In South America, huge independent empires, such as the Huari empire, were forming.

Contact between the civilizations of the world was very limited. Only a few countries traded with each other. But Islam was gradually spreading over the whole of northern Africa through conquest and trade.

NORTH AMERICA

NORTH AMERICA

In about 700, two separate town cultures began to develop in North America. One was the Temple Mound culture around the Mississippi area – a culture that traded far across the continent in copper and goods. Another was the Anasazi *pueblo* (village) culture in the southwest, where people lived in stone pueblos connected by roads. The Anasazi had an advanced religion. Elsewhere, many Native American nations grew bigger and stronger, though they were still mainly farming and hunting peoples, living either in permanent villages or as nomads. Far to the northeast, in Newfoundland, the first white men arrived – the Vikings settled there for a short time around year 1000.

CENTRAL AND SOUTH AMERICA

CENTRAL AND SOUTH AMERICA

Around 600–700, the great Mexican city of Teotihuacán was at its greatest. Decline set in around 750, both there and among the Maya further south. But the Mayan empire of city-states survived this whole period. From 900–1100 the warlike Toltecs flourished in Mexico. To the south, in Peru, the city-states of Tiahuanaco in the Andes mountains and the Huari near the coast grew larger and more developed. Tiahuanaco preceded the Inca empire. By 1000, the Huari empire was replaced by the Chimú empire which was developing around Chan Chan in northern Peru.

EUROPE

Europe was busy finding its feet during the period known as the Dark Ages. The Byzantine empire acted as a stable focus for Christendom, though its fortunes rose and fell. In the 8th century, the Muslims invaded Spain, setting up an advanced culture there that lasted 700 years. At the same time, further north, the Carolingians created the first European empire, though it declined in the 9th century after Charlemagne's death. In the rest of Europe, nations were slowly taking shape, overseen by the Catholic Church in Rome. This process was accelerated by threats from the Magyars, Vikings, and by Muslims in Spain and Anatolia. By 1100, some European nations were growing strong, more stable and prosperous. Universities were founded, church-building flourished, and towns grew in size and importance. Medieval leaders started overseas military adventures and conquests – for example, the European Crusades to win land in Palestine.

ASIA

In India, the Gupta empire collapsed in 535 and the country was disunited. Both Hindu and Buddhist influences expanded into southeast Asia. Around 775, the kingdom of Srivijaya in Sumatra conquered the Malayan peninsula, and in Cambodia the Khmer dynasty established the kingdom of Angkor in 802. In China, one of its greatest dynasties, the Tang, lasted for 300 years, producing some of the finest works of art in Chinese history. From 960 it was replaced by the Song dynasty for a further 300 years. Elsewhere, a strong Tibetan kingdom rose and fell, and rich states grew up in Thailand, Vietnam, Japan and Indonesia. In Central Asia, Turkic and Mongol nomads were growing in strength.

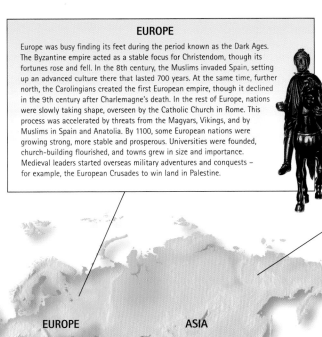

EUROPE

ASIA

MIDDLE EAST

AFRICA

AUSTRALASIA

AUSTRALASIA

Polynesians occupied new Pacific islands, moving to New Zealand around 900. In Australia, the Aborigines were untouched by outside influences.

AFRICA

By 700, the whole of northern Africa was part of the Islamic empire. In western Africa, gold-rich Ghana grew wealthy and strong, and other trading kingdoms such as Mali and Kanem-Bornu began to develop on the fertile southern edge of the Sahara desert.

MIDDLE EAST

The Sassanid empire reached its greatest extent in 579. On the death of Muhammad in 632, the Islamic empire began to expand. In 634, the Arabs conquered Persia and overthrew the Sassanian empire. But by 756, the Islamic empire started to break up. At the end of the 11th century, Jerusalem was captured by crusaders.

THE BYZANTINE EMPIRE 476–1453

Byzantium inherited the eastern half of the Roman empire, surviving nearly a thousand years until, finally, it was taken over by the Ottoman Turks.

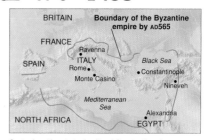

Centred on the strategic city of Constantinople, Byzantium controlled east–west trade, and for long periods, dominated the Mediterranean Sea and Black Sea.

Justinian ruled Byzantium for 38 years with his wife Theodora. They were lawmakers and reformers, and they restored the empire's power and lands. They gave shape to the sophisticated culture of Byzantium, building great churches and giving patronage to the arts and literature.

▼ Byzantium was often under attack. Its navy had a secret weapon invented by Kallinikos in 677 called 'Greek Fire', a mixture that burst into flames when it touched water. It was made from quicklime, sulphur and petroleum.

Constantinople, the eastern Roman capital, had been built by Emperor Constantine on the site of the ancient Greek port of Byzantium. When the Roman empire collapsed in the 5th century, the city became the capital of the new Byzantine empire. The edges of the Roman empire's territories had been captured by barbarians, so the early emperors of Byzantium, Anastasius (491–518) and Justinian (527–565), fought to reclaim Rome's former territories. During Justinian's long reign, he sent able generals – Belisarius, Narses and Liberius – to add north Africa, much of Italy and southern Spain to its list of reclaimed territories. However, many of these gains were soon lost under his successors.

A further revival followed when Emperor Heraclius (610–641) re-organized the empire, bringing the state and the Church closer together. He beat back the Sassanid Persians, who had occupied Syria, Palestine and Egypt. Under his rule, Constantinople became a rich centre of learning, high culture and religion. The city was well placed for controlling trade between Asia and Europe. The empire produced gold, grain, olives, silk and wine, which it traded for spices, precious stones, furs and ivory from Asia and Africa.

▲ This pictorial map shows Constantinople in 1422, not long before it fell to the Ottomans. It became a Muslim city, and was renamed Istanbul in 1453. The city stood on a promontory called the Golden Horn.

This classic Byzantine Orthodox mosaic is on the inside of a church dome in Ravenna, Italy. It shows Jesus being baptized by John the Baptist with the god of the Jordan River sitting close by.

The Byzantines made elaborate crosses, icons, caskets and other sacred relics. These became an important part of life in the Orthodox church.

▼ Saint Sophia, the Church of the Holy Wisdom, was built in Constantinople for Justinian around 530. It took 10,000 people to construct it. Later, it became a mosque, and today it is a museum.

KEY DATES

476	Fall of the last Roman emperor
491–518	Emperor Anastasius in Constantinople
527–565	Emperor Justinian's generals reconquer former territories
610–641	Emperor Heraclius expands Byzantium
633–640	Arabs take Syria, Egypt and north Africa
679	Bulgars overrun Balkan territories
976–1026	Basil II rebuilds the empire
107	Seljuk Turks take Anatolia
1204–61	Norman Crusaders capture Constantinople
1453	Fall of Byzantium to the Ottoman Turks

The Byzantine basilica of St Apollinare was built near Ravenna in Italy in the 6th century. During this period, Byzantine architecture was gradually steering away from the old Roman styles.

The Byzantine empire declined in the 8th century – the Arabs twice trying to take Constantinople itself. However, under Basil II (976–1025), the empire flourished again. Then, soon after Basil died, Anatolia was lost to the Turks and the empire again declined. It was taken over by the Crusaders for 50 years in the 13th century, but it was reclaimed again by Michael VIII in 1261. Finally, the city of Constantinople was taken by the Ottoman Turks in 1453. The sophisticated Byzantine culture had been the most lively and creative in Europe, and the Orthodox faith had spread as far as Russia and eastern Europe.

SUI AND TANG CHINA 589–907

The Sui dynasty lasted only 30 years, yet it reunited China after 370 years of disunity. This was followed by the T'ang dynasty, which lasted nearly 300 years.

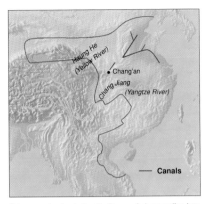

China grew in size during the Tang period, expanding into central Asia, and many big projects were taken on, such as the canal system and irrigation schemes.

The Tang people believed that dragons symbolized the energies of the Earth and that all things should be in harmony with one another. These beliefs even influenced their thinking about building practices.

From the fall of the Han to the rise of the Sui, China was divided into three kingdoms – Wei in the north, Shu in the west and Wu in the south. There was constant warfare, as well as nomad invasions from Mongolia and Tibet. Many towns were ruined, and the population fell. Devastation in the north led to migrations southwards, making the south more politically important. During this time, Buddhism became more widespread in China, bringing in many foreign ideas. Finally, in 581, a general from Wei, Yang Jian, overthrew his rulers and founded the Sui dynasty. By 589 he had unified China.

SUI DYNASTY

Yang Jian renamed himself Emperor Wen. Before he came to power, taxes were high and people were conscripted into the army for long periods of time. He cut both taxes and conscription, governing firmly from his capital, Chang'an. He also encouraged the development of agriculture by setting up irrigation schemes and redistributing land. This helped to make the country wealthy. The second Sui emperor was Yang Di. Under his rule, the Grand Canal was rebuilt to link the main rivers of China. He also had palaces and pleasure parks built and raised money for them by ordering people to pay ten years' taxes in advance. The peasants rebelled and, in 618, Yang Di was killed.

TANG DYNASTY

The second T'ang emperor, Taizong (626–649) reorganized government, cut taxes and redistributed land. The reorganization of this united empire was far in advance of anything found in other parts of the world.

Rice paddy-fields need controlled watering and large-scale drainage works. The Tang dynasty created conditions in which such large-scale projects became possible.

74

This stable period marked the beginning of nearly 300 years during which Chinese excellence in the arts, science and technology was promoted. From 640–660, T'ang China expanded into central Asia, seeking to stop troublesome nomads from taking control of the Silk Road. The Chinese travelled as far as modern-day Korea, Afghanistan and Thailand. After Taizong's time, there was a rebellion by An Lushan in Beijing in 755 that challenged T'ang rule, and the T'ang never fully recovered. Imperial rule became a formality, and the power shifted to the regional governors and courtiers. The Tibetans also defeated the Chinese in central Asia and there were more rebellions in the 9th century. By 907 the T'ang dynasty had collapsed. There followed a period of bitter civil wars that lasted until 960.

This wall-painting from a tomb shows the Tang princess Yung Tai, who was forced to commit suicide at the age of 17 for criticizing her grandmother, Empress Yu. In China, obeying and submitting to one's parents and elders was thought very important.

▲ These ceramic ornaments are examples of the foreign animals that would have been seen in the Tang capital, Chang'an. The camel carried silk, and the horse, larger than the Chinese variety, originated in central Asia. Chang'an lay at the Chinese end of the Silk Road and was the world's largest city, with two million people.

THE GRAND CANAL

Started by the Sui and completed by the Tang, the Grand Canal was an enormous undertaking. It stretched over 800km from the Huangho River to the Yangtze, and linked the major cities and capitals of the north with the rice-growing and craft-producing areas of the south. The road journey from north to south was difficult, and sea travel was hampered by typhoons and pirates. The canal allowed safe, long-distance, freight-carrying transport, to bind China's northern and central regions closer together.

KEY DATES

589 Yang Jian unites China, founding Sui dynasty
602–610 Military actions in Taiwan, Vietnam, Korea and central Asia
618 T'ang dynasty founded by Li Yuan
626–649 Emperor Taizong – expansion of T'ang China
640–660 Chinese expansion in central Asia and China
755–763 An Lushan's rebellion – T'ang power declines
870s Major peasant rebellions throughout China
907 T'ang dynasty collapses

ISLAM 622–750

Islam established itself very quickly and influenced many other civilizations. Within 150 years it had grown into a huge empire guided by religious principles.

This is a Muslim portrayal of the Archangel Gabriel (Jizreel). Gabriel is recognized by Muslims as the messenger of Allah to the prophet Muhammad.

The prophet Muhammad, who founded the religion called Islam, was born in Mecca in 570. At this time the Arab peoples worshipped many different gods. Muhammad became a successful, widely travelled trader, and was influenced by the Judeo-Christian belief in just one God. When he was 40 years old, his life changed: he saw the Archangel Gabriel in a series of visions. Muhammad then wrote down the *Quran*, the Muslim holy book, under dictation from Gabriel. He was instructed to teach about prayer, purification and *Allah*, the one God. The word *Islam* means 'surrender to Allah'.

When Muhammad started teaching, the rulers of Mecca felt threatened by his ideas. Muhammad and his followers had to flee to Medina in 622 and the Muslim calendar counts its dates from this flight – the *Hegira*. In Medina, Muhammad organized a Muslim society, building a mosque. His following grew quickly – many Arabs were poor and Islam preached a fairer society. In 630, Muhammad recaptured Mecca and became its ruler. He kept non-believers out and banned idol worship. Muhammad died in 632.

The Dome of the Rock, known as al Aqsa, in Jerusalem, was completed in 691 on the site of Solomon's Temple. It was built where Muhammad had experienced an important vision in a dream. Decorated with complex geometrical patterns, this mosque shows an early Islamic architectural style.

This page from the *Quran* was written in early Arabic lettering style in the 9th century. One aspect of the new Islamic culture was its artistic and cultural creativity.

ISLAMIC EXPANSION

The new Muslim *caliph* (leader), called for a *jihad*, or holy war. Within ten years, under Caliph Umar, the Arabs conquered Syria and Palestine (defeating the Byzantines), Mesopotamia and Persia (bringing down the Sassanids), as well as Egypt and Libya. After the death of Caliph Uthman, there were disputes between his successor, Muawiya, and Ali, Muhammad's son-in-law. Ali was murdered in 661 which led to a permanent split into two groups, the Sunnis, and the Shiites, the followers of Ali.

Muslims travelled widely, as explorers and traders, and brought ideas about Islam with them. Their faith decreed that they should make at least one pilgrimage to Mecca.

◀ At the battle of Yarmuk, in Syria, in 636, the Muslim forces defeated a Byzantine army twice their size. This was a major loss for Byzantium, and the Muslims captured Syria and Palestine, the most prosperous part of the Byzantine empire. They took Jerusalem, and established the beginnings of a large empire.

▼ Arabic knowledge of medicine, healing and surgical techniques was well advanced for this time. This picture shows doctors setting a fracture in a broken limb.

THE UMAYYAD DYNASTY

In 661, the Arabs established a capital at Damascus, and Muawiya became the first Umayyad caliph. Territorial expansion followed – Muslim armies invaded central Asia, Afghanistan, Armenia, north Africa and even Spain. They twice attacked Constantinople without success. When they invaded Europe, they were defeated by the Franks in France in 732 and had to retreat. The Umayyads organized their empire in a Byzantine style. They were tolerant and did not force conversion to Islam. Many people converted as Muslims were seen as genuine liberators, bringing an end to the old order, establishing clear laws and increasing trade. Arabic became a universal language across Islam, except in Persia which was mainly Shi'ite and retained its distinct culture. This common language helped ideas and knowledge to spread quickly from one place to another.

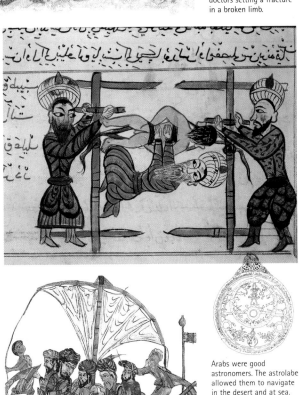

Arabs were good astronomers. The astrolabe allowed them to navigate in the desert and at sea.

The Arabs sailed in *dhows*. These wooden boats had triangular sails and carried cargo and passengers.

KEY DATES	
610	Muhammad experiences his first vision
622	The *Hegira* – the flight from Mecca to Medina – takes place
630	Muhammad takes Mecca and forms an Islamic state
636–642	Muslims take Palestine, Syria, Persia and Egypt
656–661	Caliphate of Ali – dispute between factions
661–680	Founding of Umayyad dynasty
711	Arabs invade Spain
732	Franks defeat the Arabs at Poitiers, France
750	Umayyad dynasty overthrown by the Abbasids

BULGARS AND SLAVS 600–1453

Bulgaria and Kiev had a significant influence on eastern Europe. Their adoption of Orthodox Christianity affected both their peoples and the Orthodox church.

In the mid-9th century, Cyril and his brother Methodius devised the Cyrillic alphabet, based on Greek letters, for use in writing down the Slavonic languages.

The Bulgars were the descendents of the Huns, who settled beside the Volga river in Russia, and reached the height of their power around 650. Then the Khazars from lower down the Volga destroyed their kingdom. As a result, many Bulgars migrated to the Danube area, dominating the local Slavs and founding a Bulgar state. Byzantium took action against them, especially when the Bulgars killed their emperor in battle in 811. In the 860s, two missionaries, Cyril and Methodius, were sent to convert the Bulgars and draw them into Byzantium's influence. This helped, but the quarrels did not end until the Bulgars were beaten in 1014. To punish them, Basil II had 14,000 Bulgars blinded, and the Bulgar khan died of shock.

Vladimir, Grand Prince of Kiev (c.956–1015), interviewed Catholic and Orthodox Christians, Muslims and Jews, and opted for the Orthodox faith, probably for political as much as religious advantages. Vladimir was the youngest son of Grand Prince Svyatoslav, who had brought down the Khazars. Vladimir conducted campaigns to secure Kiev's territories.

ORTHODOX DIPLOMACY

In Byzantium, the state and the church were closely linked. Religious and diplomatic missions were sent out and, in this way, Byzantium converted the Bulgars to Christianity. Catholic Rome and Orthodox Constantinople competed for influence in eastern Europe. Kiev adopted the Orthodox beliefs, and a Russian Orthodox culture was born there. Cyrillic lettering, used today by Russians and Bulgarians, was invented by Cyril the missionary and his brother Methodius. By the time Byzantium fell in 1453, Russia had become the home of Orthodoxy.

▶ When the Bulgars killed the Byzantine emperor Nicephorus in 811, they made his skull into a goblet to take to their khan, Krum. The Byzantine emperors called the Bulgar khans *tsars* – a name that was adopted later by Russian emperors.

The Church of Intercession, an example of early Orthodox church-building in Russia, was built at Bogolyubovo in 1165.

THE RISE AND FALL OF KIEV

The Slavs came from what is now Belarus. The first states in Russia were Slavic, and led by Swedish Viking traders (*Ros* or 'oarsmen'). The greatest Ros leader was Rurik, who founded Novgorod, Smolensk and Kiev. The Vikings traded with Baghdad and Constantinople, and Kiev grew rich as a trading city. The Vikings considered themselves a superior class, mixing only gradually with the Slavs. In 988, the Kievan prince Vladimir converted to Christianity, marrying a Byzantine princess. He then made the nobility and people adopt Christianity. This brought Kiev new trade, culture and respectability abroad. Under Jaroslav the Wise (1019-54) Kiev became a centre of splendour and influence that rivalled Constantinople, with diplomatic connections across

Europe. Churches were built, and the first Russian laws were written, as well as the first works of Russian art and literature. Kiev was on the steppes of the Ukraine, and vulnerable to nomadic warriors such as the Pechenegi who threatened, and the Polovtsy who sacked, the city. After Jaroslav died, the state of Kiev broke up and the Russians retreated into safer northern areas. Here a new Russia was becoming established, centred around the growing city of Moscow.

▲ A central theme of Orthodox culture was the icon, or holy image, which was believed to have spiritual and healing powers. Icon-painting spread from Byzantium, through Kiev, into later Russian culture.

▶ This 13th-century helmet belonged to the prince of a small principality called Suzdal, once part of Kievan Russia.

79

THE CAROLINGIANS 751–843

The Carolingian dynasty established Europe's first rich and powerful empire. These people were the former Germanic 'barbarians' known as the Franks.

Frankish empire in AD771
Land conquered by Charlemagne
Divisions of Charlemagne's empire in AD870

Charlemagne's empire unified most of western Europe. Its capital, Aachen, lay not far from the capital of today's European Union at Brussels.

This gold image of Charlemagne, inset with precious stones and known as a reliquary, was made in Germany around 1350 to hold parts of Charlemagne's skull.

The Franks had settled in what is now Belgium and northern France. Their leader, Clovis (481–511), of the Merovingian dynasty, established a capital at Paris. Clovis became a Christian and earned Rome's support. He united the Frankish tribes, defeated the Gauls, the Alemanni (a confederation of Germans) and the Visigoths, and created a kingdom resembling today's France. His sons consolidated this, but quarrels broke out. Power fell to Charles Martel, who led the Franks against the invading Muslims at Poitiers in 732. Charles founded the Carolingian dynasty, and in 751, under his son Pepin, the Carolingians replaced the Merovingians as Frankish rulers. In 768, Pepin's sons, Carloman and Charlemagne, inherited his kingdom. Carloman died in 771 and Charlemagne took full control. He first conquered the rest of France, and then what is now Germany, Italy and the Netherlands, creating an enormous European empire. In central Europe he quelled the Saxons and the Avars, forcing them both to accept Christianity.

CHARLEMAGNE'S CORONATION

The blessing of the Church gave a nation greater respectability. For the pope, Charlemagne's grand coronation in 800 in St Peter's Church, Rome, on Christmas Day, was a political move against Constantinople. It showed there was now a Christian empire in the west as well as in the east. Charlemagne offered to marry the Byzantine empress Irene, and missions were sent to him from Persia and the Baghdad Caliphate, as well as from the rulers of Europe. Had Charlemagne's empire been kept intact, European history may have been very different.

Pope Leo III crowned Charlemagne as Holy Roman emperor in 800.

Holy Roman emperors were crowned in the Palatine Chapel, Aachen.

THE CAROLINGIAN RENAISSANCE

Charlemagne supported the Roman church, favouring its influence in his kingdom. In return, the pope crowned Charlemagne as the first Holy Roman emperor in 800. Charlemagne was a lawmaker and founded schools, cathedrals and monasteries run by Irish, British and Italian monks. He also invited scholars, scribes, architects and philosophers to his court. His capital at Aachen became the chief centre of learning in western Christendom. Charlemagne died in 814. His successor Louis the Pious ruled successfully but, on his death in 843, the empire was divided between his three sons. The empire later became two countries: Germany and France. The Carolingians ruled Germany until 911 and France until 987.

Charlemagne was a great military leader who, once he had invaded lands, tried to improve conditions and encourage the poor to improve their standard of living.

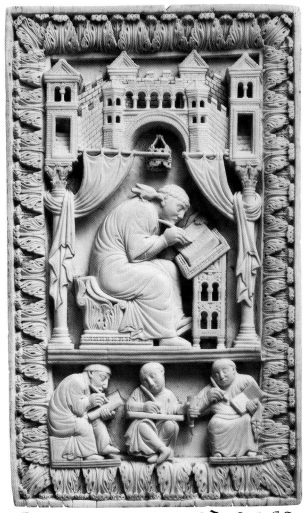

▲ The Carolingian Renaissance inspired this ivory carving of St Gregory and other scholars at work, in 850–875. The Aachen scholars created a new script called *minuscule*, with clear, rounded letters but Charlemagne never learned to write.

KEY DATES

486–510	France united by Merovingian King Clovis
732	Charles Martel beats the Arabs at Poitiers
751	Pepin, the first Carolingian king
768	Charlemagne becomes Carolingian king
782	Charlemagne defeats the Saxons
790s	Charlemagne defeats the Avars in Austria
800	Pope crowns Charlemagne
814	Charlemagne dies
843	Carolingian empire divided into three

THE ABBASID DYNASTY 750–1258

During the 500 years of rule by the Abbasid dynasty, the Islamic empire was unified, its culture flourished, and Baghdad became one of the world's greatest cities.

When Harun al-Rashid became caliph in 786, he ended a decade of uncertainty and rivalry in the Islamic empire.

In 750, there were disagreements between the Arabs as well as dissent among the invaded peoples. The Umayyads were overthrown by the Abbasid family who then ruled the Islamic world for 500 years. The Abbasids were descended from Muhammad's uncle, al-Abbas. Under al-Mansur, their first caliph, they moved their capital to the new city of Baghdad in 762, and adopted many Persian and Greek traditions. Their most famous ruler was Harun al-Rashid (786– 809), the fifth caliph. From 791 until 806, he fought a long war with the Byzantine empire, which he eventually won. Parts of the empire sought independence, but Harun al-Rashid managed to suppress them. In spite of these wars, he found time to encourage learning and the arts, bringing together Persian, Greek, Arab and Indian influences. Baghdad became a world centre for astronomy, mathematics, geography, medicine, law and philosophy. The court in Baghdad was the setting for much of *The Thousand and One Nights*, a book still

The stories for *The Thousand and One Nights* came from many different countries, including India, Syria and Egypt. The stories feature Ali Baba, Sinbad the Sailor and Aladdin.

enjoyed today. Under later caliphs, various provinces became independent but they still followed Islam, its law and culture. The Abbasid caliphs increasingly lost power and became spiritual figureheads. The Muslim empire separated into emirates, whose fortunes rose and fell at different times. Yet the Muslim world acted as one civilization with many different centres.

This elaborately decorated tile, made in Persia in the 12th century, is an example of the Islamic art in the Abbasid period, which was rich and very sophisticated.

People came to the Abbasid court in Baghdad from all over the empire, even from as far away as central Asia and Spain.

This decorated Persian bowl was made during the Abbasid dynasty. It shows how Muslim artists created new styles with intricate designs.

GHANA 700–1240

Ghana was the first truly African state. Most Africans still lived in tribal village societies, but Ghana, a centre of the gold trade, opened up new possibilities.

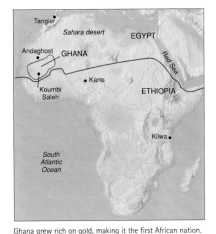

Ghana grew rich on gold, making it the first African nation. Its capital, Koumbi Saleh, was quite cosmopolitan. Gold was transported north to Morocco, Tunisia, the Nile and Arabia.

The medieval kingdom of Ghana lay further north, inland from today's nation of Ghana. Its roots lay in the 4th century, when the African Soninke tribes were ruled by the Maga, a Berber clan from Morocco. The Berbers had mastered trans-Saharan camel travel, and traded salt for gold from the Soninke. When the Arabic Muslims invaded north Africa there was an upsurge in the trade in gold, and by 700 Ghana was rich and important as a trading centre. In 770, the Soninke ousted the Maga, and built a nation under Kaya Maghan Sisse, who became Soninke king around 790.

Ghana's capital was the city of Koumbi Saleh, where Africans and Berbers met and traded. In the 9th century Arab traders described Ghana as 'the land of gold'. The gold came from Asante and Senegal, to the south and west, and trade routes led north and east to Morocco, Libya and Aksum, and so on to Europe and Asia. Ghana reached its peak in the

Prester John was the legendary king who was said to rule over a Christian empire in the heart of Africa.

10th century, controlling both the gold and salt trades. Other goods that passed through Ghana included woollen cloth and luxury items from Europe, as well as leather goods and slaves from the south. In 990, Ghana took over the neighbouring Berber kingdom of Awdaghost – Ghana was now 800km across. In 1076, however, it fell to the Almoravids, a puritanical Berber Muslim sect. The Almoravids ruled both Morocco and Spain, but they lost them in 1147, and power returned to Ghana until, in 1240, the country became part of a new African nation, Mali.

Berber and Arab traders transported goods hundreds of kilometres across the Sahara desert with camel caravans. Without traders, Ghana and its successors, Mali and Songhai, would not have become rich nations.

ANGLO-SAXON BRITAIN c.600–1066

The arrival of the Angles, Saxons and Jutes in Britain in the 5th and 6th centuries created a new people, the English, who were to dominate Britain.

Before they became Christians, the Angles buried their kings, with their possessions in ships, to take them to the afterlife. This gold clasp comes from a famous burial ship discovered at Sutton Hoo in England.

Vortigern, the British high king, hired German mercenaries, but failed to pay them. In revenge, they started to conquer Britain. Settlers followed in their wake, beaching their boats and wading ashore with cattle and sheep.

The Romans left Britain around 410. There was a brief revival of power for the now-Romanized British. In 446, the British high-king, Vortigern, invited some German Saxons from the Rhineland to enter Britain as mercenaries to support him in his struggle with the Picts. The Saxons gained a foothold in the southeast, but they were held off between 500 and 539 by the British under their leader, Arthur. After a major battle in 552, the Saxons began to take over southern and central England, and many Britons were killed or lost their lands, emigrating to Wales, Cornwall, Ireland, Scotland, Brittany in France and northwest Spain.

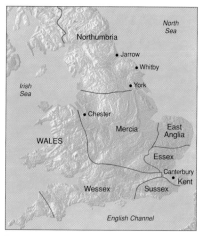

England was divided into seven kingdoms. From 878 Northumbria, East Anglia and much of Mercia came under Viking control and formed the Danelaw.

THE BIRTH OF ENGLAND

In the wake of the German invaders, many of their countrymen emigrated to England. During the 6th and 7th centuries, they slowly populated the country. British towns, villages and farms were abandoned, and the Celtic Christian church retreated with them. The Germans brought new farming and ownership patterns, and their pagan tribal groupings gradually took the shape of kingdoms. Eventually, seven kingdoms were formed: East Anglia, Mercia and Northumbria (ruled by the Angles), Essex, Sussex and Wessex (ruled by the Saxons) and Kent (ruled by the Jutes). In 597, Augustine was sent from Rome to convert the Saxons to Christianity but, by 620, the Saxons had reverted to paganism. They were later converted back by the Celtic Christians. The seven kingdoms frequently fought each other for domination and to claim the title Bretwalda (lord of Britain). In the 7th century the Northumbrian kings Edwin, Oswald and Oswy, and in the 8th century, the Mercian kings Ethelbald and Offa, gained supremacy. Egbert of Wessex was the first king of a united England in 829.

▼ This statue of King Alfred the Great stands at Wantage, his birthplace. Alfred was one of England's great leaders. He created laws based on justice and encouraged education.

STRUGGLES FOR POWER

In 789, the first Vikings appeared in England, and by the middle of the 9th century they had started to settle. When Alfred the Great was king of Wessex in 871, the Vikings were threatening to overrun his kingdom. Alfred fought nine battles against them in one year alone. He finally defeated them in 878 and made them sign the Treaty of Wedmore. which divided England in two – the Saxon west and Danelaw in the east. Alfred was a lawmaker, a scholar and a just king. In his time, texts were translated into English and *The Anglo-Saxon Chronicle*, an important history book, was begun. By 940, Danelaw had been won back from the Danes. England was reunified under Edgar (959–75), but in 1013 the Danes returned, and England was ruled until 1035 by the Dane, Canute the Great. There was better cooperation between the Danes and Saxons under Edward the Confessor but, in 1066, his son Harold, having just fought invading Norwegians in Yorkshire, was beaten by invading Normans, under Duke William.

▲ The Ruthwell Cross, carved in a Celtic style by Saxon monks in the 8th century, was richly decorated with scenes from the Gospels.

KEY DATES
446 Arrival of Jutish mercenaries led by Hengist and Horsa
560 onwards Large-scale immigration of Anglo-Saxons
597 Augustine arrives to convert the Anglo-Saxons
793 The first Viking raid, on Lindisfarne monastery
870 onwards Immigration of the Danes into Danelaw
871–99 Alfred the Great crowned king of Wessex
1013 The Danes conquer all of England
1066 The Normans, led by Duke William, conquer England

▼ Anglo-Saxon society had three classes – thanes or nobles, churls or freemen and serfs or slaves. In this picture, serfs are harvesting barley.

THE HOLY ROMAN EMPIRE 962–1440

Otto I became king of Germany in 936. He wanted to revive the old Roman empire and was crowned as the first Holy Roman emperor by the pope in 962.

The Holy Roman empire united all of the German-speaking peoples and extended its power into Italy, both to protect and to try to control the popes.

The Holy Roman empire was neither particularly holy, nor Roman. Founded by Charlemagne in 800, it was concerned with the power of kings and it was German. After Charlemagne's death the Carolingian empire gradually broke up, and France and Germany were separated. In Germany, a high king was elected as an overlord so that he could bind together the many independently ruling dukes, counts and bishops – the first of these overlords was Conrad I of Franconia, elected in 911. Later, the ambitious Otto I (936-973) wanted to revive the Roman empire. Otto brought stability by uniting all of the rulers who owed him allegiance and by defeating the Magyars.

Otto I was on the throne of Germany for 37 years. He made the Holy Roman empire a great and lasting institution by uniting his country's regional rulers and making them cooperate with him.

Otto conquered Bohemia, Austria and northern Italy. After 25 years, he had the pope crown him Emperor Augustus, founding an imperial tradition that lasted 850 years until 1806. His empire became a revived Holy Roman empire.

The Holy Roman emperor had the right to be crowned by the pope in Rome. Many popes and emperors disagreed over questions of power and authority, and this led to problems because each side wanted to interfere in the other's affairs.

When Henry IV went to see the pope at Canossa, in January 1077, to settle a dispute over power, Pope Gregory VII kept him waiting outside in a snowstorm for three days before forgiving him and removing the ban of excommunication.

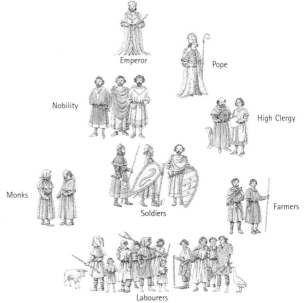

Emperor

Pope

Nobility

High Clergy

Monks

Soldiers

Farmers

Labourers

POPES AND EMPERORS

Several popes wanted help in ruling Christian Europe but often came into conflict with the emperors. Catholics had to obey the pope, so he was powerful. Popes wanted to choose emperors and emperors wanted to choose popes and control Church affairs. Finally, Emperor Henry IV and Pope Gregory VII clashed – in 1075 Gregory said Henry had no right to choose bishops. In revenge, Henry said that Gregory was no longer pope. Gregory excommunicated him, which meant Henry was no longer recognized by the Christian Church and his subjects did not have to obey him. In 1077, Henry asked to be forgiven. The quarrel over choosing bishops was finally settled in 1122, but there were more disputes, leading toward a gradual separation of church and state.

KEY DATES

911	Conrad I of Franconia is elected German king
936–973	Otto I strengthens the Holy Roman empire
955	Otto I defeats the Magyars
1056–1106	Henry IV in conflict with the pope
1122	Concordat of Worms: an agreement between emperor and pope
1200	Peak of the political power of the Roman Catholic Church
1300	Popes lose political power
1440	Holy Roman empire passes to the Austrian Habsburg dynasty

▲ The noblemen usually supported the emperor against the pope, but sometimes they rebelled. Soldiers usually supported the nobles, who gave them land; and peasant labourers were employed by soldiers and nobles. Similarly, monks supported clerics, who supported the pope. These were 'feudal' relationships, where a person gave allegiance and taxes in return for protection, land or rights. Everyone was bound into feudal relationships, throughout society.

◄ In 1122, the pope and the Holy Roman emperor signed an agreement at St Peter's Cathedral in the town of Worms, in southwestern Germany. The agreement ended a long-running dispute over who was responsible for the appointment of bishops.

THE AMERICAS 600–1200

In central America, the Toltecs came into prominence following the destruction of Teotihuacán. Meanwhile, in South America two new civilizations were developing.

By 600, Teotihuacán was in decline, and around 700 it was burned to the ground, possibly by barbarian tribes from the north. Various peoples tried to assume control, and around 900, the Toltecs established a capital at Tula. It became the centre of a military state and trading network that reached from Colorado to Colombia. In 1000, far away in Yucatán, a faction of the Toltecs invaded the Mayan empire, expanding the northern Mayan city of Chichén Itzá. The Toltec empire came to an end in 1168, when it was overrun and Tula was destroyed. Soon afterwards, the Aztecs moved into the area.

THE LATER MAYA

Many Mayan cities were abandoned around 800, though some still flourished in northern Yucatán from 900 onwards. Around 1000, Yucatán was invaded by Toltecs, who stayed there until 1221, building a copy of Tula at Chichén Itzá. Warrior-chiefs took power from the priests, and caused crafts such as pottery, art and literature to decline in quality.

The Toltecs were very militaristic, and their temples were guarded by stone statues of warriors such as this one from Tule.

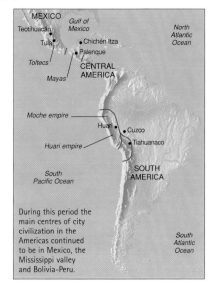

During this period the main centres of city civilization in the Americas continued to be in Mexico, the Mississippi valley and Bolivia-Peru.

The Toltecs were beaten by the Maya from Mayapán, whose Cocom dynasty dominated Yucatán for 200 years until civil war broke out in 1480. The Spanish arrived in the 16th century, but the last Maya city-state, Tayasal, did not fall until 1697.

THE PYRAMIDS OF ETOWAH

Etowah was one of the towns of the Mississippian culture in North America. This city culture spread far beyond the Mississippi valley – Etowah was near today's Atlanta, and famous as a source of mica, a transparent form of rock which could be split into fine sheets, like glass. The Etowans used tools of copper and stone, and built earthen pyramids with temples or the palaces of their chiefs on top. Their cities often had 10,000–20,000 inhabitants. They traded with Mexico and the Great Lakes area, and they made items to trade with the village-dwelling tribes of North America.

TIAHUANACO AND HUARI

Civilization in South America was based in two places. One was at Tiahuanaco, a large temple-city 3660m above sea level near Lake Titicaca in Bolivia. Between 600 and 1000, it had a population of 100,000. The people of Tiahuanaco made distinctive pottery and jewellery, massive dry-stone walls and enormous temple-stones. They created a string of towns stretching to the coast and into the Brazilian rainforests. The other civilization was Huari, which included remnants of several earlier local cultures such as Nazca and Moche. This was a powerful military empire, covering over half of modern Peru. Huari and Tiahuanaco may have followed the same religion, but Huari was militaristic and Tiahuanaco was peaceful. The two empires prospered until about 1000 when they were both abandoned, possibly because of drought.

KEY DATES	
600	Teotihuacán is sacked and burned
800	Toltec migration into central Mexico
900	Toltecs establish a city-state at Tula
1000	Tiahuanaco and Huari abandoned
1168	Tula destroyed
1200	Building of the Mississippian temple-cities
1200	Rise of the Aztecs and the Incas

This pottery figure of a god from Huari, decorated with maize, was probably honoured by farmers to help grow their crops.

This bowl made by the Mimbres people of the southwest had a hole to 'kill' the bowl. It was then buried with its owner.

▲ This is one of the many massive carved stone figures of Tiahuanaco, erected around 700. Tiahuanaco, near the southern edge of Lake Titicaca, was ruled by a priesthood according to religious principles. The city had several large temples.

▲ This earring from Huari, is made of stone inlaid with bone and shell. The Huari people also made beautiful jewellery and small objects out of gold.

◄ The Sun god Viracocha was carved on the Gateway of the Sun at Tiahuanaco around 600. This giant gateway opened into the Kalasasaya, the largest of the city's building areas and the main temple.

THE VIKINGS c.600–1000

The Vikings ransacked Europe for 200 years. But they were also traders and settlers and influenced the way of life in countries all over the continent.

Viking men and women wore everyday clothes that were both practical and fashionable. Their gold and silver jewellery was sometimes broken up and used as money.

In the 8th century, the Vikings began to venture from their homelands in Norway, Denmark and Sweden in search of adventure, treasure and better farmland. They made excellent wooden ships which could sail on rough seas and up rivers, landing easily on beaches. At first they raided rich monasteries and coastal towns, and later they sailed up the Rhine, Seine and Loire rivers to attack inland cities. Local rulers bought them off with silver and gold. Not all Vikings were raiders. Many were farmers looking for new land or traders seeking business. They were excellent sailors and traders, venturing as far as Constantinople and Baghdad in search of conquest or trade.

Viking coins minted in the 9th century were made of real silver or gold, so the coins themselves were actually worth the value they represented.

VIKING LONGSHIPS

The Vikings built superb boats, with sturdy keels acting as frames. These made the ships faster and more seaworthy. The boats were capable of being sailed or rowed. They could also be hauled by teams of men across land when necessary – even being dragged long distances overland in Russia, to get from one river to another. Or they could be beached easily without needing a harbour. A dragon's head on the bow was intended to scare off evil spirits, sea monsters and enemies.

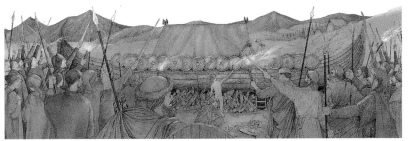

For the cremation of a Viking headman, the dead body was placed on a ship with his belongings, for use in the next life, and a slave girl was often sacrificed. The ship was set alight by a close relative, naked to symbolize how we enter and leave life naked.

VIKING TRADERS AND SETTLERS

In Britain, the Vikings settled mainly in northern and eastern England, northern Scotland, the Isle of Man and Ireland. In Ireland, they destroyed many monasteries and founded the first towns. In France, the Vikings settled in Normandy, given to them by the French king in 911 to stop their raiding. In 1066, as Normans, they invaded England, and in the early 1070s, southern Italy and Sicily. Vikings also settled in Iceland and some sailed on to Greenland and North America. Others entered the Mediterranean, raiding Spain, southern France, Italy and Byzantium. When they were beaten back by the Byzantines, Vikings sold them their services as traders and warriors instead. Swedish Vikings took over the Baltic Sea,

building trading towns such as Visby, Kiev and Novgorod. Sailing down Russia's rivers, they met Bulgar, Khazar, Byzantine and Arab traders. By 1000, the Vikings had settled down and their Nordic homelands became Christian nations. They had an enormous effect on the future of northern Europe, establishing trading routes and towns, founding Russia, influencing France, Holland, Poland, Britain and Ireland, and weakening the Carolingian empire. Their descendants, the Normans, were influential in Europe and led the Crusades. Because of Viking raiders, people had to rely on local feudal lords, exchanging work, produce and fighting men for protection. Gradually, Europe became more disunited, fighting grew frequent and the gap between the rich and poor widened.

▲ The Vikings were skilled metalworkers. This is a die-stamp, used for stamping a pattern onto hot metal. It shows two shamans with weapons, poised for ritual animal sacrifice.

▼ The Viking town in Denmark called Hedeby, was well known for its craftworkers and merchants. Hedeby was one of the ports from which the Viking traders sailed far and wide.

THE NORMANS C.900–C.1200

The Normans invaded England in 1066 and soon ruled over the Saxon and Viking English, the Welsh and the Irish. They also wielded influence further afield.

The Norman invasion of England took five years, yet it raised the Normans from provincial French vassals to become the wealthy rulers of a whole country.

The Normans were Danish overlords who lived in Normandy from 900 onwards. They had absorbed Carolingian and Christian ideas. There were not many of them, yet they were tough warrior-lords. William the Conqueror was crowned on Christmas Day 1066 – he had been only a French duke, but now he became the English king.

William the Conqueror, Duke of Normandy, was Norman king of England from 1066 to 1087.

NORMAN RULE

After the Norman invasion of 1066, many of the English protested. William put down rebellions brutally, taking English land and giving it to his Norman nobles, for them to rule the local areas. He gave land to the Church in order to gain its support, replacing English with French bishops and encouraged French traders and craftsmen to settle in England. The Normans built large castles, churches, monasteries and great cathedrals, and many towns grew up around them. The nobility spoke French while the ordinary people spoke early English. A central administration and tax system was established, and a tax assessment of the

▲ William the Conqueror was succeeded by two of his sons. William II ruled from 1087-1100 and Henry from 1100 to 1135. They established firm Norman rule, but it collapsed under the next king, Stephen, who died in 1154.

country's land and wealth, the *Domesday Book*, was made. Norman rule was harsh. They cared mainly about wealth and power, and used England as a base for foreign adventures, which the English had to finance. However, England developed economically, and within 100 years, the Normans began the invasion of Wales, Ireland and Scotland. England was changing – its landscape, towns and culture were all influenced by the Normans. By 1140 there was a disagreement over who should rule the country. This weakened the king and strengthened the nobles' power. A new Norman dynasty called the Plantagenets was founded in 1154 and their first king, Henry II, ruled England and half of France. During this time, the English class system, dominated by nobles, began to develop.

▶ The Bayeux Tapestry was made to commemorate the Norman invasion of England in 1066. Halley's Comet, shown clearly on the tapestry, came close to the Earth in that year, and it was taken as an omen that the invasion was justified.

THE NORMANS IN EUROPE

The Normans were also busy elsewhere in Europe. Around 1060, Norman soldiers under Robert Guiscard invaded Sicily and southern Italy, supporting the pope against the Byzantines and Arabs. As a result, they were favoured by the pope and often protected him. In the 13th century, they became leaders of the Crusades, the first European overseas colonial adventure. Through political marriages, and by serving as knights, papal agents, bishops and royal courtiers, Norman lords formed a feudal network which became very influential across Europe in the 13th century. In these feudal relationships, a noble who pledged allegiance and gave military support to a king was rewarded with lands and titles. Nobles then ruled estates and provinces, demanding loyalty of their followers and also rewarding them with lands and positions of power.

To honour ancient traditions, local law courts were often held outdoors. The lord of the manor was the judge. This court, or assize, held in 1072, met to decide whether some lands belonged to the Bishop of Bayeux in Normandy or to Canterbury cathedral.

THE FEUDAL SYSTEM

Under the feudal system, people held land in exchange for services. It developed in the 8th century under the Franks and was introduced to England by the Normans. In exchange for receiving estates and titles, Norman nobles paid taxes to the king, provided knights and raised armies. Nobles gave their knights land in exchange for military service and taxes. A knight had to have *villeins* (peasant workers) to manage his land. The villeins lived in villages near to the manor house. In exchange for a farm or house, they worked for the lord of the manor, giving him crops or money.

Manuscripts telling stories about knights and courtly love between lords and ladies were very popular in Norman England.

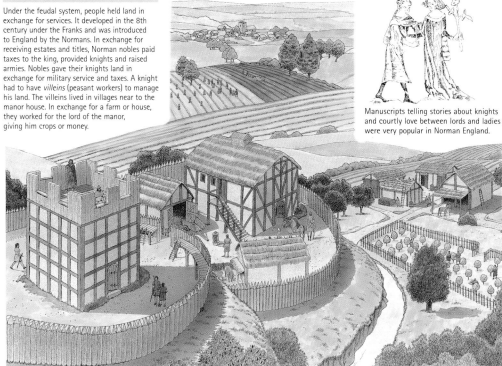

THE SELJUK TURKS 1037–1243

The Seljuks invaded the Middle East from 1037 onwards, ending Arabian domination of the Islamic world and opening the way for the Ottomans.

The Seljuks streamed down from Bokhara to Baghdad and later westwards into Anatolia, nearly to Constantinople. Anatolia (Turkey) then became Muslim, not Christian.

The Turks were originally a group of tribes living in Turkestan, central Asia. They split up in the 6th century, spreading to Russia, China, India and Persia. Some Turks abandoned the nomadic life to become administrators and mercenary warriors. They served the Abbasids, Fatimids and sometimes rose to high office. Turks such as the Seljuks, Ottomans, Mamluks, Bulgars and Khazars soon began to have great influence. They also joined forces with the Mongols. The Turkish cities of Samarkand and Bokhara grew wealthy and cultured in Islamic times.

SELJUK EXPANSION

To the east of the Caspian Sea lived a Turkic group called the Ghuzz, or Turkomans. The Seljuk broke away from the Ghuzz in 950, moving south and west. The Abbasid caliph in Baghdad was having difficulties, and he asked the Seljuks for their help. Led by Tughril Beg, the Seljuks invaded Persia and had occupied Baghdad by 1055. The Abbasid caliph appointed Tughril as sultan under him – in effect, he gave the Abbasid empire to the Seljuks. In this way, the Seljuks rose from being a simple nomadic tribe to rulers of the Islamic world.

Alp Arslan, Tughril's nephew, became sultan in 1063. He took Syria and Armenia and raided Anatolia. In 1071, the Byzantine emperor fought back. Alp Arslan hired Norman and Turkish mercenaries and marched into Armenia. The armies met at Manzikert. The Seljuks won because they pretended to have lost and ran away. When the Byzantines pursued them, they turned round and heavily defeated the Byzantine army. The Seljuks captured the Byzantine emperor and held him for ransom. This victory laid the foundation for what later became the Ottoman empire. Alp Arslan was a compassionate leader and ruled the empire well. With his blessing, many Turkomans and Seljuks moved into Anatolia.

▲ This minaret at the Jami mosque in Simnan, Iran, shows typical Seljuk patterns in its elaborate brickwork. The Seljuks became Muslims around 970, and considered themselves defenders of the Islamic faith.

▶ Like most nomads from the Asian steppes, the Seljuks were great horsemen. Using the new invention of stirrups, they could stay on horseback and fire arrows accurately in battle. This picture shows them defeating the Byzantines at the battle of Manzikert.

MALIK SHAH

The Seljuk empire reached its greatest power under the rule of Alp Arslan's son, Malik Shah (1072–92). He was a patron of the sciences and the arts and built fine mosques in his capital, Isfahan. His minister, Nizam al-Mulk, was respected as a statesman. During this time, Seljuks fully took over Anatolia (Turkey), founding the Sultanate of Rum next door to Constantinople. On Malik Shah's death, the Seljuk empire broke up into small states, and a variety of Seljuk, Mamluk and Kurdish sultanates continued through the 12th century, all under the eye of the Abbasid caliph in Baghdad. Then, in 1220, the Mongols overran the area, finally occupying Baghdad in 1258.

KEY DATES	
950	The Seljuks break away from the Ghuzz Turks
1038	Seljuks conquer Khorasan (Afghanistan)
1055	Seljuks conquer Baghdad
1071	Seljuks defeat the Byzantines at Manzikert
1072	Peak of the Seljuk empire
1081	Founding of the Seljuk sultanate of Rum
1092	Death of Malik Shah – Seljuk empire breaks up
1243	Mongol invasions: Seljuks become Mongol vassals
1258	Mongols destroy the Abbasid caliphate

▲ The Tomeh or Friday mosque was built in Isfahan, Persia in the Seljuk style. The Seljuks were great patrons of learning, architecture and culture.

▲ This is a tiled detail from the tomb of the Seljuk sultan Kaykavus I at Sivas in Turkey. The Seljuks produced beautiful and intricate patterns that were used to adorn their religious buildings.

◄ Though the Seljuks brought new life to the Abbasid empire, life in the Muslim world went on very much as before. This scene shows what a *souk*, or indoor trading hall, in Baghdad, would have looked like around the 12th century.

CHINA: THE SONG DYNASTY 960–1279

The Song (or Sung) dynasty created the third united Chinese empire, introducing many innovations and taking China into a long period of cultural eminence.

Until the Jin invaded the north in 1127, the Song ruled all of China. They were then forced to move south where they prospered for another 150 years until the Mongols invaded.

This Song temple painting from the 12th century shows the disciples of the Buddha feeding the poor.

After the fall of the Tang dynasty in 907, China had fragmented. In the Huang He valley, five emperors over 53 years tried to found new dynasties. None succeeded until Song Taizu took power in 960, founding the Song dynasty. He brought the many warlords and armies under control, and by both military and diplomatic means began to reunify China. This took 16 years and was completed by his brother, Song Taizong, the second Song emperor, in 979.

THE NORTHERN SONG PERIOD

Because China was now surrounded by other states, Song China was smaller than in Tang times. In the northwest was Xixia, which was Tibetan; in the northeast was Liao, ruled by Mongol Khitans; in the southeast was Nan Chao, a Thai state, and in the south was Annam, a Vietnamese kingdom. The Song emperors worked hard to make peace with them all.

Agriculture expanded and the population grew – especially in the south, which was now wealthy and important. By the end of the Song period there were probably around 100 million people living in China.

▼ Song artists often painted landscapes with small central features in them. This example of landscape painting from the Song period is called 'Fisherman'.

This stoneware vase with a butterfly and leaf-and-flower design is typical of the fine porcelain of the Song period. Europe did not master such artistic techniques for many centuries.

'A Buddhist Temple in the Mountains' was painted by Li Cheng in the 10th century.

THE SOUTHERN SONG PERIOD

In 1068 the prime minister, Wang Anshi, reformed the government. He simplified the tax system and reduced the size of the huge army. Although these cuts saved money, they also made invasion easier. In 1127, north China was attacked by the Jin, and the Song capital, Kaifeng, was lost. The Song withdrew to Hangzhou, south of the Yangtze, and the north was then ruled by the Jin until Kublai Khan's Mongols took over in 1234. Hangzhou became a large and beautiful city, with canals, parks and fine buildings. The Southern Song lasted until 1279 when south China was overrun by the Mongols.

The Song period saw great prosperity and advancement in new technologies, arts and literature. They invented gunpowder rockets, clocks, movable-type printing, paddle-wheel boats, magnetic compasses and water-powered machinery. Landscape painting, fine porcelain, poetry and theatre flourished. Banking and trade became important, towns grew large and new crops were introduced. Song China could have become even greater, but it was brought down by the Mongol invaders.

CHINESE PORCELAIN

Throughout the world, pottery had been made of clay, which produced a chunky and rough finish. Around 900 the Song dynasty Chinese invented porcelain, which was made from kaolin, a fine white clay. Their craftsmen made fine, smooth and delicate porcelain which, when used with special glazes and painting styles, could be beautifully decorated – making each piece a work of art. During this period, Chinese emperors had factories built to make porcelain especially for their palaces. Porcelain production soon became an enormous industry in China.

KEY DATES	
907	Fall of the Tang dynasty
960	Song Taizu founds the Song dynasty
979	Song Taizong completes unification of China
1000	Culture and the economy thrive in China
1068–86	Wang Anshi's reforms
1127	The Jin take north China: the Song retreat to Hangzhou
1234	The Mongols conquer northern China, ousting the Jin
1279	The Mongols conquer southern China: Song period ends

Song emperors had ceramic factories built to supply fine porcelain.

This porcelain wine vessel, standing on top of a warmer, was used for making mulled wine.

THE
MIDDLE AGES
1101–1460

During the Middle Ages, empires rose and fell
throughout the world. Many wars were undertaken
in the name of religion. In Europe, alliances were
made and quickly broken and a sense of nationalism
was growing. European traders ventured as far afield
as China, camel caravans trudged across the Sahara
and Venetian ships sailed the Mediterranean Sea
with their goods. These were times of faith and
fortune, of war and torture, famine and wealth. By
the end of the Middle Ages learning had come
within the reach of everyone who could read.

▲ The fortress Krak des Chevaliers, in what is now Syria, was the largest
and strongest castle built by the crusaders. It was garrisoned by 2,000
men but finally fell to the Saracens in 1271.

◄ The French king Saint Louis IX embarks in Aigues Mortes in 1248 for
the 7th Crusade to the Holy Land.

THE WORLD AT A GLANCE 1101–1460

During this period trade increased people's knowledge of many parts of the world, but it also helped to spread the Black Death, a disease carried by the fleas that lived on ships' rats. In Europe, the Black Death killed a quarter of the population.

Information about Africa was spread by Arab traders who sailed down the east coast of the continent. They carried with them stories of vast inland empires, rich with gold, and centred on large stone cities. In west Africa, the kingdom of Mali flourished.

In the Far East, the Khmer empire of Cambodia was at its height. In Japan, military rulers called shoguns were supported by samurai warriors, and were virtual dictators of their country.

The Mongols conquered much of Asia and Europe to form the largest, but short-lived, empire of all time. Their success was based on brilliant military tactics and superb horsemanship.

In the Americas, the Aztecs built their capital city of Tenochtitlan in the centre of a lake in Mexico, while in South America, the Inca empire was expanding by conquering neighbouring tribes.

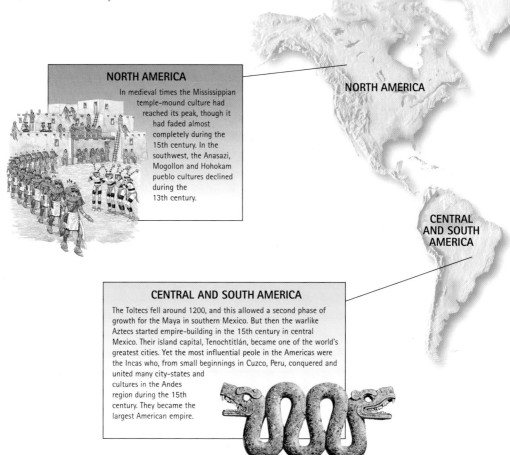

NORTH AMERICA

In medieval times the Mississippian temple-mound culture had reached its peak, though it had faded almost completely during the 15th century. In the southwest, the Anasazi, Mogollon and Hohokam pueblo cultures declined during the 13th century.

NORTH AMERICA

CENTRAL AND SOUTH AMERICA

CENTRAL AND SOUTH AMERICA

The Toltecs fell around 1200, and this allowed a second phase of growth for the Maya in southern Mexico. But then the warlike Aztecs started empire-building in the 15th century in central Mexico. Their island capital, Tenochtitlán, became one of the world's greatest cities. Yet the most influential peole in the Americas were the Incas who, from small beginnings in Cuzco, Peru, conquered and united many city-states and cultures in the Andes region during the 15th century. They became the largest American empire.

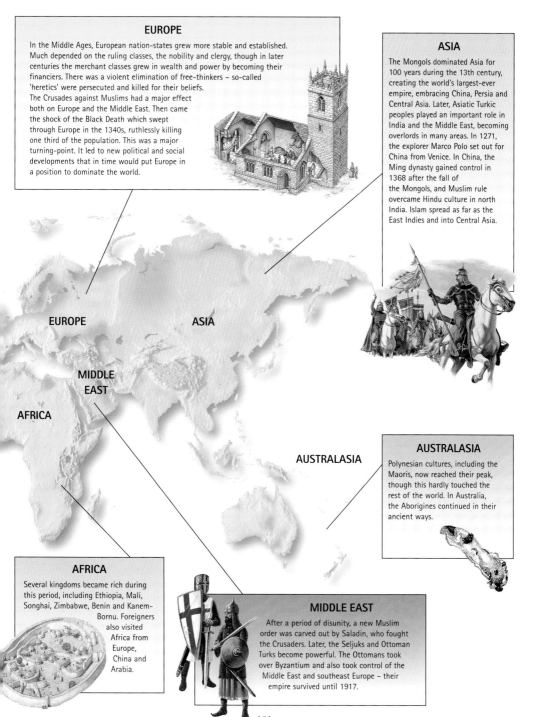

EUROPE

In the Middle Ages, European nation-states grew more stable and established. Much depended on the ruling classes, the nobility and clergy, though in later centuries the merchant classes grew in wealth and power by becoming their financiers. There was a violent elimination of free-thinkers – so-called 'heretics' were persecuted and killed for their beliefs. The Crusades against Muslims had a major effect both on Europe and the Middle East. Then came the shock of the Black Death which swept through Europe in the 1340s, ruthlessly killing one third of the population. This was a major turning-point. It led to new political and social developments that in time would put Europe in a position to dominate the world.

ASIA

The Mongols dominated Asia for 100 years during the 13th century, creating the world's largest-ever empire, embracing China, Persia and Central Asia. Later, Asiatic Turkic peoples played an important role in India and the Middle East, becoming overlords in many areas. In 1271, the explorer Marco Polo set out for China from Venice. In China, the Ming dynasty gained control in 1368 after the fall of the Mongols, and Muslim rule overcame Hindu culture in north India. Islam spread as far as the East Indies and into Central Asia.

EUROPE

ASIA

MIDDLE EAST

AFRICA

AUSTRALASIA

AUSTRALASIA

Polynesian cultures, including the Maoris, now reached their peak, though this hardly touched the rest of the world. In Australia, the Aborigines continued in their ancient ways.

AFRICA

Several kingdoms became rich during this period, including Ethiopia, Mali, Songhai, Zimbabwe, Benin and Kanem-Bornu. Foreigners also visited Africa from Europe, China and Arabia.

MIDDLE EAST

After a period of disunity, a new Muslim order was carved out by Saladin, who fought the Crusaders. Later, the Seljuks and Ottoman Turks become powerful. The Ottomans took over Byzantium and also took control of the Middle East and southeast Europe – their empire survived until 1917.

THE CRUSADES 1095–1291

Palestine, once ruled by Byzantium, had been conquered by the Muslim Arabs in 637. From Rome, the pope called on Christian leaders to fight for the Holy Land.

To Christians and Muslims, Palestine was the Holy Land, a place of pilgrimage for hundreds of years. After the Arabs conquered Palestine in 637, Christian pilgrims were still able to visit Jerusalem safely, but this changed with the arrival of the Seljuk Turks. In 1095, Pope Urban II called on Christians to free Palestine from Muslim rule. Knights and ordinary people set out, led by Peter the Hermit and Walter the Penniless. Most of them never reached Palestine, and the rest became a wild, hungry mob. In 1099, a well-disciplined Crusader army recaptured Jerusalem, massacring its inhabitants. They established four Crusader kingdoms in Palestine and Syria. At first the Saracens, as the Crusaders called the Seljuk Turks, left the Crusader kingdoms alone.

The Crusaders wore heavy armour and rode large stallions, while the Muslims, called Saracens, wore light armour and rode mares. As a result, the Crusaders looked formidable, but the Saracens were more mobile.

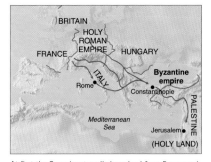

At first the Crusaders travelled overland from France and Italy to Palestine but, after having to fight the Seljuk Turks in Anatolia, they then went by sea from Venice.

But some of the Crusaders behaved badly towards the Muslims. In 1187, the Muslim sultan Saladin defeated the Crusaders and retook Jerusalem. In 1191, Richard I of England, known as the Lionheart, led an army to the Holy Land. He took Cyprus and the city of Acre, but was unable to recapture Jerusalem. Saladin respected Richard, and they eventually both signed a treaty sharing the Holy Land, including Jerusalem – the Crusaders founded a 'Second Kingdom' of the holy city, with its heart at Acre.

The Crusaders built Norman-style castles in Palestine and Syria. Krak des Chevaliers in Syria, built by the Knights Hospitallers and holding 2,000 men, was besieged by the Muslims in 1271. They starved the Crusaders into surrender.

Saladin (c.1137–93) a pious leader, united his people and led them in a *jihad* or holy war against the Crusaders.

Richard the Lionheart (1157–99), led an army of knights to the Holy Land in 1191 on the Third Crusade. They did not recapture Jerusalem, but Richard was able to secure a five-year peace treaty with Saladin. This allowed European pilgrims to visit the holy places again. When Richard tried to return to England in 1192, he was captured by Leopold of Austria, and then Henry VI, the Holy Roman emperor who held Richard for ransom for about a year. He finally reached England in 1194.

The fourth Crusade began in 1202, but the Crusaders were unable to pay for transport. In exchange for transport from Italy, they agreed to loot Constantinople. In 1212, up to 50,000 children from France and Germany set off for Palestine but most of them died of hunger or became slaves – this is known as the Children's Crusade. The Fifth Crusade to Egypt failed, and the last three crusades (1218–72) were also unsuccessful. Palestine was finally conquered in 1291 by the sultan of Egypt.

Louis IX, king of France (1226–70), was a deeply religious man. He led the Seventh Crusade against Egypt in 1248, and led the Eighth Crusade (1270), but died of the plague.

KEY DATES

1096-99	First Crusade takes Palestine and Syria
1187	Saladin wins back Jerusalem
1189-92	Third Crusade
1202-04	Fourth Crusade loots Constantinople
1212	Children's Crusade
1218-21	Fifth Crusade – a failure
1228-29	Sixth Crusade – partly successful
1291	Palestine taken by sultan of Egypt

▼ At the decisive battle of Hattin in 1187, Saladin tricked the Crusaders onto a hill on a hot day. While the Crusaders roasted in their metal armour, he surrounded and subdued them. Saladin then went on to win back Jerusalem.

HENRY OF ANJOU 1154–1189

Henry of Anjou became Henry II, the first Plantagenet king of England, in 1154. With his lands in France he became one of the most powerful rulers in Europe.

Henry II (1133–89) was a man of great humour but he also had a violent temper. Through his strong rule he brought about a period of peace and prosperity to England and France.

Eleanor of Aquitaine's marriage to Louis VII of France was annulled because they had no children. She then became Henry II's wife.

▲▶ Thomas à Becket (c.1118–70), Henry's chancellor, became Archbishop of Canterbury in 1162. He frequently opposed the king and in 1170 was murdered in Canterbury Cathedral (right). This was a mistake that Henry much regretted.

Henry of Anjou was William the Conqueror's great-grandson. His mother Matilda was the widow of the Holy Roman emperor Henry V, who had died in 1125. She was the daughter of Henry I of England, who named her his heir after his sons had died. Henry I wanted to strengthen his hold on Normandy, so in 1128, he had Matilda marry Count Geoffrey of Anjou, in France. In 1127, Henry had forced the English nobles to accept a woman as heir to the thrones of England and Normandy, but they were angry that Matilda had married into a French royal house. When Henry died in 1135, the Church and nobility split, and most threw their support behind Matilda's cousin Stephen as king. Civil war broke out in 1139, but in the end, Stephen remained king. He was later forced to make Matilda and Geoffrey's son, Henry of Anjou, his heir.

Henry ruled over a greater area of France than the French king Louis VII. He also ruled England, and eventually spread his influence to Wales, Scotland and Ireland.

When Henry of Anjou became Henry II of England at the age of 21, he inherited the French provinces of Anjou, Maine and Touraine from his father and Normandy and Brittany from his mother. In 1152, he married Eleanor, the abandoned wife of the French king Louis VII, thus gaining Aquitaine. As a result of this he ruled England and two thirds of France.

HENRY AND BECKET

Henry was a very energetic ruler and travelled widely throughout his kingdom. He was well-educated and cultured, and his court at Chinon in France was attended by many erudite scholars and troubadours (minstrels). Henry brought his nobles firmly under control, improved the laws of England and forced the Scots and Welsh to obey him. When Norman nobles took control in Ireland, he subdued them and made himself king of Ireland in 1172. Henry chose capable ministers, among them Thomas à Becket, who became his chancellor. When Henry made him Archbishop of Canterbury, Becket began to assert the rights of the Church. After years of quarrels, Henry is said to have exclaimed, "Who will rid me of this turbulent priest?" Four knights took him at his word and killed Becket. Henry later did penance for this crime.

Eleanor of Aquitaine died in 1204. Her tomb in the abbey church at Frontrevault, in western France, lies next to that of one of her sons, Richard I. Her husband Henry II, who died in 1189, lies nearby.

LIFE IN A CASTLE

Castles were large buildings that were cold and draughty to live in. They were military fortresses that also housed the lord's soldiers and servants. Towns soon grew up outside the castle walls. In the lord's dwellings, the lady's servants lived in the top room, where linen and clothes were stored. Under this was the master bedroom, where the lord and lady would sleep. Below this was the solar, the lord's living room, and on the ground floor were the great hall and a secure storeroom for the master's weapons, monies and valuables.

After the murder of Becket, the pope demanded that Henry do penance and be flogged. This was done, and Henry expressed his regrets. Later he was pardoned.

Henry's empire was a family possession, not a country, and he planned to divide it between his four sons. They squabbled over this and then revolted against him. Two of them died, leaving Richard (the Lionheart) and John. Richard became king of England in 1189, and was followed after his death in 1199 by John. Although Henry had been a great and creative king, who had written the common law of England, he died in 1189 feeling that his life had been a failure. After his death, his sons lost most of his French lands and the new order that Henry had built in England soon disintegrated.

KEY DATES	
1122	Eleanor of Aquitaine is born
1133	Henry of Anjou born
1139	Eleanor of Aquitaine marries Louis VII of France; marriage annulled
1152	Henry marries Eleanor of Aquitaine
1154	Henry becomes king of England
1157	Submission of the king of Scotland
1162	Thomas à Becket becomes Archbishop of Canterbury
1166–76	Legal reforms in England
1170	Murder of Thomas à Becket
1171	Henry becomes king of Ireland
1173	Thomas à Becket made a saint
1174	Rebellions by Henry's sons
1189	Henry dies in France

IRELAND 700–1350

This period of Irish history saw increasingly permanent domination by foreigners, following invasions first by the Vikings and then by the English.

▲ Strongbow, or Richard de Clare, Earl of Pembroke invaded Ireland in 1170 from Norman-dominated Pembroke in Wales. In 1171 he became king of Leinster.

▼ Art MacMurrough Kavanagh, king of Leinster, rides to make peace with the Earl of Gloucester during the Norman invasions.

Ireland was peopled mainly by Gaelic Celts who lived in about 150 *tuath* or tribes. They frequently feuded and warred, and this became a hindrance to Ireland's prosperity. Then, in 432, one man arrived who changed the course of Irish history – St Patrick. He travelled around Ireland converting Irish chiefs to Christianity and preaching peace. By 600, Ireland had become Europe's main Christian centre, and Irish monks preached across Europe. In 795, the Vikings invaded, and for the next 40 years, raided and destroyed monasteries. By 840, they began to settle, founding towns such as Dublin, Waterford, Cork and Limerick. From these, they traded and mixed with the Irish people, adopting many of their customs.

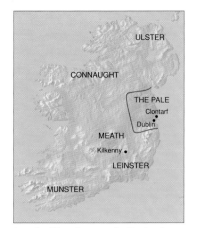

In medieval times there were five kingdoms in Ireland. All that was left of direct Norman rule was a small area around Dublin called the Pale.

The rest of Ireland was still traditionally Irish. By now, the five largest kingdoms were Ulster, Leinster, Munster, Connaught and Meath. In 976, Brian Boru, king of Munster, set about invading his neighbours. By 1011, he dominated Ireland, but on his death other local kings fought to be high king. The last strong high king was Turlough O'Connor of Connaught. After he died in 1156, two kings became rivals. One of these, Dermot MacMurrough of Leinster, asked for help from the Normans in England.

THE COMING OF THE ENGLISH

The Earl of Pembroke, or 'Strongbow', supported Dermot MacMurrough in return for marrying his daughter and inheriting Leinster. In 1170, Strongbow and other Norman nobles invaded, seizing Irish lands for themselves. This alarmed the king of England, Henry II, who proclaimed himself overlord of Ireland. Many Irish, fearing chaos, supported him and the Norman nobles submitted. Like the Vikings before them, many Normans soon adopted the customs of the Irish. However, in 1366, Lionel, Edward III's son who governed Ireland, ordered the Irish-Norman families to stop speaking Gaelic and marrying Irish women. This demand was not accepted and the Irish-Normans now looked upon the English as interfering foreigners. By the late 15th century English rule existed only in the Dublin area, called 'the English Pale'.

KEY DATES

432	St Patrick introduces Christianity to Ireland
795	The start of Viking raids – destruction of Irish monasteries
840	Vikings settle, establishing coastal trading towns
1014	Brian Boru, king of Munster, defeats Vikings at the Battle of Clontarf
1148	Richard de Clare becomes Earl of Pembroke
1166	Rory O'Connor becomes first king of Ireland since 1014
1170	Norman invasion of Ireland led by Richard de Clare
1171	Richard de Clare becomes king of Leinster; Henry II annexes Ireland
1366	Irish-Normans revolt against English orders banning Gaelic and mixed marriages
1530s	Henry VIII reimposes English control

During the unsuccessful English campaigns in Ireland between 1367 and 1400, ships had to carry provisions across the Irish Sea to the English troops.

▼ On the Rock of Cashel, in County Tipperary, stand the ruins of St Patrick's Cathedral. Given to the Church in 1101, the cross (far left) is where traditionally the kings of Munster were crowned.

SHOGUNS AND SAMURAI 1200–1500

The shoguns were generals who acted as governmental dictators, and the samurai were Japanese knights. They both dominated Japan for nearly 700 years.

A samurai's main weapons were a bow made of boxwood or bamboo and one or two single-edged swords. Samurai were strictly trained from childhood, following a code called *bushido* – the warrior's way.

The Fujiwara family had held power in Japan for 300 years from the 9th century. However, their influence broke down when they ran out of daughters, the traditional brides of the emperor. For a time, some of the former emperors ruled. Then the Taira clan took over briefly until a rival clan, the Minamoto, rallied under Minamoto Yoritomo and seized power. Yoritomo assumed the title *sei-i dai shogun*, which means 'barbarian-conquering great general'. In 1192, he set up the Kamakura shogunate, through which he ruled Japan from his estate, Kamakura, near Edo (Tokyo). His powers were unlimited. From that time on, shoguns ruled Japan as military dictators until 1868. When Yoritomo died in 1199, the Hojo family, a branch of the Taira clan, became regents to the shoguns, and held power in an unofficial capacity until the Kamakura shogunate ended in 1333.

Minamoto Yoritomo (1147–99) was an ambitious nobleman who saw his chance in the chaos that followed the breakdown of the power of the Fujiwara. Yoritomo ruthlessly crushed his enemies, including many of his own family.

Japanese government was complicated. The emperor was a ceremonial figure to whom everyone bowed down, but the shogun had the real power. The regents to the emperors and shoguns also had influence, as did the *daimyos* or lords, who jostled for position at court and frequently battled over land. As a result, a class of warriors grew up called *samurai*, who fought for the daimyos.

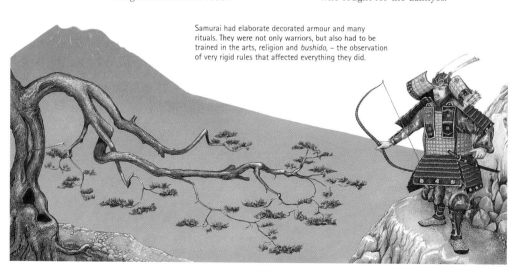

Samurai had elaborate decorated armour and many rituals. They were not only warriors, but also had to be trained in the arts, religion and *bushido*, – the observation of very rigid rules that affected everything they did.

During the 12th century, Zen, a branch of Buddhism, spread from China to Japan. It had simple but strict rules, which the samurai followed. Buddhist shrines, like this gateway, were also built in the Chinese style.

KNIGHTS OF JAPAN

The samurai were knights who were prepared to fight to the death for their daimyos, to whom they swore undying loyalty. Like European knights, samurai believed in truth and honour, and had a strict code of conduct called *bushido*. Before combat, a samurai would shout his name and those of his ancestors, and boast of his heroic deeds. In battle he fought hand to hand, often using two swords at once. If defeated or captured by his enemy, he had to commit ritual suicide (*hara-kiri*) in order to save face. At times, rivalry between samurai was destructive.

In 1333, the Ashikaga clan overthrew the Kamakura shogunate and the emperor, putting a new emperor in place. He appointed them as shoguns, this time in Kyoto. However, there was frequent samurai fighting between daimyos. This increased until, in 1467–77, the Onin civil war broke out, and Japan split into nearly 400 clan-states. The Kyoto emperors became powerless and impoverished. Despite this, trade and culture centred on the daimyo estates grew in Japan. For ordinary people, the daimyo wars brought high taxes, insecurity and disruption to their lives.

As with European knights and Muslim warriors, religion and war were very closely connected for the samurai. He took a long time to dress and arm himself for battle, and there were strict rules of cleanliness and ritual.

THE SAMURAI IN BATTLE

Samurai battles were very ritualistic. They involved prayer and posturing (making oneself look strong) beforehand, with shouting and noise-making, using rattles and gongs to frighten the enemy. Individual samurai would undertake duels and contests. Often, battles were like a dance or a ceremonial game of chess. However, samurai warfare was deadly once they joined in full battle. During the Ashikaga period (1338–1573), much of the fighting deteriorated into meaningless squabbles for honour and plots of land.

EUROPEAN TRADE 1100–1450

During the early Middle Ages a new commercial order was developing in Europe. Merchants and bankers thrived and influencied the decisions of kings.

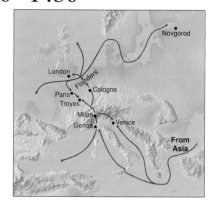

In the 12th century, cities and ports grew up on trade routes in Europe. Italian merchants attended fairs such as that at Troyes to buy Flemish cloth and sell Asian goods.

The early Middle Ages was a time of growth for Europe. Population was increasing, and more land was cultivated to grow food. This created agricultural surpluses for trading. Towns grew larger, with regular trade fairs at places like Troyes, Lyons, Antwerp, Frankfurt, Leipzig, London, Krakow and Kiev. River links and shipping routes were busier. Instead of exchanging goods (bartering), money was used, and people entered business increasingly for profit. Jewish traders, Knights Templars and certain business families specialized in money-lending and the safekeeping of valuables. Italy was the richest part of Europe. Venice and Genoa were large independent seaports and banking centres, buying spices, silks and other luxuries from the East. Goods from Asia came through Byzantium, Egypt and Syria, and from Africa through Tunisia and Morocco. They were traded for cloth, furs, hides, iron, linen, timber, silver and slaves.

The perils of travel in medieval times are shown in this drawing of a highwayman robbing a traveller of his money. Highwaymen often lay in wait for their victims at roadsides.

In a medieval town, markets were usually held once a week. Livestock, food, metals, cloth, leather and woodwork were all sold there, and country people met to discuss local affairs.

Most of Europe's money was silver, but the Asian countries traded in gold. This caused problems, so the Templars, Jewish traders and Italian merchants invented banking, with bills of exchange and 'promissory notes' which could be used instead of cash. Early industries grew up in the Rhineland (Germany), northern France, Flanders and England, importing materials like copper, alum, wool and charcoal, and exporting goods and clothes.

THE GROWTH OF COMMERCE

A new class of merchants and skilled craftsmen appeared. Merchants grew rich through buying and selling, but they also risked losing money because of roadside robbery or piracy on the high seas where cargoes and fortunes could be lost. Trading companies, cities and organizations like the Hanseatic League in the Baltic Sea worked together to protect trade, and opened offices in ports and market-places. To protect their trade the Venetians and Genoese became Mediterranean naval powers. Around 1350, in Genoa, insurance services were offered, to protect traders against loss and bankruptcy. Banking families such as the Fuggers in Augsburg, Germany, and the Medicis in Florence, Italy, grew in wealth and influence. A new commercial order was developing, and kings, nobles and clerics slowly lost power as they grew dependent on merchants and indebted to bankers. Soon, this new class was to influence the decisions of kings.

In Europe, posthouses and taverns were built along main roads. They provided refreshments, places to stay and a change of horse for merchants, pilgrims and other travellers.

THE HANSEATIC LEAGUE

In 1241, two German towns, Hamburg and Lübeck, set up a *hansa* or trading association, which developed into the Hanseatic League in 1260, and involved many former Viking towns. They carried food and raw materials from eastern Europe in exchange for manufactured goods from the west. The Hanseatic League dominated trade between England, Scandinavia, Germany and Russia in the 14th century.

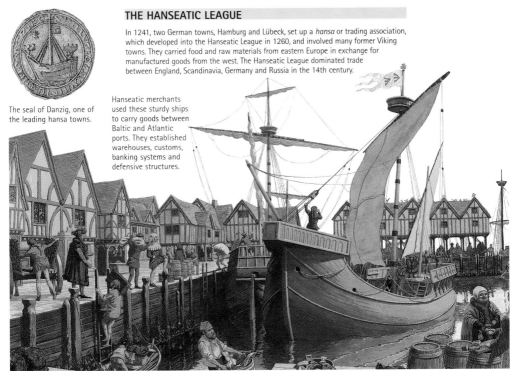

The seal of Danzig, one of the leading hansa towns.

Hanseatic merchants used these sturdy ships to carry goods between Baltic and Atlantic ports. They established warehouses, customs, banking systems and defensive structures.

CHARTER AND PARLIAMENT 1215–1485

In 13th-century England there was a growing struggle between the kings and lords. The absolute power of rulers was being questioned by those they ruled.

King John (1199-1216) quarrelled with his nobles, who turned against him, forcing him to sign the Magna Carta.

King John of England, the youngest son of Henry II, was given to violent outbursts of temper. Not surprisingly, he soon fell out with his barons in English-ruled Anjou and Poitiers, and he lost those lands to France. In England, he taxed his barons heavily and ruled so harshly that they rebelled. The barons threatened John, and demanded that he accept their traditional rights and obey the law.

The great seal of King John was affixed to the bottom of the Magna Carta. John's seal showed his consent and so turned the charter into the law of the land.

THE MAGNA CARTA

In 1215, the barons met King John in a meadow called Runnymede, beside the Thames River. There, they forced him to put his seal to the Magna Carta, which means 'great charter'. This charter covered many important areas, including weights and measures, the powers of sheriffs, and the legal rights of freemen and boroughs (towns). The king agreed to obey the law himself and he was not allowed to raise taxes without the agreement of his Great Council of nobles. No sooner had John agreed to the charter than he went back on his word. A civil war broke out, but John soon died, leaving the throne to his young son who became Henry III. The charter was reissued, and in 1225, it became the law of England. Henry III was incompetent and he spent large sums of money, so the barons got together again, this time led by Simon de Montfort. They forced Henry to agree to consult the Great Council in all major matters. Like his father, Henry III went back on the deal, but de Montfort defeated him in battle at Lewes. Simon de Montfort and the Council then ruled England in Henry's name.

In 1215, John was forced to put his seal to the Magna Carta at Runnymede. John did not actually sign the charter, and possibly could not even write.

THE POWER OF PARLIAMENT

In 1265, Simon de Montfort called a new Parliament of two chambers, the House of Lords (previously the Great Council of nobles and bishops) and the House of Commons. The House of Commons was made up of two knights from every shire and, representing the people, two burgesses from every borough. Later, Edward I (1272–1307), a successful ruler, reformed England's law and administration, creating a Model Parliament which included even more representatives from the country. However, the king still held power. In 1388, there was a major clash and the 'Merciless' Parliament removed some of King Richard II's rights.

As time went on, Parliament's powers gradually grew. The House of Commons slowly gained greater power, though Parliament still represented mainly the richer classes. Only in the 20th century did full-scale democracy arrive.

KEY DATES	
1215	King John reluctantly affixes his seal to the Magna Carta
1216	King John dies. His nine-year old son, Henry III, becomes king
1225	The Magna Carta becomes the law of England
1227	Henry III, now aged 20, begins to rule
1258	Law reforms – the Provisions of Oxford
1265	Simon de Montfort's Parliament is called
1272	Edward I becomes king of England
1295	Edward I's Model Parliament
1307	Edward II becomes king of England
1388	The 'Merciless' Parliament (against Richard II)

▶ Simon de Montfort was a Norman baron who became earl of Leicester. In 1264-65 he virtually ruled the country on behalf of the king.

▲ Henry III is pictured at his coronation in 1216. He ruled for 55 years, yet he lost much of his power as king because he was not a good ruler. He was more interested in the arts and in building churches.

Bishop Lord Lady Knight Merchant Nun

Peasant

Queen

King

These were the different social classes of the time, in order of power from the king downwards. The largest number of people were peasants, who had no power at all. Some lords and priests treated them fairly, allowing them to voice their concerns, but this was rare.

BENIN AND ZIMBABWE 1100–1480

Benin was an advanced kingdom in the tropical forests of western Africa. Zimbabwe was a gold-mining centre in the high grasslands of southeast Africa.

Benin was situated in what is now southeastern Nigeria. It was the longest-lasting of the forest kingdoms of rainforested western Africa. Its capital, Benin City, was founded in about AD900 and was at its most prosperous in the 15th century. The city had wide streets lined with large wooden houses and was enclosed within walls 40km long. The palace of the *oba* (king) was richly decorated with bronze plaques and carvings. The city's busy merchants dealt in cloth, ivory, metals (especially bronze), palm oil and pepper. Benin was famous for its art, especially sculptures using pottery, ivory or brass.

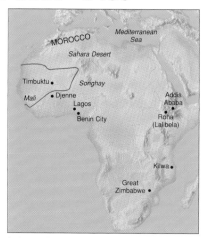

During medieval times, there were four main kingdoms that flourished in Africa: Mali (later overwhelmed by Songhay), Ethiopia, Benin and Zimbabwe.

This lifelike ivory mask shows an *oba* or king of Benin. The oba would have hung it round his waist on ceremonial occasions.

This Benin bronze shows an oba seated on his throne, with two subjects. kneeling before him. Benin craftsmen cast bronzes by the 'lost wax' process. A wax model was carved, then covered with clay to make a mould. The wax would be melted away, and molten bronze would be poured into the mould. Many copies could then be made using this process.

Benin flourished under the leadership of Oba Eware the Great, who ruled from 1440 to 1473. He modernized and expanded Benin. Usually, warring African states made slaves of their prisoners, but Benin avoided this – so when the Portuguese began buying slaves from western Africa in the 16th century, Benin did not join in the slave trade. This protected it against European colonialization until 1897.

Many of the peoples of western Africa lived in tribal villages, herding animals and growing crops. The grasslands of central Africa (shown here) were very different environments from the tropical forests of the west.

ZIMBABWE

Zimbabwe grew prosperous from its large reserves of copper and gold. Dug from over one thousand mines, much of it was bought from the 10th century onwards by Arab traders on the east coast. They built the only towns in southern Africa, and Zimbabwe is best known for its walled palace city, Great Zimbabwe, built between 1100 and 1400. However, little is known of the Zimbabweans. They were not great warriors, so Zimbabwe did not expand its borders by military means.

Around 1450, Zimbabwe was absorbed into the Shona kingdom of Rozvi (Mwenemutapa), named after a great chief, Mwene Mutapa. This warrior kingdom took control of most of what is Zimbabwe and Mozambique today. It continued gold and copper trading with the Arabs and grew rich from this. This changed when the Portuguese settlers tried to gain control of the mines. Rozvi fought against this for some time, though by 1629, the mines had fallen under Portuguese control. Nevertheless, Rozvi survived until the 1830s.

This is a 14th-century bronze head of an *oni*, or king, of Ife. He is wearing the headdress of a sea god. Ife was a kingdom that once bordered Benin.

GREAT ZIMBABWE

One intriguing African mystery is the walled city of Great Zimbabwe, after which modern Zimbabwe is named. The massive stone structures were built of granite blocks between the 11th and 14th centuries, but nobody knows why or by whom. A *zimbabwe* is a stone-built enclosure, of which there were many in southeast Africa, though this was the largest and grandest.

The ruins of the Great Enclosure can be seen today on the site of the city of Great Zimbabwe.

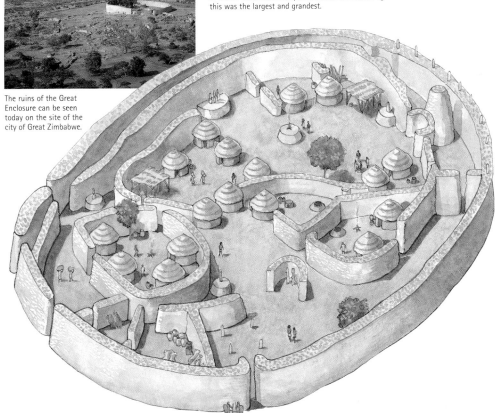

THE MONGOL EMPIRE 1206–1405

The Mongols created the largest empire in history. Their presence was felt strongly in China, Russia and Islam, though their empire was not very long-lasting.

At its greatest extent in the 13th century during the reign of Kublai Khan, the Mongol empire extended from the Pacific Ocean to the Black Sea.

Genghis Khan (c.1162–1227) was a great leader, general and organizer. During one campaign, his army travelled at breakneck speed – 440km in three days. He died after a fall from a horse.

In 1180, a 13-year-old boy was made leader of his tribe when his father was poisoned. The boy was named Temujin, and his tribe, the Yakka Mongols, were a warlike nomadic people in Mongolia. Two thirds of the tribe promptly deserted him, but soon Temujin reunited them and went on to take over other Mongol tribes. In 1206, at a meeting of the *khans* (chiefs), Temujin was hailed as Genghis Khan, 'Emperor of All Men'. He promised that future generations of Mongols would lead lives of luxury. Genghis Khan began a career of conquest by training a ruthless, fast-moving and well disciplined army. His hordes terrified their opponents, killing anyone who did not surrender or change sides. In a series of outstanding campaigns, Genghis Khan conquered Turkestan, north China and Korea, then swung westward to overrun Afghanistan, Persia and parts of Russia. Some of his success came from the fact that his opponents were not united.

MONGOL EXPANSION

After Genghis died, Ogodai and Monke Khan conquered Armenia, Tibet and more of China, then ravaged eastern Europe. His grandson, Kublai Khan, completed the conquest of China. He made himself first emperor of the Yuan dynasty (1271–1368). Some aspects of Mongol rule were good – they gave women status, encouraged scholars, respected different religions and helped trade. They opened the Asian Silk Roads to East–West travellers. Some aspects were not so good – their ruthless armies destroyed cities and massacred many people. However, the Song in southern China resisted the Mongols for 20 years before they fell, and the Delhi Sultanate stopped them invading India. By 1260, Mongol expansion had ended.

In battle, the Mongols were unstoppable. Their bows fired further than any had before, their horses were fast and their tactics tricked many of their opponents.

The Mongols were a nomadic people from the bleak plains of Mongolia who lived in portable yurts, large, round tents made of hides or cloth. They herded cattle, sheep, goats and horses. Even when they invaded cities, their army stayed outside in yurt encampments.

THE BARBAROUS TAMERLANE

From 1275, a Venetian merchant called Marco Polo spent 17 years at the court of Kublai Khan. His stories gave Europeans their first real picture of China and its wealth. After Kublai Khan's death in 1294, the mighty Mongol empire began to break up. Some khans, such as the Chagatais in Turkestan, the Ilkhans in Persia and the Golden Horde in southern Russia, kept smaller empires for themselves. Cruel though the Mongols were, none was as barbarous as the great Mongol–Turkish ruler of Samarkand, Tamerlane, or Timur (1336–1405). He and his army went on the rampage between 1361 and 1405, and brutally overran Persia, Armenia, Georgia, Mesopotamia, Azerbaijan and the Golden Horde.

Despite his cruel reputation, Tamerlane was a great patron of the arts, astronomy and architecture in Samarkand. Generally, however, the Mongols left no lasting mark on the world, except for the destruction they brought. China and Russia became poor, the Muslim world was in turmoil and even European countries like Poland and Serbia suffered greatly. After Tamerlane's death in 1405, the great, bloodstained Mongol adventure was over, except in Russia and Turkestan.

In battle the Mongols wore light armour made of leather and iron. They were so fast and ruthless that most of their opponents gave up in fear. Big silken flags streamed behind them. Anyone who opposed them was destined to die.

MONGOL SPORTS

The Mongols loved horse-riding, wrestling and archery. The great khans encouraged sport as a way of developing battle skills and discovering talented soldiers. There were many sporting contests, and promotion in the army could be gained from success in these. Sport also gave a training in teamwork, which was one of the Mongols' greatest strengths.

From an early age, Mongol boys practised archery and wrestling.

The Mongols adopted the ancient Persian game of polo.

MEDIEVAL EXPLORERS 1270–1490

In the Middle Ages, many bold men made long, and often dangerous, journeys to distant lands. These new contacts improved trade and spread political influence.

Prince Henry the Navigator (1394–1460) was responsible for the city of Ceuta in Morocco. This led him to become increasingly fascinated with ships. He sponsored expeditions and the work that led to the building of a new ship, the caravel. He encouraged more precise mapmaking and the invention of seafaring instruments. The sailors he trained were the first Europeans to undertake long sea voyages.

Camel caravans took Muslim travellers and traders across the deserts of Africa and Asia, making them some of the most travelled people of the medieval period.

The first medieval explorers were the Vikings, who went as far as America, Morocco and Baghdad. The first account of central Asia was written by a Franciscan friar, John of Pian del Carpine, who visited the Mongol khan on behalf of Pope Innocent IV in 1245. The best-known European traveller was Marco Polo, a young Venetian who journeyed to meet Kublai Khan in China and worked there for many years. Returning in 1295, he composed a vivid account of his travels.

Between 1325 and 1350, Ibn Battuta, a Moroccan lawyer, travelled to Russia, central Asia, India, southern China and Africa, writing detailed descriptions of his travels. Admiral Zheng He was sent by the Chinese Ming emperor Yongle on seven naval expeditions between 1405 and 1433. His fleet sailed to Indonesia, India, Persia, Mecca and eastern Africa, establishing diplomatic relations and extending China's political influence over maritime Asia. Zheng He took back gifts to the emperor, including spices and exotic animals.

PRINCE HENRY THE NAVIGATOR

Henry was a son of the king of Portugal. At the age of 21, he discovered treasures in Morocco that had been carried overland from Songhai and Senegal in west Africa. He was curious to know if these places could be reached by sea. So, between 1424 and 1434, Henry paid Portuguese sailors to explore the coast of Africa. Encouraged by their discoveries, he built a school of navigation at Sagres in Portugal, to train sailors for further voyages of discovery.

Kublai Khan sent Marco Polo on various journeys, including to the Chinese borders of Tibet. Polo told of how they burned bamboo on their campfire, which caused loud crackling noises that terrified the horses. However, the noise also scared off wild animals.

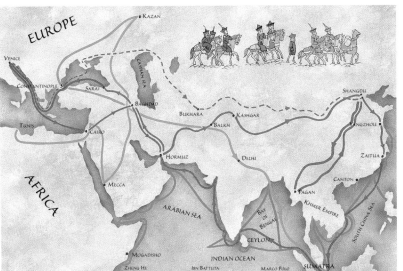

The incredible journeys of medieval travellers covered thousands of kilometres. The greatest of these travellers were Marco Polo, Ibn Battuta and Zheng He.

Marco Polo first visited China with his father, a Venetian trader. He stayed there longer, playing an active role in the court of Kublai Khan and being sent on missions for the khan around China and to Pagan in Burma.

Marco Polo was away from Venice for 25 years. His overland journey to China took four years, and the return journey by sea from China to Persia, then overland, took three. He acted as a regional governor and ambassador for the khan while in China. The khan welcomed many foreigners, and he found Europeans to be very unusual, exotic visitors.

By the time Prince Henry died in 1460, Portuguese explorers had reached what is now Sierra Leone. Henry's work inspired later Portuguese explorers to sail further down the coast of western Africa, seeking a sea route to India and the Far East. The world was now on the verge of a great expansion of international contact. The Chinese could have been the first international travellers, but its emperors preferred isolation, and traders were discouraged from travel. Muslims had also travelled far and wide, though by 1500 they had lost their urge to expand further. Meanwhile, the Europeans were about to change their inward-looking policies and seek new horizons.

Ibn Battuta (1304–68) was a lifelong traveller from northern Africa who wrote lengthy accounts of his journeys. He travelled to Africa and Russia, to Morocco and India, and by sea to south China. His stories were the most accurate and useful of all the accounts written by medieval travellers.

Admiral Zheng He's fleet of huge ocean-going junks were specially built for his expeditions. On his first voyage, his fleet consisted of 62 of these ships.

THE HUNDRED YEARS WAR 1337–1453

The Hundred Years War was a series of short, costly wars in which the English kings tried to dominate France, but met great resistance from the French.

John of Gaunt (Ghent in Belgium) was one of the sons of Edward III. As regent (1377–86) for his nephew Richard II, he was the most powerful man in England.

▲ Edward, Prince of Wales, father of Richard II, got his nickname the Black Prince from the colour of his armour.

▶ Edward III, invaded France in 1346. His army of 10,000 men defeated a French army twice its size at Crécy. The English longbows easily outshot the French crossbows.

In 1328, Charles IV of France died without a direct heir. The French barons gave the throne to his cousin, Philip VI, but Charles's nephew, Edward III of England, challenged him, and Philip confiscated Edward's French lands. In 1337, war broke out. At the start of the conflict, which actually lasted 116 years, the English defeated a French fleet in the English Channel at Sluys, then invaded France, winning a major battle at Crécy and capturing Calais. Both sides ran out of money and had to agree to a truce, which lasted from 1347 until 1355. In 1355, a fresh English invasion took place, led by Edward's heir, Edward, nicknamed the Black Prince. He won a resounding victory at Poitiers. The Treaty of Brétigny in 1360 gave England large parts of France. But a new campaign followed and England lost most of her French possessions.

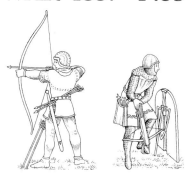

The English longbow (left) shot further and faster than ever before. The French crossbow (right) was easier to load and fire than a longbow, but much slower.

THE CHILD KINGS AND A TRUCE

In the late 1360s, the French and English thrones were inherited by children, Charles VI of France and Richard II of England. Richard's uncle, John of Gaunt (1340–99), ruled for him. In 1396, Richard II married Charles VI's daughter, Isabelle, and a 20-year truce was agreed.

nombre .&+ t ce que te fcay
& leurs befoignues & ordon
nances et ce que te &uile
ny et determineray en ce

vhle & france. &y ple & la
futaille & crecy entre le roy &
france et le roy dangleterre.

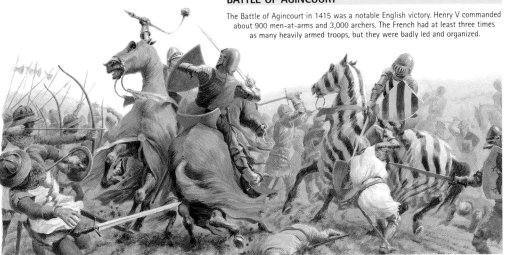

BATTLE OF AGINCOURT

The Battle of Agincourt in 1415 was a notable English victory. Henry V commanded about 900 men-at-arms and 3,000 archers. The French had at least three times as many heavily armed troops, but they were badly led and organized.

THE END OF A COSTLY WAR

After a long truce the war began again in 1415. Henry V (1387–1422), England's adventurous king, revived his country's old claim to the French throne. England still held Calais and parts of Bordeaux. Henry captured Harfleur in Normandy and heavily defeated the French at Agincourt. Henry next occupied much of northern France. Charles VI made him heir to the French throne in 1420. He also married Charles's daughter, Catherine of Valois. Henry died just 15 months later, leaving the throne to his infant son, Henry VI. Charles VI died soon after.

In support of the claim, Henry's uncle, John, Duke of Bedford, besieged Orléans. The French forces, led by a 17-year-old peasant girl, Joan of Arc, successfully defended the town. Joan claimed she saw visions and heard voices telling her to free France. She escorted the new but uncrowned king, Charles VII, to Reims to be crowned. However, Joan was soon defeated at Paris and captured by the Burgundians. They sold her to the English, who burned her as a witch. There was sporadic fighting for some years after. The French recaptured their lands by 1453, ending the war. Only Calais remained English. This had been a kings' war, but it was the people who had paid the price.

KEY DATES

E = English victory, F = French victory

1340	Battle of Sluys (E), at sea
1346	Battle of Crécy (E)
1347	Battle of Calais (E)
1356	Battle of Poitiers (E)
1372	Battle of La Rochelle (F), at sea
1415	Battle of Agincourt (E)
1428	Battle of Orléans (F)
1450	Battle of Formigny (F)
1451	Battle of Bordeaux (F)

At the age of 17, Joan of Arc (1412-31) led the French against the English, during France's darkest hour. The English accused her of being a witch, because she claimed she had visions and heard voices telling her to drive the English out of France.

Joan of Arc (Jeanne d'Arc) was burned at the stake in 1431. Six hundred years later, in 1920, she was made a saint.

THE BLACK DEATH 1347–1351

The Black Death was one of the worst disasters in history. It resulted in the death of around a third of the population of the Middle East and Europe.

The Black Death was carried by rat fleas. It possibly spread from an area in south China or southeast Asia.

Rats were common in houses, ships and food stores, so the disease spread rapidly through the population.

In the art of the time, the Black Death was depicted as a skeleton riding furiously on horseback.

The Black Death killed about 25 million people in Europe alone, and probably many millions more in Asia. It was a form of bubonic plague and took its name from spots of blood that formed under the skin and turned black. There were also swellings ('buboes') in the groin and armpits. Victims usually died horribly within a few hours of the symptoms appearing. The plague was carried by rat fleas, which could also live on humans. The Black Death later developed into pneumonic plague, which spread directly from person to person through touching or sneezing.

The disease was carried from south China or Burma, through central Asia, along the Silk Road to Baghdad and the Crimea by Mongol armies. In 1347, it arrived by ship at Genoa, in Italy. It then spread west and north, reaching Paris and London in 1348, and Scandinavia and Russia in 1349. There was no protection against it, and it killed rich and poor alike.

European towns were filthy, with rubbish, rats and human excrement in the streets. Human waste was thrown out of windows and trodden underfoot. The lack of any basic hygiene was the reason that the plague spread so fast.

THE IMMEDIATE EFFECTS

The Black Death devastated whole regions: houses stood empty, villages and towns were abandoned, and people in some trades and even some whole areas were completely wiped out. Baghdad and Mecca were emptied. Fields were littered with unburied corpses because doctors, priests and the people who had buried the corpses died themselves. Society and economy in Europe began to disintegrate.

▶ The Black Death spread through Europe from Genoa. Some areas, such as Ireland and parts of France, lost only 10 per cent of their population, but other areas such as northern Italy, eastern England and Norway lost as much as 50 per cent.

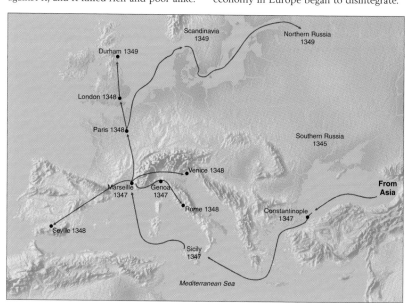

Scandinavia 1349
Northern Russia 1349
Durham 1349
London 1348
Paris 1348
Southern Russia 1345
Venice 1348
Marseille 1347
Genoa 1347
Rome 1348
From Asia
Constantinople 1347
Seville 1348
Sicily 1347
Mediterranean Sea

THE LONG-TERM EFFECTS

The Black Death were widespread. It destroyed many people's faith in God. To them it appeared to have no logic, killing good as well as wicked people. Farms were abandoned and churches were empty. Until the onset of the Black Death, Europe usually had a surplus of labour and low wages, but the shortage of workers now made wages soar. Many country people began moving into the empty towns, working for actual money for the first time. The already weak feudal system collapsed. There were revolts. Europe and the Muslim world were in shock. Over the next one hundred years, many things changed. The medieval period was making way for a new, more questioning, world.

People burned the clothes of the dead to try to stop the plague spreading. This failed, however, because the real cause of the disease were the fleas that lived on rats that were rife at the time.

▲ It was important to remove diseased bodies quickly, even when people were still bewailing the loss of their loved ones. Criers went around the streets calling "Bring out your dead!"

◄ At night, plague carts were loaded with corpses to be taken away and buried. The Black Death spread quickly in towns because of the crowded housing conditions and lack of hygiene. Even isolated monasteries did not escape since the disease was carried there by infected people pleading for help.

CHINA: THE MING DYNASTY 1368–1644

After a long campaign, the Mongols were driven out of China. There then followed 150 years of peace and prosperity under the Ming dynasty.

Emperor Hong Wu (1328–98) reorganized the administration of China, setting up colleges for training mandarins (civil servants). Candidates for these posts had to pass examinations in literature and philosophy.

Kublai Khan was a great Chinese emperor, but he was a foreigner. When he died in 1294, he was followed by a series of feeble Yuan emperors, famines and much hardship. The last Yuan emperor, Sun Ti, was a bad ruler. The Chinese people were tired of being ruled harshly by foreigners. They found a Chinese ruler in Zhu Yuan-hang, who had been a monk and, during bad times, a beggar. As a rebel bandit chief, he had a ready-made army. He also proved to be an excellent general.

After a 13-year campaign, he captured Beijing, drove the Mongols back to Mongolia, and became emperor. He founded the Ming ('bright') dynasty, and took the name Hong Wu ('very warlike'). He moved the capital south to the fortified city of Nanjing. Hong Wu ruled China for 30 years as a dictator, guarding against Mongol incursions and restoring

▼ Inside Beijing, the Ming emperor Yongle built the Forbidden City, which only the emperor and his household were allowed to use. This is a typical building inside the imperial complex.

Art, literature and ceramics had developed during the Song and the Yuan dynasties. This vase demonstrates another period of excellence in the arts under the Ming.

order and prosperity to his country.

Hong Wu left his throne to a grandson, Jianwen, but he was overthrown four years later by his uncle, Zhu Di, who became Emperor Yongle – pronounced *Yong-lay* – (1360–1424) in 1403.

PEACE UNDER THE MING

China grew great again under Yongle, who was emperor from 1403 to 1424. Roads, towns and canals were rebuilt, and when he moved to Beijing, he built the great halls, palaces and temples of the Forbidden City. Learning and the arts flourished. Trade and industry were encouraged and, unusually, China looked outwards, exporting goods and spreading Chinese influence abroad. The Muslim admiral Zheng He was sent on long voyages to India, Islam and Africa. After Yongle's reign, however, China lost interest in other countries. Many Chinese settled in southeast Asia, becoming involved with the growing 'China trade'. Government administration was improved and, apart from problems with piracy and Mongol attacks, flourished for a century.

From 1517 onwards, the Portuguese and other Europeans arrived on the coast, trading mainly at Guangzhou (Canton). In the late 16th century there was a series of emperors who were disliked and wasteful, and there were attacks on the borders. Trade declined, corruption and banditry grew, and there was famine and rebellion. In 1592, the Japanese invaded neighbouring Korea, threatening the security of China. Rebels eventually took over much of China, and in 1644, the Ming dynasty finally fell.

Gardening and landscaping developed into a very special art form in China and Japan. Water was an important ingredient in this exquisite Chinese ornamental garden.

KEY DATES	
1353–54	The Black Death breaks out across China
1368	The Ming dynasty is founded by Zhu Yuanzhang
1403–24	The reign of Ming emperor Yongle
1517	Arrival of the first Europeans traders in southern China
1552–55	Major attacks on shipping by pirates off the China coast
1582	Growing corruption and decline
1592	The Japanese invade Korea, threatening China's security
1644	Fall of the Ming dynasty

This brush-holder, from the Ming period, is made of carved lacquer. Lacquer is a thick varnish painted in many layers onto wood. It sets hard, making a very strong material often used by the Chinese.

Landscape painting also became a highly developed art form under the Ming. This classic Ming landscape painting by Tang Yin is entitled *Dreaming of Immortality in a Thatched Cottage*.

THE KHMER EMPIRE 802–1444

The Khmer empire was created in 802, when the Khmer people were united by Jayavarman II. It reached its peak under Suryavarman I and Suryavarman II.

The Khmer lived in what is now Cambodia. Their armies conquered many of the surrounding lands, dominating mainland southeast Asia during the 12th century.

Around 400, the Khmer had created a state called Chen-la which was at its strongest around 700 under Jayavarman I. Previously Hindu, the Khmer adopted Buddhism during this time. Chen-la declined, and after a brief occupation by the Javanese, a new Khmer state was created in 802 by Rajah Jayavarman II. He was a 'god-king' or *devarajah* (like the Tibetan Dalai Lama today). He ruled from a city called Angkor Thom, near a lake called Tonle Sap. The Khmers wrote books on paper, palm leaves and vellum. Fire, rot and termites have long since destroyed them, but it is possible to learn about the Khmers from Chinese histories, and from the many carvings in the ruins of Angkor Thom ('great city') and Angkor Wat ('great temple') nearby.

The temple complex of Angkor Wat was richly decorated with many carved sandstone figures. After the temple was abandoned in the 15th century, they were swallowed up by the jungle and not rediscovered until the 19th century.

The building of Angkor Thom, originally called Yasodharapura, was started just before 900. The richly decorated temple complex of Angkor Wat was built between 1113 and 1150.

▼ Angkor Wat, a huge temple complex built of red sandstone, was surrounded by walls and a moat 180 metres wide and 4km long. The temple had three main enclosures (representing the outer world) surrounding an inner holy shrine.

▲ Many of the temple carvings at Angkor Wat show the daily lives of the Khmer people as well as telling the stories of their sacred myths and battles.

The Khmer armies, which may have included hundreds of war elephants, fought many battles and conquered most of the surrounding lands, including Thailand and Champa (southern Vietnam). The empire reached its peak between 1010 and 1150, under Suryavarman I and Suryavarman II. In the 13th century, the people grew tired of serving the devarajahs through forced labour, and Khmer life began to break down. In 1444, invading Thai armies forced the Khmer to abandon Angkor. From then on Cambodia was dominated by the Thai kingdom of Siam.

This masterpiece of carved architecture is one tower of the Bayon temple, built in the 12th century, in the capital city, Angkor Thom.

KHMER DAILY LIFE

The Khmer were builders, craftspeople, fishermen, farmers and warriors. Many lived in houses perched on stilts around Tonle Sap. Their main food was rice, and their special irrigation systems produced three crops a year. The kings were still Hindus, but most of the population were Buddhists. They held elaborate religious ceremonies in connection with the seasons of the year. They traded with India and Java, and also with China, bartering spices and rhinoceros horn for porcelain and lacquerware. The royal women of the court wore skirts, leaving the upper part of the body bare. They were encouraged to study law, astrology and languages. Men wore only a loose loin-covering.

KEY DATES	
c.400	Founding of Chen-la, after the fall of Funan
c.700	Chen-la reaches its peak of development
802	Jayavarman II founds the Khmer nation by uniting the people
880s	The Khmer invade the Mon and Thai peoples
900	Angkor Thom founded
1050–1150	The Khmer empire at its high point under Suryavarman I and Suryavarman II
1113–50	Angkor Wat is built
c.1215	Death of last Angkor king, Jayavarman VII; empire starts to fall into decline
1444	Angkor abandoned after Thai invasions led by Ayutthaya

These heavenly dancers were carved on one of the walls at Angkor Wat in about 1200.

THE
RENAISSANCE

1461–1600

This period marks the start of modern history. Muslims still dominated much of Europe and Asia. The Ottomans in the Middle East and the Moghuls in India took Islamic culture to a new height. The Aztecs and Incas dominated the Americas. In Europe a new world was coming into being. Europeans questioned their traditions and beliefs. They sailed the oceans, explored new ideas, and European society changed greatly – it became more materialistic, free-thinking and complex.

▲ The Inca celebrated two festivals of the Sun. One was in June, the other in December. The emperor led the ceremonies, attended by officials from all over the empire, in the great square at Cuzco.

◀ This is a detail from *Madonna of the Magnificat*, painted by the Italian Renaissance artist Sandro Botticelli in 1465.

THE WORLD AT A GLANCE 1461–1600

Europeans started to emerge from the narrow confines of the Middle Ages to travel beyond their continent. In 1461, European seafarers, traders and colonists were on the brink of setting out to find new routes to the Far East, and to explore and exploit the rest of the world. For the first time, continents were brought into direct contact with each other.

In Mexico and South America, the Aztec and Inca empires were at their height, but with the arrival of the Spanish, the Aztec capital Tenochtitlan was destroyed and the Inca forced to retreat to the highlands of Peru. By 1535, the Spaniards had turned the people of South and Central America into slaves and the original inhabitants were nearly wiped out by disease and ill-use. The invaders turned their attention north, but it was some years before North America would feel the real effects of their arrival.

African civilizations too came under European influence, but it was confined to the coast. The heart of Africa remained undisturbed. China was still ruled by the Ming. Although the arts flourished, society had begun to stagnate under their rule.

In Europe, the movement now called the Renaissance was fuelled by Greek scholars fleeing from the fall of Constantinople, who brought with them the knowledge of ancient Greece and Rome.

NORTH AMERICA

Europeans first arrived here around 1500, though colonies were not properly started until the 17th century. The Mississippian culture was in decline from the 1450s and the Pueblo peoples of the southwest, friends with the Aztecs, were now past their peak. Other native peoples were embroiled in their own political and religious problems, as well as matters of trade with other groups, unaware all the time of the white man's impending threat to their way of life.

NORTH AMERICA

CENTRAL AND SOUTH AMERICA

CENTRAL AND SOUTH AMERICA

Disaster struck South America. The richly advanced civilizations of Mexico and the Andean regions were generally on an upswing when the Spaniards arrived. But both the Aztecs, in the 1520s, and the Inca in the 1530s, were quickly subjugated by these strange foreigners, whom they had welcomed at first. Trickery, followed by European diseases, killed millions. The Spanish and Portuguese quickly took over, establishing plantations, mines and cities in the search for gold, wealth and glory. The majority of early immigrants were actually Africans, brought over as slaves to run the plantations. But it was the Latino bosses and priests who, by 1600, ran what was quickly becoming Latin America. Those indigenous Americans who survived were suddenly the subjects of new masters.

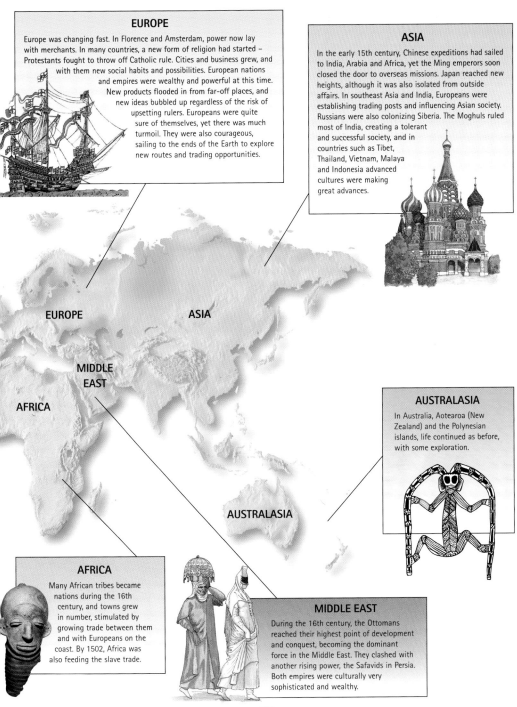

EUROPE

Europe was changing fast. In Florence and Amsterdam, power now lay with merchants. In many countries, a new form of religion had started – Protestants fought to throw off Catholic rule. Cities and business grew, and with them new social habits and possibilities. European nations and empires were wealthy and powerful at this time. New products flooded in from far-off places, and new ideas bubbled up regardless of the risk of upsetting rulers. Europeans were quite sure of themselves, yet there was much turmoil. They were also courageous, sailing to the ends of the Earth to explore new routes and trading opportunities.

ASIA

In the early 15th century, Chinese expeditions had sailed to India, Arabia and Africa, yet the Ming emperors soon closed the door to overseas missions. Japan reached new heights, although it was also isolated from outside affairs. In southeast Asia and India, Europeans were establishing trading posts and influencing Asian society. Russians were also colonizing Siberia. The Moghuls ruled most of India, creating a tolerant and successful society, and in countries such as Tibet, Thailand, Vietnam, Malaya and Indonesia advanced cultures were making great advances.

EUROPE

ASIA

MIDDLE EAST

AFRICA

AUSTRALASIA

In Australia, Aotearoa (New Zealand) and the Polynesian islands, life continued as before, with some exploration.

AUSTRALASIA

AFRICA

Many African tribes became nations during the 16th century, and towns grew in number, stimulated by growing trade between them and with Europeans on the coast. By 1502, Africa was also feeding the slave trade.

MIDDLE EAST

During the 16th century, the Ottomans reached their highest point of development and conquest, becoming the dominant force in the Middle East. They clashed with another rising power, the Safavids in Persia. Both empires were culturally very sophisticated and wealthy.

THE AZTECS 1430–1520

In the 15th century, the Aztecs dominated Mexico from their wondrous city of Tenochtitlan, dominated by pyramids, on an island in the middle of a lake.

By 1500, the Aztecs controlled a large empire in Mexico. They had started to expand in 1430, under the emperor Itzcoatl. Tenochtitlan had a population of about 300,000 around 1500, when it was at its most powerful under Montezuma II. In order to feed them all, food was grown on artificial islands, or *chinampas*, built up in Lake Texcoco, in the middle of which the city stood. Conquered lands provided maize, beans and cocoa, cotton cloth, and gold, silver and jade for Aztec craftworkers. Traders bought turquoise from the Pueblo Indians in the north, while from the south came brightly coloured feathers, which were used to make elaborately decorated capes, fans, headdresses and shields. Aztec society was organized along military lines. All the young men served in the army from the age of 17 to 22. Some stayed on longer than this, because even a peasant could rise to be an army commander if he was good enough.

The Aztecs dominated the centre of Mexico from coast to coast, including a number of cities, and they also influenced much wider areas to the north and south.

HUMAN SACRIFICES

One of the main tasks of the army was to take many prisoners-in-war. The prisoners were sacrificed in Tenochtitlan, at the huge pyramid-temples in the middle of the city. Religious blood-sacrifice was important to the Aztecs who sacrificed to many different gods. All of these gods were believed to need a great deal of human blood – especially the god of war, Huitzilopochtli. This armed aggression and human sacrifice were gradually turned the Aztecs' neighbours against them.

▲ Aztec priests were a special class of people in Aztec society, responsible for running a full calendar of elaborate ceremonies and religious sacrifices. For human sacrifices, they used knives with blades made from very sharp stone, such as chalcedony, flint or obsidian.

▶ Ordinary Aztecs lived in huts with thatched roofs. They ate maize pancakes, with spicy bean and vegetable fillings, very like Mexican tortillas today.

This ceremonial headdress of the 16th century is made mainly of quetzal feathers. Parrot feathers in brown, crimson, white and blue were also used.

RISE AND FALL OF THE AZTECS

The Aztecs traded far and wide around Mexico, into what is now the USA and south to Colombia. They sold high-value items made by craftspeople – clothing, jewellery, household and ceremonial items. They also exacted tribute – payments made by cities to stop the Aztecs invading them. The capital, Tenochtitlan, was one of the world's best-planned cities. The streets and canals were laid out in a grid pattern on its lake island, and arranged around a huge ceremonial area of pyramids, temples, palaces and gardens. Three wide causeways linked the city to the mainland. But the Aztecs' greed for sacrificial victims meant that, when the Spanish arrived in 1520, their neighbouring societies helped them conquer the Aztecs by the following year.

The emperor was treated like a god, and he could be spoken to only by priests and nobles. Ordinary people had to keep their eyes on the ground when he travelled through the capital.

◄ This terracotta statue shows the hideously grinning skull face of the Aztec god of death. The Aztecs also used human skulls to make masks. They encrusted them with turquoise and seashells and lined them inside with red leather.

▼ Three long causeways linked Tenochtitlan to the mainland. Traders travelled far and wide from the city, and some of them acted as spies for the emperor. The causeways were also a good defence for the city. When the Spanish arrived, it was trickery and disease, not direct attack, that helped them overcome the Aztecs.

THE INCA EMPIRE 1438–1535

For a century, the Incas ruled a vast, well-organized empire in the Andes mountains of South America. Their empire was obliterated by the Spaniards.

This golden pendant made by the Incas has markings showing mathematical patterns. These had a religious and calendrical significance for the Incas.

The Inca ruler was known as the *Sapa Inca*. He was believed to be descended from Inti, the Sun god, who gave him the right to rule. He was also worshipped as a god himself. The Sapa Inca ran the country from Cuzco, thought to be Inti's home. Royal officials directed everything in all parts of the empire. They looked after the affairs of the cities, and made sure the factories and workshops that produced pottery, textiles and decorative metal objects, as well as the farms, were all working efficiently. Writing was unknown to the Incas, so they kept all their records on *quipus*. These were cords with knots tied in them to convey information, such as records of population and taxes. At its greatest period in 1525, the empire stretched for 3,500km. The cities, towns and villages were all linked by a network of roads. Communication throughout the empire was provided by relay runners.

▲ A *quipu* was a length of string or cord, from which several strings hung. These were in different colours, and each had knots in it. Each knot represented a piece of information, usually a number. An Inca would hold the long cord outstretched and 'read' the information in the downward rows.

▶ To grow crops in the foothills of the Andes, the Incas cut terraces into the slopes with wooden tools. They grazed their alpacas and llamas on higher ground, and grew maize, pumpkins, quinoa, beans and fruit lower down.

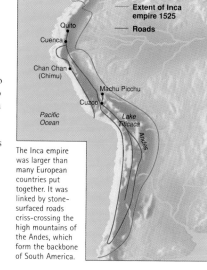

The Inca empire was larger than many European countries put together. It was linked by stone-surfaced roads criss-crossing the high mountains of the Andes, which form the backbone of South America.

INCA EXPANSION

When Pachacuti became the Sapa Inca in 1438, he began to expand his lands around Cuzco. In 1450, he conquered the Titicaca basin, and in 1463 he went to war against the Lupaca and Colla tribes. Under his son Topa's command, the Inca army defeated the neighbouring Chimu empire in 1466, and Topa continued to expand the empire after he became the tenth Sapa Inca in 1471. During the next 15 years, he conquered lands far to the south, and later took control of lands to the north and west.

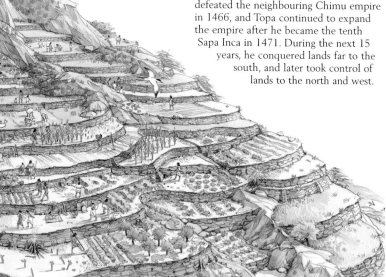

RISE AND FALL OF THE INCAS

The Incas reached a very efficient level of organization, and invented ingenious ways of farming on steep slopes, and building bridges, roads and towns in the high mountain areas. They achieved all this without being able to write.

Topa Inca built many of the roads and towns. Topa's son, Huayna Capac, the Sapa Inca from 1493, further expanded the empire, building a second capital at Quito. When he died in 1525, the empire was divided between his sons: Huascar ruled the south and Atahualpa the north. This division led to civil war, just before the Spaniards landed in 1532. Because they were able to use the roads and the Incas were arguing among themselves, the Spaniards destroyed the empire by 1535.

KEY DATES	
1200	Manco Capac establishes the Inca dynasty and capital of Cuzco
1350	Local expansion of the Incas under Mayta Capa
1438	Pachacuti becomes the Sapa Inca
1450	Pachacuti greatly enlarges the Inca empire
1466	Topa Inca overruns the Chimu empire
1485	Topa Inca conquers Chile and Peru
1493	Quito becomes the second capital
1525	Huayna Capa dies and civil war breaks out between Cuzco and Quito
1532	The Spaniards invade the Inca empire
1535	Spaniards destroy the Inca empire

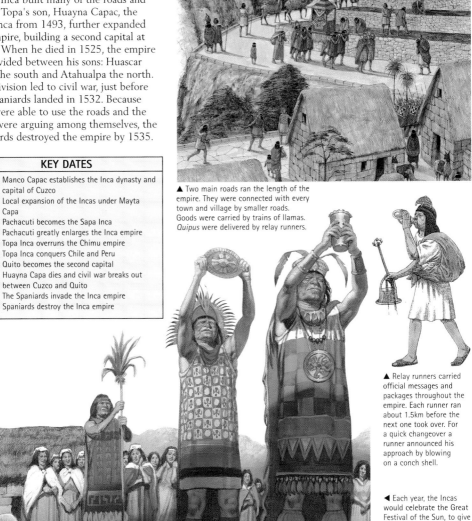

▲ Two main roads ran the length of the empire. They were connected with every town and village by smaller roads. Goods were carried by trains of llamas. *Quipus* were delivered by relay runners.

▲ Relay runners carried official messages and packages throughout the empire. Each runner ran about 1.5km before the next one took over. For a quick changeover a runner announced his approach by blowing on a conch shell.

◄ Each year, the Incas would celebrate the Great Festival of the Sun, to give thanks for the growth of crops and continuation of life, and to pray for blessings in the future – not unlike the Christian festival of Easter.

THE RECONQUEST OF SPAIN 1469–1516

The reconquest of Muslim-ruled Spain by the Spanish began in the 12th century. The country was fully reunited 300 years later, under Ferdinand and Isabella.

Ferdinand succeeded to the throne of Aragon in 1479. He was a tough politician and ruled Spain jointly with his wife, Isabella.

Isabella inherited the kingdom of Castile in 1474. She and her husband, Ferdinand, eventually ruled over the whole of Spain.

After the fall of the Roman empire, Spain had been ruled by the Visigoths for 300 years. Then came the invading Berbers (Moors) from northern Africa in 711, establishing a Muslim caliphate which lasted from 756 until 1031. At this time, Christians in the north of Spain started pushing southwards. They started a *reconqvista* (reconquest) which, by 1235, had limited the Muslims to Granada in the south of the country.

However, Catholic Spain was divided into several kingdoms – Leon, Castile, Navarre and Aragon. In the 15th century, Leon had joined with Castile, making Castile and Aragon the two largest. The first step toward finally uniting Spain was made in 1469 when Ferdinand, heir to Aragon, married Isabella of Castile. When the king of Castile died in 1474, Isabella and Ferdinand succeeded him as joint rulers of his kingdom. Five years later, Ferdinand inherited Aragon and made Isabella joint ruler of Aragon as well.

▼ The Christian armies of Aragon and Castile defeated the Moors in 1492, and the Moors were driven back to north Africa where they were shown no mercy.

Spain was divided for much of the 15th century, though the uniting of Aragon and Castile in 1479 made the eventual union of Spain almost inevitable.

THE SPANISH INQUISITION

With the two kingdoms united, Spain grew more powerful. Both Ferdinand and Isabella were devout Catholics. Under their rule the Spanish Inquisition was established. This was a religious court that severely punished people suspected of heresy (disagreement with the Catholic Church's teachings). It operated with great severity; people were tried in secret and tortured until they confessed. Those who did confess could be fined, while those who refused were either imprisoned or burnt to death to expunge their sins.

Boadbil, the last Moorish emir of Granada, leaves the city after the conquest by Aragon and Castile in 1492, ending a long era of Muslim rule in Spain.

During the Spanish Inquisition, books that were written by people suspected of heresy were burnt. This painting by Pedro Berruguete not only celebrates the Catholic victory in Spain but also vividly illustrates the power of the Inquisition.

THE REUNIFICATION OF SPAIN

In 1492, 14 years after the Spanish Inquisition began, Moorish Granada was recaptured by Aragon and Castile. Many Muslims and Jews were expelled or forcibly converted – as many as 200,000 Jews left the country. This persecution resulted in many skilled and able people moving away to France, Germany or the Ottoman empire.

In the same year, Ferdinand and Isabella sponsored the voyage of Christopher Columbus – they were seeking a sea-route to India and China, but found the Americas. This began a period of Spanish conquest that brought about the downfall of the Aztecs, Maya and Incas.

Ferdinand and Isabella had five daughters, one of which, Catherine of Aragon, married Henry VIII of England. But Ferdinand and Isabella had no son, and descent passed through their daughter Joanna the Mad. When Isabella died in 1504, Ferdinand acted as regent for the young Joanna. In 1515, Navarre joined Castile, and Ferdinand finally became king of a united Spain. Joanna's son, Charles V, eventually became the Habsburg emperor, the most powerful ruler in Europe. Under his rule, Spain experienced its golden age.

KEY DATES

1248	The Christians reconquer most of Spain
1469	The marriage of Ferdinand and Isabella
1474	Isabella inherits Castile
1478	The Spanish Inquisition is established
1479	Aragon and Castile are united
1492	The conquest of Granada – end of Muslim rule in southern Spain. Christopher Columbus' expedition to India is financed by Isabella
1504	Isabella dies
1515	Navarre joins Castile – Spain is finally united
1516	Ferdinand dies

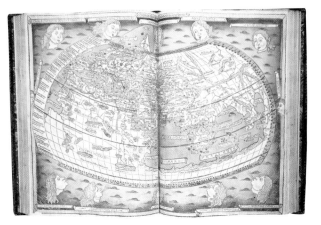

A map of the world taken from Ptolemy's *Geographia*, shows how the world was understood in 1486, before world exploration by Europeans was properly underway.

ITALY 1460–1530

During this period Italy was divided into small states. This allowed for great variation – some states were progressive while others were more conservative.

To further the ambitions of her father (a Borgia pope), Lucretia Borgia (1480-1519) was married three times. With her third husband, the Duke of Ferrara, she devoted herself to the patronage of art and literature, to charitable works and the care of children.

Many Italian states, such as Florence, Venice and Rome, were really large cities. Others were ruled by dukes, as in Mantua, Milan, Urbino and Ferrara. Most of these states were ruled by families who had grown rich from trade and commerce in the late Middle Ages.

The most powerful family of the time was that of the de Medici of Florence. They had made a great fortune during the 14th century through banking and moneylending. The best-known de Medici is Lorenzo, who became joint ruler of Florence with his brother in 1469. He was a clever statesman and banker and also a patron of writers, artists, philosophers and scientists. He was keen to promote his family and saw his second son become pope. Under Lorenzo's influence, Florence became one of the most beautiful and prosperous cities in Italy, and a centre of the Renaissance. Lorenzo helped to make the form of Italian spoken in Florence into the language of the whole country.

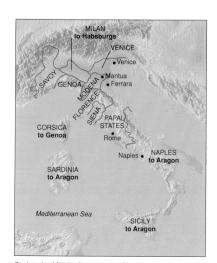

During the Middle Ages, much of Italy was controlled by the Holy Roman Empire. Following a power struggle between emperors and popes, many cities formed their own independent states.

Another famous family was that of the Borgias. Two Borgias became popes. One, Rodrigo, had many illegitimate children and wanted them all to be powerful. But, on his death, the family's power collapsed.

The de Medici villa at Florence was built by Giuliano da Sangallo, a modern Renaissance architect, for Lorenzo the Magnificent, in 1480.

LORENZO DE MEDICI

In 1469, when he was 20 years old, Lorenzo became the joint ruler of Florence with his brother Giuliano. He was the grandson of Cosimo de Medici, who was the second de Medici to hold power over Florence. Lorenzo's brother was killed in a plot by a rival family in 1478. Lorenzo did everything he could to promote his family – his second son Giovanni became Pope Leo X – and to build a large gathering of scholars and creative people. He was the first patron of the artist Michaelangelo. He maintained and expanded the family traditions in banking, patronage and government.

Lorenzo de Medici (also known as *Magnifico Signore*) ruled Florence from 1478 to 1492.

The magnificent city of Florence was at the height of its powers during the late 15th century. Ruled by the de Medicis, it was home to many great artists, architects, writers and scientists of the Renaissance. Florence also became one of Europe's main business and banking centres.

The Sforzas were a great family of Milan. Ludovico Sforza was a man of taste, but also one with ruthless ambition. He ruled as regent for his nephew, the duke of Milan, but made himself the real centre of power. He made alliances with Rodrigo Borgia and married a daughter of the powerful d'Este family, from Ferrara. Ludovico's court attracted great artists of all types, among them Leonardo da Vinci.

Families like the de Medici represented 'new money', with new values and ideas. They paid for exploration, centres of learning, public works and new imported products. People travelled to Italy to learn new ideas, which were taken back to other parts of Europe, while Europeans flocked to Florence, Venice and Milan to gain support for their own ideas. Although the future centres of modernity were to be in northwest Europe, much of the energy of the early Renaissance came from the city-states of Italy.

Raphael was a painter and architect who created a new realistic style in art. This is his *Deposition of Christ*, which he painted in 1507 at the age of 24. The following year, Pope Julius II asked him to do a major work in the Vatican in Rome.

Wealthy Renaissance people enjoyed a very comfortable life. In addition to palaces or large city houses, many had country villas where they welcomed groups of visitors. They would spend time hunting, holding parties, discussing literature and writing poetry.

EUROPEAN EXPLORERS 1453–1600

In the second half of the 15th century, European sailors and navigators planned voyages which would take them far beyond the limits of the world they knew.

In 1488 Bartholomeu Dias (1450-1500) explored the coast of Africa. Gales blew his ships round the Cape of Good Hope, but his crew would go no further.

▲ Vasco da Gama (1469-1525) rounded the Cape of Good Hope in 1497, and sailed up the east coast of Africa. With the help of an Indian sailor he then crossed the Indian Ocean to Calicut in India. He sailed there again to defend Portuguese interests and was made viceroy to India in 1524.

This urge to explore was partly a result of a new interest in the world encouraged by the Renaissance, but the main intention was to bypass the Islamic world in order to set up new trading links with India and the Far East, the source of spices and other luxuries. Until the fall of the Byzantine empire in 1453, spices were brought overland to Constantinople and then carried across the Mediterranean to different countries in Europe. In spite of their expense, spices were an essential part of everyday life. There was no refrigeration so the only way to preserve meat was by salting it. Adding spices helped to hide the salty taste, and spices also concealed the taste of meat which had gone bad despite being salted.

When the Portuguese explored the west coast of Africa in the 1460s, they set up harbours and forts, trading with the Africans in gold, ivory and silver. Gradually they sailed farther south, and Bartholomeu Dias reached the tip of southern Africa in 1488. Nine years later, he helped Vasco da Gama plan a voyage around the Cape of Good Hope to Calicut in India.

A sailor's personal property from the year 1536, salvaged from the wreck of Henry VIII's flagship, *Mary Rose*. It includes a pouch, whistle, rosary and comb.

Vasco da Gama was followed by Pedro Cabral who returned from India with a cargo of pepper. This encouraged other navigators to try and sail further east. In 1517, the Portuguese had reached China, and nearly 30 years later they had arrived in Japan. The Portuguese were driven not only by trading possibilities but also by a determination to spread Christianity to the peoples of the East.

► Vasco da Gama's small ships were a development of the traditional caravel, with its triangular lateen sail. His ships had both square and lateen sails, making them more manoeuvrable and adaptable on the oceans.

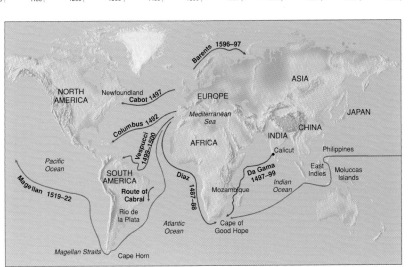

900 | 1100 | 1200 | 1300 | 1400 | 1500 | 1600 | 1700 | 1750 | 1800 | 1850 | 1900 | 1950 | 2000

Barents 1596–97

NORTH AMERICA

Newfoundland Cabot 1497

EUROPE

ASIA

Columbus 1492

Mediterranean Sea

JAPAN

Vespucci 1499–1500

AFRICA

CHINA

INDIA

Calicut

Philippines

Pacific Ocean

SOUTH AMERICA

Diaz

Da Gama 1497–99

East Indies

Moluccas Islands

Magellan 1519–22

Route of Cabral

1487–88

Mozambique

Indian Ocean

Rio de la Plata

Atlantic Ocean

Cape of Good Hope

Magellan Straits

Cape Horn

◀ Navigators from Europe tried many routes to reach the Spice Islands, the Moluccas. They discovered more than they expected, and by the end of the century had begun to form trading companies.

▲ Ferdinand Magellan (1480–1521) led the first expedition to sail round the world in 1519. The voyage took three years. He gave the Pacific Ocean its name.

WESTWARD EXPLORATION

While the Portuguese sailed east, the Spanish sailed west. Columbus discovered the West Indies in 1492. Amerigo Vespucci reached South America in 1499. On a second voyage in 1501, he realized that he had found a new continent. In 1497, John Cabot, a Venetian sponsored by England, discovered Newfoundland in Canada, and in 1535, Jacques Cartier sailed up the St Lawrence River, claiming the area for France. Ferdinand Magellan rounded South America in 1519 and crossed into the Pacific. He died in the Philippines, but some of his crew returned to Spain in 1522 – the first explorers to sail round the world.

CHRISTOPHER COLUMBUS

In 1492, Queen Isabella sponsored Christopher Columbus, a navigator from Genoa in Italy, to find a western route to India. However, it is possible he knew of America from Viking tales he heard in Iceland. Most people believed the world to be much smaller than it really was. When Columbus reached a group of islands across the Atlantic, he called them the West Indies. They were in fact the islands of the Caribbean. Columbus made three more voyages there, but it is not known whether he really knew if these were America or Asia.

Christopher Columbus (1451–1506) first went to sea at the age of fourteen. He was shipwrecked and washed up on the coast of Portugal.

◀ When Christopher Columbus and his crew landed on Guanahani in the Bahamas, he claimed it for Spain.

141

TUDOR ENGLAND 1485–1603

During the Tudor period, England grew great and powerful, throwing off the past and the influence of Rome, and sowing the seeds of an imperial future.

Henry Tudor came to power after the end of the Wars of the Roses.

Henry VIII was a strong ruler who brought about great changes in England.

T he Tudors, a Welsh family, rose to power after the confusion of a long civil war, the Wars of the Roses (1455–85). The first Tudor king, Henry VII, banned private armies and put down any lords who opposed him. He strengthened and enriched both the Crown and England. In 1509, when the young Henry VIII became king, England was an important power in Europe. Henry married Catherine of Aragon, daughter of Spain's Ferdinand and Isabella, and spent 15 years as a pleasure-seeking Renaissance-style ruler, while Thomas Wolsey ran the government. After wars against France and Scotland in 1513, Henry became more politically aware. He and Catherine had only one living child, Mary, and Henry wanted a male heir, so he asked the pope's permission to divorce Catherine. He was refused. At this time,

Henry VIII loved banquets. He was well-educated, played several musical instruments and wrote songs. He also enjoyed lively discussions on religion, art and politics.

new religious ideas and demands for Church reform were common, so Henry broke away from Rome. He made himself head of the Church in England in 1534, divorced Catherine and closed the monasteries, selling their lands to pay for wars and other ventures.

DISSOLUTION OF THE MONASTERIES

Between 1536 and 1540 Henry closed 800 monasteries, turning out 10,000 monks and nuns and selling or making gifts of their lands. He did this to break the power of Rome in England, and to raise money. He founded the Protestant Church of England, though he was not enthusiastically Protestant – Protestantism really developed under Elizabeth I.

Henry VIII rebuilt the English navy and his pride and joy was the *Mary Rose*. In 1536, he went to watch it sail on the Solent. However, the ship's balance was affected by the 700 sailors standing on deck, and it capsized and sank!

Henry married six times, and during his reign, strengthened English control of Wales and Ireland, established a large navy and planned various colonial and commercial ventures. He was succeeded in 1547 by his only son, Edward VI (1537–53), who died at the age of 16. During his reign, the Church of England grew stronger. He was succeeded by his half-sister Mary I (1516–58), Henry's eldest daughter, who reigned for five years and tried to restore Catholicism.

THE FIRST ELIZABETHANS

When Mary died, her sister Elizabeth I came to the throne. Elizabeth was popular and intelligent. She refused to marry and made her own decisions. The Catholic Mary Queen of Scots, Elizabeth's cousin, was found guilty of plotting against her, yet Elizabeth resisted pressure to have her executed for many years. Elizabeth aided European Protestants and sent out English pirates against Spanish ships and colonies. She made a settlement between English Catholics and Protestants, and fought a war with Spain, defeating the Spanish Armada. England began to develop overseas ventures, and at home its industries and economy grew. This was Shakespeare's time, when English culture and society flowered, preparing the ground for an English period of imperial greatness.

MARY, QUEEN OF SCOTS 1542–87

Mary Stuart became queen of Scotland in 1542 when she was just one week old. Her father, James V, was the nephew of Henry VIII and this encouraged Catholic Mary to claim the English throne. She was educated in France and married the heir to the French throne in 1558. After his death in 1560, Mary returned to Scotland where she was unpopular. She abdicated and fled to England in 1568. As a focus for Catholic dissent against Elizabeth, Mary became involved in plots and was imprisoned in Fotheringay Castle, where she was executed in 1587 on a charge of treason.

Elizabeth I became queen of England and Ireland in 1558. She ruled for 45 years and, due to her active involvement in government, England went through a period of stability, and cultural and economic expansion.

THE PORTUGUESE EMPIRE 1520–1600

Portuguese seafarers and traders paved the way for European colonialism around the world. At its height, their trading empire spanned the whole globe.

▲ The Portuguese were the first Europeans to trade with west African countries. This brass plaque from Benin shows Portuguese men symbolically holding up the pillars supporting the palace of the oba of Benin.

This ornamental African mask from Benin shows the oba (king) wearing a headdress carved with representations of Portuguese merchants.

The Portuguese were the leading seafaring explorers of Europe. They had long been fisherpeople, accustomed to the high seas. Henry the Navigator began the training of sailors in the mid-15th century, sending ships down the western coast of Africa. There were large profits at stake in the trade in exotic goods. Portuguese explorers reached the East Indies (Indonesia) in the early 16th century, following the Muslim trade-routes to the Moluccas (Spice Islands), which were rich in the spices such as cinnamon, cloves and nutmeg, that Europe wanted. To control this valuable trade, the Portuguese conquered the Moluccas and seized many of the best-placed ports in the Indian Ocean. They also visited China. Because Portuguese traders needed to sail around Africa in order to return to Lisbon, forts were set up at various places along the African coast to supply and protect the ships.

▼ The Portuguese empire at its greatest extent in about 1600 was far-flung, but very profitable. Trading posts and ports to service ships were positioned in strategic locations along the major trade routes.

▲ Benin craftspeople carved items such as this 16th-century ivory salt-cellar for export to Europe. Around the base are figures of Portuguese noblemen.

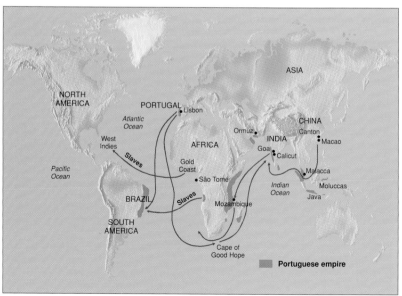

ASIA

NORTH AMERICA

PORTUGAL · Lisbon

Atlantic Ocean

Ormuz

CHINA

Canton

INDIA

West Indies

AFRICA

Goa

Macao

Slaves

Gold Coast

Calicut

Pacific Ocean

· São Tomé

Malacca

Indian Ocean

Moluccas

BRAZIL

Slaves

Mozambique

Java

SOUTH AMERICA

Cape of Good Hope

Portuguese empire

A ILHA E CIDADE DE GOA METROPOLITANA DA INDIA E PARTES ORIENTAIS QVE ESTA EN 15 GRAOS DA BANDA DO NORTE

THE START OF THE SLAVE TRADE

From Africa, the Portuguese bought gold and also slaves to work on their newly established sugar plantations. The first plantations were on the African island of Sâo Tomé. When the slaves there revolted in the 1570s, the Portuguese established plantations in Brazil. They had conquered a large part of this country and they transported African slaves there to work. This was the beginning of the transatlantic slave trade.

At its height in the 16th century, the Portuguese empire did not possess large areas of colonial land like the Spaniards, but they did hold well-placed, valuable trading posts and plantations. These included Angola and Mozambique, the islands of Cape Verde, Madeira and the Azores, the bases of Ormuz (Persia), Goa and Calicut (India), Colombo (Sri Lanka), and trading posts in the Far East, such as Macao (China), the Celebes, Java and Malacca.

KEY DATES	
1419	The Portuguese reach Madeira
1471	The Portuguese reach Asante and Benin
1487	Dias rounds the Cape of Good Hope
1498	Vasco da Gama reaches India
1500	Cabral explores the coast of Brazil
1505–20	Asian trading posts founded in Goa and Malacca
1520	Magellan discovers the Moluccas (Spice Islands)
1530	First Portuguese colony established in Brazil
1534	First African slaves are landed in Brazil

The port and city of Goa in India was an important link in the Portuguese trading empire. It is shown here in a map made in 1595 by a Portuguese-Dutch engraver, Johannes Baptista van Doetechum the Younger.

Before the Portuguese arrived in the Moluccas its rulers enjoyed high profits from the lucrative spice trade. Under Portuguese rule the local rulers were bypassed. Spices from the Moluccas included cloves, nutmeg, pepper, cinnamon and ginger.

145

THE REFORMATION 1520–1600

During the Reformation, a new kind of Christianity, with many new groups and sects, developed. This led to social divisions and eventually to war across Europe.

John Calvin (1509–64) was born in France and was originally named Jean Chauvin. He was a strict Protestant and believed that God had already ordained the future and that only those chosen by God (the Elect) would be saved.

Europe suffered a series of violent religious civil wars. There were many massacres, and people accused of being heretics were burnt at the stake.

By the early 16th century, the new ideas of the Renaissance led some people to challenge the teachings of the Roman Catholic Church. The way its leaders ran the Church was strongly criticized. Priests, monks and nuns no longer led lives of poverty, celibacy and simplicity, and popes and bishops were too interested in money and power. People sought Church reform. This became known as 'the Reformation'. It had started quietly over 100 years before, but it took on impetus in 1517 when Martin Luther, a German priest, nailed a list of 95 statements (theses) to the church door at Wittenberg, criticizing the role of the Church. Luther hated the sale of 'indulgences' – forgiveness of sins sold for money. He hoped that his list would lead to healthy debate, but he was accused of heresy (going against Church beliefs). Luther was excommunicated from the Catholic Church in 1521.

The Reformation in the 16th century meant that Europe was divided roughly north–south over religious beliefs – Protestant to the north and Roman Catholic to the south. This division also happened within individual countries such as France, and later led to civil war.

THE EARLY PROTESTANTS

Luther had gained support in Germany and Switzerland, setting up his own Lutheran church. Other groups, such as Quakers, Anabaptists, Mennonites and Moravian Hussites did the same. After 1529, they were all called Protestants. Ulrich Zwingli led the Reformation in Switzerland. His views were more extreme, and this led to a civil war in which Zwingli was killed. Zwingli was followed by John Calvin, who gained followers in France, Germany and Holland. He established the Reformation in Switzerland and influenced John Knox, who took the Reformation to Scotland. Some groups pooled all their property to form communities, taking over whole towns.

▲ Martin Luther (1483–1546) believed that people were saved by faith alone, and he wanted faith to be based on the Bible, not on corrupt religious traditions. He believed that church services should be in the local language, not in Latin. The 16th-century cartoon on the right shows the devil dictating Luther's sermons to him.

The Council of Trent met three times between 1545 and 1563. The Council tried to reform the Catholic Church and stop the spread of Protestantism.

▲ The Catholic Church used pictures for teaching, and this woodcut illustration, from Germany in 1470, shows a good Catholic on his deathbed, being given the last rites.

THE COUNTER-REFORMATION

In 1522, Pope Adrian VI admitted there were many problems in the Roman Catholic Church, but following his death, nothing more was done until 1534, when Paul III became pope. This was the year Henry VIII of England broke away from Rome. Paul began to reform the Church in a movement known as Counter-Reformation. He began by encouraging the preaching and missionary work of an Italian order of friars called the Capuchins. Six years later, he approved the founding of the Society of the Jesus, or Jesuits, which had been founded by Ignatius Loyola, to spread Catholicism. He also called together a group known as the Council of Trent in 1545 to decide on further Church reforms. The council decided to enforce vows of poverty and set up Church colleges (seminaries) to educate monks, nuns and priests. All this led to a revival of Catholic faith and active opposition to the Protestants.

However, the religious dispute in Europe grew into a political one when Philip II of Spain tried to restore Catholicism in England, France and Holland by force. Other rulers took sides. Civil war erupted in France, and Protestant Holland revolted against Spanish domination. Eventually the Thirty Years War broke out in 1618.

▼ Pope Julius II was a notable patron of the arts during the early 16th century. However, his lack of interest in reform caused people to criticize the way that the Church was run.

KEY DATES	
1517	Luther's 95 Theses, announced at Wittenberg, Germany
1522	Luther's Bible is published in German
1523	Zwingli's Programme of Reform established in Switzerland
1530s	Protestant social movements and revolts in Germany
1534	England separates from the Roman Church
1540s	Calvin establishes Protestant church in Geneva
1545	The first Council of Trent – the Counter-Reformation begins
1562-98	The Huguenot Wars in France
1566	Calvinist church founded in the Netherlands
1580s	Increase of tension between European rulers
1618	Outbreak of the Thirty Years' War (until 1648)

THE OTTOMAN EMPIRE 1453–1600

Following the taking of Constantinople in 1453, the Ottoman empire soon became a force to be reckoned with in the Middle East and around the Mediterranean.

When Constantinople fell to Mehmet II in 1453, the Ottoman empire began its golden age. The former Byzantine capital was renamed Istanbul, becoming the centre of an enormous empire which, at its peak around 1680, stretched from Algeria to Persia and Hungary to Arabia. The Ottoman empire, founded by Osman I in 1301, extended into Europe by 1389. The Mongols halted its expansion for a while but, after taking Constantinople, Mehmet II quickly conquered 12 kingdoms and 200 cities in Anatolia and the Balkans. Then Selim I gained Syria, Arabia and Egypt between 1512 and 1520.

▲ The Ottoman *spahi* or cavalry knights were given land in return for providing military service, becoming a local ruling class across the empire.

▼ By 1566, the Ottoman empire stretched into three continents. Suleiman had built up a strong navy and won control of the Mediterranean. He also dominated the Red Sea and Persian Gulf.

SULEIMAN THE MAGNIFICENT

Suleiman the Magnificent ruled for 46 years from 1520. He conquered Belgrade and Hungary but failed in his siege of Vienna, the capital of the Holy Roman Empire. Later he took Mesopotamia, Armenia and the Caucasus region. The Ottomans gained control of the eastern Mediterranean and Black Sea (thereby dominating Venetian and Genoan trade), and also northern Africa and the Ukraine.

Women in the Ottoman empire led a secluded life. Outside their home they had to wear a veil and could meet only men from their own families.

To his own people, Suleiman was known as *Qanuni*, the Lawgiver, because he reformed the Ottoman administration and the legal system. He gave shape to the Ottoman empire, enriching everything from architecture to courtly life. He was a poet, scholar and patron of the arts, and he rebuilt much of Istanbul.

Europeans called him Suleiman the Magnificent because of the splendour of his court and his military victories in Europe. These included a series of campaigns in which he captured Belgrade in Yugoslavia and threw the Crusader Knights of St John out of Rhodes in 1522. His greatest victory was at Mohacs in Hungary in 1526, his siege of Vienna threatened the heart of Europe, and he took the Muslim holy city of Mecca in 1538. Meanwhile, the Turkish fleet, under the pirate Barbarossa (Khayr ad-Din Pasha), attacked and ravaged the coasts of Spain, Italy and Greece.

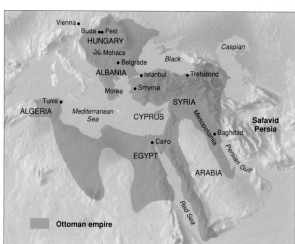

Vienna ●
Buda ●● Pest
HUNGARY
✕ Mohacs
● Belgrade   *Black*
ALBANIA ● Istanbul   ● Trebizond
Morea   ● Smyrna
Tunis ●   **SYRIA**
ALGERIA   *Mediterranean Sea*   **CYPRUS**
Caspian
Safavid Persia
● Baghdad
● Cairo
EGYPT
ARABIA
Mesopotamia
Persian Gulf
Red Sea

■ **Ottoman empire**

Suleiman the Magnificent, born in 1495, became sultan in 1520 and turned the Ottoman empire into a rich and vast Sunni Muslim empire straddling three continents.

MUSLIM WARS

Suleiman waged three campaigns in the east against the Safavid empire of Persia. This was a war between Muslims – between the Sunni Ottomans and Shi'ite Persians. Suleiman took Baghdad, but the eastern border of the empire was never secure. The wars between the two empires lasted throughout the 16th century and diverted Ottoman attention so they did not advance further into Europe.

THE START OF A SLOW DECLINE

When Suleiman died, his son Selim II became sultan. Selim led a life of leisure while his ministers and generals ran the empire. The Ottomans themselves were not large in number. They relied on taking Russian and north African slaves, and conscripting one in five boys from their European territories, to train them as administrators and soldiers. Ordinary people were left alone as long as they were obedient and paid taxes, and no one was forcibly converted to Islam. The Ottomans relied on Greeks, Armenians, Venetians and other foreigners as traders, making the Ottoman empire international in character. However, by 1600, the empire had begun a long, slow decline.

▲ Suleiman's greatest victory was at the battle of Mohacs in 1526 when he crushed the Hungarian army. His army was able to overwhelm an alliance of central European nations and killed the king of Bohemia.

▼ Suleiman's failure to capture Vienna, the capital of the Holy Roman Empire, in 1529 prevented him invading further into Germany and central Europe. Ottoman advances therefore halted. The use of cannons was a fairly recent development in warfare.

KEY DATES

1453	The Ottomans take Constantinople
c1460	Greece, Serbia and Bosnia taken
1512–20	Selim I takes Syria, Arabia and Egypt
1522	Suleiman takes Rhodes from the Knights of St John
1526	Battle of Mohacs: Hungary taken
1529	Siege of Vienna (fails)
1534	Suleiman takes Baghdad and Armenia
1538	Suleiman takes the holy city of Mecca
1540s onwards	The flowering of Ottoman culture
1566	Death of Suleiman
1600	Ottoman begins slow decline

INDIA: THE MOGHULS 1504–1605

The Islamic world was changing. India, a divided subcontinent, was invaded by the Moghuls. They established a strong empire in the north of India.

Babur, a descendant of Genghis Khan and Tamerlane, led a tribe in Turkestan called the Moghuls – the name Moghul is a variation of the word Mongol. Driven out by the Uzbeks, they invaded Kabul in Afghanistan in 1504. Then they turned their eyes on India, a patchwork of often-warring Hindu and Muslim states. After an experimental attack in 1519, 12,000 Moghuls swept through the Khyber pass into India in 1526, invading the Delhi sultanate, the greatest power in India.

Babur, born in Ferghana, Turkestan, was the first Moghul emperor in India. He died in Agra in 1530.

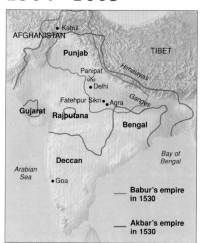

Expanding outwards from Delhi, the Moghul empire grew to cover all of northern India and much of central India. Although it was Muslim-ruled, it accommodated the many faiths and cultures of India.

Babur and his followers were Muslims. When they invaded India, the Ottoman empire supplied them with guns and soldiers. Babur's troops also rode swift horses which easily outmanoeuvred the Indians' slower elephants. This helped them to defeat a much large Indian army at a battle in which the sultan of Delhi was killed. After this victory, Babur made Delhi his capital. When Babur died in 1530, his son Humayun became ruler.

◀ Painted by a Persian, this picture shows Babur (left), his ancestor Tamerlane and Babur's son Humayun (right).

▲ Babur had a full-scale account of India written down. It details the nature, people and customs of his empire.

Humayun invaded western India, but in 1540, the Surs chased out the Moghuls, forcing them back into Persia. Humayun returned in 1555, overcame the Surs and moved back to Delhi. A year later, before he was able to win back the whole empire, Humayun was killed in an accident.

AKBAR EXPANDS THE EMPIRE

Humayun was succeeded by Babur's grandson, Akbar. He became emperor at the age of 13 and ruled until his death in 1605. Akbar was a great military leader and wise ruler. His army pushed west into Gujarat and east into Bengal. This was the richest province in the north of India. It produced rice and silk, which provided Akbar with his main source of income. By 1576, Akbar controlled all of northern India.

Although Akbar was a Muslim, many of his subjects were Hindus, and to keep the peace, he married a Hindu princess. He believed in religious tolerance, and made a settlement with the Hindus, bringing them into government and encouraging their overseas trade. He set up a well-organized empire with professional administrators.

MOGHUL GREATNESS

During this period, India traded profitably with Africa, the Ottomans, Europe and the Far East. The Portuguese now had trading posts and ports in India. The country also had the world's largest textile industry. Akbar welcomed Christian Jesuits and Persian artists to his court, and he tried to create a new religion for India without success. He built schools for the children and also a new capital city at Fatehpur Sikri. The city combined Muslim and Hindu styles of architecture.

KEY DATES

1504	The Moghuls seize Kabul
1526	Delhi becomes the Moghul capital in India
1556	Akbar the Great, the greatest Moghul emperor, begins reign
1571	Fatehpur Sikri becomes the new capital
1605	Jahangir becomes Moghul emperor (Nur Jahan rules 1611-22)
1628	Shah Jahan, Moghul emperor
1658	Aurangzeb, the last great Mogul emperor
1707	Beginning of the decline of the Moghuls
1803	The fall of the last Moghul stronghold to the English

AKBAR, THE THIRD MOGUL EMPEROR

Akbar inherited the Moghul empire at the age of 13, and he ruled for nearly 50 years. He invaded Rajasthan, Gujarat, Bengal, Kashmir and the Deccan to rule most of India. He taxed farming peasants less, encouraged traders and introduced a very efficient government and military service. This served later Moghul emperors and their people well. Though Akbar could not read, he welcomed scholars of all religions, artists and foreign travellers to his court. His greatest success was in making peace with the Hindu majority of the Indian population, ending many Hindu–Muslim conflicts.

Akbar ruled India at the same time as Elizabeth I ruled England and Philip II was king of Spain. Akbar even attempted to start his own Reformation, by inventing a new religion which drew on other religions. However, this was not adopted by his people.

◄ Although some local rulers rebelled against Akbar's rule, they were soon defeated. Here, the rebel Bahadur Khan is shown yielding to Akbar.

▼ At Fatehpur Sikri, Akbar built a capital city in a mixture of Muslim, Hindu and other architectural styles as the centre for his new religion. He died in 1605 and was buried in this tomb.

THE CONQUISTADORES 1519–1550

The Spanish conquistadores were adventurers and soldiers who invaded Central and South America. In doing so, they destroyed the Aztec and Inca empires.

After destroying the Aztecs, Hernán Cortés returned to Spain where he died in poverty.

Francisco Pizarro marched on the Incas in 1532. He founded Lima before being murdered in 1541.

Soon after the navigators had found the Americas, Spanish adventurers, known as conquistadores (conquerors) followed them. After conquering many Caribbean islands, they explored the American mainland, hoping to find treasure. In 1519, about 500 Spanish soldiers, led by Hernán Cortés, reached the Aztec city of Tenochtitlan, where at first, they were welcomed. It is thought that the Aztec emperor, Montezuma II, had been awaiting the return of the god-king Quetzalcóatl, and he may have believed Cortés was he. The Spaniards tricked and captured Montezuma, and Cortés ruled in his place. When Cortés left, the Aztecs rebelled and defeated the remaining Spaniards. With the help of an interpreter, Cortés then won the support of neighbouring tribes who had been conquered by the Aztecs. In 1521, he returned to Tenochtitlan with a native army and destroyed the city.

At first Montezuma welcomed Cortés to Tenochtitlan, showering him with gifts. This goodwill soon died when the Spaniards seized power. Eventually, most of the Aztecs died of diseases brought by the foreigners.

THE END OF THE INCA EMPIRE

Another conquistador, Francisco Pizarro, landed in Peru in 1532 seeking to conquer the Incas. An Inca civil war was already in progress between Huascar and Atahualpa, the sons of Huayna Capac. Atahualpa killed Huascar with the Spaniards' help, but Pizarro then had Atahualpa executed. The Incas soon surrendered and by 1533 their vast empire was in Spanish hands.

THE CAPTURE OF ATAHUALPA

In 1532, Pizarro, with only 159 men against a large Inca army, kidnapped the Inca leader, Atahualpa. He was god of the Incas, and that made Pizarro more powerful than the gods. The Inca soon yielded, and Atahualpa was executed. Like the Aztecs, the Inca were tricked into submission, and a whole civilization died.

THE SPANISH EMPIRE 1535–1600

Spain's occupation of large areas of the Americas brought harsh conditions and disease to the Native Americans. By 1600, Spain had the largest empire.

After the fall of the Aztecs and Incas, the king of Spain added their territories to his empire. The Aztec empire became the Viceroyalty of New Spain in 1535. Later, in the 16th century, it also included parts of California, Arizona and New Mexico. The land of the Incas became the Viceroyalty of Peru. Many people from Spain emigrated to live in this new Spanish empire. The colonies were ruled by a Council of the Indies based in Spain. Many of the laws made for the colonies show that the Spanish government tried to make sure the Native Americans were not ill-treated. But it was impossible to prevent the colonial Spaniards from treating them very cruelly. The Native Americans were forced to mine silver and work as slaves. Millions died because they had no resistance to European diseases such as the measles and smallpox. The colonists were followed by Spanish missionaries, who destroyed temples and idols and set up Catholic churches in their place, trying to convert the Native Americans.

The conquistadores were followed by missionaries, who sought to convert the Native Americans – by force, if necessary. They destroyed the temples and made the people build churches in their place.

The Spaniards forced the Native Americans to mine gold and silver, which was then sent back to Spain. The harsh conditions and new diseases brought by the Spanish meant that the population of Mexico fell disastrously from 25 million in 1500 to just one million in 1600.

The Spanish empire continued to expand under Philip II (1556–98). Most of the Philippine Islands were conquered in 1571. Then, in 1578, King Sebastian of Portugal was killed in Morocco. Philip was Sebastian's closest relative, so he inherited the Portuguese empire. By 1600, the Spanish had the world's largest empire, but they were losing power. Philip's opposition to the Protestants in Europe led him into expensive wars which used up the gold and silver from the Americas.

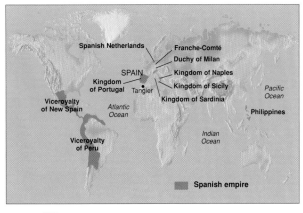

▲ The Spanish took new foods, such as pineapples, tomatoes, potatoes, cocoa, peppers and sunflowers back to Europe.

▶ The Spanish empire was large and yielded vast wealth, especially from gold and silver mined in Mexico and Peru.

Spanish Netherlands
Franche-Comté
Duchy of Milan
SPAIN
Kingdom of Naples
Kingdom of Portugal   Tangier
Kingdom of Sicily
Kingdom of Sardinia
Pacific Ocean
Viceroyalty of New Spain
Atlantic Ocean
Philippines
Indian Ocean
Viceroyalty of Peru
Spanish empire

RUSSIA 1462–1613

During this period, Russia grew from being a collection of small principalities into a great country. Its isolation ended, enabling it to play a major role in history.

Ivan III was the first ruler of all Russia. He came to the throne of Muscovy in 1462, making Moscow his capital. When he died in 1505, he had set Russia on a new course.

▲ Ivan III adopted the Byzantine symbol of the double-headed eagle as his own emblem – both Byzantium and Russia looked east and west.

After the decline of Kiev around 1060, Russia survived as an assortment of separate small principalities such as Novgorod, Smolensk, Kiev and Vladimir. This suddenly changed when the Mongols under Batu Khan invaded in 1238. They burned Moscow and damaged Kiev. The Khanate of the Golden Horde (or Tartars) dominated Russia by demanding tribute in money and soldiers, and the Russians cooperated to avoid trouble. In the 14th century, Kiev was absorbed into Lithuania for a time. In 1263, Muscovy (Moscow) had a new ruler, Prince Daniel, who gradually expanded its territories.

Slowly, Muscovy began to dominate the other Russian states. In 1380, the Muscovites defeated the Golden Horde, although the Tartars carried on raiding Moscow and demanding tribute until 1480, when Ivan III overpowered them. Ivan III, or Ivan the Great, came to the throne of Muscovy in 1462. He expanded Muscovy and gave it a sense of pride, introduced a legal code and declared himself 'ruler of all Russia'. In 1472, he married Sophia, the niece of the last Byzantine emperor, and appointed himself as the protector of the Eastern Orthodox Church, calling Moscow 'the third Rome'.

St Basil's cathedral in Moscow was built between 1555 and 1560 to celebrate Ivan IV's victories in Kazan and Astrakhan in the east, It became a major centre of the Orthodox faith.

By 1480, Ivan III had brought Novgorod and other cities under his control. He rebuilt Moscow's famous Kremlin (citadel). When he died in 1505, he was succeeded by his son Vasili, who ruled until 1533. Vasili was succeeded in turn by Ivan IV, his three-year-old son.

▼ The boyars of Russia had been independent of central control until Ivan the Terrible brought them under his control. Then they joined the growing trade with the West in fur, timber and other raw materials.

IVAN THE TERRIBLE

Ivan IV, or 'Ivan the Terrible' was the
Grand Prince of Muscovy from 1533 to
1584. He was crowned as the first *tsar*
(emperor) in 1547. His harsh upbringing
left him with a violent and unpredictable
character, but his nickname meant 'awe-
inspiring' rather than 'terrible'. He
improved the legal system as well as
reforming trading links with England and
other European countries – Russia had
until then been isolated. He captured
Kazan and Astrakhan from the Tartars,
pushing on toward Siberia. Ivan reduced
the power of the boyars (the nobility) by
instituting a kind of secret police, to bring
the country under stronger control. He set
many patterns for the future, establishing
strong central control by the tsars. In
1581, in a fit of anger, he foolishly killed
his heir and son Ivan, and so was
succeeded by his second son, Fyodor
who was mentally unstable.

THE ROMANOV TSARS

When Ivan IV died in 1584, Boris
Gudunov ruled as regent until Fyodor died
in 1598. Boris made himself tsar, against
the great opposition of the boyars. He
promoted foreign trade and defeated the
Swedes, who sought to invade Russia. But
he died in 1605, and Russia entered eight
years of civil war, as rival forces fought for
the throne. Eventually, Ivan IV's great-
nephew Mikhail Romanov (1596–1645)
gained the throne in 1613. He was tsar
for 30 years, and founded the Romanov
dynasty, which ruled until 1917.

▲ The Kremlin was the
centre of Moscow. It was
like a fort and many
palaces, churches and
cathedrals were rebuilt
within the protection of
its walls by Ivan III.
It became the symbol of
the centralized power
of the tsars.

◄ Ivan the Terrible visited
the seat of the patriarch
of the Russian Orthodox
Church at Zagorsk in order
to have himself anointed
and confirmed as the head
of the Orthodox Church.

Ivan IV was a strong ruler
who truly set the course
of Russia's expansion.
Known as the Ivan
the Terrible, he was a
formidable personality.

KEY DATES

1238	Invasion of Russia by the Mongols
1263	Muscovy begins to grow larger
1462–1505	Ivan III, the Great, strengthens Muscovy
1472	Ivan III appoints himself protector of Eastern Orthodox Church
1480	End of Tartar dominance of Russia
1505–33	Vasili rule as tsar
1533–84	Ivan IV, the Terrible, expands Russia
1584–98	Fyodor is tsar and Boris Gudunov regent
1598–1605	Boris Gudunov rules as tsar
1605–13	Civil war between rival boyars
1613	Mikhail Romanov, first of the Romanovs, becomes tsar

DUTCH INDEPENDENCE 1477–1648

The Netherlands was a fast-developing Protestant area with a promising future, but ruled by Catholic Spain. The Dutch wanted to control their own affairs.

William of Orange ('the Silent') became Spanish governor of part of the Netherlands in 1559, but he turned against the Spanish crown, leading the Dutch Revolt from 1567 to 1572. He became a Calvinist in 1573 and was declared an outlaw. He was killed in 1584 by a fanatical Catholic, Balthasar Gérards.

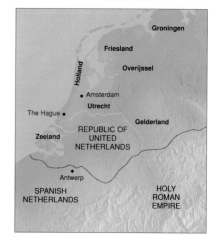

The United Provinces grew richer as the marshy land was drained and developed. As a Protestant country with growing trade and industry, independence from Spain, an old-fashioned imperial power, became necessary.

After the collapse of Charlemagne's empire in the 9th century, the Netherlands, made up of 17 provinces in what is now Belgium, Luxembourg and the Netherlands, were fragmented as possessions of various ruling families. In the 14th and 15th centuries, the dukes of Burgundy, Philip the Bold and John the Fearless, acquired Flanders (Belgium) and the Netherlands. These lands stayed under Burgundy's control until Charles V, inheritor of Burgundian lands and a member of the Habsburg dynasty, made them a Spanish possession in 1516. This did not suit the people of the Netherlands, since most of them were Protestants. The fight for independence started when Charles's son Philip II became king of Spain in 1556. He resisted the Protestant tide and tried to take complete control. He sent the Duke of Alba as governor to the Netherlands with orders to use terror, if necessary, to crush any opposition.

The Duke of Alba executed two leaders of the independence movement, and this resulted in the Dutch Revolts, which were led by William of Orange. The more ruthless the Duke of Alba became, the more opposition grew. There were public executions, towns were pillaged and whole populations massacred. The Dutch used many guerrilla tactics, such as the flooding of the lowlands, to prevent movement. In 1576, Spanish troops sacked Antwerp, one of Europe's richest ports, and ended its prosperity.

▲ A cartoon of the time shows the aristocratic Duke of Alba trying to stamp out heresy in the Netherlands by trampling on the bodies of executed Protestants.

▶ During the siege of Louvain in 1571, the heroic Dutch successfully used every possible means to overcome the superior armed might of the Spanish.

STRUGGLE AND INDEPENDENCE

Many merchants and bankers moved to
Amsterdam, rebuilding it into a fine city
defended by canals and a growing navy.
They developed modern trade, banking
and industry, becoming one of Europe's
main Protestant centres. Spain brought the
Catholic southern provinces (Belgium)
back under its control, but in 1581 seven
Protestant northern provinces declared
themselves independent. Fortunately for
them, Spain was busy fighting France,
England and the Ottomans, and so were
unable to stop the Dutch.

This struggle for independence was a
religious war and a fight between modern
Dutch town-dwelling burghers and the
traditional Spanish royal hierarchy. Led by
William of Orange, the Dutch declared
the Republic of the United Netherlands.
A truce followed in 1609, though it was
not until 1648 that Spain officially
recognized Dutch independence.

▶ The plundering of the rich city of Antwerp by the
Spanish in 1576 was the last straw for the Dutch. From
then on, they were determined to be rid of the Spanish.

KEY DATES

1477 The Netherlands become a Habsburg possession
1516 The Spanish take control of the Netherlands
1568 The Dutch Revolt begins
1576 The sack of Antwerp – a turning-point
1581 The Northern Provinces declare independence
1609 Truce – the Dutch effectively win the war
1648 Dutch independence fully recognized

▲ Battle is joined on
the Zuider Zee, east of
Amsterdam, between the
naval might of Spain and
the small boats of the
Dutch in 1573. As with
the Armada, the smaller
boats out-manoeuvred
the Spanish vessels and
sank many of them.

157

NORTH AMERICA 1460–1600

North America was a land of many different peoples, each with their own traditions, way of life and culture. The arrival of the Europeans was disastrous for them.

The tribes of the Iroquois wore masks during important tribal ceremonies. The masks represented the spirits of mythological creatures.

▲ The French explorer Jacques Cartier (1491–1557) sailed up the St Lawrence River in what is now Canada and claimed the area for France. One of his men drew this map of the town of Hochelaga, part of the Huron nation, now the city of Montreal.

When the Europeans first arrived in America in the 16th century, there were millions of Native Americans in hundreds of tribes and many nations. They did not believe that they owned the land but thought that it was held in common for the entire tribe. Each tribe had its own customs, language and way of life, according to where it lived. For example, on the Great Plains where wild animals such as bison were plentiful, the Cheyenne and Pawnee lived a nomadic lifestyle, hunting and trapping. Hunters on the Great Plains sometimes camouflaged themselves in animal skins when they went in search of prey. The animals they caught provided them with meat, and also with skins for clothing and shelters. Tribes who lived on the coast or by lakes made wooden canoes and went fishing. Other tribes in the woodlands were village-dwelling farmers, who grew crops, herded domestic animals, and hunted and fished.

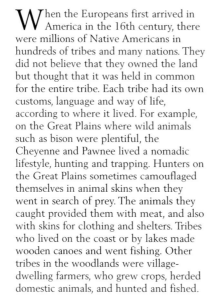

▶ The Miami tribe of Ohio made clothing from hides and furs. Skins were cleaned and stretched and then cut and sewn into garments and moccasins. Women did most of the domestic work and crop-growing, but they also held power in tribal decision-making.

Some Native American nations built totems to the spirits of nature, often with an eagle at the top to represent the far-seeing powers of Great Spirit.

In the southwest, people living in villages called *pueblos*, grew crops of maize, squash and beans by building dams to irrigate the dry land. They had roads, complex societies, as well as strong religious traditions, and they traded with the Aztecs and other native peoples.

Along the Mississippi River, an advanced city civilization had thrived, although it was in decline from 1450 onwards. The Mississippians supplied Native American nations with tools, cloth, valuables and goods brought from far away.

People on the east coast lived by farming maize, beans and tobacco in plots around their villages, and they engaged in local trade and barter. In the northeast, Native American fields and clearings reminded European settlers of home – with the result that the region gained the name 'New England'. Many tribes were part of confederations or nations related by blood, tradition or political agreements. Sometimes disagreements between the tribes led to bitter war.

The people of the northeastern woodlands made decorated moccasins and ceremonial pipes which were used to celebrate special occasions.

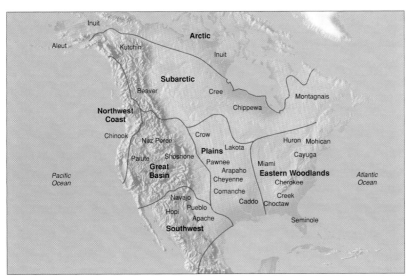

The American nations were very diverse. The map shows where the main tribes of Native Americans lived in 1500, before Europeans arrived and started driving them off their own lands. At this time there were about six million Native North Americans. These numbers fell drastically as the colonists spread west across the continent.

▼ The Chippewa lived in wigwams made of bent branches and covered with an outer layer of skins or birchbark to fend off the winter cold.

THE ARRIVAL OF THE EUROPEANS

Like the Aztecs and Incas, none of the Native American tribes had horses or wheeled transport before the Europeans arrived. Their knowledge of metal was limited and most of their tools were made from wood or stone. Their weapons were bows and arrows, slingshots and spears. At first, some tribes were friendly with the Europeans, even helping them to survive. Yet things changed disastrously for the native peoples when more aggressive European settlers arrived. Whole villages of Native Americans died from European diseases, such as smallpox and the measles. Others were killed in disputes and the rest were driven off their lands.

▶ The nomadic Plains Indians lived in *tipis*. In the evenings, stories were told, both to entertain and to pass on the history, customs, laws and ways of the tribe. They also held tribal councils to settle disputes and decide the tribe's future.

TRADE AND EMPIRE

1601–1707

The Europeans were now beginning to take over
the world. The biggest impact was in the
Americas. British and French settlers occupied
the east coast of North America, and Spanish
conquistadores had already taken over Central
and South America. European trading posts were
now dotted around the world; only Japan kept
them out. In Europe, this century brought a
tragic mixture of wars, revolution and
devastation, as well as enormous growth and
progress in the sciences and arts.

▲ In 1620, a ship called the *Mayflower* sailed from Plymouth in England
carrying pilgrims to a new life in North America.

◀ The Taj Mahal near Agra in India was built in the 17th century by
Shah Jehan as a mausoleum for his wife, Mumtaz Mahal.

161

THE WORLD AT A GLANCE 1601–1707

The 17th century was the age of the absolute ruler. In Europe, India, China and Japan, power was concentrated in the hands of the kings, emperors and shoguns who ruled the land. The great exception was in England where an elected, rebellious Parliament overthrew and executed the king, Charles I. Although his son, Charles II, was later invited to take the throne, he was only granted limited powers.

At this time, although embroiled in wars, Europe spread its influence worldwide, while countries such as India and China enriched Europe with their products, art and ideas.

Many thousands of Europeans went overseas to North America to seek a better life, or to try and found communities where they could worship as they wished, free from the interference of hostile governments. The 17th century also saw another kind of movement of people. The terrible trade in slaves tore millions of Africans from their homes and transported them across the Atlantic ocean to toil in the American plantations.

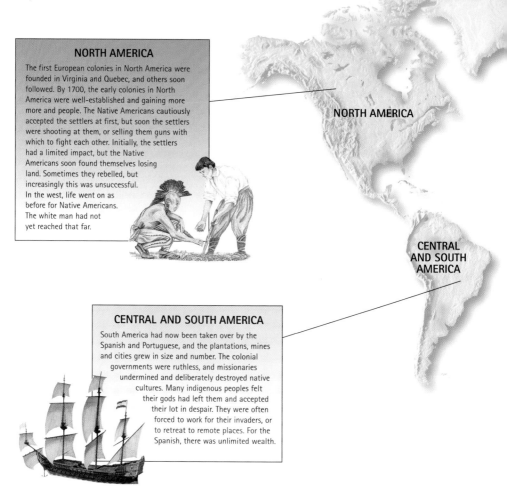

NORTH AMERICA

The first European colonies in North America were founded in Virginia and Quebec, and others soon followed. By 1700, the early colonies in North America were well-established and gaining more more and people. The Native Americans cautiously accepted the settlers at first, but soon the settlers were shooting at them, or selling them guns with which to fight each other. Initially, the settlers had a limited impact, but the Native Americans soon found themselves losing land. Sometimes they rebelled, but increasingly this was unsuccessful. In the west, life went on as before for Native Americans. The white man had not yet reached that far.

NORTH AMERICA

CENTRAL AND SOUTH AMERICA

CENTRAL AND SOUTH AMERICA

South America had now been taken over by the Spanish and Portuguese, and the plantations, mines and cities grew in size and number. The colonial governments were ruthless, and missionaries undermined and deliberately destroyed native cultures. Many indigenous peoples felt their gods had left them and accepted their lot in despair. They were often forced to work for their invaders, or to retreat to remote places. For the Spanish, there was unlimited wealth.

EUROPE

During the Thirty Years War, many countries in Europe were devastated by troops and cannon, as rulers fought for power. Rivalry between Catholics and Protestants caused much bloodletting, and in England, a civil war. Yet rulers, while causing much of the turmoil of this century, also grew rich and powerful. They built great palaces and estates and became patrons for music, science and the arts. Underneath, European society was transforming itself, with people moving into cities, reading more books and exchanging new ideas in the streets and coffee-shops. Their attitudes were changing faster than those of the rulers, and this was to lead to trouble. The ports, banks and warehouses became busy as Europe's trade with the world expanded.

ASIA

The Manchus invaded China and set up the Qing dynasty, which would last until 1911. But Europeans were knocking at their door, looking for trade. Japan kept them out, while China allowed access to Canton only, and India and southeast Asia let them in. A fight for control of India and the East Indies broke out between rival European trading companies. In India, friction between Hindus and Muslims grew stronger, and the Moghul empire weakened. Asian products were sought by Europeans, bringing wealth and big changes to the affected countries. In the more isolated parts of Asia, though, people had not yet encountered their first Europeans.

EUROPE

ASIA

MIDDLE
EAST

AFRICA

AUSTRALASIA

Australia, called 'Terra Incognita' (meanding 'unknown land'), and New Zealand, were first visited by Dutch sailors in the 17th century. However, life for the Aborigines, Maoris and Polynesians carried on undisturbed. This relatively isolated part of the world was as yet untouched by Europeans or Asians.

AUSTRALASIA

AFRICA

Africa lost much of its population through the slave trade, though its chiefs gained in wealth as a result, and new trading nations grew up, such as Asante and Congo. European settlers moved into South Africa, and trade with Europe, particularly in west Africa, increased.

MIDDLE EAST

The Ottomans and the Safavids in Persia continued to dominate the Middle East, though both were now past their peak. The Ottoman empire was beginning a very long, slow decline, to be gradually eaten away from the inside as well as the outside. The Persians thrived on contact with India and Asia, but had little to do with Europeans.

JAPAN IN ISOLATION 1603–1716

The Tokugawa shoguns brought stability to Japan after years of chaos. Fearing disruptive influences from foreigners, they sealed Japan from the outside world.

Shinto religious traditions remained strong under the Tokugawas, though the role of the temples in politics and the economy was reduced.

In 1603, Tokugawa Ieyasu, the head of a leading Japanese family, became shogun of Japan mainly by military force and political manoeuvring. He established his government at Edo (later renamed Tokyo) and began to change what was then a small fishing village into an enormous fortress-city. From Edo he ran most of the country's affairs. Ieyasu retired in 1605, but continued to control the government until he died in 1616.

After 150 years of disruption and civil war between rival *daimyos* (lords), the Tokugawa family took strong control of the country, removing any troublesome *daimyos* and restricting foreign influences. Since 1540, European merchants and Catholic priests from Spain and Portugal had visited Japan. Nagasaki in the south, ruled by a rebel *daimyo*, had become an isolated base for them.

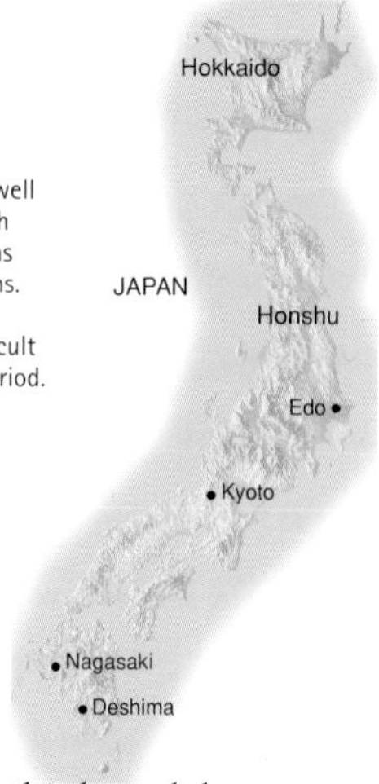

Japan is a fertile and well populated country with many valleys and plains separated by mountains. These geographical extremes made it difficult to unify during this period.

The 'foreign devils' alarmed the Tokugawa rulers, who thought the strange visitors would introduce disruptive ideas and divide the country again. The foreigners did indeed change the ideas of the people around Nagasaki. Tokugawa Iemitsu, a later shogun, persecuted the newly converted Japanese Christians when they rebelled in 1638. He had 37,000 of them killed, and banned their religion.

▲ There were important technical and cultural advances in Japan during this time. However, due to Japan's 'closed door' policy to foreigners, these advances were not seen by the outside world. These exquisite Japanese porcelain figures date from this period.

▶ Nijo castle in Kyoto was built in the 17th century for the Tokugawa Bakufu, the ambassador to the emperor. Even though the emperor was by now largely powerless, it was still important for the shogun to remain on friendly terms with him.

Map labels: Hokkaido · JAPAN · Honshu · Edo · Kyoto · Nagasaki · Deshima

JAPAN BECOMES PROSPEROUS

Following the rebellion by Japanese Christians in Nagasaki, only a few Dutch and Chinese traders were allowed into Japan. Japanese people were not allowed to go abroad, and Japanese who lived away from the country were not allowed to return. Christian priests were ordered to leave or be killed, and their churches were torn down. Japanese Christians were executed. Life became very regulated and orderly, and the country was sealed off from outside influences. Tokugawa rule gave Japan almost 250 years of peace.

Japan grew more prosperous because it now operated as one country. Merchants and farmers were encouraged to expand their businesses, while traditional *daimyos* and samurai warriors lost their positions and grew poor. As in Europe, Japan was changing from being a feudal society to a trading economy. Cities and towns grew larger and the population expanded greatly during the 17th and 18th centuries. Though Japanese society still kept its strict rules of behaviour, people were becoming better educated.

There were temporary setbacks to Japan's growth during this period. In 1684, the fifth Tokugawa shogun Tsunayoshi introduced some reforms inspired by Buddhist scholars. They were not popular. In 1703, the capital, Edo (Tokyo), was destroyed by an earthquake and fire. However, in 1716, a reforming shogun, Yoshimune, came to power and Japan's isolation from the rest of the world began to break down.

▲ The Tosho-gu temple at Nikko was built in the 17th century. It was dedicated to Ieyasu, who, after his death, was looked on as a saint.

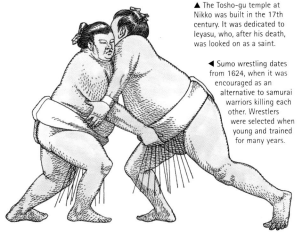

◀ Sumo wrestling dates from 1624, when it was encouraged as an alternative to samurai warriors killing each other. Wrestlers were selected when young and trained for many years.

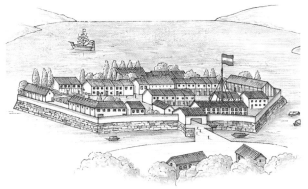

◀ The Dutch were permitted to occupy the island of Deshima in Nagasaki Bay as a trading base. A few ships were allowed to visit each year, exchanging foreign goods for Japanese silks and other products. The Dutch were not allowed to cross onto the Japanese mainland.

KEY DATES	
1603	Ieyasu founds the Tokugawa Shogunate
1609	Small Dutch trading base established on the island of Deshima in Nagasaki Bay
1612	Persecution of Nagasaki Christians begins
1638	Portuguese traders banned and expelled
1638	The Shimabara rebellion in Nagasaki
1684	Hardship after Tokugawa Tsunayoshi's reforms
1703	Edo destroyed by earthquake and fire
1716	Yoshimune, a reformer, comes to power

THE STUARTS 1603 –1649

The Stuart dynasty came from Scotland. In England, they faced a complicated political situation which led to six years of civil war and the downfall of a king.

Apparently James I stammered and dribbled. But he was an intelligent king who did his best in a difficult situation, and during his time, England and Scotland moved closer to being united. He was not popular as he believed in the right of the king to rule as he wished.

Queen Elizabeth I, the last Tudor monarch of England, died in 1603 without an heir. James VI of Scotland, son of Mary Queen of Scots, succeeded her as James I of England. James was descended from Henry VIII's sister and Elizabeth's aunt Margaret Tudor, who had married the Scottish king, James IV, in 1503. His family, the Stuarts, had ruled Scotland for over 200 years.

England and Scotland now had the same king, but they still remained separate countries. James dreamed of uniting them but many English and Scottish people opposed this. He tried to make peace between Catholics, Anglicans and Puritans. The Puritans were extreme Protestants who wished to abolish church ceremony and music, bishops, church hierarchies and other 'popish' traditions. James angered them by refusing to go as far as they wanted. But he ordered a new translation of the Bible, the King James Bible, to try to bring Christians together.

As England's prosperity grew during Tudor and Stuart times, many towns were rebuilt. They were not planned, but rebuilt along existing winding streets.

JAMES THE SPENDER

James made peace with Catholic Spain to try and ease tensions between European Catholics and Protestants, and Britain was at peace for 20 years. But in 1624 James was drawn into the Thirty Years War in Germany on the Protestant side, in support of his son-in-law, Frederick, a German prince. James got deeply into debt. The costs of running the country were growing and James himself was a lavish spender. He believed Parliament should obey him and grant whatever he asked for. But Parliament and the king's ministers had grown stronger in Tudor times, and he fell out with them when his demands for more money were refused.

THE GUNPOWDER PLOT

Catholics in England were frustrated over Protestant intolerance towards them and, although James I tried to please everyone, opinions pulled in conflicting directions. Some Catholics saw violence as the only way to gain toleration for Catholics, though many disliked this idea. A small group plotted to kill both the king and parliamentarians by blowing up Parliament during its ceremonial opening on November 5, 1605. One of the conspirators was Guy Fawkes, who was discovered guarding barrels of gunpowder in the cellars of Parliament. He and the other plotters were arrested, tortured and horribly put to death. After this, attitudes towards Catholics hardened.

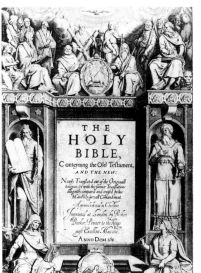

The King James Bible, or Authorized Version, published in 1611, was carefully translated under James I's guidance, in order to serve as one Bible for Anglicans, Puritans and Catholics. It was admired because of the beauty of its language, and has survived to this day. It is still used in some churches.

KEY DATES

1603	James I becomes king of England
1605	The Gunpowder Plot to blow up Parliament
1608	James disagrees with Parliament over money
1621	James again disagrees with Parliament
1625	Charles I becomes king
1629	Charles closes Parliament
1637	Charles's court splits after a crisis
1640	Charles recalls Parliament – clashes follow
1642	The English Civil War begins
1649	Charles I is executed by the parliamentarians

Charles left London and raised an army. He was finally defeated and handed power to Parliament. He escaped and continued the Civil War, but was recaptured, held prisoner and executed in 1649. For 12 years, during the English Revolution and Civil War, England had no king.

▼ During Tudor and Stuart times, wealthy people gained more power and influence. However, disagreements increased between the different groups, especially over money, business and religious matters.

CHARLES I

James I tried to please everyone. He was unpopular in England because he made mistakes, and because he was Scottish and his Danish wife, Anne, was Catholic. His belief in the rights of the king was also disliked. When he died in 1625, his son Charles became king and inherited his unpopularity.

Charles I also disliked parliamentary interference, and handled some situations badly. People started to take sides, and supported either the king or Parliament. This became a battle between traditional and modern ideas. When, in 1629, Parliament refused to give Charles more money and allow him to rule in his own way, he sent the parliamentarians home and tried to govern without them.

Charles ruled without Parliament for eleven years, but his court and ministers were divided over many important questions. Charles also angered the Scots, who thought he had become too English, and lost their support. Parliament, called back in 1640, then united against him. It tried to limit his powers and suppress his supporters. In 1642, Charles tried to arrest five parliamentary leaders, but Parliament, including the nobility, totally opposed him.

THE THIRTY YEARS WAR 1618–1648

The Thirty Years War was the world's first modern war. Starting as a religious conflict between Catholics and Protestants, it ended as a fight for power in Europe.

Ferdinand II of Austria was a determined Roman Catholic who believed it was his right to force his religion on others.

Frederick, the 'Winter King' of Bohemia for only one year, was also the ruler of a German state called the Palatinate.

In 1618, tensions exploded in Bohemia between Catholics and Protestants, and between the Habsburgs and other royal houses. Ferdinand II, the Holy Roman emperor, had inherited the Bohemian throne in 1617 and two years later, in 1619, the Austrian throne. Until that time, the Habsburgs had been neutral in matters of religion. Bohemia had long been Protestant, but Ferdinand was Catholic, and he unwisely forced Bohemia to become Catholic. This resulted in the Bohemians revolting against him.

In 1619, the German rulers who elected the Holy Roman emperor met at Prague. They deposed Ferdinand II as king of Bohemia and made Frederick, a Protestant, king in his place. The outcome was a whole series of wars, fought mainly in Germany, which eventually involved most of Europe for the next thirty years.

At first the Catholics won most of the battles, with Spanish Habsburg help and money. In 1625, the Danes joined the Protestant side, but to no avail. The Catholics had two outstanding generals, Count Wallenstein and Count Tilly, whose troops fought well, and by 1629, the Protestant allies were in trouble.

The use of guns and cannon increased the destruction and cost of the war. The matchlock musket was improved by the Swedes to make it lighter and faster to reload.

SWEDEN ENTERS THE WAR

Frederick fled and a Catholic prince, Maximilian of Bavaria, was appointed king of Bohemia. The struggle then moved northwards. Led by Wallenstein, the emperor's army defeated the Danes and overran northern Germany. It seemed that nothing could stop Ferdinand from forcing Germany to become Catholic until, in 1630, Protestant Gustavus Adolphus of Sweden entered the war. He took back northern Germany, soundly defeating the Catholics in battles at Breitenfeld and Lützen. But the battles took their toll. Tilly was killed at Breitenfeld and Gustavus Adolphus died at Lützen.

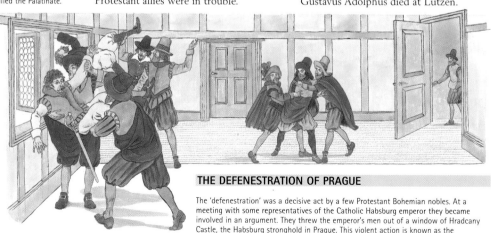

THE DEFENESTRATION OF PRAGUE

The 'defenestration' was a decisive act by a few Protestant Bohemian nobles. At a meeting with some representatives of the Catholic Habsburg emperor they became involved in an argument. They threw the emperor's men out of a window of Hradcany Castle, the Habsburg stronghold in Prague. This violent action is known as the 'Defenestration of Prague' and sparked the Thirty Years War in 1618.

The French entered the war in 1635, a year after the Swedes were beaten at Nördlingen. The French minister Cardinal Richelieu had already supported the Protestants because he opposed the ambitious Habsburgs. The same year, the German Protestant princes withdrew from the war, bankrupt and defeated. Many alliances switched, and the conflict grew complicated. Different countries had different aims. The French advanced into Catholic Bavaria to overcome the Spanish Habsburgs and Sweden defeated the Austrian Habsburgs. When the French and Swedes were poised ready to take over Bavaria and threaten Austria, the Habsburg emperor asked for peace.

THE RESULTS OF THE WAR

During this long war, large guns and mercenary troops had been used. This had been expensive and caused great devastation. Troops looted whole areas of Germany and even at times switched sides. Germany was in ruins, and the Netherlands and Switzerland gained independence; however, France, Sweden and Holland grew stronger. Some states gained land and others lost it. One German state, Brandenburg–Prussia, grew stronger and was to become even more important. The Habsburgs lost their power, and the Holy Roman empire grew weaker. Germany broke down into 300 small states. Many European governments became secular, which meant that they no longer forced religious beliefs on their subjects. The Peace of Westphalia, which ended the war, was the first major European treaty of modern times.

▲ One of the worst events of the Thirty Years War was the destruction of the German city of Magdeburg by the Catholics under Count Tilly in 1631. Until then, Tilly had been highly respected across Europe.

▶ The Catholic count Albrecht Wallenstein (1583–1634) was an outstanding general. He became rich from the war, and tried to build his own empire in northern Germany. This made him very unpopular with the emperor and eventually led to his downfall.

▼ Wallenstein and his men were murdered at Eger in Germany in 1634, when it was discovered he was using the war as a way of growing rich and becoming powerful.

KEY DATES

1618–20 Bohemian revolt against Austria
1625–27 Denmark joins the Protestants
1629 Protestant Germans losing the war
1630 Gustavus Adolphus of Sweden joins the war, overrunning northern Germany
1631 Tilly storms and destroys Magdeburg
1631–32 Protestant victories at Breitenfeld and Lützen
1634 Protestants are defeated at Nördlingen. Count Wallenstein is murdered
1635 Protestant Germans make peace – France joins the war
1645 French and Swedish victories in Germany
1648 The Peace of Westphalia treaty ends the war

FRANCE AND RICHELIEU 1624–1661

Louis XIII became king at the age of nine. He later appointed as his chief minister the man who was to make France the leading nation in Europe.

Marie de Medici (1573–1642) had been queen of France, then regent to her son Louis XIII. She clung to power and was banished in 1617. Richelieu helped her make peace with her son in 1620. But when she tried to replace Louis in 1630, she was permanently exiled to Brussels.

Louis XIII was the son of Henry IV and the second king of the Bourbon line. He became king as a boy in 1610 and assumed power in 1617. He was very influenced by Cardinal Richelieu, but he outlasted Richelieu by one year, dying in 1643 and leaving the throne to his young son, Louis XIV.

In 1624, Louis XIII of France appointed Cardinal Richelieu as his chief minister. They worked together for eighteen years. Richelieu's ambition was to unify France into one centrally ruled country and make it great. Regional dukes held great power, and he set about breaking their influence. In 1628, he also dealt harshly with the troublesome French Protestant Huguenots. Richelieu was disliked by Catholic leaders, nobles and judges because he stopped many of their privileges, and the high taxes he levied caused many revolts by the people. He believed in strong control, and used force to get his way.

The clothing of the French nobility was very elaborate. Wigs, hats and clothes were a sign of status. This was a French army officer's clothing when on campaign.

Abroad, Austria and Spain were the main threats to France. The Habsburgs ruled both countries and, if they combined forces, France would be vulnerable. By 1631, in the Thirty Years War, Habsburg Austria controlled most of Germany and threatened to dominate Europe.

CARDINAL RICHELIEU

Armand du Plessis, the duke of Richelieu (1585–1642), became a bishop in 1607 and a cardinal in 1622. He entered the council of the regent, Marie de Medici, in 1616, and became chief minister in 1624. Richelieu believed in 'absolutism' – the right of the king to do what he wanted. He believed the king was responsible to God, not to the Church, lords or people. Richelieu used spies effectively and suppressed all opposition. He trained his successor, Cardinal Mazarin, who continued Richelieu's policies and ruled as regent for the young Louis XIV until 1661. In many European countries, this was a time when chief ministers were very powerful.

La Rochelle was
the stronghold
of the Protestant
Huguenots, who had
developed their own army and navy.
Richelieu besieged the port in 1628 and broke
their power. In this painting, Louis XIII is depicted
visiting the scene of the siege in October of that year.

FRANCE BECOMES STRONGER

To weaken Austria, Richelieu paid
Sweden, the Netherlands and Denmark
to fight a common enemy, the Habsburgs.
In 1635, France declared war on Spain
(which ruled Belgium and Burgundy). The
fighting went on until 1648 and outlasted
Richelieu, but his plans succeeded. He
tried to extend France to what he thought
were its natural frontiers – the Pyrenees
mountains and the Rhine River.

When Richelieu died in 1642, his
follower Cardinal Mazarin continued his
policies. France replaced Spain as Europe's
great power. A revolt by the French
nobility, called the Fronde, was put down
in 1653. When Louis XIV came to the
throne he was only five, and Mazarin ruled
as regent. By the end of Mazarin's life, in
1661, France had changed greatly. It had
grown larger, stronger and richer, its armies
had become the finest in Europe, and
Louis XIV was to be its greatest king.

▶ The royal flag of the ruling Bourbon kings of
France acted as the French flag until 1790, the
time of the French Revolution.

▼ Richelieu allowed the Protestant Huguenots
religious freedom, but he fought to break their
political and military power. This grisly massacre
of Huguenots was initiated by Richelieu.

EAST INDIA COMPANIES 1600–1700

The East India Companies were powerful trading organizations set up by the English, Dutch and French to protect their business interests in southeast Asia.

The ships of the East India Companies, first used for trading, were also converted into warships for use against pirates, Asians and ships from other companies.

In 1600, the English East India Company was formed in London. Its purpose was to unite the English merchants doing business in southeast Asia. There was cut-throat competition for trade in this area which had first been controlled by the Spaniards and the Portuguese. In the 17th century, the contest for this lucrative trade with the East was between the Dutch, English and French.

The Netherlands followed England and set up a Dutch East India Company in 1602, with its headquarters in Amsterdam and also at Batavia (Jakarta) on the island of Java. The French formed their own East India company later, in 1664.

These organizations became immensely powerful. Trading was only one of their activities – they also had a political influence. They armed their ships to fight at sea and maintained private armies. The East India companies set up military as well as trading bases and made treaties with local rulers around them. They waged war on neighbouring nations and on each other. In many ways they behaved like independent states.

In the 17th century many European travellers visited India. Through them, knowledge of the impressive history and culture of India began to reach Europe.

The English lost the contest to control the spice trade in the East Indies to the Dutch. India then became the centre of their activities. By 1700, England had sole trading rights in India, with a number of key ports, notably Calcutta, Madras and Bombay. The Dutch had ports on the Cape in South Africa, in Persia, Ceylon, Malaya and Japan, and also dominated the Spice Islands (now Indonesia). The French were less successful in their attempt to dominate India. Many private fortunes were made. Sailors and traders often died of disease or fighting. Some made homes in Asia, founding European centres in India, southeast Asia and China.

▲ In 1652 the Dutch founded a base at the Cape of Good Hope (Cape Town) as a staging post for ships on the long voyage from Europe to the Far East. This later became a Dutch colony.

▶ The English colony of Madras was a major port for exporting cotton goods It was also the centre of a region noted for making cloth with brightly coloured designs and scenes from Indian life.

THE DUTCH EMPIRE 1660–1664

The Dutch empire was founded on worldwide trade. In the 17th century, their huge merchant fleet enabled them to become a powerful trading nation.

▲ Peter Stuyvesant was the harsh governor of the New Netherland colony in North America from 1647 to 1664. He was hated both by the Native Americans and the colonists. In 1664, the colonists surrendered gladly to a small English fleet without a fight.

▼ The Dutchman Adrian Reland made this folding map of Java around 1715. Java had been ruled by many different local rulers until the Dutch East Indies Company took control in 1619. Java remained a Dutch colony until 1949.

By the end of the 16th century, the port of Amsterdam was Europe's busiest, with warehouses, banks and trading houses, and a large fleet of ships. Frustrated with their exclusion from South America by the Spanish and Portuguese, the Dutch headed for the Far East. They founded an East India Company for their traders and took control of trade from the Spice Islands or 'East Indies', seizing Java and the Moluccas from the Portuguese.

The Dutch East India Company established its headquarters at Batavia (Jakarta) on the island of Java (now part of Indonesia) in 1619. The company maintained an army and a powerful fleet of ships which drove the English and the Portuguese out of the East Indies and seized Ceylon, the port of Malacca and several ports in India. The company even set up a trading post in Japan – the only Europeans allowed to do so.

In 1652, the Dutch occupied the Cape of Good Hope on the southern tip of Africa as a midway point on the long journey from the Far East to Europe. From there, Dutch ships were able to take the shortest route to the East Indies, straight across the Indian Ocean.

Amsterdam was the centre of European banking in the 17th century. A bank was founded there in 1609 for the depositing and lending of money to finance trade.

EXPANSION AND CONTRACTION

The huge merchant fleet of the Netherlands was also busy elsewhere. In 1621, the Dutch West India Company was founded across the Atlantic, and by 1623, 800 Dutch ships were engaged in the Caribbean, trading in sugar, tobacco, animal hides and slaves. The company established a colony in Guiana, and they captured Curacao and, for a while, controlled northeastern Brazil.

In North America, the company founded the colony of New Netherland along the Hudson River in 1624. From there they exported furs, timber and other goods bought from Native Americans.

Eventually, the Dutch lost their naval supremacy to the English and their empire suffered. They lost Ceylon, Malacca and the Cape to the English, and were left only with their southeast Asian empire.

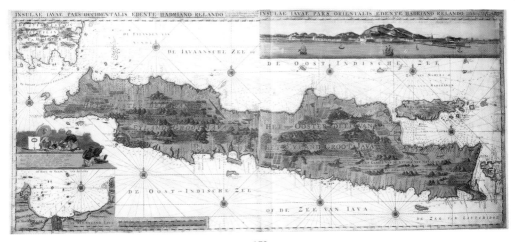

ENGLISH CIVIL WAR 1642–1660

The English Civil War was fought between supporters of the king and supporters of Parliament. For five years the country was run by a dictator, Oliver Cromwell.

During the Civil War, the west and north generally supported the king and the south and east supported Parliament, though there were local divisions across the country. The first major battle took place at Edgehill in 1642; the last at Worcester in 1651.

Charles I (1600-49) came to the throne of England in 1625, the same year that he married Henrietta Maria of France. His belief in the 'divine right' of the king first led to clashes with Parliament and eventually the English Civil War.

▲ Oliver Cromwell (1599–1658) went to college in Cambridge and studied law in London. He was first elected to Parliament in 1628 representing Cambridge. He recruited and trained Parliament's New Model Army. He was a strict Puritan and believed that God had chosen him to perform His will.

The English Civil War was fought between supporters of King Charles I and supporters of Parliament. Like his father, James I, Charles believed in 'divine right', claiming that his right to rule came directly from God. This belief put Charles at odds with Parliament.

Charles became king in 1625 and immediately began to quarrel with Parliament over his right to imprison people who opposed him, religion and taxes. In 1629, he dissolved Parliament, and, for 11 years, tried to rule alone.

In 1637, Charles attempted to impose the Anglican form of public worship on the Scots. The Presbyterian Scots rebelled, raising an army that, in 1640, occupied part of northern England. Charles recalled Parliament to ask for money to put down the rebellion by the Scots, but Parliament demanded reforms. Civil war broke out after Charles tried to arrest his five leading parliamentary opponents. In 1642, fighting broke out all over the country between Royalists (supporters of the king), known as Cavaliers, and supporters of Parliament, known as Roundheads.

The king made Oxford his capital and his forces at first held the advantage. However, Parliament secured the support of the Scottish army, and in the long run, proved superior, for it had the money to maintain a professional army. This New Model Army led by Sir Thomas Fairfax decisively defeated Charles's forces at Naseby in 1645. The king surrendered in 1646 after Oxford fell to the Roundheads.

▶ Charles's Cavalier forces were crushingly defeated by the New Model Army of the Roundheads at the battle of Naseby in 1645. This was the decisive victory for Parliamentary forces during the English Civil War.

174

Charles was imprisoned on the Isle of Wight, where he plotted to begin the war again with Scottish help. A second phase of fighting broke out, with Royalist risings and an attempted invasion by the Scots, but it failed. In 1648, parliamentarians who still respected the king were removed from Parliament by Oliver Cromwell. The remaining Rump Parliament, as it was called, found Charles guilty of treason and executed him in 1649.

OLIVER CROMWELL

After Charles' execution, Parliament abolished the monarchy and England became a Commonwealth. Parliament governed the country but it quarrelled with the army, and its members argued. In 1653, Oliver Cromwell emerged as a strong leader and ruled the country as Lord Protector. Cromwell clashed with some parliamentarians and was forced to govern with the help of army generals. He fought a war with the Dutch over trade and control of the seas, took control of Ireland and planned colonial expansion.

His dictatorship was not universally popular because of his use of force and the high taxes charged. But he introduced education reforms and gave more equality to the English people. In 1658, Cromwell died and was succeeded by his son Richard. He was not an effective ruler and the army removed him. The English people wanted a king again, and in 1660, the son of Charles I took the throne as Charles II.

THE TRIAL OF CHARLES I

Charles was unpopular because he married a Catholic. He had also imposed high taxes to pay for wars that people did not want, as well as trying to limit the powers of Parliament, dissolving it for 11 years. However, at his trial and execution, he behaved with great dignity and this won him some sympathy. At his execution, Charles put on an extra shirt so that people would not think that, when he shivered from the cold, he was shivering with fear. His body was secretly buried by his supporters at Windsor Castle.

◀ The seal of the House of Commons depicts the Commonwealth Parliament in session in 1651.

▼ Shortly after the end of the Civil War, two great disasters happened in London. The first was the Great Plague, which arrived from Europe in 1664–65, and killed about 20 per cent of the population of London. Then, in 1666, the Great Fire destroyed most of the city.

CHINA: THE QING DYNASTY 1644–1770

The Qing dynasty was founded by the Manchus, a Siberian people living in Manchuria. The Qing dynasty was to rule China from 1644 to 1911.

The Manchus came to conquer China from lands lying to the north of the Great Wall. During the Manchu period, the size and population of China grew and the troublesome Mongols were finally defeated.

This intricate gold flower-shaped brooch was made during the Manchu period in China. It is typical of the many fine products of the time that China exported to the rest of the world.

▼ The grand houses and ornamental gardens of the upper class Qing Chinese. are depicted in this ebony panelled Coromandel screen, made in 1672.

The Ming dynasty of emperors had ruled China since 1368. But heavy taxation had made their rule unpopular and rebellions broke out all over. The last Ming emperor, Chongzhen, hanged himself as peasant rebels overran his capital, Beijing. In the confusion that followed, the Manchu chieftain Dorgon led an army south from his homeland of Manchuria. He occupied Beijing and set up the Qing ('pure') dynasty. His nephew Shunzhi was the first Qing emperor.

Resistance to the Manchus continued in China's southern provinces and 40 years went by before all of China submitted to their rule. The Manchus lived separately from the Chinese in closed-off areas. Marriage between Chinese and Manchus was forbidden. Chinese men were even compelled to wear their long hair in *queues* (pigtails) to show they were inferior to the Manchus.

However, both Chinese and Manchus were employed as civil servants to run the empire. As time passed, the Manchus adopted Chinese customs. In this way, they were accepted quite easily. They were small in number, so they had to be careful not to be too excessive in their treatment of the Chinese. They brought new life and efficiency to the country without disturbing the nation's customs.

A RICH AND POWERFUL EMPIRE

At first China prospered under the Qing. The empire grew and trade increased particularly with Europe. Chinese silk and porcelain were the finest in the world and their cotton goods were cheap and of high quality. Huge quantities of Chinese tea were sold abroad when tea-drinking became fashionable in Europe during the 18th century.

The empire became so rich and powerful that its rulers were able to treat the rest of the world with contempt. Under Emperor Kangxi (1661–1722), foreign merchants were forced to kneel whenever his commands were read out. The Manchus also forced several nations into vassal status, including Tibet, Annam (now Vietnam), Burma, Mongolia and Turkestan, making the Chinese empire the world's largest at the time. They made a deal with the Russians over land and trade.

Early on, there were some rebellions in southeast China and amongst ethnic minorities, who protested against Chinese people moving into their areas. But, on the whole, the Qing period brought peace, prosperity and security to China. The population grew dramatically from 100 million in 1650 to 300 million in 1800, and Chinese (Han) people spread out to the west and southwest of China. However, in the late 18th century, corruption and decline began to set in.

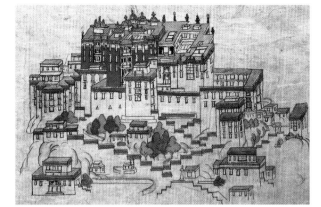

▲ Tibet (Xizang) was ruled by a Buddhist leader called the Dalai Lama. The third Dalai Lama rebuilt the Potala monastery in Lhasa, the capital, as his residence in 1645. The Dalai Lamas came under the influence of the Mongols, but by the middle of the 18th century, Tibet was part of the Chinese empire.

◄ This enamelled porcelain vessel from the late 17th century imitated the shape and designs of the bronze ritual vessels of ancient Shang China.

◄ The Chinese silk industry employed thousands of workers, especially women, to weave silk into cloth on looms. Silk cloth was made for use in China and for export to Europe. Cotton was also imported and then made into cloth for export. The weavers of the port of Su-Chou were particularly famous for their silks.

KEY DATES

1644   The Manchus found the Qing dynasty in Beijing
1644–60 Manchu forces conquer most of China
1661   The island of Formosa is captured from the Dutch by supporters of the defeated Ming
1661   Kangxi becomes second Qing emperor
1674–81 Rebellions in the south, soon suppressed
1683   Manchu forces capture the island of Formosa from supporters of defeated Ming
1689   Russians swap Siberian land for trade in China
1696   The Manchus defeat the Mongols in Mongolia
1717–20 War against the Mongols for the control of Tibet
1750s   Chinese invade Tibet and Turkestan
1760s   Chinese invade Burma, making it a vassal state

THE OTTOMAN EMPIRE 1602–1783

After the reign of Suleiman the Magnificent, the Ottoman empire entered a long and slow decline. Nevertheless, the empire survived until 1923.

In 1565, Suleiman the Magnificent decided to invade Malta, occupied at the time by the Crusader Knights of St John. Although the Turks greatly outnumbered the Knights, their invasion was not successful and they had to withdraw after several months. Suleiman died in 1566. In 1571, when the Ottomans tried to invade Venetian-ruled Cyprus, their invasion force was destroyed by a combined fleet from the navies of Venice, Spain and the Papal States at Lepanto off the coast of Greece. In 1602, a long and costly war broke out with Safavid Persia, with no gain. Plagues and economic crises also hit Istanbul. Once profitable trade routes linking Asia, Africa and Europe were bypassed as new sea routes around Africa and land routes through Siberia opened.

Sultan Osman II ruled from 1618 to 1622. He was young, strict and fond of archery. He restricted the power of the Janissaries (senior army officers) but they took over, had him killed and replaced him with Mustafa I.

THE EMPIRE FADES

The Thirty Years War in Europe gave the Ottomans some peace. But when, in 1656, they tried to invade Crete, the Venetians blocked the Dardanelles (the narrow sea passage from the Mediterranean to the Black Sea), threatening Istanbul itself. This caused panic, and the sultan, Ibrahim, was deposed by army officers. A new grand vizier (chief minister), Mehmet Kuprili, took charge. He reformed the economy and army and Ottoman fortunes revived.

The next vizier, Kara Mustafa, tried to invade Habsburg Vienna for a second time in 1683. The defenders of Vienna held out for two months until an army of Germans and Poles arrived to defeat the Turks. The Austrians invaded Hungary, the Venetians took part of Greece, and the Russians threatened Azov in the Ukraine. Another vizier, Mustafa Kuprili, took office in 1690. He managed to drive back the Austrians, but he was killed in 1691. During the 1690s, the Ottomans finally lost Hungary and Azov. Their European empire was saved only because Austria went to war with France.

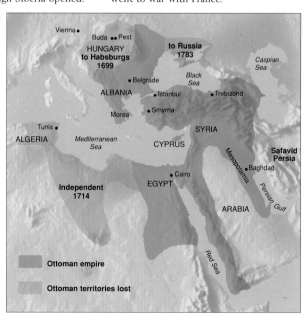

▲ Sultan Mustafa I (1591–1639) was mentally unstable. He ruled twice – 1617–18 and 1622–23.

▶ The Ottoman empire was still large, yet it was slowly falling apart at the seams as it ceased to be prosperous.

Ottoman empire

Ottoman territories lost

THE EMPIRE SHRINKS

In 1710-20, the Ottomans regained Azov and Greece, but they lost Serbia and parts of Armenia. Additionally, they lost control of most of northern Africa – Algeria, Tunisia and Libya. These countries officially remained Ottoman, but actually became independent. In 1736, the Russians attacked again, and by 1783, they had taken the Crimea and most of the Ukraine – the Ottomans no longer controlled the Black Sea. In Anatolia, local chiefs were rebelling and in Istanbul people were worried about the future.

The Ottoman empire was still strong, but it had lost much of its trade and wealth. The progress made in the early days of the Ottoman empire in religion, the arts and social advances, slowed. The Ottomans' only friends, the Moghuls, were also in decline, while the Europeans were advancing rapidly. But the Ottoman empire was not finished yet.

▶ A Turkish miniature, made in 1610, shows a festival of musicians called to entertain the sultan in Istanbul. To keep the sultans separate from politics and the people, they were looked after lavishly. The authority of the sultans was finally weakened by a series of bloody contests for power among ruling families.

▼ The siege of Vienna in 1683 marked the farthest point of the Ottoman Turks' advance into Europe. The defenders of Vienna held out for two months, just long enough for a slow-moving army of Germans and Poles to arrive. The Turks were utterly defeated in a 15-hour battle on September 12, 1683.

SLAVERY AND PIRATES 1517–1810

The early development of many colonies in the Americas was carried out by pirates, owners of the sugar plantations and millions of African slaves.

From ports such as Bristol, finished goods were shipped for sale in western Africa. Once the goods had been sold in Africa, the ship would load up with slaves and take them to them to the West Indies. The final leg of the voyage would bring a cargo of sugar back to Europe.

Within a hundred years of Columbus' first landing in 1492, most of the native peoples of the Caribbean islands, the Arawaks and Caribs, had died as a result of European mistreatment and diseases. By the early 17th century, the Caribbean was a battleground. The Spanish, French, English and Dutch all fought for the islands they called the West Indies. Some islands changed hands several times in a fierce contest for trade and for land to establish European colonies.

English, French and Dutch 'privateers' went buccaneering to make their fortune. They were often supported by their governments since they caused trouble for the Spanish, captured islands, established settlements and made good profits. Some were later sent out as admirals or colonial governors. Francis Drake sailed round the world in 1577–80, raiding Spanish ships and returning home rich. Captain Kidd was ordered to put down piracy, but joined the pirates instead. Edward Teach (Blackbeard) and Captain Morgan raided Spanish settlements and galleons in the Caribbean. They paved the way for the establishment of colonies. The Spanish lost a lot of gold to the pirates, but this did not stop their colonialization of the Americas.

THE SLAVE TRADE

In Europe, tea and coffee were becoming fashionable drinks and this led to a huge demand for sugar to sweeten them. Sugar grew well in the West Indian climate, but its cultivation needed many workers. Local workers could not be found, because many of the original islanders had died out. So the colonists imported slave labour from western Africa.

Europeans saw nothing wrong in using Africans as slaves. They were bought cheaply, crammed into ships and then sold to plantation owners. Two-thirds of them died either on the voyage or from disease, ill-treatment and overwork. Even so, by 1800, there were nine million African slaves in the Americas.

West Africa was rich in gold. Arabs called the area 'Guinea' and Europeans borrowed the word. In 1663, a golden coin of 'Guinea gold' was struck by order of Charles I.

Newly captured slaves were chained together by the neck or feet. Iron collars stopped the slaves from running away.

▲ Iron manacles (handcuffs) which could not be opened without special tools were used to hold slaves' arms together.

▶ Whole families and villages of Africans were shipped to the Americas as slaves. Many of them did not survive the journey and western Africa, the Congo and Angola lost much of their population.

Slaves harvested the sugar cane on the plantations in the Caribbean. Landowners grew very wealthy, often returning to Europe where they lived well, and leaving their plantations in the hands of managers.

THE TRIANGLE OF TRADE

The European-owned sugar plantations in the Caribbean were often very large. They had warehouses, boatyards, churches, slave quarters and the landowner's grand house. A triangle of trade developed, taking finished goods from Europe to western Africa, slaves from western Africa to the Americas and plantation products back to Europe. The profitable markets in Europe for sugar, tobacco, oils and other products were exploited. Piracy, plantations and slavery were driven by the urge for profit, and profits helped Europe's economy grow. Slavery continued into the 19th century. Most of today's Afro-Americans the descendants of slave ancestors.

▶ Long before Europeans arrived, the Arabs had traded slaves on the eastern African coast. When the Portuguese arrived they used the slaves in their colonial ventures.

HENRY MORGAN

Welshman Captain Morgan (1635–88) was the scourge of the Caribbean between the 1660s and 1680s. He organized fleets of buccaneers, attacking Spanish galleons in mid-ocean and seized their treasures. Much of the booty went back to England, to reward investors who supported his voyages. He captured Porto Bello in 1668, sacked Maracaibo in 1669 and took Panama in 1671. Later, he was knighted for his services against the Spaniards, and made lieutenant-governor of Jamaica in 1674. He died in 1688, aged 53. Buccaneers like Morgan helped England's economy grow much richer.

AFRICAN STATES 1550–1700

In the 17th century, Africa was a patchwork of different peoples and kingdoms, each with its own customs, forms of government, language and gods.

This ram's head mask is from the west African kingdom of Benin, famous for its bronzes. Masks represented gods and spirits, and were used in the annual ceremonies of sacrifice and dancing.

D uring this period, the nations of Africa were developing rapidly. Had the Europeans not arrived, the African nations would have probably advanced their cultures much further. Although Europeans did not have a great influence until the 19th century, they bought gold, exotic items and slaves, and sold guns, cloth, tools and finished goods. By doing so, traditional African trade and society were changed. Some areas, such as West Africa, lost many people to slavery. Social divisions increased as chieftains and merchants made profitable deals with the Europeans. Some chiefs even sold their own people into slavery.

The largest African state was Songhai. European traders on the coast took the gold and slave trade away from Songhai, and its wealth collapsed. In 1591 a Moroccan army crossed the Sahara and invaded the country. South of the Sahara, new states had grown up, including Mossi, the city-states of Hausaland, and Kanem-Bornu and Darfur. These Muslim states traded with the Ottomans and Arabs.

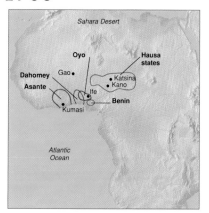

Gao, Katsina and Kano adopted the Muslim faith, brought to western Africa across the Sahara by the Arabs. The coastal kingdoms kept their own religions. Much of northeast Africa was under Ottoman control.

In the east, Christian Ethiopia was surrounded by Muslim countries. Muslims in parts of the country rebelled, ravaging Ethiopia. The Portuguese then arrived, driving out the Muslims in 1543, and Ethiopia was left in peace. Along the east and west coasts, the Portuguese built forts and slave depots. These attracted Africans to the coasts and encouraged chiefs to grow rich by joining in the slave trade.

▲ This Asante helmet was decorated with gold animal horns and charms. Europeans were unable to buy slaves with gold from the Asante because they had all they needed. Instead they bought them with guns and increased the Asante military power.

▶ The Portuguese built forts around the coast of Africa. This pictorial map, made in 1646, shows the fort at Mombasa on the east coast (now in Kenya).

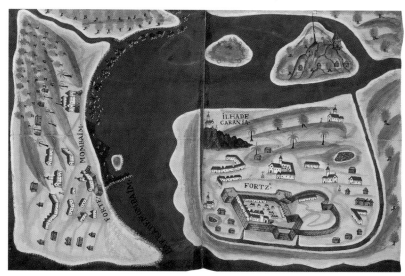

DAHOMEY AND ASANTE

A number of states occupied the forest zone along the west African coast. In 1625, a new kingdom called Allada was founded by King Akaba. Between 1645 and 1685, it merged with two other kingdoms to become Dahomey. This new state grew wealthy from the gold and slave trades. Dahomey was overrun in 1747 by Yorubas from Oyo (now in Nigeria). Dahomey became notorious to Europeans because, when its chief died, thousands of slaves were sacrificed so they could accompany him to the afterlife.

West of Dahomey lay Asante. In 1689, Osei Tutu founded the powerful Asante confederacy and built its capital at Kumasi. It grew wealthy from trade in cola nuts, gold and slaves. The important Portuguese-controlled fort and trading post at Elmira in Asante was taken over by the Dutch in 1637.

Africa provided the slaves needed to work the rapidly growing plantations in the Americas. Millions were shipped across the Atlantic. Many died either during slave wars between different African states to capture slaves or on the terrible voyage across the Atlantic ocean. To lose such an enormous number of its people was a catastrophe for Africa.

▲ A tribal celebration in the kingdom of Lovango in the Congo region in 1686. After the arrival of the Europeans, tribal security and unity gave way to increased social distrust and control by greedy chiefs.

▶ A European trader offers brandy to the chief of the Alcaty tribe, in Senegal, western Africa, in exchange for water, around 1690.

KEY DATES

1570	Rise of Kanem-Bornu as a major nation
1575	Portuguese first settle in Angola
1588	The English Guinea Company is founded
1600	Mwenemutapa at its zenith
1625	New kingdom of Allada set up by King Akaba
1637	Dutch drive Portuguese from the Gold Coast
1652	Dutch East Indies Company founds Cape Town
1660s	Rise of Bambara kingdoms in western Africa
1685	Founding of Dahomey from three kingdoms
1689	Osei Tutu founds the Asante empire
1701	Military expansion of Asante by Osei Tutu

◀ An *oba* (ruler) of Benin rides in a procession of his people. Once the richest state in western Africa, by the 18th century the kingdom of Benin was on the wane. It was overwhelmed by the growing strength of the Yoruba people and the kingdom of Oyo.

IRELAND 1540–1800

English Protestant rule in Ireland was finally and forcibly imposed during the 17th century. There was resistance but this was brutally crushed by the English.

The Irish never liked English rule. Henry II of England had conquered most of Ireland in 1171, and for the next 400 years English monarchs had struggled to maintain their authority there. Relations became more strained as time passed. The problem was mainly religious. The Irish were Catholic and the English had become Protestant. Irish priests encouraged rebellion by teaching that the English were heretics with no rightful authority over Ireland. But the English took strong measures to keep the Irish under their control. They dissolved many old monasteries and sold the land to families who supported their rule. The Irish reacted with frequent revolts. In 1556, Mary I sent troops into central Ireland to forcibly remove some of the native Irish and give their land to English settlers.

▲ James Butler, the Duke of Ormonde (1610–88), governed Ireland for Charles I of England.

▼ The town of Drogheda was beseiged in 1641 by Catholic Irish forces led by Sir Phelim O'Neill.

PLANTATIONS AND REVOLT

The established hold of the English was further extended in 1580. English colonists were promised wealth and opportunity, and they quickly developed the land and new towns. But their colony was destroyed in 1598 by an Irish attack. A revolt broke out in Ulster, a purely Irish area, but was suppressed by 1603. The English started a plantation there, mostly with Puritan Scots settlers, strengthened by fortified towns such as Londonderry. Some Irish fought back, but many left. By the mid-17th century, the Catholics of Ulster were outnumbered by Protestants.

In 1642, an Irish uprising began, and thousands of Protestant settlers were killed. Engaged in the English Civil War, Cromwell only tackled the uprising in 1649. When he arrived with a large army, the Irish were crushed with a brutality that has never been forgiven. Local people were moved to poor land in the west of the country, and English soldiers were given the land to settle. Catholics now owned less than half the land in Ireland.

HARSH PROTESTANT RULE

Irish hopes were briefly raised when the Catholic James II became king of England. His daughter married William of Orange from Holland, commander of a grand alliance of countries fighting France. William became king of England in 1688. James, the 'Old Pretender' escaped to Ireland. Eventually James's army (the Jacobites) met William's at the battle of the Boyne in 1690 and William triumphed.

This series of events marked a turning-point in Irish history. Harsh laws were introduced that banned Catholics from owning guns. They were also forbidden to be involved in politics, to hold land, to receive education and even to own large horses. Catholics converting to the Protestant faith were given land taken from those that remained Catholic. Communities broke apart, with some Irish accepting their lot, others resisting and yet more leaving the country. But, while the 18th century was a relatively peaceful period, new trouble was brewing. When Wolf Tone led a rebellion in the 1790s, many Irish people were killed, a French invasion was fought off, and the rebellion cruelly put down. However, the English were forced to realize that the Irish Catholics were there to stay.

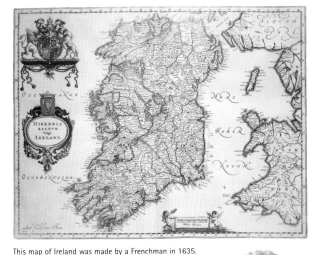

This map of Ireland was made by a Frenchman in 1635. Fourteen years later, Cromwell arrived with a large army to brutally suppress an Irish uprising against English rule. Many Irish people were moved to poor land in the west.

KEY DATES

1556	Mary 1 starts Protestant plantations in Ireland
1580	Further plantation settlements established
1598	Revolts across Ireland, especially in Ulster
1642	Irish uprising against English control
1649	Cromwell's suppression of the Irish revolt
1690	Battle of the Boyne – a Protestant victory
1798	Wolf Tone's nationalist rebellion

Being Catholic, James II was the great hope of the Irish Catholics. However, European power-politics became caught up in the Irish question, and the English, under William III, had to defeat James.

THE BATTLE OF THE BOYNE

This decisive battle took place near Drogheda in 1690. The army of the recently deposed James II, last of the Stuart kings, was outnumbered by the Protestant army of William III. When William's troops crossed the Boyne River, James's troops fled. James went into exile in France, while William's rule in England was strengthened by the victory.

THE GREAT NORTHERN WAR 1700–1721

Following a war between Sweden and other northern European countries, Sweden lost most of its empire and Russia became the leading power in the Baltic.

This 17th-century painting shows King Charles XI of Sweden (1655–97) and his family. The future Charles XII is being held by his mother, Queen Eleonora.

The Great Northern War was fought between Sweden and other northern European powers led by Peter the Great of Russia. At stake was control of the Baltic Sea and the lands around it. In 1700, Sweden was attacked by Denmark, Saxony, Poland and Russia. Sweden's Charles XII was only 18, and his enemies hoped to take advantage of his inexperience. But Charles proved a born leader. He defeated the Russians at Narva in Estonia, forcing Saxony, Poland and Denmark out of the war and putting a new king on the Polish throne. Eight years later Charles invaded Russia. But the bitter winter of 1708–09 set in, and the Russians retreated, destroying everything as they went. The Swedes ran short of food, struggling against repeated Russian attacks. By the spring, Charles's army was reduced to half its size.

This map shows the Swedish empire at its greatest extent in 1660. Sweden was the largest military power in northern Europe and was in an ideal position to invade Russia in 1708.

At the battle of Poltava in June 1709, the Russians beat the Swedes and Charles fled to Turkey. He returned to Sweden in 1714, beating off a Danish invasion in 1716. He invaded Norway and was killed there in 1718. Without Charles, and exhausted by 20 years of fighting, the Swedes agreed peace terms in 1721.

▲ This bronze plaque shows the taking of Narva in Estonia by the Swedes. During the battle, 40,000 Russian soldiers were crushingly defeated by and army of 8,000 Swedes. This was a tremendous victory for the young Charles XII of Sweden.

▶ The Battle of Poltava, near Kiev in the Ukraine in 1709, brought Sweden's power and dominance in the region to an end. Peter the Great's army was larger and better equipped and the Swedes were tired, hungry and far from home.

THE SPANISH SUCCESSION 1701–1713

When Charles II of Spain died in 1700 he left no heir. The question of who should succeed him led to the War of the Spanish Succession.

John Churchill, Duke of Marlborough (1650–1722), was made commander of the allied forces in 1702. He won great battles at Blenheim, Ramillies, Oudenarde and Malplaquet.

Prince Eugène of Savoy (1663–1736) fought the Turks at the siege of Vienna in 1683. By 1701, he had become commander-in-chief of the Austrian forces and fought at the battles of Blenheim and Oudenarde.

The French Bourbons and the Austrian Habsburgs both claimed the Spanish throne. Before Charles II died in 1700, they had signed an agreement dividing his empire. But Charles's will left his lands to Philip of Anjou, the grandson of Louis XIV of France. Louis ignored his earlier agreement with the Habsburgs, and chose to back Philip instead. But an alliance between France and Spain was not acceptable to every country in Europe.

By 1701, western Europe was at war. Organized by William III of England, England, the Netherlands, most German states and Austria formed a grand alliance against France. In 1704, a French army was overwhelmed at Blenheim by a combined force under the Duke of Marlborough. He won three more victories over the French in the Spanish Netherlands. In 1706, an Austrian army under Prince Eugène of Savoy drove the French from Italy.

At the Treaty of Utrecht in 1713, France retained her frontiers. Austria took the Spanish Netherlands and Naples, England gained Gibraltar and Newfoundland. Philip V remained king of Spain.

The allies then invaded Spain but the French forces pushed them out again, allowing Louis' grandson Philip V to remain on the Spanish throne. The long war had exhausted both sides and, in 1713, peace was signed at Utrecht.

THE BATTLE OF BLENHEIM

In 1704, the battle of Blenheim was fought in Bavaria between four armies and several nations. The French and Bavarians were marching on Vienna. The armies of Marlborough and Eugène intercepted them at Blenheim, and in the ensuing battle, 12,000 allies and 30,000 French and Bavarians were killed. However, it was a victory for Marlborough and Eugène, and Vienna was saved.

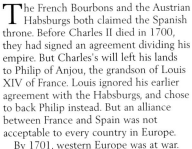

COLONIAL AMERICA 1600–1700

Settlers were arriving on the North American continent in large numbers. These European peoples shaped the character of future life in the 'New World'.

▲ William Penn (1644–1718) was a wealthy Quaker who founded Pennsylvania in 1681. He set out to welcome people who had suffered religious persecution and hardship.

▼ The Quaker Society of Friends was founded in England in the mid-117th century. They were Puritans and disliked priestly control of the Church. Quakers, including women, were encouraged to preach and speak out.

The French and Spanish made up the majority of the earliest European settlers in North America, but they were later overtaken by the English and Germans. The majority of them were Protestants who had suffered religious persecution in Europe. Within 20 years of the first Puritans arriving in America there were 20,000 English people living in Massachusetts. The colony grew and developed rapidly, with Boston as its capital. Some of these colonists moved to Rhode Island and Connecticut.

In 1625, at the mouth of the Hudson River, New York had begun as a Dutch colony. When the English took over in 1664, English, German and a variety of other nationalities settled there. It soon grew into a large cosmopolitan city of traders and craftspeople. Further down the coast in 1681, in repayment of a debt, the English king gave Pennsylvania to a group of Quakers led by William Penn. Penn was a religious idealist and dreamed of a 'holy experiment' – a new society. He assisted poor people from Europe to settle in the colony. Many English, Scottish, Irish and German settlers moved there to start a new life.

Settlers worked hard to build a new life. This is a small family farm in Maryland (previously New Sweden). The family kept cattle, pigs and chickens, and grew wheat, vegetables, tobacco and cotton.

Further south, the Carolinas and Virginia grew in size after the English Civil War, when King Charles II granted land there to his royalist supporters. They established profitable plantations growing tobacco, cotton, rice and indigo. The settlers imported slaves from Africa to work the land from 1619 onwards. Soon the majority of the people were slaves.

The Puritans of New England had a high regard for education. In 1636, the Massachusetts government founded Harvard College in Cambridge.

PIONEERING SETTLERS

In the southwest, Spanish-Mexican pioneers pushed up into New Mexico, building a capital at Santa Fe in 1609. This was a colony of forts, mines and trading posts. With Florida also in their hands, the Spanish might have taken the whole of North America, but Spain lost its control over the seas and they missed their chance. The French had settled around the St Lawrence, the Great Lakes and the Mississippi. As colonists, traders, fur-trappers and pioneers, they were small in number. By 1700, there were 12 English colonies along the Atlantic coast, with some 250,000 English compared with only 20,000 French. Germans, Dutch, Swedes, Lithuanians, Bohemians and other nationalities each found homes in different areas. The new America was being built by hard-working, ordinary people rather than distant European governments.

NATIVE PEOPLES

At first, the Native Americans and European settlers both gained from mixing together – in some cases co-existing peacefully with each other. But as more settlers arrived, native lands were seized. There were several atrocities, and native distrust of and resistance to the settlers grew. Local conflicts arose, leading to war in the 1670s. The settlers won, and native resistance declined. Some native peoples were actively driven from their homelands. As European takeover became certain, a gradual tide of migrations began.

▼ The first elected representatives of the colony of Virginia, together with its governor and council, met in 1619 at Jamestown to make the laws.

▼ Fur was an important commodity that the settlers exported to Europe. Here, two French fur traders meet Native Americans near Lake Superior.

SALEM WITCH TRIAL

In 1692, several young girls in the town of Salem, Massachusetts, claimed that they had been bewitched by a West Indian slave called Tituba. Most people of the time believed in witchcraft and the Puritans of Salem took fright. This led to the trial and execution of 14 women and 6 men accused of witchcraft. Several people died in prison, and 150 more awaited trial. Eventually, the madness was stopped by the governor, William Phips, and by a respected Congregational preacher, Increase Mather.

REVOLUTION AND INDEPENDENCE

1708–1835

The 18th century is often called 'the century of revolutions'. In the years 1708 to 1835, there were revolutions against governments and growing colonial power in many parts of the world; some were successful, some were not. Political revolutions happened because people felt dissatisfied with the way their country was run. There were also revolutions in farming techniques and industry, in science, technology and medicine, in transport, and in the arts, especially literature.

▲ The Jacobite (Stuart) rebellion against the Hanoverian rule in England ended at the battle of Culloden in 1746, when the Jacobites were defeated by English troops led by the king's son, the Duke of Cumberland.

◄ Generals Rochambeau and Washington give orders for the attack at the siege of Yorktown during the American Revolutionary War in 1781.

THE WORLD AT A GLANCE 1708–1835

In North America, the United States won its independence from British rule, but this brought problems for the Native Americans. Many people emigrated from Europe and took up more and more land. In South and Central America, the colonies fought for freedom from Spain and Portugal and won.

In Europe, Prussia and Russia rose to become major European powers, while the French Revolution of 1789 marked the end of the monarchy in France.

In Africa, the Fulani, Zulu and Buganda peoples established new kingdoms. African states in the north threw off Ottoman control. The Moghul empire in India collapsed and Britain and France fought for control of its land. China conquered Tibet, but faced problems at home. Japan banned contact with the West. In the Pacific, the arrival of Europeans threatened the traditional way of life.

NORTH AMERICA

The 18th century saw the birth of the United States of America and of Canada. The American Revolutionary War of the 1780s had been caused by bad British colonial government. The USA became the world's first proper democratic, constitutionally ruled state, with a declaration of rights embracing everyone (except Native Americans and slaves). A declaration of independence was made, and after a while, the new republic began to spread its wings westwards, reaching toward the Pacific ocean. Migrants from war-torn Europe, seeking a new future, swelled the population. American towns, trade and culture took shape and grew larger and richer. The British held on to Canada, which eventually gained greater control of its own affairs. Meanwhile, many Native Americans in the east were thrown off their lands, migrating westwards. In the south, slaves worked the cotton and tobacco plantations, catering for the appetites of Europe and fuelling the wealth of their landowning masters.

NORTH AMERICA

CENTRAL
AND SOUTH
AMERICA

CENTRAL AND SOUTH AMERICA

The Napoleonic Wars in Europe forced Latin Americans to think for themselves, and in the early 19th century new independence movements fought against the Spaniards and Portuguese for control of their colonies. The riches of the mines and slave-run plantations had declined in importance, and Latin Americans now had to fight for a place in a fast-changing world. But the independence movements were run by the landowners, so there was little gain for the ordinary people. Native peoples suffered greatly under the rule of Latinos.

EUROPE

For much of the 18th century a gap was developing in European society. Wealthy, autocratic rulers lived in their great palaces, while the growing middle classes with 'new money' developed a different, forward-thinking outlook. Society changed greatly. Cities grew, bankers and inventors were busy, foreign goods and ideas came in. New inventions enabled factories to start making manufactured goods in large quantities. During the Napoleonic wars, the old order was swept away across much of Europe, and the rule of law and business grew stronger. Russia expanded into the Far East, knocking on China's door. Europe now dominated the world, mainly as a result of trade, industry, bravado and cannons, and its influence was still growing.

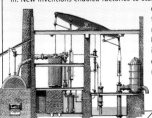

ASIA

During this time, India was slowly taken over by the British. China resisted such changes, growing conservative and refusing to entertain new ideas and foreign contact. Japan was still isolated, yet modernizing faster than China. Other Asian countries found themselves with both new friends and new enemies in the Europeans, who meddled in their affairs, always to their own advantage. Rivalry between Russia, China and Britain for control of Central Asia grew stronger. Asian traditions and stability were being undermined, and if Asian rulers resisted, the Europeans came in by the back door.

EUROPE

ASIA

MIDDLE EAST

AFRICA

AUSTRALASIA

Following the explorations of Captain Cook, Australia and New Zealand became targets for British colonization. Settlers started arriving in the early 19th century. The Maoris, who were warriors, fought back, but the Aborigines of Australia, who lived simpler lives, were helpless and easily overridden.

AUSTRALASIA

AFRICA

Though Europeans and Arabs controlled a few coastal colonies, many African nations were now strong. However, the power of many of them came from trade with Europeans. Some tribes dominated others, and some, such as the Zulus and Asante, were aggressive toward their neighbours. African disunity made it easier for Europeans to turn one nation against another.

MIDDLE EAST

The Middle East was weak at this time, owing to the decline of the Ottomans. In north Africa and Egypt, Ottoman control was lost. Persia remained stable, largely unaffected by outside influences.

AUSTRIA AND PRUSSIA 1711–1786

The Austrian empire was by now passing its peak, and Brandenburg–Prussia was growing stronger. Both empires tried to dominate the other states of Germany.

Maria Theresa was Habsburg empress from 1740 to 1780. She slowly improved conditions in the Austrian empire with the help of well-chosen ministers, reforming local government, education and the army.

Charles VI, Archduke of Austria, became Holy Roman emperor in 1711. This made him the most powerful man in Europe, adding the lands of the Holy Roman empire to Austrian territory. After Charles died in 1740, three men claimed that they, not Charles's daughter Maria Theresa, should be crowned. The rivals were Charles of Bavaria, Philip V of Spain and Augustus of Saxony.

The situation became more complicated as other European states joined in. The War of the Austrian Succession (1740–48) began when the Prussians invaded the Austrian province of Silesia. Prussia was supported by France, Bavaria, Saxony, Sardinia and Spain. But Britain, Hungary and the Netherlands backed Maria Theresa. In the end, Maria Theresa kept her throne, Austria was weakened and Prussia kept Silesia. The balance of power in Germany shifted to Prussia, and the Holy Roman empire declined. Austria was large but losing power. Over a century later, in 1870, it was Prussia that united Germany, and Austria was left out.

The Schonbrunn imperial summer palace in Vienna, built between 1696 and 1730, is an enormous and grand example of decorative Rococo architecture.

BRANDENBURG–PRUSSIA

The old Hohenzollern dynasty of Brandenburg inherited Prussia in 1618. By 1700, Brandenburg–Prussia had become a leading Protestant power, with Berlin as its capital. Its electors (kings) built an efficient government and helped its industries to thrive. Prussia's rise to power began under Frederick William I (reigned 1713–40), who built up its army. His successor in 1740, Frederick the Great, used the army to challenge Austria, France and Russia. During his reign, he doubled the size of Prussia, improved its business and industry, and made it a cultural centre of the Enlightenment. Over the next 100 years, Prussia gained more lands, increasingly dominating Poland and northern Germany.

▲ Frederick the Great was the elector of Prussia from 1740 to 1786. He was stern, brave and ambitious. Under his leadership, Prussia became a strong nation. He established religious tolerance in Prussia and freed his serfs. But many men died as a result of the wars he undertook.

▶ In the Battle of Fontenoy in Belgium in 1745, France had a major victory over Austria and its allies. In this painting, the French king Louis XV points to the victor of the battle, Marshal Saxe.

SCOTLAND: THE JACOBITES 1701–1746

In the early 18th century, the grievances of the Scots, added to Stuart claims to the English throne, led to two fateful and bloody Scottish rebellions.

Bonnie Prince Charlie (Charles Edward Stuart) was half-Scots, half-Polish and raised in Rome. He arrived in Scotland to lead the Forty-Five Rebellion, and was beaten at the battle of Culloden.

Flora MacDonald was a daughter of a laird who worked with the English. Despite this, she supported Bonnie Prince Charlie and when he was fleeing, she disguised him as her maid, and helped him to escape.

▲ The Jacobites were beaten at Culloden by English troops led by the Duke of Cumberland. He had all the wounded killed, and the others were chased and punished.

When James II died in 1688, the Stuarts lost their hold on the English throne. Scottish highlanders wanted a Scottish king. Meanwhile, the English were deliberately trying to break down the highland clan system, requiring the lairds (clan chiefs) to live away from their homes in Edinburgh or London. As a result, the lairds needed more money, so they raised rents and began evicting people off the land. Family feeling in the clans broke down, and clansfolk became tenants, without clan rights.

In England, Queen Anne died in 1714. Her cousin George of Hanover (from Germany) became the new king. He was the great-grandson of James I of England and a Protestant, but he was a foreigner. Some people felt that the Scot, James Stuart, had a better claim. He was not only a Stuart but a Catholic. Also, many Scots were unhappy because their nation had been joined with England to form a 'United Kingdom' in 1707. The Jacobites invaded England in 1715 and were defeated at Preston in Lancashire.

The Jacobites supported James Stuart. They planned rebellions both in England and Scotland, but these failed. James Stuart returned from France, but too late: 26 soldiers were executed and 700 sent to the West Indies as a punishment. In 1745 there was another uprising. James's son, popularly known as 'Bonnie Prince Charlie', landed secretly in Scotland and led the uprising. After overrunning Scotland, his army invaded England. They reached Derby but did not travel further south. In 1746, the Jacobites were cruelly defeated at the battle of Culloden.

Bonnie Prince Charlie fled, returning to France in disguise. The English gained control of the Highlands, and their revenge was severe. Highland lairds were executed and clansfolk disarmed. Until 1782, they were forbidden to wear kilts or play bagpipes. Over the years, clan lands were forcibly cleared of people to make way for grazing sheep, to earn money by supplying wool to the growing woollen mills of England. Clansfolk were sent to live in the cities, Ulster or the colonies.

▼ Bonnie Prince Charlie travelled from France to land secretly in the Hebridean islands off northwest Scotland, on his way to lead the rebellion of 1745.

AGRICULTURAL REVOLUTION 1650–1800

During the 18th century, the landscape changed dramatically in parts of Europe, especially in England, as new, profitable farming methods were introduced.

In many villages, the poorer people were forced to leave their homes to clear space for the new enclosed fields and modern farming methods.

This old cartoon shows a farmworker, who is trying to carry all the tools he needed to use on the new farms of the 18th century.

European farming methods had not changed for centuries. But by the 18th century, landowners, botanists and breeders, particularly in England, were all discussing better ways of running farms and growing crops. Scientists investigated animal-breeding, land management and raising crops. Cities and industries were growing larger, and there was more money to be made in farming. As profits rose, landowners studied and experimented even more. All this led to an agricultural revolution.

New ploughs were designed, and in 1701, the English farmer Jethro Tull invented the horse-drawn seed drill, which allowed the mechanized planting of seeds in rows for ease of weeding. By rotating crops, soil fertility was increased, and by careful breeding, animals were improved. These methods all required financial investment and larger farms.

The rural landscape changed greatly during the 18th century. In many parts of England, land had been farmed in large, open medieval fields. Villagers rented strips of these fields, where they worked alongside their neighbours. This system provided enough food to keep countryfolk alive, but it did not produce a surplus to sell to town-dwellers for profit.

▲ Thomas William Coke (1752–1842), the Earl of Leicester, was a wealthy landowner and a member of Parliament. He was famous as a leader in the Agricultural Revolution.

▶ Each year, Thomas Coke held a conference at his country house, Holkham Hall, to which landowners and breeders from all over Europe would come to discuss farming methods. Coke himself created new improved breeds of sheep.

196

The British Royal Agricultural Society held outdoor meetings each year, to show pedigree animals and discuss farming. This meeting near Bristol took place in the early 19th century.

THE ACTS OF ENCLOSURE

Landlords decided that their fields could be more efficiently farmed if they were enclosed. Hedges and walls were built across open fields, to create smaller, easily worked units. The Acts of Enclosure passed by Parliament between 1759 and 1801 also meant that common grazing land was enclosed. In total, three million hectares of land were enclosed in England during the Agricultural Revolution.

Many tenants lost their livelihoods, and were forced to move to towns. Rich landlords established enormous estates with grand houses. Their farms grew large and some estates were redesigned as beautiful parkland by famous landscape gardeners like Lancelot 'Capability' Brown. These changes were supported by the government, which itself was made up of landowners. But it brought much hardship to ordinary farming people.

KEY DATES

1701 Jethro Tull invents seed drill for faster planting
1730 Lord Townshend introduces the system of four-crop rotation
1737 Linnaeus develops a system of plant classification
1754 Charles Bonnet publishes a study of the food value of various crops
1804 French scientist Sussure explains how plants grow

Experimental breeding of farm animals, produced new, improved strains, such as this Old English breed of pig.

Using crop rotation, soil fertility was increased, especially by sowing clover every fourth year, which put goodness back into the soil and rested it. This improved the crops planted in the other three years.

THE SEVEN YEARS WAR 1756–1763

The Seven Years War was a battle between the European powers for continental dominance, and for control at sea and of colonies overseas.

William Pitt, the 1st Earl of Chatham (1708–78) was British secretary of state from 1756 to 1761. He directed the British involvement in the Seven Years War with a keen sense of strategy.

▼ The Seven Years War was costly in lives and money to all the participants and fought on a large scale, as this skirmish between Prussian and the British soldiers demonstrates.

For much of the 18th century Austria, Prussia, Russia and France each wanted to take control of Europe. This was unfinished business left over from the War of the Austrian Succession, which ended in 1748. But none of the European powers was strong enough to win on its own, so they built alliances. As a result, there was an uneasy balance of power.

Austria, France, Sweden, Russia and Spain were opposed to Prussia, Britain and Hanover. Austria wanted to recapture Silesia from Prussia, and England and France were already fighting over their Indian and Canadian colonies. But wars were expensive in time, money, weapons and lives, and they drained the warring states' resources. Fighting started in 1756 and lasted for seven years. At first, it seemed as if the Austrians and French would be the victors.

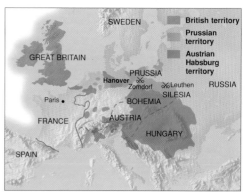

The Seven Years War involved many nations, each of which had its own aims. Prussia and Britain gained the most. Prussia kept Silesia, and Britain gained greater control of the seas, and of Canada and India.

The British, under their secretary of state, Pitt the Elder, joined the Prussians. Prussian victories in 1757 at the battles of Rossbach (against France), Leuthen (against Austria) and Zorndorf (against Russia), together with British successes over the French at Plassey in India and at Quebec in Canada, restored the balance of power.

HOW THE WAR ENDED

In 1759, a British–Prussian army defeated the French at Minden in Germany, the British navy defeated the French fleet at Quiberon Bay. In 1760, the British took Montreal in Canada. Then, in 1761, William Pitt the Elder was forced to resign because his policies were unpopular with other politicians. Elizabeth, the tsarina of Russia, died in 1762, and the new tsar, Peter III, withdrew Russia from the war. However, this did not bring an end to hostilities. What actually ended them was the expense and destruction they brought to all sides as they ran out of money and military materials.

▼ The Battle of Zorndorf was fought between the Russians and the Prussians in 1758. The battle was fierce, and neither side really won, though Prussia benefited most, since they fended off a Russian invasion.

Ministers and diplomats now controlled governments and, after such prolonged deprivations, many countries preferred to talk than to make war. In the Treaty of Paris in 1763, it was agreed that Britain would gain French lands in Canada and India, while the Prussians would keep the rich province of Silesia.

KEY DATES

1756	The Seven Years War breaks out
1757	Battle of Plassey – British control of India grows
1757-58	Prussia battles for survival – victories at battles of Rossbach and Leuthen
1759	British gains in Canada and at sea
1759	Battle of Minden – British–Prussian victory
1740–48	War of the Austrian Succession
1760	British take Montreal, Canada
1762	Russia withdraws from the war
1763	Treaty of Paris ends the war

In the battle of Quiberon Bay in November 1759, off Brittany, the British navy defeated the French and, from then on, dominated the high seas.

This medal was made in honour of the alliance made at the palace of Versailles in 1756 between Austria and France.

199

NORTH AMERICA 1675–1791

The mid-18th century saw a conflict for control of
North America between settlers and the Native
Americans, and between the English and the French.

Joseph Brant, also
known as Thayendanega,
(1742–1807), was born a
Mohawk. He fought with
the British when he was
young, and became friends
with an English official,
who gave him an English
name and education.
Later he visited London
and was received at court.

French and British colonists had been
fighting for many years. First there was
King Philip's War (1675–76), in which the
New England Wampanoag tribes rose up
against the settlers. The Wampanoag lost,
but not before killing 10 percent of adult
males in Massachusetts. King William's
War (1689–97), between English and
French settlers, did not achieve much. In
Queen Anne's War (1702–13), the English
took Acadia (Nova Scotia) and destroyed
Spanish St Augustin in Florida. Finally, in
King George's War (1744–48), the British
captured Louisbourg, a French fort, but
it was returned in 1748 in exchange for
Madras in India.

These wars were mostly connected with
European conflicts. Each side had one
long-term aim: they wanted to control
North America. Each side was helped by
Native Americans, who fought in all the
wars, hoping in return to receive support
in their own disputes with colonists who
were taking their land. But the Native
Americans generally lost out to the
settlers, who did not respect them. For
example, from 1730 to 1755, the
Shawnee and Delaware
peoples were forced by the
settlers to leave their lands.

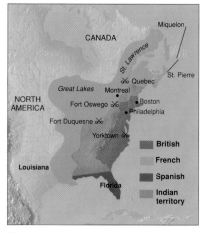

This map shows European possessions in North America
in 1756, at the beginning of the Seven Years War. By
1763, Britain controlled most of France's lands.

PONTIAC'S REBELLION

In 1763, there was a Native American
uprising called Pontiac's Rebellion. Pontiac
was chief of the Ottawa people and of a
confederacy of Algonquin tribes. With
some religious zeal, the tribes attacked
places from the Great Lakes to Virginia.
Some 200 settlers were killed. The British
retaliated, and in 1766, Pontiac made
peace. He was assassinated in 1769 by a
British-paid Native American in Illinois.

CAPTURE OF ACADIA

Acadia, or Nova Scotia, was claimed by the French
in 1603 and settled by them. Britain also claimed
it, attacking it several times during the 17th
century. Finally, they captured it in 1710, though
the French held on to Cape Breton Island nearby. In
the late 1750s, the British threw out 6,000 of the
Acadians, as they considered them a security risk.
Many went to Louisiana, settling around the mouth
of the Mississippi River, where they later became
known as Cajuns. Nova Scotia was populated
instead by Scottish people who had lost
their lands in the Highland Clearances.

The British taking of Quebec in 1759 meant the beginning of the end of New France. The battle took place in the fields outside the city. The British and French generals, James Wolfe and the Marquis de Montcalm, both died during the fighting.

CANADA

In 1754, the French and Indian War (part of the Seven Years War) was fought. French colonists had settled in the Ohio valley, and the British claimed it for themselves, so the French built a chain of forts and refused to leave. The French won some important battles in 1755 (Fort Duquesne) and 1756 (Fort Oswego). But the British captured Acadia in 1755, Quebec in 1759, and Montreal in 1760. The Treaty of Paris in 1763 gave Britain many former French colonies, and New France (Lower Canada) became British. Britain now controlled all of the lands east of the Mississippi River, and some French lands were given to Spain in exchange for Florida, which became British.

In 1791, the British Constitutional Act split the territory held by Quebec into the colonies of Upper and Lower Canada. This was done to strengthen Canada after the American Revolutionary War (1775–83), during which the new state of USA was founded. Upper Canada was English-speaking and Lower Canada French-speaking. The British had been successful against the French, but they misunderstood the American settlers, losing the 'Thirteen Colonies' by 1781, in the American Revolutionary War. Some 40,000 British loyalist settlers moved to Canada from the USA.

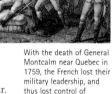

With the death of General Montcalm near Quebec in 1759, the French lost their military leadership, and thus lost control of Canada.

KEY DATES

1675–76 King Philip's War
1686–97 King William's War
1710 Acadia taken by the English
1739–41 The British fight Spanish Florida
1743–48 King George's War
1755–63 French and Indian War
1763–66 Pontiac's Rebellion
1760 British gain control of Canada
1775 American Revolutionary War begins

In 1775, Ethan Allen and a band of 83 men attacked the British garrison at Fort Ticonderoga. This was one of the first military actions in the American Revolutionary War.

TRADE WITH CHINA 1700–1830

Trade with China was profitable, yet the government there did not want 'barbarian' influences introduced. European merchants looked for other ways to trade.

China reached its largest size during the reign of Qianlong, spreading its tentacles into central Asia and Tibet. This expansion was expensive and brought few benefits except that it kept out the British and Russians.

Qianlong (1711–95) ruled China for 60 years from 1735. He was a philosopher-emperor who supported the arts, wrote poetry and created libraries.

Throughout the 18th century, Chinese silk, cottons, tea, lacquerware and porcelain were highly prized in Europe, but they were expensive and in short supply. Merchants from Portugal, Britain, Italy and the Netherlands tried to expand the China trade. But the powerful Chinese emperors, who controlled all contact between their people and foreigners, were simply not interested. Qianlong, emperor for 60 years, was a scholar and traditionalist who had no time for 'barbarians'. The problem for the Europeans was that they had to pay for everything in silver, as Chinese traders were not allowed to exchange foreign for Chinese goods. Also, the Europeans were permitted to trade only in Guangzhou (Canton), where they were penned up in 'factories' (fortified warehouses), and traded through Chinese intermediaries. European traders were very competitive, and they fought to get the best Chinese goods and to sail them home to Europe as quickly as possible to fetch the highest prices.

▲ These Chinese maps from around 1800 show China, the 'Middle Kingdom', sitting at the centre of the world. At the time, China was isolated – though the world was knocking at its door.

▶ In 1793, the British diplomat Lord Macartney visited the Chinese emperor to encourage trade relations. Such relations were rejected, so people resorted to illegal deals. Both China and Britain had little respect for each other.

THE OPIUM TRADE

Soon European merchants looked for other ways to trade. Opium had long been used in China for medicinal purposes, and the merchants formed links with Chinese drug dealers, selling them vast quantities of opium (5,000 barrels per year by the 1820s), from countries such as Burma. In return, they received precious Chinese goods for Europe. The trade grew steadily in the late 18th century, and the Qing government tried to stop it. By the 1830s, opium use was spreading through China, making people lazy, harming society and the economy, and costing China dearly.

THE QING DYNASTY

The Qing emperors were not keen to develop trade because they had urgent problems at home. Years of peace and prosperity had led to a growth in the population (400 million by 1800), and now there were food shortages. Taxes were high, corruption was growing, and the population was moving from place to place.

The Qing were very conservative, remote and stubborn. As result, there were protests and uprisings, often organized by secret societies with political ambitions. The White Lotus sect caused a peasant rebellion which lasted from 1795 to 1804. The effect of this was to weaken people's respect for the Qing dynasty. Foreigners – Russians, Japanese, Tibetans and other ethnic minorities, as well as Europeans in their clippers and gunboats – were also nibbling at China's edges.

EUROPEAN INTERVENTION

The Qing emperors were brought up to believe that China was the centre of the world. They described their country as 'the Middle Kingdom, surrounded by barbarians'. When a British ambassador, Lord Macartney, travelled to Beijing in 1793, Emperor Qianlong refused to discuss trade. From then on, the foreigners decided to get their way by other means, and the opium trade was increased. By 1800, for many of the Chinese, there were aspects of life that were oppressive, and opium, which was smoked like tobacco, provided an escape. When, in 1839, the Chinese tried to stop the trade, the British went to war. Even China's control of the world supply of tea was almost at an end. During the 1830s, the Englishman Robert Fortune stole several tea plants while travelling in China. He took them to India and set up rival plantations there.

The foreign trading stations or 'factories' at Guangzhou (Canton) were the only places where trading with China was permitted. Europeans could not travel outside their compound, and they could trade only during certain months.

▲ The Temple of Heaven was rebuilt in 1751 during Qianlong's reign. The wooden prayer hall was enormous and highly decorated, and the roof was covered with blue ceramic tiles.

◄ Macao was a Portuguese colony on a peninsula not far from Guangzhou. It had been established in 1557, with imperial permission, and was a centre for Chinese and Japanese trade.

AFRICA 1700–1830

Africa was now strongly affected by its increasing trade with the Europeans and Arabs, and many African kingdoms grew strong and rich as a result.

Shaka Zulu became leader of the Zulus in 1816. He taught them battle skills and expanded Zulu lands in southeast Africa.

During the 18th century, the continent of Africa was relatively peaceful. In the north, the Ottoman empire, which controlled Egypt, continued to decline. The Asante people on the west coast grew increasingly rich by selling slaves. In the southeast, the Portuguese were slowly building up a colony in Mozambique. The lands of the east coast (now Kenya) were ruled from Oman, a kingdom to the north on the Arabian Sea. At the southern tip, the Cape of Good Hope, Dutch settlers began to explore the territory inland.

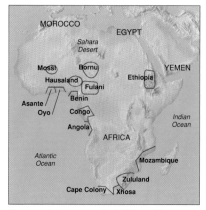

Many new states were growing in Africa and there was much movement of peoples. Europeans and Arabs had small coastal colonies, but their influence inland was mainly felt through trade, rather than invasion.

NEW AFRICAN STATES

During the 18th century, an average of 35,000 slaves each year were being sent from western Africa to the Americas. But, by the end of the century, the British were having second thoughts, and in 1787, they established Sierra Leone as a refuge for freed slaves. In 1822, Liberia was founded for freed slaves from the USA. Most European countries stopped slave trading in the earlier 19th century, though Portugal continued until 1882.

The Yao and Nyamwezi empires in eastern Africa virtually emptied that area to provide slaves. Asante and Oyo dominated west African slaving into the 19th century, when they started selling timber, ivory, hides, gold and beeswax to the Europeans instead. This changed west African farming practice of growing 'cash crops' for export. Meanwhile, in eastern Africa, slaves continued to be sent by the Omani Arabs to Arabia and India.

The Zulu nation in southern Africa, led by King Shaka, fought constantly with their neighbours. The bloodshed was so great that the years from 1818 to 1828 became known as *mfecane*, or the time of troubles. There were migrations from the Sudan, the Tutsi moved into Rwanda, and the Masai into Kenya from further north.

Zulu warriors were armed with stabbing spears known as *assegai*. They wore battle head-dresses and ornamental shields to frighten their enemies and also to recognize each other in battle.

AFRICAN MUSLIM STATES

On the southern edge of the Sahara, there was an Islamic revival. Many Muslims expected a *mahdi* or saviour to appear, and various African caliphs, moved by this possibility, founded new, well-organized states such as Sokoto, Mossi, Tukulor and Samori in inland western Africa. In Egypt, Mehmet Ali Pasha took control from the Mamluks in 1811, modernized the country and invaded Sudan in the 1820s.

Africa was changing rapidly. Mostly, it still belonged to Africans, but they were not united against their common threat, the Arabs and Europeans. As a result, Africa was vulnerable.

▲ The Hausa city of Kano in northern Nigeria was captured in 1809 by the Muslim leader Usman ' dan Fodio, of the Hausa kingdom of Gobir. The Hausa cities converted to Islam, becoming part of an Afro-Islamic state called the Sokoto Caliphate.

Mehmet Ali Pasha (1769–1849) was Ottoman governor of Egypt, but he made Egypt virtually independent of the Ottomans and invaded the lands up the Nile River in Sudan, making Egypt the leading power in the eastern Mediterranean. He ruled Egypt from 1810 to 1828.

MASSACRE OF THE MAMLUKS

The Mamluks were originally slaves, captured in the 9th century by Muslim armies in the Caucasus and Russia. They were mostly Cossacks and Chechens by origin, trained to serve as soldiers and administrators in Egypt. By the 13th century, they had become palace guards and ministers, and then they overthrew the sultan, ruling Egypt from 1249 to 1517. When the Ottomans took Egypt, the Mamluks became the ruling class under the Ottomans. As Ottoman power declined in the 18th century, they regained power in Egypt. After Mehmet Ali Pasha conquered the Mamluks in 1811 and took control of Egypt, he invited all the surviving Mamluk commanders to a banquet in Cairo where he had them massacred.

MODERNIZING RUSSIA 1730–1796

The rulers who followed Peter the Great continued his strategy of Westernization and expansion, making Russia into a great European power.

Peter III was tsar for half a year. A grandson of Peter the Great, he did not have the character to be tsar, and he was not liked. Tsarina Elizabeth forced him to marry Catherine.

▼ Winter was often a good time to travel in Russia because the snow made progress faster. Catherine the Great travelled in an enclosed sledge drawn by horses.

When Peter the Great died in 1725, his wife became Tsarina Catherine I. However, she died after only a few years. Anna Ivanovna ruled for ten years from 1730, continuing Peter's pro-Western policies, and welcoming many foreigners at court. But the Russian people suffered, since the tsarina's friends in St Petersburg cared more about music, poetry and wars against the Ottomans or in Europe, than about peasants and their welfare.

From 1741, Peter's daughter, Elizabeth (1709–62), made Russia more westward-looking and industrial, and declared war on Prussia in the Seven Years War. Tsarina Elizabeth forced Peter, the heir to the Russian throne, to marry in 1745. His wife, Catherine, was born into a poor but noble Prussian family, and like many women at the time, had to accept the man chosen as her husband. When Elizabeth died in 1762, Peter III ruled briefly.

Catherine the Great (1729–96) ruled Russia for 34 years. Other European leaders respected Catherine for her achievements in foreign policy, but feared her power.

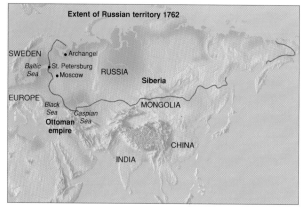

Extent of Russian territory 1762

SWEDEN • Archangel
Baltic • St. Petersburg
Sea • Moscow RUSSIA
Siberia
EUROPE
Black Sea Caspian Sea MONGOLIA
Ottoman empire
CHINA
INDIA

CATHERINE THE GREAT

Peter III was a weak man and Catherine despised him. Six months after his coronation, he was killed in a brawl. Catherine declared herself empress and ruled in his place. Although she was intelligent and cultured, she carried her private ruthlessness into public life.

To support Catherine's wars and her lavish court, Russia was drained of wealth by taxes and young men to fight. She planned to improve education and social conditions, yet there were few educated officials to carry this out. She asked the nobility for help, and gave them extra powers. This made the peasants' situation even worse, and led to Pugachev's Rebellion in 1773–74. Rebels took the city of Kazan, promising to abolish landlords, serfdom, taxes and military service. But Pugachev and his supporters were brutally crushed.

◄ From the 16th to the 18th centuries, the Russian empire had more than doubled in size. During Catherine's reign it gained ports on the Baltic and Black Sea coasts.

FOREIGN POLICY

Catherine's appointment of a reform commission of ministers in the 1760s failed, so she chose autocratic rule, dividing the country into regions, each ruled by nobles. Then she left the nobles to look after Russia's home affairs.

Her claims to greatness came from the way she expanded Russia's lands. This strategy of expansion was masterminded by two ministers, Count Alexander Suvarov and Grigori Potemkin. In the north and west, new lands were won by a war with Sweden in 1790. And most of Poland was seized when it was partitioned (divided up). These gains gave Russia important seaports on the Baltic coast.

In the south, Russia took Azov, on the Black Sea, from the Ottomans, then the Crimea and, by 1792, the whole northern shore of the Black Sea. The Ottomans no longer controlled the Black Sea and Russia built up a powerful navy. To the east, Russia's gradual development of Siberia was also stepped up.

But Catherine was terribly cruel. Courtiers were flogged and peasants who dared to complain about their miserable conditions were punished. Many poor people faced starvation, yet Catherine continued to collect heavy taxes to pay for her wars and extravagant lifestyle.

Life at the Russian court was rich and elegant, sheltered from reality and out of touch. In contrast, the peasants lived in poverty. When Catherine the Great travelled through Russia in 1787 to see how her subjects lived, the streets of the towns were lined with healthy, well-dressed actors. The real peasants were kept hidden from view.

KEY DATES

1741 Elizabeth becomes tsarina
1756–63 Russia joins the Seven Years War
1761 Catherine the Great becomes tsarina
1772 First partition of Poland
1783 Russia annexes Crimea
1792 Russia gains Black Sea coast
1793–95 Second and Third partitions of Poland
1796 Death of Catherine the Great

This painting of the inside of the Winter Palace in St Petersburg, shows how impressive life in St Petersburg was. Tropical plants grew indoors while people sometimes froze to death just outside.

EXPLORATION IN OCEANIA 1642–1820

The exploration of Oceania developed quite late compared with other parts of the world. It was pioneered by Tasman, Cook and other explorers.

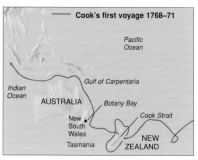

— Cook's first voyage 1768–71

On Cook's first voyage he sailed from the tip of South America to New Zealand and proved there was no large continent in between as many people thought.

Between 1768 and 1779 the navigator Captain James Cook (1728–79) made three voyages of discovery to the Pacific. In 1770, he landed at Botany Bay and claimed Australia for Britain.

During the 17th century, Dutch seamen explored the southern Pacific and Indian oceans. By the 1620s they had found the northern and western coast of Australia, naming it 'New Holland'.

In 1642, the Dutchman Abel Tasman (1603–59) discovered the island of Tasmania. He had sailed from Mauritius and travelled so far south that he did not sight Australia. Farther to the east, Tasman later reached the south island of New Zealand. After a fight with its Maori inhabitants he returned to Batavia in the Dutch East Indies, discovering Tonga and Fiji on the way. The next year, he sailed along the northern coast of Australia.

In 1688 and 1699, the English navigator William Dampier explored the western and northwestern coastline of Australia. These explorers proved that Australia was an island, but they did not settle there. The Pacific remained largely unknown as it was too distant and too poor to attract trading interest from the Europeans.

The first scientific exploration of these southern lands was undertaken by Captain James Cook, who made three voyages. The first voyage (1768–71) took him around New Zealand. Then he landed at Botany Bay in Australia, claiming it for Britain. On his second voyage (1772–75), he explored many Pacific islands and Antarctica. On his last voyage, begun in 1776, he visited New Zealand, Tonga, Tahiti and finally Hawaii, where he was killed in a quarrel with the islanders.

THE VOYAGES OF CAPTAIN COOK

Jean-François La Pérouse (1741–88) was sent by Louis XVI to sail round the world on a scientific expedition. He travelled the oceans with a crew of scientists, charting, observing and collecting samples while visiting Canada, Siberia and Australia. His ships disappeared in 1788.

Captain Cook was commissioned to sail to Tahiti to observe a passage of Venus in front of the Sun. After this, he was secretly sent south to chart New Zealand and Australia for the British government. On his second voyage, he was the first explorer to visit the Antarctic, but he was driven back by pack ice. Cook discovered the value of carrying vegetables and fruit for his sailors, so preventing scurvy (caused by lack of vitamin C). He also took well-trained artists with him as he was determined that the findings should be scientifically recorded. He died in Hawaii in 1779 while on his third voyage.

NATIVE PEOPLES

The 'new' lands explored by Cook had been inhabited for hundreds of years. The Maoris lived in New Zealand, and the Aborigines lived in Australia. Both peoples lived according to ancient traditions. Understandably, they were wary of Cook and his men – the first Europeans that they had ever seen.

Aborigines had lived in Australia for thousands of years, spread out over a vast continent. They lived by foraging and hunting, and using their advanced knowledge of nature. They were so different from Europeans that there was such a clash of culture that Aboriginal culture was later almost wiped out.

The Maoris, it is thought, had sailed to Aotearoa (New Zealand) from Polynesia around AD750, and were farmers, warriors and village-dwellers. As the Europeans moved into their land, they resisted.

The first settlers in Australia arrived in 1788. They were convicts who had been transported there from Britain as a punishment for their crimes. Free settlers started to arrive in 1793. In New Zealand, whalers, hunters and traders were soon followed by missionaries. Many of the early settlers came from Scotland, Ireland and Wales. The settlers introduced diseases which often killed the local peoples who had no resistance to them.

KEY DATES

1642–44 Abel Tasman's voyages to Tasmania and New Zealand

1688/1699 William Dampier explores western and northwestern coastline of Australia.

1766–68 Bougainville discovers Polynesia and Melanesia

1768–71 Cook's first voyage

1772–75 Cook's second voyage

1776–79 Cook's third voyage

1829 Britain annexes all of Australia

1840 Britain claims New Zealand

▲ The Maoris were skilled sailors and craftworkers who decorated their canoes with elaborate religious carvings. When Cook arrived, there were about 100,000 Maoris in New Zealand. Many were killed in later wars against British settlers and troops.

In 1779, while on his third voyage to the Pacific, Captain Cook was killed in a skirmish with Hawaiians over the theft of a boat. Initially, the British had been welcome, but after this event, his crews had to sail home without their captain.

THE FOUNDING OF THE USA 1763–1789

People in the thirteen colonies in America were dissatisfied with British rule. They fought for their independence, and a new nation was born.

George Washington (1732–99) served in the British army in America, then was made the commander in chief of the new American army, fighting the British. In 1789, he became the first president of the United States.

A t the end of the Seven Years War in 1763, both the British government in London and the English colonists in America felt satisfied. They had defeated France and gained territory from them in Canada, and also land as far west as the Mississippi River. With the French threat gone, the colonists no longer needed Britain to defend them.

But the British wanted to govern the old French territories and collect higher taxes to pay for soldiers to defend these newly won lands. They raised taxes levied in the thirteen colonies. Local colonial assemblies argued that it was unfair for Britain to tax the American colonies, since they had no say in running the British government. They said 'taxation without representation is tyranny'. The colonies banned all British imports, and on July 4, 1776, representatives from all 13 colonies adopted the Declaration of Independence, claiming the right to rule themselves.

The Boston Tea Party in 1773 was a symbolic protest against British taxation in America. A band of colonists dressed up as Mohawks, boarded three ships in Boston harbour and threw tea chests into the sea. The British resorted to punishment, closing Boston harbour until money was paid for the lost tea. But this only made things even worse.

▲ The British soldiers were well-drilled professionals, while the Americans were mostly volunteers. But the Americans were highly motivated because they felt strongly about their cause. On the left is a uniformed British grenadier, and on the right is an American revolutionary soldier.

The battle of Bunker Hill, near Boston, in 1775, was the first major battle of the Revolution. The British won, but they lost more than twice as many men as the American colonists.

INDEPENDENCE

Guided by the ideas of Thomas Jefferson, and influenced by the Enlightenment, the American Declaration of Independence stated in 1776: "We hold these truths to be self-evident, that all men are created equal, that they are endowed by their Creator with certain inalienable rights, that among these are Life, Liberty and the pursuit of Happiness."

The American Revolutionary War had begun in 1775. At first the British were successful, despite the problems of fighting nearly 5,000 kilometres from home. But the Americans had an advantage because they were fighting on home territory, and they believed in their cause. Six years after the conflict began, the British army surrendered at Yorktown, Virginia, in 1781, having been defeated by George Washington's troops. Britain eventually recognized American independence in the Treaty of Paris, 1783.

KEY DATES

1763	End of the Seven Years War. British troops sent to North America
1764	Sugar Act taxes imported molasses
1765	Stamp Act adds tax on documents
1775	American Revolutionary War begins. Battle of Bunker Hill takes place
1776	American Declaration of Independence
1781	British army surrenders at Yorktown
1783	Britain recognizes American independence
1787	Draft American Constitution drawn up
1789	American Constitution becomes law. George Washington becomes first president of USA
1801	Thomas Jefferson becomes president

THE US CONSTITUTION

In 1783, after signing the peace treaty with the British, the people of the new United States of America had to decide on the best way to run their country. They decided to have a president, elected every four years. He would rule with the help of a Congress (divided into a House of Representatives and a Senate made up of representatives from the states), and a Supreme Court. The draft Constitution (set of legal rules) for the new government contained three important statements about the American nation.

First, it was to be a union. The colonists who had fought against the British would stay together to govern their own country. Second, each of the states would hold their own assembly, and run a state government as they liked. Third, neither the president, the Congress, nor the Supreme Court would ever be allowed to control the central government of America on their own. A system of checks and balances would make sure that power was shared among these three areas of government.

These were new ideas influenced by the Enlightenment, and never tried out before. The revolutionary Constitution became law in 1789. This new nation, with its short history and its people with many bad memories from their own past, was the world's first proper democratic republic, ruled according to collectively agreed laws. Only 150 years later, it was to become the world's leading nation.

The draft Constitution was worked out at a series of conventions in 1787. Of the 55 delegates attending, 39 signed the document. Once the draft was agreed, copies were sent to each state to be agreed by its leaders.

A Liberty Medal was struck to mark the victory of the Americans over the British in 1781.

The Liberty Bell in Philadelphia was made to symbolize American Independence.

Thomas Jefferson (1743–1826) became the third President in 1801. He was a political leader, whose ideas greatly affected American politics.

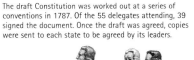

THE FRENCH REVOLUTION 1789–1799

In 1789, the discontented people of France overthrew their king, demanding freedom and equality. The revolution that followed changed France forever.

Marie Antoinette (1755–93) was Louis XVI's Austrian wife. The people thought she was arrogant and extravagant.

▲ Maximilien Robespierre (1758–94) trained as a lawyer. He became the leader of a revolutionary group called the Jacobins in 1793. He was head of the Committee of Public Safety and helped protect France from invasion. In 1794, he was accused of treason and executed.

▶ On July 14, 1789, the people of Paris stormed the Bastille, a prison where many popular leaders had been imprisoned by the king. This was the real outbreak of the revolution. Other countries feared that revolution would spread across Europe.

The French Revolution had been building up for years. It was caused by bad government and enormous differences between the rich and the poor, encouraged by new Enlightenment ideas about people's rights and hastened by the American Revolution.

In the 18th century, France was in crisis. Food was scarce, prices were high, and the government was facing bankruptcy. To get more money, Louis could either borrow it or raise state taxes. But first he needed approval and support from a traditional assembly, the Estates-Général, which had not met for 175 years.

At the assembly, the representatives of the professional classes rebelled against the nobles and clergy. They took an oath to start a new National Assembly and demand reform. They wrote a new constitution abolishing the old order, nationalising Church lands and reorganizing local government. Louis sent troops to try and dismiss the Assembly.

Louis XVI (1754–93) became king in 1774. He was shy, and preferred hunting and the good life to governing his country.

When the citizens of Paris heard this, they rebelled. On July 14, 1789, a mob stormed the Bastille, the king's prison in Paris. The riot marked the beginning of a bloody revolution in which the rebels demanded, 'Liberty, Equality, Fraternity'.

THE STRUGGLE FOR POWER

Louis XVI fled, but was captured and imprisoned. In 1792, the monarchy was abolished and in the following year, Louis and his wife, Marie Antoinette, were tried and executed. By then, the revolutionary government was at war with most other European states, who were afraid that revolution might spread to their countries.

As often happens in revolutions, chaos broke out, and there was a struggle for power. The new revolutionary government began rounding up its rivals, royalist or popular, calling them 'enemies of the revolution'. There was a political battle between two groups, the Jacobins and Girondins, which the Jacobins won. They then dominated a new ruling body, called the Committee of Public Safety. The committee mobilized French armies against invasion, and from September 1793 to July 1794, they executed anyone who opposed them in a Reign of Terror.

During the Terror, around 18,000 lost their heads to the guillotine. Soon, one man, Robespierre, wielded dictatorial power. Even he was not safe, and in 1794, he was accused of treason and executed.

THE DIRECTORY

A new constitution was written in 1795 and a weak government, called The Directory, was formed. War had already broken out, and French revolutionary armies had conquered the Netherlands and south Germany. A young general, Napoleon Bonaparte, took over the army, invading Italy, Switzerland and Egypt. The Directory came to rely on him. He grew popular and powerful, and in 1799 he removed the Directory and took control.

The so-called *sans culottes* (named because they did not wear knee-breeches), preserved public order in the streets during the Reign of Terror. Many people lost their lives as a result of the hatred of the *sans culottes*.

KEY DATES

1788	Estates-Général called to a meeting
1789	National Assembly and storming of the Bastille
1789	Declaration of the Rights of Man
1791	The New Constitution and Legislative Assembly
1792	The Revolutionary Wars and French Republic
1793-94	The Reign of Terror
1794	Robespierre's dictatorship. Holland invaded
1795-99	The Directory rules France
1796	Napoleon becomes chief army commander
1799	Napoleon takes power

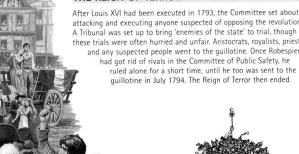

THE REIGN OF TERROR

After Louis XVI had been executed in 1793, the Committee set about attacking and executing anyone suspected of opposing the revolution. A Tribunal was set up to bring 'enemies of the state' to trial, though these trials were often hurried and unfair. Aristocrats, royalists, priests and any suspected people went to the guillotine. Once Robespierre had got rid of rivals in the Committee of Public Safety, he ruled alone for a short time, until he too was sent to the guillotine in July 1794. The Reign of Terror then ended.

Members of the lower classes celebrate the end of the Reign of Terror by dancing around a tree decorated with rosettes in the national colours.

THE NAPOLEONIC WARS 1797–1815

Restoring order after the French Revolution, Napoleon attempted to change the whole of Europe. But Britain stood against him and Napoleon was finally exiled.

In this cartoon, drawn in 1803, Napoleon is depicted straddling the world while the comparatively tiny John Bull (representing Britain) tries to fight him off.

Napoleon was born in Corsica, the second son of an Italian lawyer. As a young man, he had joined the French army, and his courage and quick thinking led to rapid promotion. At the age of 26, he became a general. He led a number of successful campaigns, capturing northern Italy in 1797. The Directory feared he was now too powerful and popular. They offered him the job of invading Britain. Napoleon suggested invading Egypt, to disrupt the British trade route to India. He did invade Egypt, but his plan failed after Nelson destroyed his fleet in 1798.

In 1799, Napoleon returned to France and seized control. He dismissed the government, appointing three officials, called consuls, to run the country. Napoleon made himself first consul, and for the next 15 years, ruled France. In 1804, he crowned himself emperor.

Napoleon introduced many lasting reforms, bringing new laws, a better educational system, a reorganized government and a new national bank.

In 1799, Napoleon (1769–1821), already a war hero, took over the government by force. Though many disagreed, France was in disorder and Napoleon became First Consul.

He was a brilliant general, moving his troops quickly and using new battle tactics. He also had a very large army, since Robespierre had introduced a conscript system in which all adult men were forced to serve. The army numbered 750,000 soldiers in 1799, and another two million men joined up between 1803 and 1815. Napoleon used this massive force to try and conquer Europe.

THE BATTLE OF MARENGO

One of Napoleon's many military successes, the battle of Marengo, was fought against the Austrians in Italy in 1800. Napoleon was a brilliant leader, inspiring his troops with speeches, 'leading from the front' and using very innovative tactics. He modernized warfare, using cannon and large armies, and outwitting his opponents. His control of Europe pushed many countries into the modern world.

Napoleon wanted to create a society based on skill rather than on noble birth. To encourage achievement he founded the Légion d'Honneur in 1802 'for outstanding service to the state'. Members of the Légion received a medal and a pension for the remainder of their lives.

THE NAPOLEONIC WARS

Napoleon defeated Austria and Russia at Austerlitz in 1805, Prussia at Jena in 1806, and Russia faced a second defeat at Friedland in 1807. Napoleon created new republics allied to France and ruled by placing his relations in positions of power. He also created Europe-wide laws and governments – called the Continental System.

In 1805, Britain won a major sea battle against France at Trafalgar. The British admiral, Horatio Nelson (1758–1805) died, but his victory saved Britain from invasion. In 1808, Napoleon invaded Spain, beginning the Peninsular Wars in which Britain supported Spain and Portugal.

The British sent troops led by the Duke of Wellington to Spain. There, he won battles at Salamanca (1812) and Vittoria (1813), pushing the French out of Spain.

Napoleon's disastrous invasion of Russia in 1812 left over 500,000 French dead of cold or hunger or killed. In 1813, he was also crushingly defeated at Leipzig by a combined European force, led by the Prussian general, von Blücher. Finally, in 1814, France was invaded and Napoleon was sent into exile. He escaped and was finally defeated by Wellington and von Blücher at Waterloo in Belgium in 1815. He died in exile on the remote South Atlantic island of St Helena in 1821.

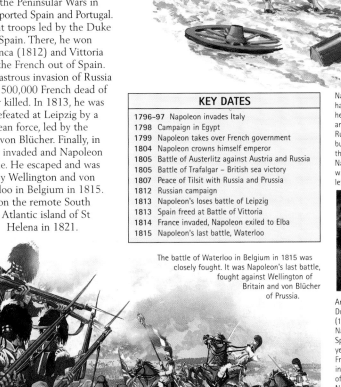

KEY DATES	
1796–97	Napoleon invades Italy
1798	Campaign in Egypt
1799	Napoleon takes over French government
1804	Napoleon crowns himself emperor
1805	Battle of Austerlitz against Austria and Russia
1805	Battle of Trafalgar – British sea victory
1807	Peace of Tilsit with Russia and Prussia
1812	Russian campaign
1813	Napoleon's loses battle of Leipzig
1813	Spain freed at Battle of Vittoria
1814	France invaded, Napoleon exiled to Elba
1815	Napoleon's last battle, Waterloo

The battle of Waterloo in Belgium in 1815 was closely fought. It was Napoleon's last battle, fought against Wellington of Britain and von Blücher of Prussia.

Napoleon believed Russia had allied with Britain, so he invaded. When his army reached Moscow, the Russians had already burned it down. Eventually the winter took its toll. Napoleon entered Russia with 510,000 men and left with only 10,000.

Arthur Wellesley, Duke of Wellington (1769–1862), fought Napoleon's armies in Spain where it took four years to push out the French. Wellington was involved in the Congress of Vienna after the Napoleonic Wars. A national hero, he became British prime minister in 1828.

THE END OF SLAVERY 1792–1888

The European colonies in the Americas depended heavily on slave labour. But by the mid-18th century many people were questioning the morality of this.

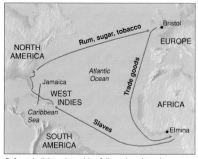

Before abolition, slave ships followed a triangular Atlantic sailing route, taking goods to Africa, slaves to the Americas and products such as sugar back to Europe.

William Wilberforce (1759–1833) was member of Parliament for Hull, a busy slaving port. The trade horrified him. He and other humanitarian Christians campaigned against the slave trade from 1784 onwards. Trading was banned throughout the British empire in 1807.

Throughout the 18th century, Britain, France and Spain grew rich on taxes and profits from their colonies. Much of this wealth was created by slave labour. Denmark, Sweden, Prussia, Holland and Genoa (Piedmont) also traded in slaves. Africans were sold to Europeans by slave dealers and local rulers, who saw slave-trading as a means of punishing criminals, getting rid of enemies, disposing of captives and getting rich. Nobody knows how many slaves were sold in all, but historians have estimated that 45 million slaves were shipped from Africa between 1450 and 1870, although only 15 million survived. Many Europeans disliked the slave trade, but at the time they believed it was the only way to supply labour to colonial plantations.

Fortunately, some decided to protest, saying it was against God's law and human decency. Rousseau, a French philosopher, wrote in *The Social Contract*, in 1764, "Man is born free, but everywhere he is in chains." His writings inspired the revolutions in France and America, and individual freedom became regarded as a social right, not a gift from the king. Rousseau's ideas also inspired people to fight on behalf of others who were unable to help themselves. Politicians, clergy and ordinary people began to think how they might help the slaves. But moral arguments did not have as much force as the profits that slavery generated.

▲ Some slaves escaped from plantations and set up their own villages in remote areas. In 1739, a group of escaped Jamaican slaves, called the 'Maroons', rebelled against the British.

▶ Conditions on slaving ships were appalling and unhealthy and many slaves died. Slaves were stacked on dark shelves and floors in the holds of ships, hardly able to move.

ENDING THE SLAVE TRADE

Between 1777 and 1804, slavery was made illegal in the northern United States. Denmark withdrew from slave trading in 1792 and Britain in 1807. But slave smuggling continued. The British navy clamped down on slave-trading from 1815 onwards, but slavery itself was still legal elsewhere. A slave revolt in the French colony of Santo Domingo in 1791–93 led to abolition by France, but in 1803, they made slavery legal again. In 1831, a slave uprising in Virginia led by Nat Turner led to harsh new laws and increased support for slavery amongst white southerners.

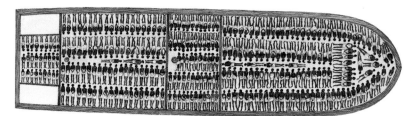

PHILANTHROPY

In Britain, Thomas Clarkson (1760–1846) and William Wilberforce had led an anti-slavery campaign and, in 1807, the British part of the trade was abolished. However, slaves were not actually freed for some time. Wilberforce died just before all of the slaves in British hands were freed. Europeans had by now grown disgusted with slavery, and the British navy blocked the trade by stopping slave ships.

Slavery continued in Cuba, Costa Rica, Brazil and the southern United States. The large plantations had been built on slave labour, and plantation owners were reluctant to change. Also, Europe enjoyed cheap, slave-grown cotton and tobacco from the southern states of the USA.

In the USA, northerners supported emancipation while southerners wanted to keep their slaves. The 1831 slave revolt in Virginia led to harsh laws to control slaves in the southern states. Slavery was finally banned in the USA in 1863, in Cuba in 1886 and in Brazil in 1888. The Arabic slave trade in Africa ended in 1873.

◄ The leader of the Virginia slave revolt of 1831, Nat Turner (1800–31), killed his master and 57 whites, and encouraged 60 slaves to revolt. Their revolt lasted some months. He and his followers were eventually captured and hanged.

The economy of the southern states of USA relied on black slave labour. Cotton-picking was one of the slaves' main jobs. The cotton was profitably exported to supply the cotton mills of industrial Europe.

KEY DATES

1517 Regular slave trading started by Spain
1592 British slave trading begins
1739 Jamaican 'Maroon' slave revolt
1760s Slave trading at its peak
1791–1801 Santo Domingo slave revolt
1792 Danish slave trading abolished
1807 British slave trade abolished
1834 Slavery abolished in British colonies
1865 13th amendment abolishes slavery
1888 Slavery abolished in Brazil

THE SLAVES' REVOLT IN SANTO DOMINGO

The French Revolution spread to the French colonies overseas. In 1791, the National Assembly in Paris decided to give the vote to slaves in Santo Domingo (now Haiti) in the Caribbean. Plantation owners refused to obey. When they heard this, about 100,000 slaves rebelled. Many slave owners were killed, houses destroyed, and sugar and coffee plantations set on fire. Napoleon sent troops to the island and there was a long civil war led by Toussaint l'Ouverture (1746–1803), an ex-slave who declared himself ruler of the island in 1801.

THE BRITISH IN INDIA 1774–1858

The hold on India by the British East India Company gradually grew stronger. The British came to dominate Indian society, becoming its ruling caste.

This working model, called 'Tipu's Tiger', shows a tiger devouring a European. It was made for Tipu Sahib of Mysore. Between 1767 and 1799, with French support, he tried to resist British control of his lands.

By 1750, the British East India Company controlled the very profitable trade between Britain, India and the Far East. Its officials were skilful businessmen who had built up knowledge of Indian affairs, especially through Indians they employed. They made friends with many Indian princes, and struck bargains with both the friends and enemies of the declining Moghul rulers. Many British people in India lived rather like princes themselves. By working for the East India Company many of them became extremely rich. Some of these so-called *nabobs* built fine houses in Calcutta and other places, designed by British architects, furnishing them with expensive luxuries from England, India and the colonies. In Calcutta, they held meetings, tea parties and dances, as if they were back home. Gradually, wives and families travelled to India to share this English way of life.

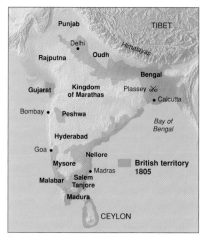

By 1805, the British controlled the rich cloth-making districts of Bengal in northeastern India, as well as the prosperous coastal lands in the south.

However, some British people were attracted to Indian art, culture and architecture, preferring to wear Indian clothes, at least at home. They learned Indian languages and studied Indian religions and writings, taking Indian ideas back to Britain when they returned.

▲ Tipu Sahib (1749–99) of Mysore owned an ivory chess set which was made up of pieces with Indian princes and men on one side, and East India Company administrators and soldiers on the other.

▶ At first, the British mixed more easily with Indians than they did later on. Here, the Scottish governor Sir David Ochterlony smokes a hookah and presides over an Indian musical performance.

218

BRITISH EXPANSION

By 1780, the East India Company controlled many of the more prosperous parts of India, but in 1784 the British government stopped further expansion. The company's bosses thought otherwise. When Indian states fought each other, the company often simply moved in. Around 1800, Napoleon's ambition to build an empire in India scared the British, and the government changed its policy. From 1803 to 1815, the company fought the Marathas, who ruled central India, breaking their power. In many cases they took a 'soft approach', using trade to favour certain Indian states and stationing troops there 'for their protection'.

The company fought in Burma, where the local rulers threatened Bengal, and also on the Northwest Frontier and in Afghanistan, where they feared Russian influence. In 1843–49, they annexed Sind and the Punjab. Whenever a dynasty failed, or if a state was weakly governed, the company moved in. During the 1830s, the company's governor pompously overruled several Indian traditions, and introduced missionaries to convert Indians to Christianity. The company built roads, railways and buildings, and expanded British businesses, insisting on using English as the language of education and business. As a result, Indian opposition gradually grew stronger.

THE INDIAN MUTINY

Trouble broke out among the sepoys, the Indian soldiers in the company's army. Sparked by a terrible famine, the Indian Mutiny started in 1857. Several towns, including the capital, Delhi, were captured by the sepoys, and British men, women and children were massacred. The mutiny was suppressed violently by British troops. Each side now became suspicious of the other side. The British started to live a more separate life, and Indians were 'kept in their place'. The British government took control of the East India Company in 1858, and closed it down. While India was perhaps the richest and most developed European colony of all, the British had to work very hard to control it.

Some Indian rajahs and princes made friends with the British and gained many advantages as a result. To be protected by British soldiers guaranteed a prince's power, and the British gained from the deal by having easy influence and trade in a prince's state without having to govern it.

HOMES FOR NABOBS

Nabobs were officers of the East India Company who had gained fortunes in India. Many nabobs had themselves grown up in tough conditions, and had gone India to escape hard times, seek a fortune or build a new life. They worked hard, risking their lives through war or disease. They lived in conditions that reflected the opulence of Indian rulers combined with the trappings of British aristocrats. They built great mansions in cities like Calcutta and Delhi, and had many servants.

Unification and Colonization

1836–1913

The world map changed greatly during this
period – new nations were formed and some
were unified. Africa was carved up by
colonialists, and China's power was fractured.
There were more revolutions in Europe. The
USA, Canada and Russia occupied areas on their
furthest frontiers. Railways, telegraph wires and
steamships made the world suddenly seem
smaller. New cities such as New York, Buenos
Aires, Johannesburg, Bombay and Shanghai
became centres in a new global order.

▲ The coming of the railroad opened up North America, but also led to
the first national strike. The strike spread along the railway, from coast to
coast, uniting the workers in their fight for a decent wage.

◀ During the Second Boer War in South Africa, the Boers (Dutch
settlers) were finally defeated by the British in 1902.

THE WORLD AT A GLANCE 1836–1913

In North America, settlers travelled west to colonize the vast lands taken over by the United States and Canada. However, the opening up of these new territories caused much hardship for the native peoples whose way of life was being threatened.

In Africa, religious wars strengthened the influence of Islam in the kingdoms of the north. European explorers and missionaries began to visit lands in the centre. Led by a desire to exploit the resources of Africa, European powers quickly established colonies throughout the continent. The power of the great trading nations of Europe grew.

In Asia, Europeans also took control of India, Burma and southeast Asia, and began to trade with China and Japan. Europe's expansion into other continents did not stop internal conflicts, and many wars were fought between countries or empires wanting more power and territory.

NORTH AMERICA

USA grew strong during this period. Its territories now extended west to Texas and California, and the 'Wild West' was being opened up by railroads, settlers and soldiers. This took place at great cost to the Native Americans, who were killed off or squeezed into small, isolated reservations. Despite attempts to revive their fortunes, their culture was dying, and it gained little respect from the new Americans. In the 1860s the American civil war broke out, a destructive modern-style war over political principles. One result of it was the abolition of slavery in the USA. The cities of the east and the midwest then grew larger and more industrial, and ever more settlers arrived from Europe. Canada was united, and it pushed west too, becoming a prosperous independent dominion within the British empire. By 1900, North America had become wealthy and strong. The USA even became an imperial power itself. Its financiers, corporations and armies were to help the USA dominate the world in the later 20th century.

NORTH AMERICA

CENTRAL AND SOUTH AMERICA

CENTRAL AND SOUTH AMERICA

Latin America developed more slowly than North America, partially because of its dictatorial governments and controlling landowners. After the independence wars of the 1820s, a second wave of changes arose in the 1860s–1880s, when South American countries fought each other. There followed a spate of development brought by railways, population growth and increasing wealth earned from exports. But the old Spanish ways lived on, in the form of tough governments, rich landowners in their *haciendas* (ranches) and a large mass of poor people.

EUROPE

This was Europe's century. Europe's incessant wars almost stopped, and its armies went overseas, staking out claims to empires elsewhere. Industrial cities grew large, interlaced with railways and telegraph wires. Politicians, industrialists and the middle classes gained increasing power. The new working classes formed workers' movements, leading, by 1905, to the first, unsuccessful, workers' revolution in Russia. Immense achievements were made in engineering, science, ideas, the arts, and in exploring the world. Europe now governed and financed the world, and grew rich as a result. Yet times were hard for some – there were famines, strikes, economic downturns and mass emigrations. These hardships led eventually to another new invention - social welfare systems for the poor.

ASIA

Trouble hit China and Japan in the mid-19th century. Foreign traders forced their way in and in China major rebellions broke out. The isolationist Qing dynasty in China eventually fell in 1911. Japan adopted Western modernization. In India, British rule became total – though not without being challenged by an Indian mutiny first. The West now dominated the East. For some Asians, employees of Westerners, this was advantageous. But many Asians simply became cheap labour on plantations and in Asian colonial cities. Railways, missionaries, soldiers and traders opened up the interiors of Asian countries. But Asian traditions survived more than those of other cultures elsewhere in the world.

EUROPE

ASIA

MIDDLE EAST

AFRICA

AUSTRALASIA

British settlers took over most of Australasia, and, in growing numbers, overwhelmed the indigenous peoples. The nations of Australia and New Zealand appeared on the map as exporters of food, wool and gold.

AUSTRALASIA

AFRICA

First came explorers, then traders, missionaries, governors and administrators. In the 1880s Europe parcelled up Africa and took over. Gold rushes made South Africa rich, ruled by whites. The slave trade was now finished, but all of Africa fell to European exploitation and government instead – dominated by the British and the French.

MIDDLE EAST

The long, slow decline of the Ottomans continued, and the Persians had to fight the British to fend them off. The Middle East became something of a backwater, held in check by traditional rule, and by-passed by change. But, by the same token, it also avoided colonialization.

INDUSTRIAL REVOLUTION 1836–1913

The Industrial Revolution is the name given to a period when great changes took place in Britain, and people began to use steam power to make goods in factories.

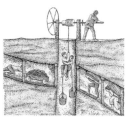

D uring the 18th century, many people in Britain worked at home, usually producing goods by hand. There were also many farmers and farm labourers who worked on the land to grow crops to feed their families. By the middle of the 19th century, all this had changed. Many British people now lived in towns and worked in enormous factories, or in shops, offices, railways and other businesses designed to serve the inhabitants of these industrial centres. Leading the world, British inventors continued to develop revolutionary new machines which performed traditional tasks such as spinning and weaving much faster than they could be done by hand. Machines were also used to make iron and steel. These metals were in turn used to make more machines, weapons and tools.

▼ The new factories were built near canals and railways so that raw materials could be delivered, and finished goods taken away. Rows of terraced cottages were built to house the workers.

Many children worked in mines and factories, but this was banned by most countries by 1900.

The British inventor Isambard Kingdom Brunel (1806–59) built railways, bridges, tunnels, viaducts, railway stations, ports and the world's largest ship.

Jobs in factories, such as textile mills, often required skill rather than strength. Women were as good as men for such work and many single women gained independence by earning a wage for themselves.

Four factors brought about the change: coal mining, a canal system, capital (money) and cheap labour. Coal was used to smelt iron and steel and to make steam to power the new machines. Barges carried raw materials and finished goods along the canals. The profits from Britain's colonies gave merchants the money to invest. And badly paid farm workers flocked to the towns for better paid work.

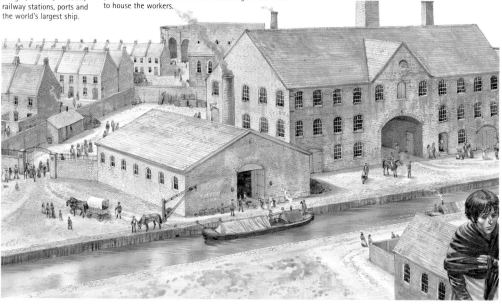

BUSINESS BOOM

New coal mines were dug to supply coal for steam engines and coke for ironworks. By the middle of the 19th century, Britain's canal and rail systems linked all the major industrial cities. The new machines made goods faster and more cheaply. Factory and mine owners made huge profits, some of which they spent on more machines, so creating new jobs. Investors saved small amounts of money in banks which then lent large amounts to industrialists. This developing capitalist system raised money to build factories, offices and houses.

For many workers life in the factories and mines was hard and dangerous. Men, women and children worked 13 or more hours a day, often for low wages. Many workers were killed or injured by unsafe machinery before new safety laws were enforced. Towns grew rapidly and without proper planning, leaving some areas without drains or clean water. Diseases such as cholera (from dirty water) became common and killed thousands of people.

In time, laws to shorten working hours and prohibit child labour were introduced. Trade unions, at first banned, campaigned for better pay and conditions for workers. In time, reformers won better working conditions and schooling for all children. Slums were cleared and new laws were brought in to control factories and houses.

The arrival of the railway opened up North America but also led to the first national strike – the Great Strike of 1877. When railroad workers had their wages cut, their protests stopped the trains. Finally, the army was called in.

In 1842, James Nasmyth (1808–90) invented the steam hammer, used to make parts for the new steamships. It was worked by a double action steam engine.

▶ A big step forward in steel-making was made by Henry Bessemer (1818–98). In a Bessemer Converter, hot air was blasted through melted iron to convert it into steel. Steel was stronger and more useful than iron, but before Bessemer's invention in 1856, it was very expensive to make.

KEY DATES

1837 Queen Victoria comes to the British throne
1838 Brunel builds the steamship, the *Great Western*
1842 James Nasmyth invents first steam hammer
1850s British industrial cities linked by rail and canal
1851 'Great Exhibition' held at Crystal Palace
1868 First Trades Union Congress held in Manchester
1870 Suez Canal completed, easing travel to India
1893 Independent Labour Party established
1900 USA and Germany both overtake Britain's steel production

THE OPIUM WARS 1830–1864

European merchants used the addictive power of opium to gain important trading links with China – a country that wished to remain closed to foreigners.

Ships, like this British merchant ship in Lintin harbour in 1834, carried some of the enormous quantities of opium traded at this time by Europeans in their quest for precious Chinese goods.

The Chinese had almost no contact with the rest of the world for centuries. Many European merchants were extremely keen to trade, especially in the rare Chinese silks and porcelain that were so popular in Europe. However, the Chinese government allowed trading to take place at only one port, Guangzhou (Canton). To get around this problem, foreign merchants began to smuggle the drug opium into the country so that the Chinese were forced into trading their precious goods in exchange for the drug. The Chinese government tried to stop this, and in 1839, Chinese officials, under the orders of the Chinese high commissioner of Guangzhou, Lim Tse-hsu, visited the British warehouses where they seized and burned up to 20,000 chests of opium.

The British would not tolerate what they saw as the confiscation of private property, and in response, they sent warships which threatened the Chinese and besieged the port. The Chinese refused to pay compensation, banned trade with Britain, and fired on the British forces. Thus started the first of the opium wars (1839–42) fought by the Chinese and the British.

Hong Kong Island became a British colony in 1842. It soon grew into a centre of trade. In 1860, the Kowloon Peninsula was added, and in 1898, the British gained the New Territories on a 99-year lease.

The wife of an opium-smoker publicly destroys her husband's pipe. The sale or smoking of opium had been banned in China by orders of the emperor from the early 18th century onwards.

TREATY OF NANKING

The war was one-sided because the British had superior forces, and they bombarded Guangzhou and captured Hong Kong from the Chinese. When this first war was over, the British forced the Chinese to sign the Treaty of Nanking (Nanjing) which opened up Chinese ports to Britain. China also had to pay compensation and gave the island of Hong Kong to the British.

Britain's aggressive approach to the Chinese owed much to the British foreign secretary of that time, Henry Temple, 3rd Viscount Palmerston. He was always ready to use force in what he saw as the defence of British interests overseas. In this, and later 'unequal treaties', the Chinese were forced to give in to European demands. The Chinese were afraid that foreign trade meant that the country would come under foreign influence.

SOCIAL UNREST

Trouble, largely promoted by the British, erupted again in the mid-1850s and resulted in the Second Opium War (1856–60). This war was also eventually won by the British and it ended with another treaty. The Treaty of Tientsin was signed in 1858, and it forced the Chinese to open even more ports to trade with European merchants. Other countries, such as France and the United States, signed more of these 'unequal treaties', gaining their citizens special rights and increasing Western influence in China. Eager merchants and missionaries rushed in.

At the same time, the huge Chinese empire was gradually breaking down. The ruling Qing dynasty was faced with rebellions started by starving peasants. The Taiping Rebellion (1851–64) was begun by people who wanted the land to be divided equally between the ordinary people. The foreign powers helped to crush the rebellion because they wanted the Qing dynasty to continue so that the treaties would be honoured.

KEY DATES

1839 Chinese officials destroy British opium stocks
1839 Outbreak of First Opium War
1842 Chinese sign the Treaty of Nanking
1842 Hong Kong island becomes British territory
1844 Treaty of Wanghia with United States
1851 The Taiping Rebellion breaks out
1856 Outbreak of Second Opium War
1858 Chinese sign the Treaty of Tientsin
1898 Britain obtains 99-year lease on New Territories

▲ Britain's vastly superior navy was easily able to destroy Chinese junks during the opium wars.

▼ The Taiping Rebellion (1851–64) was crushed by the Chinese leaders with help from foreign powers who wanted Qing rule to continue.

YEAR OF REVOLUTION 1848

In 1848, rebellions and protests broke out in many parts of Europe. They demonstrated how unhappy people were with their rulers.

Giuseppe Mazzini (1805–72), seen here in prison, was a tireless campaigner for democracy and the unification of Italy.

The reasons for many of these rebellions were similar to those that sparked the French Revolution. One of the main reasons was that people in many countries across Europe began to feel they were more important than 'the state' and that they should have a say in their own government. In response to the rebellions and violent protests, rulers tried to restore older systems of government, but the events of 1848 showed that change was inevitable.

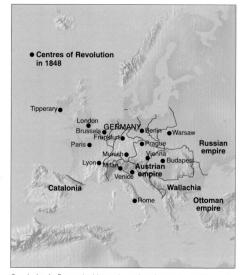

● Centres of Revolution in 1848

Tipperary ●
London ●
Brussels ● GERMANY ● Berlin ● Warsaw
Frankfurt ●
Paris ● ● Prague   Russian empire
Munich ● ● Vienna
Lyon ● Milan ● ● Budapest
Venice   Austrian empire
Catalonia   Wallachia
● Rome   Ottoman empire

Revolution in Europe had been simmering since 1815, and in 1848, most European countries experienced rebellions. The map shows where the most serious outbreaks were.

One powerful reason for the revolutions of 1848 was nationalism – the desire of people who spoke the same language to form their own independent nations. Nationalism was especially strong in Italy and Germany, which were divided into many small states, and in parts of the Austrian empire. Other rebellions were led by people who wanted cheaper food, or changes in land laws which would give the land to working people.

▲ In February 1848, Paris revolutionaries demanding 'Bread or Death' stormed government buildings in Paris. They overthrew King Louis-Philippe, and declared a republic with Louis Napoleon, nephew of Napoleon Bonaparte, as 'prince-president'.

▶ In Britain, the last and biggest Chartist demonstration took place in 1848. The People's Charter demanded political reforms, including votes for all men. A large crowd gathered in London, but the meeting ended without violence.

CHARTISM

In some countries, people were demanding the right to vote. This was one of the reforms that the Chartist movement in Britain wanted. The 'People's Charter' was first published there in May 1838. A petition said to have 1,200,000 signatures on it was handed in to Parliament in June 1839 but was rejected a month later. By February 1848, and following the revolution in France, a final petition was formed. When it was complete it was said to have over three million names on it. On April 10, 1848 a mass march travelled across London to the Houses of Parliament to present the petition. Again, the petition was rejected and Chartism became a spent force.

Recent changes had made rebellion easier. More people were able to read and newspapers told them what was happening in other countries. Few police forces existed, so troops had to be used against rioters. Most of the revolts of 1848 failed in their immediate demands, but over the next few years, nationalist feeling grew stronger and many governments began to see that democratic reforms would soon be necessary.

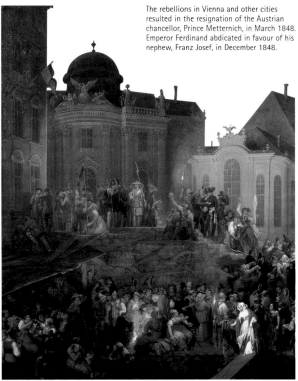

The rebellions in Vienna and other cities resulted in the resignation of the Austrian chancellor, Prince Metternich, in March 1848. Emperor Ferdinand abdicated in favour of his nephew, Franz Josef, in December 1848.

◄ Frankfurt in Germany also witnessed street fighting and rebellion before the people finally succeeded in forcing a change in their country's leadership.

REVOLUTION IN EUROPE

In France, the Second Republic was founded with Louis Napoleon, nephew of Napoleon Bonaparte, as 'prince-president'. In the separate Italian states, revolts were widespread but were crushed by the end of the year. The Austrian chancellor, Prince Metternich, resigned and the emperor Ferdinand abdicated in favour of Franz Josef.

There were uprisings in Berlin, Vienna, Prague, Budapest, Catalonia, Wallachia, Poland and Britain. In Germany, the National Assembly met at Frankfurt, and in the Netherlands a new constitution was introduced.

In Belgium, the *Communist Manifesto*, written by Karl Marx and Friedrich Engels, was published. Elsewhere in Europe, the armies and peasants remained loyal to their monarchs. Revolts were crushed in Prussia and Italy, though there were some reforms.

JAPAN 1853–1913

Under the Tokugawas, Japan had been closed to foreigners for more than 200 years. In the early 19th century, it began to experience Western influence.

After 1868, the Meiji government improved educational standards so that, by 1914, the Japanese were among the best-educated people in the world.

▲ Commodore Matthew Perry (1794–1858) is known as the man who opened up Japan to trade with the USA and the rest of the world. In 1853, he sailed to Japan with four warships and signed the Treaty of Kanagawa with the Japanese.

▶ This Japanese woodblock print shows Yokohama harbour, Japan, in the late 19th century. Following the Treaty of Kanagawa, the Japanese agreed to open ports to trade with the USA and several European countries.

During the first half of the 17th century, Japan's rulers decided that contact with the West must end. They feared Christian missionaries would bring European armies to invade Japan. They therefore banned almost all foreigners from entering Japan, and the Japanese from leaving their country. As a result, people in the West were unable to appreciate the great beauty of the Japanese art of this period until the mid- to late 19th century. In 1853, the 13th President of the United States, Millard Fillmore, sent four warships, under the command of Commodore Matthew Perry, on an historic voyage from America to Japan with the aim of opening up trade there.

The warships anchored in Tokyo Bay. The threat of American naval power helped Perry persuade the Japanese to resume trading with the West. The Japanese were impressed by Matthew Perry's steamships and by the other machinery he showed them. The two countries went on a year later in 1854 to sign the Treaty of Kanagawa, in which they agreed to open two ports to American trade.

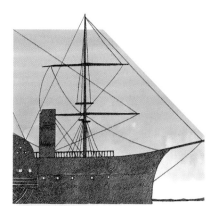

The black ships of Commodore Perry's fleet were the first steamships that the Japanese had ever seen. They realized that they would be unable to beat them.

Soon similar 'unequal treaties' had been signed with Britain, the Netherlands and Russia. The Tokugawa were criticized by their opponents for allowing these unequal treaties to be signed and for many other problems they could not solve.

RESTORATION OF THE EMPEROR

People were tired of the near total isolation that the Tokugawa family had imposed for so long. Finally, in 1868, the Tokugawa were overthrown and the emperor, Mutsuhito, was restored as ruler (the Meiji Restoration). Now that their country had opened up to the West, the Japanese began to modernize.

Although the Japanese wanted to keep some of their traditions they were also keen to learn from the industrial nations of the West. They changed and adapted both their government and their schools. Improvements in education meant that by 1914 the Japanese were among the best-educated people in the world. They began to import machines and introduced new industries such as cotton manufacture. Many Japanese people adopted European fashions. They learned to play European music and dressed in European clothes. At the same time, foreigners gradually learned to respect Japanese success and culture.

With industrialization, the Japanese soon began to expand their country. They tried to take over Korea and this led to a war with China in 1894. Japan also fought Russia over this issue in 1904–05 and finally annexed Korea in 1910. This helped make Japan the most powerful nation in its region. By 1913, Japan had become an industrial power of great importance, the first country in Asia to make such advances.

▲ Russian soldiers flee after the battle of Mukden, in which the Japanese won a decisive victory in March 1905. This costly defeat sapped the Russian desire to fight.

▼ In May 1905, Japan's fleet, led by Admiral Togo, annihilated the Russian fleet. This led to the Treaty of Portsmouth and gave the Japanese control over Korea.

AMERICAN CIVIL WAR 1861–1865

Around the middle of the 19th century, the United States was a divided country, and the largest division was between the north and the south.

Union soldier

General Ulysses S. Grant (1822–85) was appointed commander of the northern Union forces in 1863. He was a tough and determined soldier.

Robert E. Lee (1807–70) was in the US army when civil war broke out. He resigned and first advised, and then took command of the southern Confederate troops.

In the United States around 1850, the north had nearly all of the trade, industry, railways and cities while the south was a land of farms, especially cotton and tobacco plantations, that relied on slave labour. However, slavery was banned in the north.

This division caused quarrels when the laws were drawn up for the new states and territories in the west of America. Anti-slavery campaigners in the north believed that slavery should be completely banned. The Kansas–Nebraska Act (1854) gave the new states the right to choose.

Abraham Lincoln (1809–65) was elected president of the USA in 1860. He belonged to the Republican Party, which opposed slavery, although he was not an abolitionist himself. Many southern states refused to live under such a government, and led by Jefferson Davis (1808–89), they announced in December 1860 that they were seceding from (leaving) the Union and forming the Confederate States of America. The United States government declared that they had no right to do this.

Confederate soldier

Union soldiers wore the blue uniform of the US army. The Confederates usually wore grey.

The southern states believed that they had the right to make their own laws without interference from the federal government. They needed a slave labour force to work in the plantations and were certain that the economy of the south would be ruined if slaves were freed.

BATTLE OF GETTYSBURG

The battle of Gettysburg (July 1–3, 1863) was a turning-point in the Civil War. The battle was the bloodiest ever fought on American soil, but was an important Union victory by General George Meade, who stopped the invasion of the north by General Robert E. Lee's Confederate army. From this point onwards, the south's chances of winning the war declined.

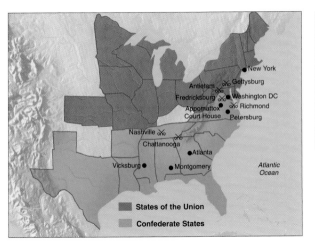

◀ This map shows the United States at the beginning of the American Civil War. Eleven of the 34 US states made up the Confederacy. Most of the battles were fought in the east and southeast.

▲ The battle of Spotsylvania, Virginia, in May 1864 was one of the many Union victories of the American Civil War. In all more than 600,000 soldiers died on both sides in the conflict.

THE TWO SIDES

The north (Union), made up of 23 states, had more men, more money and more industry than the south. The north also controlled the navy and started a naval blockade that prevented the south receiving help or supplies from abroad. The 11 states of the south (the Confederacy) were much weaker, but they had the benefit of good generals and a great fighting spirit. Civil war broke out on April 12, 1861 when the forces of the south opened fire on Fort Sumter in South Carolina. The Confederates won a number of victories early in the war.

The south won the first battles in 1861, including Fredericksburg and Chancellorsville, but the turning-point in the struggle came in July 1863 when the north won the biggest battle of the war, at Gettysburg. The Union forces, under the command of General George Meade, stopped an invasion of the north by General Robert E. Lee's Confederate army. More than 21,000 Confederate soldiers and more than 22,000 Union soldiers were killed or wounded.

Union flag

Confederate flag

During the American Civil War, the Confederates rejected the Stars and Stripes of the USA and adopted their own flags.

For the first time in history railways paid a vital part in warfare by moving troops, ammunition and supplies swiftly over great distances.

Harriet Tubman (1820–1913) was an escaped slave who made trips through southern territory, helping slaves escape.

THE END OF THE CIVIL WAR 1865

Slavery was completely abolished in 1865, with the thirteenth amendment to the Constitution. The country was reunited, but new problems emerged.

In 1864, in spite of Lee's skilful tactics, General Grant captured Richmond, the capital of the south. General Sherman marched through Georgia and the other southern states, capturing Atlanta. He followed this victory with a 'march to the sea', during which he destroyed towns and farms. Short of men, money, weapons and food, Lee surrendered on April 9, 1865, ending the civil war. More than 600,000 soldiers had died, many from diseases such as typhoid. Five days later, Abraham Lincoln was assassinated in Washington.

The American Civil War settled two great questions. Firstly, it confirmed that the United States of America was a single nation and that no state had the right to break away. Secondly, it brought slavery in the southern states to an end. After the American Civil War, arguments raged over how the south should be 'reconstructed'. Ideas included the opening of schools and the building of railways. Abraham Lincoln's successor, Andrew Johnson (1808–75), a Democrat, wanted better conditions for black Americans. The Republicans wanted a harsher policy, and it was they who won in the end.

General Lee surrendered to Grant at Appomattox Court House, Virginia on April 9, 1865. His men were outnumbered, exhausted and starving.

General Lee's presentation sword was not handed over to Grant during the surrender ceremony, as was customary. Instead, it remained by his side.

The people of the south resisted most of the aspects of the Reconstruction. Many ex-slaves who had fought on the Union side returned home expecting more freedom in the south. However, the Ku Klux Klan and other racist organizations began a campaign of murder and terrorism in 1866 with the aim of stopping black Americans gaining civil rights. Northern troops withdrew, Reconstruction ended and the Democrats took over the south.

THE GETTYSBURG ADDRESS

In November 1863, President Abraham Lincoln was invited to make a 'few appropriate remarks' at the dedication of a national cemetery at Gettysburg. His speech lasted about two minutes and is today regarded as a masterpiece. Abraham Lincoln summed up the central issue of the war – the survival of a nation dedicated to freedom.

Abraham Lincoln (1809–65) was the 16th president of the United States. Many people believe he was the greatest of all of the presidents. 'Honest Abe' was known for his integrity and the force of his arguments.

234

CANADA 1763–1913

The peace terms of 1763 effectively gave Canada over to British rule. In 1791, the British Constitutional Act split Canada into British- and French-speaking territories.

Louis Joseph Papineau (1786–1871) was a French-Canadian politician. He led the French-speaking Canadians' demand for reform and equality.

William Lyon Mackenzie (1795–1861) was a member of Canada's Reform party. He wanted Canada to have more freedom from British rule. He led the 1837 rebellion in Upper Canada.

Opposition to British rule in Canada grew during the 1830s. Rebellions broke out in both Upper and Lower Canada in 1837, led by William Lyon Mackenzie and Louis Papineau respectively. The rebels wanted self-government and, although they had some support, the most influential people in the colonies did not agree with them. The rebels were soon defeated by British troops. The British government sent Lord Durham to Canada to investigate the causes of the rebellions. His report said that Upper and Lower Canada should be united and should have control over their own affairs.

The 1840 Act of Union united the two colonies which became known as the Province of Canada. However, many Canadians still felt that these reforms did not go far enough. This was partly because the Canadians were concerned that the United States might invade if Canada looked weak. In 1867, the British North America Act was passed, and Canada became self-governing. The act united four Canadian provinces in a dominion. The French Canadians of Quebec were promised equality, and French and English both became official languages.

Winnipeg, a centre of the fur trade, was still a small town in 1870. In that year, the settlement became the capital of the province of Manitoba.

WESTERN TERRITORIES

The vast lands to the west, which belonged to the Hudson Bay Company, later became part of Canada as well. The northwest territories joined the dominion in 1870, followed by Yukon territory in 1898. The Yukon had been the location of the famous gold rush in 1896, which led to tens of thousands of prospectors making their way over the Rocky Mountains to the goldfields, and they hoped, great wealth. Completion of the Canadian Pacific Railway in 1885 united the country. Unlike the American railways, it formed one continuous system from the St Lawrence River to the Pacific Ocean.

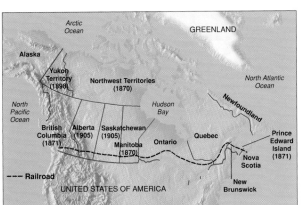

◀ The British North America Act of 1867 united the provinces of Nova Scotia, New Brunswick, Ontario (formerly Upper Canada) and Quebec (Lower Canada) in the Dominion of Canada.

▲ The Canadian Pacific railway was completed in 1885. It linked the east and west coasts, reducing the journey time from five months to five days.

235

ITALY 1833–1878

The birth of the Italian nation was brought about with the help of an aristocrat, Count Camillo Cavour, and a man of the people, Giuseppe Garibaldi.

Victor Emmanuel II (1820–78) was the popular king of Piedmont Sardinia. He eventually became king of the whole of Italy.

▼ Piedmont Sardinia took the lead in uniting Italy in 1859–60. Nice and Savoy were given to France in 1860.

In the early 19th century, Italy was made up of a number of small states. Apart from the kingdom of Piedmont Sardinia and Rome, which was ruled by the pope, these states were governed by foreign countries. In the 1830s, an independence movement known as the *Risorgimento* ('resurrection') began to grow. In 1848, revolutions against foreign rule broke out in many Italian cities and states, but they were quickly suppressed. In 1849, Victor Emmanuel II came to the throne of Piedmont Sardinia, a northern state, and made Turin his capital. He was a very popular man, perhaps because he was often seen to be restricting the powers of the clergy who were less well-regarded than in the south. He was affectionately known as 'the cavalier king'.

The rebellion in Venice in 1848 was one of the last in Italy to hold out. Severely weakened by hunger and disease, the people of Venice gave up in August 1849.

SKILFUL POLITICIAN

Count Camillo Cavour, an Italian aristocrat with very liberal views, became the chief minister of the kingdom of Piedmont Sardinia in 1852. He made an alliance with France in 1858, and together, they defeated the Austrians in 1859. Austria ceded Lombardy to France who then handed it to Piedmont in exchange for Savoy and Nice. Most of northern Italy then joined with Piedmont Sardinia.

In 1860 rebellion broke out in southern Italy, which at this time was part of the kingdom of the Two Sicilies. Giuseppe Garibaldi led a revolt and conquered the kingdom. His men were known as Redshirts because of their dress. They faithfully followed their romantic and patriotic leader. It took them a mere three months to conquer the whole of Sicily.

Cavour was now very concerned that Garibaldi, and his seemingly unstoppable men, would attack Rome, which might in turn lead to Austria or France coming to the aid of the pope. Cavour invaded the Papal States (but not Rome) and then marched his army south. Garibaldi's forces had taken Naples, and Cavour, being careful to go around Rome itself, finally met up with him.

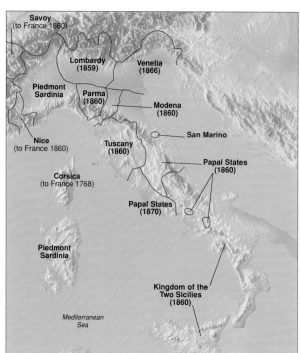

Savoy (to France 1860)

Lombardy (1859)

Venetia (1866)

Piedmont Sardinia

Parma (1860)

Modena (1860)

San Marino

Nice (to France 1860)

Tuscany (1860)

Papal States (1860)

Corsica (to France 1768)

Papal States (1870)

Piedmont Sardinia

Kingdom of the Two Sicilies (1860)

Mediterranean Sea

Giuseppe Garibaldi (1807–82) was a patriot who fought against foreign rule in Italy. With his Redshirts, he conquered the kingdom of the Two Sicilies in 1860, and it became part of the kingdom of Italy.

Count Camillo Cavour (1810–61) was the politician who made most of the plans for a unified Italy. He was also able to harness the talents of Giuseppe Garibaldi to help his own plans.

AGREEMENT AND UNITY

Count Cavour reached a detailed agreement with Garibaldi and his Redshirt soldiers which allowed the kingdom of northern Italy to take over Sicily, Naples and the Papal States. In February 1861, the first national parliament was held in Turin and one month later Victor Emmanuel II was proclaimed king of all Italy.

Two small areas were not included. Venice was still part of the Austrian empire and Rome was ruled by the pope but occupied by France. Venice was given to Italy after Austria was defeated in the Austro–Prussian War (1866). In Rome, Pope Pius IX was totally unwilling to bend to what he still saw as a northern king. The Franco–Prussian War of 1870 forced the French to withdraw their garrison in Rome for other duties and the Italian army immediately took over Rome. The city then became the capital of Italy. Pope Pius would not negotiate and thought of himself as a prisoner in the Vatican until he died in 1878. The people of Rome wanted unity and so it was that the ruling house of Piedmont Sardinia reigned over a totally united country.

KEY DATES

1830s Mazzini founds the 'Young Italy' movement
1848 Revolutions break out in Europe
1849 Victor Emmanuel II is king of Piedmont Sardinia
1852 Cavour is chief minister of Piedmont Sardinia
1859 Piedmont Sardinia and France defeat Austrians
1860 Garibaldi and his army conquers Sicily
1861 First national Italian parliament held
1870 Rome joins greater Italy

▼ A meeting between Victor Emmanuel II and Garibaldi at Teano, northeast of Naples, in 1860, eventually led to the unification of Italy.

GERMANY 1848–1871

In the second half of the 19th century the military might of France was overtaken by a German state, Prussia, and a new and powerful Germany emerged.

The diplomatic skills of Otto von Bismarck (1815–98), the chief minister of Prussia, kept his enemies isolated.

▲ Napoleon III (1808–73) became emperor of France in 1852. He was captured at the battle of Sedan during the Franco-Prussian War and sent into exile in 1871.

Afterward the failure of the revolutions of 1848, the German Confederation, made up of over 40 states, stayed as disunited as it had been for centuries. The two strongest states, Austria and Prussia, jostled for power over the whole of Germany. Although at first weaker, Prussia's trade and industry grew in the 1850s. Its increasing strength was supported by the Prussian Kaiser and his new prime minister, Otto von Bismarck.

Austria and Prussia went to war against Denmark over control of the duchies of Schleswig and Holstein. Although both duchies belonged to the royal family of Denmark, many Germans lived there. Denmark was defeated and both duchies now came under German control but Austria and Prussia soon fell out over how they should be administered.

WHO WOULD LEAD GERMANY?

In 1866, Bismarck dissolved the German Confederation and Austria declared war on Prussia, confident of victory. They had, however, not taken sufficient account of the skill and strength of the Prussian army. The Prussian forces swept through Austrian territory at an alarming speed, and the power of the Austrian Habsburg empire was forever weakened when the Austrians were defeated on July 3, 1866 at the battle of Sadowa. Bismarck then set up the North German Confederation, with Prussia as the most powerful member.

The Peace of Prague was an excellent example of the skilful diplomacy and statesmanship of Bismarck. He knew that it would be dangerous to humble Austria and he wanted to make an ally and not an enemy. Accordingly, the Habsburgs only lost the two duchies, which they were not that keen to have anyway, and Venice. Prussia did, however, make huge gains within the rest of Germany.

▶ In September 1870, during the Franco-Prussian War the Prussian army laid siege to Paris. Rather than make a full assault on the city, the Prussians simply surrounded it and waited. The poor were soon facing starvation while the wealthy were reduced to eating the animals from the Tuileries Zoo.

THE BATTLE OF SEDAN

The battle of Sedan in northeast France, on September 1–2, 1870, was the scene of an unequal conflict between Prussian forces and the French. The French forces were outnumbered by two to one. Although Leboeuf, the French war minister, had claimed that the French preparation was total, when the battle began, it was found that not all of the French riflemen even had a rifle. Surrounded and unable to break out, Napoleon III, along with 85,000 French troops, were finally forced to surrender.

THE FRANCO–PRUSSIAN WAR

The French ruler, Napoleon III, a poorly supported, ill-advised leader, felt threatened by Prussia's increasing power and he demanded Germany hand over some of their territory to balance out the Prussian gains. Bismarck ignored this demand and Napoleon's threats only served to bring the previously reluctant southern German states behind Prussia.

Bismarck provoked the French when he altered the report of a conversation between the Prussian king and the French ambassador so that it looked like an insult to France. When the document, the 'Ems Telegram' was published in 1870, the French emperor Napoleon III was furious and declared war. In the Franco–Prussian war, Prussia defeated France in 1871 and took over Alsace and Lorraine. The remaining German states also joined in 1871. Bismarck then formed the German Second Reich, with the king of Prussia, William I, as emperor.

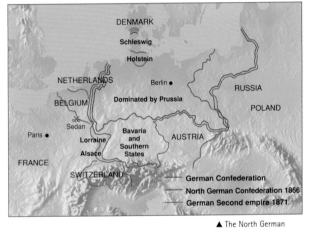

▲ The North German Confederation, dominated by Prussia, was formed in 1867. It was a union of states in which the members kept their own governments, but military and foreign policy was decided by a federal government.

KEY DATES

1852	Napoleon III becomes emperor of France
1862	Bismarck becomes Prussian prime minister
1864	Denmark plans to take over Schleswig-Holstein
1866	Schleswig-Holstein taken over by Prussia
1867	North German Confederation formed
1870	Outbreak of the Franco–Prussian war
1870	French defeat at the Battle of Sedan, Napoleon III captured
1870	Prussian siege of Paris begins
1871	Franco-Prussian war ends at Peace of Frankfurt
1871	Second German Reich proclaimed at Versailles
1873	Napoleon III dies in exile

◄ This cartoon shows Bismarck and Kaiser Wilhelm riding on Napoleon III as a pig in their triumphal entry into Paris in 1871.

SCRAMBLE FOR AFRICA 1880–1912

With their greater wealth and technology, the major European powers were able to conquer large parts of the world and claim the territory as their own.

▲ This cartoon shows the German eagle, poised to take as much of Africa as it can. Germany was just one of many European powers seeking new lands.

▼ During the latter part of the 19th century, rivalry between the different European powers played a large part in the scramble for Africa.

Towards the end of the 19th century, the European powers ceased to squabble among themselves for territories and trade within Europe itself. With the sudden emergence of the new force of Germany under the political control of Otto von Bismarck, all European nations looked further afield for economic gain. Rival European nations now rushed to carve out their respective colonies in Africa. This process became known as the 'scramble for Africa'.

Britain and France undoubtedly led the scramble, but Germany, Belgium and Italy were very close behind. Numerous conflicts flared up between Britain and France over colonies in western Africa. Where Britain had earlier been happy to control a relatively small number of coastal towns and ports, by the end of the century they had taken over all of what is now Ghana and Nigeria, and effectively controlled Sierra Leone and the Gambia.

Dr David Livingstone, lost while seeking the source of the Nile River, had a historic meeting with the journalist H. M. Stanley by Lake Tanganyika in 1871.

THE SUEZ CANAL

Opened in 1869, the Suez canal cut the sea journey between Britain and India from three months to three weeks. The Khedive of Egypt was in financial difficulties and the British bought his half of the shares in the Suez Canal in 1875.

Relations between Britain and France worsened when the British occupied Egypt in 1882 to protect their interests during a local uprising against the Europeans. In 1885, General Gordon and many British soldiers were killed when the Mahdi, the leader in the Sudan, took Khartoum on the White Nile. The Italians invaded Eritrea (now part of Ethiopia) and King Leopold of the Belgians took over the Congo.

Europeans traded guns in exchange for gold and ivory. The guns had a devastating effect in Africa.

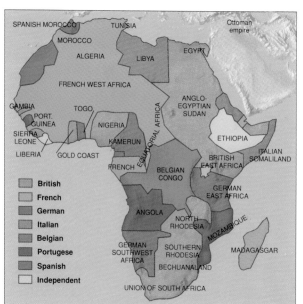

SPANISH MOROCCO
TUNISIA
Ottoman empire
MOROCCO
ALGERIA
LIBYA
EGYPT
FRENCH WEST AFRICA
ANGLO-EGYPTIAN SUDAN
GAMBIA
PORT. GUINEA
TOGO
NIGERIA
SIERRA LEONE
KAMERUN
EQUATORIAL AFRICA
ETHIOPIA
LIBERIA
GOLD COAST
FRENCH
BELGIAN CONGO
BRITISH EAST AFRICA
ITALIAN SOMALILAND
GERMAN EAST AFRICA
ANGOLA
NORTH RHODESIA
MOZAMBIQUE
GERMAN SOUTHWEST AFRICA
SOUTHERN RHODESIA
MADAGASGAR
BECHUANALAND
UNION OF SOUTH AFRICA

- British
- French
- German
- Italian
- Belgian
- Portugese
- Spanish
- Independent

CONSTANT EXPANSION

The scramble for Africa became a formal process at a conference in Berlin in 1884. The rival European countries cut up Africa like a cake. Only Liberia and Ethiopia, which defeated an Italian invasion, remained independent. The colonization of Africa had a number of effects on Africans. The Europeans took no notice of the different African nations when the new borders were drawn. The Europeans brought new forms of government to Africa, but few Africans could vote. Profits made in the colonies went back to Europe, and European colonists often took the best farmland.

KEY DATES	
1869	Suez Canal opens to shipping
1875	Britain buys Egyptian shares in Suez Canal
1876	Leopold II of Belgium takes over the Congo
1882	British occupy Egypt to protect the Suez Canal
1884	European nations meet in Berlin to divide Africa among themselves
1885	The Mahdi besieges Khartoum
1898	British defeat the Mahdi's troops at Omdurman
1893	The French take Timbuktu, Mali, western Africa
1899	British–Egyptian rule of Sudan
1912	The African National Congress (ANC) formed in South Africa

▲ The French conquest of Mali in western Africa was symbolized by the raising of the French flag in Timbuktu in 1893. Their advance along the Niger River was held up by the resistance of the local people, the Mande.

◄ Built by Frenchman, Ferdinand de Lesseps, the Suez Canal considerably reduced the journey from Britain to India. In 1875, the British, under the leadership of Disraeli, heard that the Khedive (viceroy) of Egypt faced bankruptcy and they bought his share of the canal for £4 million.

IRELAND 1800–1913

Britain's restrictions on Free Trade had a terrible effect on the Irish when disease wiped out their staple food crop. One million died and one million emigrated.

Daniel O'Connell (1775–1847) was a fighter for the rights of Catholic people in Britain. He was the first Irish Catholic to be elected to the British parliament and served from 1829 to 1847.

▲ Irish tenant farmers were ruined when the potato blight struck in 1845. The harvest was poor and they could not pay their rent. Many of the farmers and their families starved to death.

Most of the people of Ireland made a living by farming small plots of rented land or working large estates for Anglo-Irish landlords. They rarely had enough to eat. Around half lived almost entirely on potatoes. The British Corn Laws kept the price of wheat high by taxing any wheat imported. Powerful Anglo–Irish landlords favoured the Corn Laws because they made large profits from the wheat grown on their land in Ireland, all of which was shipped to England. Should the staple food, potatoes, fail, the people could not afford to buy grain from anywhere else because of this tax.

Disaster struck in 1845 and 1846 when a potato blight ruined the potato crop. Although Ireland grew enough corn to feed its people, none of it was available for them to eat as most of it was exported to England. Because of the Corn Laws, the Irish could not afford to import what should have been cheap foreign corn. There was nothing to replace the potatoes and many people starved to death.

On 6 May 1882, in Phoenix Park in Dublin, Lord Frederick Cavendish, the Irish chief secretary, and T. H. Burke, his under-secretary, were stabbed to death by Irish Nationalists. Five were later hanged for this offence.

THE BRITISH RESPONSE

The British prime minister, Sir Robert Peel, repealed (ended) the Corn Laws which gradually brought down the price of bread. But it was too late to save many Irish people. About one million died and one million more emigrated. The potato famine increased Irish feelings of hatred towards the British. In 1870, they began to demand their own parliament, which had been abolished in 1801.

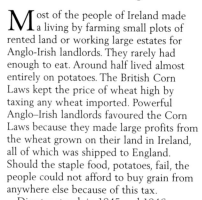

▶ Most Irish people lived a hard life with little food and comfort. Their homes in which were often little different from the barns that their Anglo–Irish landlords kept their cattle.

During the potato famine, many Irish people had to choose between possible starvation or leaving their country. About one million people starved to death and another million emigrated over the next five years, mostly to England, Scotland and Wales, as well as the United States. A typhoid epidemic in 1846–47 is thought to have killed another 350,000 Irish people.

Charles Stewart Parnell was the leader of the Irish Nationalists in the British parliament. He led the struggle for Irish home rule and supported the Land League which wanted land to be given to Irish farmers.

The Irish Republican Brotherhood, or Fenians, was founded by James Stephens (1825–1901) in 1858. It was an organization that wanted to set up an Irish republic.

IRISH LEADERS

The demands of Irish politicians, particularly Charles Parnell (1846–91), became increasing vocal in the British parliament. Parnell had entered parliament in 1875 and became president of the Irish Land League in 1879. His party demanded rent reductions and resisted the evictions of tenant farmers. The Irish politicians, and the strength of public feeling among the Irish, led to some law reforms, especially relating to the rights to own land.

However, these reforms were not enough to keep the Irish happy with British rule. Almost all the Irish wanted home rule, or self-government. After the failure of both the 1886 and 1893 Home Rule Bills, the British parliament finally passed the third Home Rule Bill in 1912, but it was not put into operation because of the outbreak of World War I in 1914.

▼ The Fenians sometimes resorted to acts of violence in Britain. In 1867, they attacked a police van in Manchester to rescue their comrades.

KEY DATES	
1801	Irish parliament abolished by the British
1829	Daniel O'Connell enters parliament
1845	First potato blight leads to widespread famine
1846	Second potato blight causes worse famine
1846	Typhoid epidemic kills 350,000 Irish people
1875	Charles Parnell enters the British parliament
1879	Parnell becomes president of the Land League
1912	Third Home Rule Bill passed but not enacted

SOUTHEAST ASIA 1800–1913

Southeast Asia was dominated by the Dutch, French and British in the late 19th century. They grew rich on the profits from crops grown by local people.

Southeast Asia was colonized by Europeans who set up plantations which were worked by the native population. The French colony of Indochina included Cambodia, Laos and Vietnam. The French gradually conquered the area during the 19th century despite local resistance. In Annam, the emperor Ham Nghi waged a guerrilla war until 1888.

The Dutch had been established in Indonesia since the 1620s. They had already taken over Indonesian trade, and from 1830, they also took over agriculture. The peasant farmers were forced to grow the crops the Dutch wanted, especially coffee and indigo (a plant from which a blue dye was made). By 1900, a nationalist movement was growing inside Indonesia itself. The Indonesians made efforts to improve education and to regain some control over their business and trade.

Faced with Burmese expansion at the end of the 18th century, the British colonized Burma and the Malay Peninsula in the 19th century because they wanted to protect India, which they regarded as the most valuable part of their empire.

Rubber packing in Colombo, Ceylon in the late 19th century. Rubber plants were introduced to southeast Asia by the British from seeds collected in Brazil.

The Burmese resisted British rule in a series of bloody wars between 1824 and 1885, but by 1886, Britain controlled the whole of the country and made it into a province of India. It was not until 1937 that Burma was separated from India and regained some independence.

In Malaya, the situation was calmer because of British rule through the local sultans. During the early part of the 19th century, the British East India Company had set up trading posts, and in 1826, Singapore, Malacca and Penang were united to form the Straits Settlements.

In Malaya, the British ruled through the local sultans. This beautiful mural of the tree of life comes from a family home in Sarawak, now part of Malaysia.

The merchant ships of the British East India Company were known as East Indiamen.

▲ Indonesian princes and Dutch colonists benefited from the profits made by growing cash crops on the islands. For ordinary Indonesians, this way of life meant great hardship.

▶ Tea was one of the important cash crops grown on large British-owned estates in India.

BRITISH INFLUENCE

In later years, the British went on to become responsible for other states in the Malay peninsula and formed the Federated Malay States in 1896, with the capital at Kuala Lumpur. Demand for rubber grew rapidly in the 19th century but the only source of supply was South America. Rubber seeds were collected in Brazil and shipped to Kew Gardens, London, where they were raised. In 1877, 2,000 young plants were shipped and distributed to countries such as Ceylon, Malaysia and Indonesia, where the plants flourished.

By the 1880s, British engineers, surveyors and architects were helping to build railways, roads, bridges, factories and government buildings in southeast Asia. They drew on the experience gained from the Industrial Revolution in Britain. Banking and investment were geared to financing the empire by trading raw materials from the colonies for home-made manufactured goods.

The British also worked out how to improve the techniques used for mining the large deposits of tin and other precious metals which had been discovered in Malaya and other countries. Towards the end of the 19th century, many people went to live and work in southeast Asia as traders, soldiers, engineers, diplomats and government administrators.

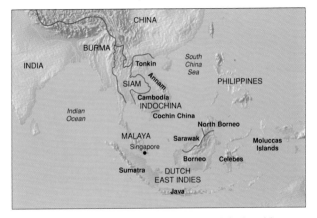

KEY DATES

1813   East India Company's trade monopoly ends
1819   Thomas Raffles of the East India Company founds Singapore as a free port
1824   British and Dutch interests settled by treaty
1859   French naval forces capture the citadel in Saigon
1867   Singapore and the Straits Settlements apply to be a Crown colony
1877   Kew Gardens, London, grow rubber plants from Brazilian seeds
1884–1885 Chinese–French War
1885   At the Treaty of Tientsin China recognizes French rule over Annam and Tonkin
1886   British annexe Upper Burma
1887   Union of Indochina formed from Vietnam, Cambodia and Laos
1898   USA takes Philippines from the Spanish

▲ Southeast Asia was dominated by three European powers in the late 19th century – the French, British and Dutch controlled every country except Siam.

▼ The French gradually conquered Indochina during the 19th century. Their forces captured the citadel in Saigon, Annam, on February 17, 1859. In 1862, the French signed a treaty with the local leader, Tu Doc.

THE BRITISH EMPIRE 1815–1913

During the 19th century, the British extended and consolidated their empire. Britain had taken over more land than any other nation in history.

When William IV died in 1837, the English crown passed to his niece, Victoria, who was just 18 years old. When Victoria died in 1901, her reign had lasted 63 years, the longest in British history.

▼ Between 1870 and 1913, the British empire expanded further to take in land in Africa and southeast Asia, providing jobs for many British people. At its height, it included a quarter of the world's land and people.

At its height, during the reign of Queen Victoria, the British empire included a quarter of the world's land and people. From the end of the Napoleonic Wars in 1815 to the start of World War I in 1914, Britain acquired so many new colonies that the empire stretched around the world. Britain was able to control this vast empire by its domination of the seas and world trade routes. Throughout the 19th century, British naval strength was unbeatable and its boats constantly patrolled countries belonging to the empire.

Because the empire covered both hemispheres it was known as 'the empire on which the Sun never sets'. Colonies in the Caribbean, Africa, Asia, Australasia and the Pacific were ruled from London and were all united under the British monarch. Strategic harbours such as Gibraltar, Hong Kong, Singapore and Aden came into British hands, and vital trading routes such as the Cape route to India, or the Suez Canal (via Egypt) to the spice and rubber plantations of southeast Asia were also controlled by Britain.

Soldiers from the countries that were part of the British empire were frequently used to make sure that British power and influence continued and expanded.

RAW MATERIALS

The empire provided the British with raw materials for manufacturing industry and British demand for colonial products such as silk, spices, rubber, cotton, tea, coffee and sugar led to the gradual takeover of many countries. Several countries became colonies when the British government acquired a bankrupt trading company.

India was an example of a country where the British had come to trade and stayed to rule. It was the most prized colony in the empire. In 1850, India remained under the rule of the British East India Company. After the rebellion, of 1857, India was placed under the rule of the British government, and its policies were more cautious. British officials left control of local affairs to the princes.

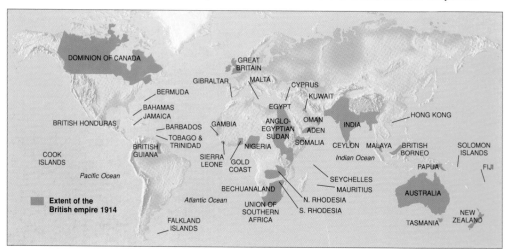

DOMINION OF CANADA
GREAT BRITAIN
GIBRALTAR
MALTA
CYPRUS
KUWAIT
BERMUDA
BAHAMAS
EGYPT
JAMAICA
HONG KONG
BRITISH HONDURAS
BARBADOS
GAMBIA
ANGLO-EGYPTIAN SUDAN
OMAN
ADEN
INDIA
TOBAGO & TRINIDAD
NIGERIA
SOMALIA
CEYLON
MALAYA
BRITISH BORNEO
SOLOMON ISLANDS
BRITISH GUIANA
COOK ISLANDS
SIERRA LEONE
GOLD COAST
Indian Ocean
PAPUA
FIJI
Pacific Ocean
SEYCHELLES
BECHUANALAND
MAURITIUS
AUSTRALIA
Extent of the British empire 1914
Atlantic Ocean
UNION OF SOUTHERN AFRICA
N. RHODESIA
S. RHODESIA
NEW ZEALAND
FALKLAND ISLANDS
TASMANIA

CONSOLIDATION

The British subjugated Egypt in 1883 to guard the Suez Canal and the route to India. After a rebellion in the south of Egypt led by a religious leader, the Mahdi, Britain entered to Sudan in 1898. The British set up trade links throughout the empire by appointing an agent in every port. They organized local produce for export and markets for British imports. The British navy protected their interests and kept the sea routes safe for shipping.

British influence extended into mainland settlements in Central and South America and into China where it had trading outposts. Queen Victoria, herself empress of India since 1876, was a keen supporter of a foreign policy that pursued colonial expansion and upheld the empire. As more British people emigrated to countries within the empire, so these lands were given more freedom to govern themselves. Many colonies, notably Canada, Australia and South Africa became dominions rather than colonies and were allowed self-government.

KEY DATES	
1824	Penal colony established in Brisbane, Australia
1829	Britain claims western Australia
1837	Victoria becomes queen of England
1850	Australian Colonies Government Act gives limited independence to Australia
1852	New Zealand is granted a constitution
1857	Indian mutiny against British rule begins
1867	British North American Act grants home rule to Canada
1875	Britain buys controlling interest in Suez Canal
1876	Queen Victoria becomes empress of India
1884	Britain annexes southeastern New Guinea
1890	Zanzibar becomes a British protectorate
1901	New South Wales, Queensland, Victoria, south Australia, western Australia and Tasmania become the Commonwealth of Australia.
1901	Queen Victoria dies
1907	Dominion of New Zealand is founded

END OF EMPIRE

Towards the end of the 19th century, some colonies began to break away from British rule. Home rule was granted to Canada in 1867, and independence to Australia in 1901. Both countries became dominions, although they remained part of the British empire. The gradual loosening of ties with the British empire reflected the fact that Britain had ceased to be the leading industrial nation in the world. Germany and the United States had overtaken it, with France and Russia close behind.

The British government passed the Australian Colonies Government Act in 1850. This gave limited independence to the country. In 1901, the colonies of New South Wales, Queensland, Victoria, south Australia, western Australia and Tasmania became the Commonwealth of Australia.

◄ A 19th-century cartoon shows the colonies of the British empire constantly worrying the imperial lion.

▼ In 1897, Victoria celebrated her Diamond Jubilee. The guests of honour included Indian princes, African chiefs, Pacific Islanders and Chinese from Hong Kong.

USA: THE PLAINS WARS 1849–1913

The wide-open plains of the American midwest, that had once seemed vast and endless. In the 1800s, they became the scene of a struggle for land ownership.

The Pawnee were one of the 'Plains nations'. They lived by hunting buffalo.

General George Custer (1839–76) died in the Battle of the Little Bighorn.

Sitting Bull (1831–90) was a Dakota (Sioux) medicine man and war chief.

Many groups of Native Americans lived on the Great Plains of the American west and had done so for thousands of years. This vast area stretched from the Mississippi River in the east to the Rocky mountains in the west, and from Canada in the north to Texas in the south. Until the 17th century, many Plains tribes were farmers. They grew maize, beans and other foods, but they also hunted buffalo on foot using bows and arrows. Their way of life on the plains began to change during the 17th century when the Spanish introduced the horse.

With horses, the Native Americans could follow the buffalo with ease. The buffalo not only provided them with meat, but also with tools and weapons fashioned from the animals' bones, and tepees and clothing made with the skins. Some of the larger groups of Native Americans became known as the 'Plains nations'. Early white settlers forced some groups to move west from their original homelands east of the Mississippi River.

WESTWARD HO!

After the civil war, the land between the Mississippi River and the Rocky mountains was thought of as a wilderness of plains and mountains. The government encouraged pioneers to migrate westward. Settlers travelled west together in wagon trains for protection on the long journey across plains, rivers and mountains. The journey could take up to eight months.

The Native Americans depended on buffalo for their food, clothing and shelter. Many buffalo were also killed to supply meat to workers lay track for the railways.

SETTLERS MOVE WEST

The government encouraged people to migrate westward. Under the Homestead Act of 1862, a family could have 65 hectares for a small fee, provided they did not sell the land for five years. More land was given to those who made improvements by drilling wells or planting trees. The Act encouraged farmers to move into and settle on the Great Plains.

The government also encouraged the building of railways, which carried people into unsettled regions. It gave land to the railways so generously that many lines were built simply to obtain land. By 1869, the Union Pacific Railroad was completed, joining America from coast to coast.

STRUGGLE FOR SURVIVAL

The opening of the railways soon changed the face of America. They brought even more settlers to the traditional homelands of the Native Americans. The two different kinds of society came into conflict. When local Native American chiefs signed land agreements with the settlers they meant different things to the two sides. The settlers' idea of private property meant nothing to the Native Americans who thought they could still use the land for hunting. A struggle for survival began. Many Native Americans bought guns and attacked the settlers' homesteads, their wagon trains, the railways and the US cavalry.

Starting in 1866, a series of wars took place. The US president Rutherford B. Hayes stated in 1877, "Many, if not most, of our Indian wars had their origin in broken promises and acts of injustice." Killing the buffalo, on which the Plains nations depended for food, was enough to destroy the Native Americans. There were about 15 million buffalo in 1860, but by 1885, only 2,000 were left. The survivors of the Plains nations were forced onto reservations, often with poor land on which they were expected to grow crops.

Virginia City in Nevada did not exist until 1859 when gold and silver were found nearby. By 1876, it was a large town, but people left when the gold and silver ran out.

The Native Americans were used to hunting and did not want to farm. They were not allowed to become American citizens and had few civil rights. Fierce battles with soldiers resulted in the deaths of thousands of the Native American groups. The last battle was at Wounded Knee in South Dakota in 1890, when soldiers slaughtered 200 Sioux. Soon, all the groups were moved onto the reservations and the Native American way of life was finished for ever.

Gold was discovered in California in 1848. Within a few months a gold rush had started, and by 1855, the town of San Francisco had grown rapidly from 800 to 50,000 people.

▲ The possibility of making their fortune attracted people of many nationalities to the American goldfields. Thousands of Chinese people travelled to California in the 1850s and the 1870s to work as labourers.

◀ In the 1830s, the Chickasaw tribe was forced to move to a reservation in Oklahoma where they were told that the land was theirs 'as long as the grass grows and the waters run'. But the central and western parts were thinly populated and sought after by white settlers. In 1906, the Chickasaw rose up to stop their land from being taken, but were suppressed by the United States Cavalry.

AUSTRALIA 1788–1913

The original inhabitants of Australia, the Aborigines, faced a growing threat to their way of life as white settlers encroached ever further into their territories.

Aborigines led a way of life based around tribal territories and customs. Although the spread of white settlements destroyed much of this, they still kept a strong cultural identity.

The colonies were granted self-government before 1890. New South Wales originally occupied the whole of eastern Australia, but was eventually divided.

During the 19th century, the new nation of Australia was created. More than 174,000 convicts had been shipped from Britain to Australia, mainly to Sydney, to pass their sentence in work gangs, for periods varying from a few years to life. Transportation to the colonies had begun during the reign of Elizabeth I, was an extension of the older punishment of banishment, and it did not end until 1868.

For many convicts, Britain held only bitter memories and so it was that many of them settled in Australia after their release. Early settlements were founded along the coast but explorers gradually opened up the interior. They were followed by pioneers looking for grazing land for the ever-growing flocks of sheep.

As the wool industry grew, so did the demand for land. Many drove their sheep beyond the official settlement limits, earning themselves the name 'squatters'. Though they were later granted grazing rights the name stuck. These early farmers gradually spread into the interior, acquiring land as they went, but eventually coming into conflict with the native Australians, the Aborigines.

▲ Robert O'Hara Burke (1820–61) and William Wills (1834–61) were the first white men to cross Australia. Their expedition contained 18 men and set out in 1860 to travel north from Melbourne to the Gulf of Carpentaria. They suffered terribly from starvation and exhaustion on the way back and only one man survived.

▶ On arrival in Australia, emigrants were housed at first in large wooden buildings. This one was designed to accommodate more than 70 people.

ABORIGINAL PEOPLE

Australia's first inhabitants, the Aboriginal people, arrived 50,000 years ago from southeast Asia. They lived in nomadic groups, travelling around their territories, hunting with spears and boomerangs, fishing from canoes and gathering fruits and vegetables. They had no written language but passed on valuable knowledge by word of mouth and in song.

When the British settled in Australia, Aboriginal culture was threatened and their land was taken over by squatters. In the late 18th century, there were more than 300,000 Aborigines. Many were killed or driven off their land by settlers, and the population fell to under 45,000.

In Van Diemen's Land, later renamed Tasmania, the Aboriginal population was completely wiped out by the 1870s. Some had perished from European diseases and the white settlers had murdered the rest.

THE GOLD RUSH

In 1851, many people rushed to Australia at the news that gold had been found in New South Wales and Victoria. This event became known as the Gold Rush. Melbourne, the capital of Victoria, became a wealthy city and Australia's population more than doubled. In 1854, gold miners at the Eureka Stockade rebelled against their colonial rulers, putting on pressure for reform and self-government.

GROWING UNREST

Squatter settlement also created problems when the immigrants and ex-convicts demanded that land be made available for smallholdings. Many failed to gain land because of opposition from existing squatters. At the same time a sense of nationalism was growing. Britain had granted self-government to all her colonies by the 1890s, and the leaders of the colonies had come to realize that some form of union was needed.

None of the Australian colonies were willing to give up their individual independence, so in 1890, after fierce arguments, the colonies agreed to unite in a federation. The Commonwealth of Australia was proclaimed on the first day of 1901 and the city of Canberra was chosen as the federal capital.

▲ In 1851, thousands of people from many countries moved to Australia after they heard that gold had been found in New South Wales and Victoria.

▶ Ned Kelly (1855–80) and his gang were bushrangers roamed the country staging hold-ups and raiding banks. Kelly often wore homemade armour. He was hanged in 1880.

KEY DATES

1797	Sheep farming introduced to Australia
1836	City of Adelaide founded
1851	Gold Rush starts in New South Wales
1854	Rebellion of gold miners at Eureka stockade
1855	Van Diemen's Land renamed Tasmania
1860	Burke and Wills set out to cross Australia
1868	Britain stops sending convicts to Australia
1880	The outlaw Ned Kelly is captured and hanged
1901	Commonwealth of Australia declared

SHEEP FARMING

Introduced to Australia in 1797, sheep farming became the major agricultural activity in the country. Because the land was often far from fertile, great areas of pasture were needed to keep the sheep healthy and well fed. This meant that more and more land was taken from the Aborigines.

THE WORLD
AT WAR
1914–1949

In the years from 1914 to 1949 the world went
through a period of rapid, intense and painful
change. The Great War, the 'war to end all wars',
was followed by a massive worldwide influenza
epidemic. The 1917 revolution in Russia made
that country the world's first socialist state.
Then came the Great Depression, a collapse of
capitalism, leading to mass unemployment
worldwide. This, followed by World War II,
meant that European world-dominance was
replaced by that of the USA and USSR.

▲ World War I saw the first widespread use of aerial warfare. These early
aeroplanes were used to spy on enemy positions and drop bombs.

◄ After the defeat of Nazi Germany in 1945, the victors, Marshal Zhukov
(USSR), General Eisenhower (USA) and Field Marshall Montgomery
(Britain) meet in the ruins of Berlin.

THE WORLD AT A GLANCE 1914–1949

Almost the whole world was affected by World War I, the Great Depression and World War II. In North America, the USA adopted a policy of isolation between the wars, but joined the Allies in World War II. In South America, right wing governments came to power in Argentina and Brazil.

In Europe, civil wars broke out in Ireland, Spain and Greece, and revolution in Russia led to civil war there, too. In the Middle East, the Ottoman empire collapsed after World War I, and Israel was founded in 1948 as a homeland for the Jewish people.

Italy's attempts to build an empire in Africa failed. Many countries began clamouring for independence. India gained independence from Britain but it was partitioned to form Pakistan. Civil war divided China, while Japanese expansion was one of the causes of World War II and the Pacific became a battle zone. Science, in the form of an atom bomb, ended the war.

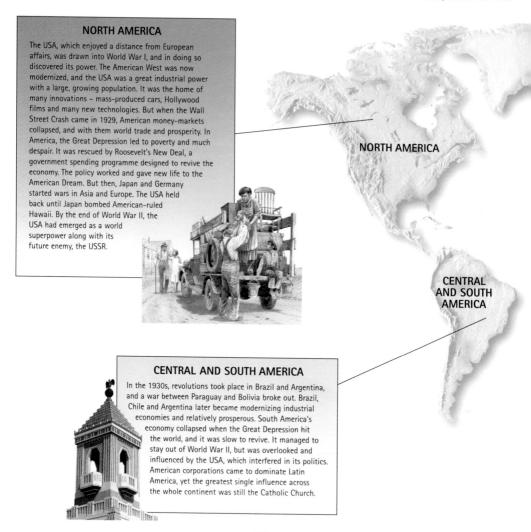

NORTH AMERICA

The USA, which enjoyed a distance from European affairs, was drawn into World War I, and in doing so discovered its power. The American West was now modernized, and the USA was a great industrial power with a large, growing population. It was the home of many innovations – mass-produced cars, Hollywood films and many new technologies. But when the Wall Street Crash came in 1929, American money-markets collapsed, and with them world trade and prosperity. In America, the Great Depression led to poverty and much despair. It was rescued by Roosevelt's New Deal, a government spending programme designed to revive the economy. The policy worked and gave new life to the American Dream. But then, Japan and Germany started wars in Asia and Europe. The USA held back until Japan bombed American-ruled Hawaii. By the end of World War II, the USA had emerged as a world superpower along with its future enemy, the USSR.

NORTH AMERICA

CENTRAL AND SOUTH AMERICA

CENTRAL AND SOUTH AMERICA

In the 1930s, revolutions took place in Brazil and Argentina, and a war between Paraguay and Bolivia broke out. Brazil, Chile and Argentina later became modernizing industrial economies and relatively prosperous. South America's economy collapsed when the Great Depression hit the world, and it was slow to revive. It managed to stay out of World War II, but was overlooked and influenced by the USA, which interfered in its politics. American corporations came to dominate Latin America, yet the greatest single influence across the whole continent was still the Catholic Church.

EUROPE

The fall of the Habsburgs and Ottomans put many new countries on the map. Ireland gained independence and Poland reappeared as an independent country. The Russian Revolution turned the USSR into a massive power, with large-scale industrialization and collectivization of farms under the dictatorship of Stalin. Germany, though it lost the Great War, grew strong again under Hitler, taking over much of Europe in World War II. Europe was vulnerable as a result of the Depression, and there was a desire for peace and to appease the Nazis. Yet, through these difficult times Europe came to lead the way with reforms in the creation of social welfare, social insurance and education systems. After World War II, much of Europe was devastated, and American aid was provided for its recovery. Colonies abroad were being made independent, public opinion held sway, and Europe approached 1950 shell-shocked by the violence of the previous decades.

ASIA

After the Chinese Revolution of 1911, life for the people did not improve. In the 1930s, China became a dictatorship, opposed by Mao Zedong's communists. The Japanese invaded in 1937, and China was devastated. Mao's communists fought back and took power in 1948. Before World War II Japan had risen to military and industrial greatness. Its aggressive expansion during the war was finally halted by two atom bombs and occupation by the USA. India avoided the war, but Indians could no longer tolerate British rule, and in 1947 India and Pakistan separated and gained independence. Indonesia and the Philippines also gained independence.

EUROPE

ASIA

MIDDLE EAST

AFRICA

AUSTRALASIA

As more settlers arrived, Australia and New Zealand developed into richer countries, exporting agricultural products and metals. Auckland, Sydney and Melbourne joined the list of world cities. After World War II, many European immigrants moved there. Polynesia suffered from the war – the islands were dragged into the modern world.

AUSTRALASIA

AFRICA

Under colonial administration, African states were rapidly modernized. South Africa became a strong white-ruled nation. Except in north Africa, World War II did not greatly affect the continent.

MIDDLE EAST

After the fall of the Ottoman empire, the Middle East was split up into separate countries, governed by the British and French. The discovery of oil made Iraq, Iran, Kuwait and Arabia economically important. British and French rule ended after World War II, and the Arab states became independent. Controversially, the Jewish state of Israel was formed in their midst.

THE START OF WORLD WAR I 1914

The assassination of Archduke Franz Ferdinand, heir to the Austro-Hungarian empire, in Sarajevo in June 1914 triggered the bloodiest conflict in human history.

Jealous of Britain's trade and colonies, Germany, which already had the world's largest army, had begun to build up its navy. Kaiser Wilhelm II's ambition to acquire more colonies overseas and his aggressive foreign policy also worried other European countries. In the years leading up to 1914, Britain and Germany competed to build bigger and better ships for their navies. The rivalry between European countries over trade, colonies and military power had also been growing, and the European powers had grouped in defensive alliances.

A British recruiting poster at the start of World War I featured the war minister, Lord Kitchener.

Under Kaiser Wilhelm II (1859-1941), Germany constructed a naval battle fleet to rival Britain's.

MAKING ALLIANCES

The main alliance was the Triple Alliance, of Germany, Italy and Austria–Hungary. In this alliance, an attack on any one country would bring its allies to its defence. This was aimed at blocking any aggressive Russian moves in the Balkans. Another alliance, the Triple Entente, was made between Britain, France and Russia. It was not a military alliance, but its members had agreed to co-operate against any aggression from Germany.

World War I began after a Serb terrorist, Gavrilo Princip, killed the heir to the Austro–Hungarian throne, Archduke Franz Ferdinand, in Sarajevo on June 28, 1914.

HOW THE WAR BEGAN

The war began when a Serb terrorist, Gavrilo Princip, shot dead the heir to the Austro–Hungarian empire, Archduke Franz Ferdinand, and his wife in Sarajevo on June 28, 1914. This led Austria to declare war on Serbia on July 28. Russia's tsar, Nicholas II, mobilized his country's troops to defend Serbia from Austria. In return, Germany declared war on Russia on August 1. Russian armies were defeated by the Germans at Tannenberg and in the battle of the Masurian Lakes. To the south, the Austro–Hungarian armies were defeated by the Russians in September.

A WAR ON TWO FRONTS

Germany had always dreaded a war on two fronts, so it put the Schlieffen Plan into operation. Drawn up by General von Schlieffen, the plan aimed to defeat France in six weeks so that Germany could concentrate its forces against Russia.

On August 3, Germany declared war on Russia's ally, France. When the German army marched into neutral Belgium to attack the French from the north, they were faced with determined Belgian resistance. This slowed down their advance and allowed the French, under General Joffré, time to reorganize their forces.

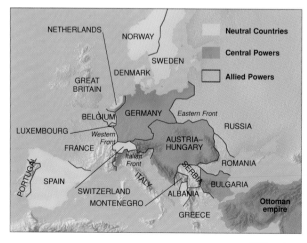

◀ In 1914, Europe divided into two. Britain, France and Russia, known as the Allies, combined to fight the Central Powers comprising Germany, Italy, Austria–Hungary and its allies. Fighting took place simultaneously on an eastern front and a western front.

GERMANY INVADES FRANCE

The British then acted upon the Treaty of London (1839), in which they had agreed to protect Belgian neutrality. It was on these grounds that Britain declared war on Germany on August 4. Britain went to Belgium's defence and sent the 100,000-strong British Expeditionary Force to France to help slow the German advance at Mons and Charleroi.

However, in the face of a determined German advance, Joffré retreated until he was behind the Marne River. Here, the French forces halted the Germans on September 8. Both sides then took up defensive positions, and within three months, a line of trenches was dug from the Channel to the Swiss frontier.

During the war, Britain, France and Russia were known as the Allies, or Allied Powers. Germany, Italy, Austria–Hungary, and their allies were known as the Central Powers. Both sides raced to manufacture more and more weapons, such as poison gas. They thought that by using these weapons they would shorten the war, but it lasted for four years and was the bloodiest conflict in human history. It has been estimated that the direct cost of the war was £40 billion and the total number of men killed or wounded amounted to about 30 million.

◀ In 1914, Britain was the only country which did not have a huge reserve of trained men. Volunteers flocked to join up at army recruiting offices.

The French army had the difficult task of defending hundreds of kilometres of frontier against the enemy.

In 1914, the German army was the largest and best trained in the world.

KEY DATES

June 28	Archduke Franz Ferdinand assassinated at Sarajevo by a Serbian terrorist
July 28	Austria declares war on Serbia. Russia mobilizes its troops to defend Serbia
Aug 1	Germany declares war on Russia
Aug 3	Germany declares war on France
Aug 4	Germany invades Belgium
	Britain declares war on Germany
Sept 8	German advance on Paris stopped at the Marne River

Britain had the smallest army in 1914, but it was made up of professionals.

◀ Motivated by patriotism and inspired by the call for volunteers to defend their countries in August 1914, millions of men of all ages across Europe joined up to fight the common enemy.

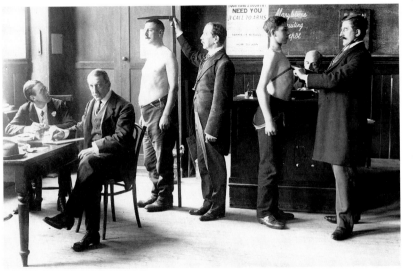

BATTLES OF WORLD WAR I 1914–1917

In a series of horrific battles along the Western Front, millions of lives were lost for the gain of only a few kilometres. The war soon reached a stalemate.

The Western Front stretched across Belgium and north-eastern France. Millions of soldiers were killed in battles along it between 1914 and 1918.

Gas masks were introduced in World War I to protect the troops against poison-gas attacks by the enemy.

During World War I, fighting took place in several areas. The Western Front was between Germany and northern France, and the Eastern Front between Germany and the Russian forces. There was also fighting at sea and in the Middle East, where the Allied Powers attacked the Ottoman empire. In Africa, British and French troops attacked German colonies.

On the Western Front, French and British troops, together with thousands of men from the British Empire, occupied a network of deep trenches from September 1914. Facing them, across a few hundred metres of ground known as 'no man's land', were trenches occupied by the Germans. Millions of men were killed on the Western Front in battles including Ypres, Verdun and the Somme. One of the worst was at Passchendaele in 1917. It was fought in torrential rain and the troops had to wade through mud up to waist-level. In 102 days, the Allies advanced just eight kilometres at a cost of 400,000 lives.

▲ Only 12 years after the Wright brothers made their pioneering flight in North Carolina, aircraft were being used in warfare. Although control of the air was not a deciding factor in World War I, the war led to many advances in flight technology.

▶ In September 1914, the German advance towards Paris was stopped short of the capital when the Allies precariously held the line of the Marne River. The French government fled to Bordeaux. The Allied line held and in their great counterattack, known as the first battle of the Marne and regarded as one of the decisive battles of the war, the Allies drove the Germans back to the line of the Aisne River.

For four years the Western Front did not move more than 32 kilometres in any direction. Barbed wire, machine-guns and artillery defences made attack futile. Tanks, first used in 1916, could crush barbed wire or machine-guns, but they were unreliable. Aircraft were more successful, and were used to spy out enemy troops, target shells and drop bombs. The Eastern Front ran from the Baltic to the Black Sea and also had lines of trenches to which the Russians retreated in September 1914.

The war along the Western Front was fought from trenches guarded by barbed wire and machine-guns. The conditions were appalling, with knee-deep mud, constant shelling, sniping and raids. The battles of the Somme and Verdun in France in 1916 cost over two million casualties, but neither side was able to advance more than a few hundred metres.

▲ Invented by two British scientists, the first tanks were used in the battle of the Somme in 1916. Fitted with machine-guns, they terrified the German soldiers but suffered from too many mechanical failures to be fully effective.

THE WAR AT SEA

There were only two major sea battles in World War I. The first, in 1914, was when a German fleet was destroyed by the Royal Navy off the Falkland Islands. In 1916, the battle of Jutland took place and both Germany and Britain claimed victory. However, the German fleet never left its port of Kiel again until the end of the war, when it surrendered to the Allies.

German submarines, called U-boats, attacked shipping bound for Britain and France. U-boats sank hundreds of Allied ships, nearly bringing Britain to its knees. When the USS *Housatonic* was sunk in 1917, the USA declared war on Germany.

Jutland was the major sea battle of World War I. Although the German fleet inflicted far more serious losses than they had sustained, Britain and Germany both claimed victory. After the battle, on May 31, 1916, the German High Seas fleet escaped in darkness and returned to port, where they remained for the rest of the war.

DISASTER AT GALLIPOLI

Turkish officer

Australian private

During 1915, in an attempt to assist the Russians on the Eastern Front, Allied forces bombarded Turkish forts guarding the Dardanelles. Allied troops, including ANZAC forces from Australia and New Zealand, then landed at Gallipoli to try to capture the strategic positions overlooking the narrow straits. But due to mismanagement, the Allied powers grossly underestimated the strength of the Turkish forces and the Australians alone suffered the loss of 8,587 men killed and 19,367 wounded.

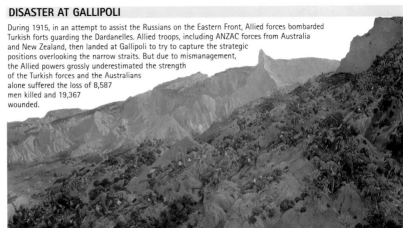

IRELAND: CIVIL UNREST 1916–1923

Irish frustration at Home Rule being first granted and then delayed by World War I led to rebellion and civil war. Southern Ireland became self-governing in 1921.

James Connolly (1868–1916) led the Irish Citizen Army. After the Easter Rising, he was executed, even though he was already mortally wounded.

▲ On Easter Monday 1916, the republicans made their headquarters inside Dublin's General Post Office. Fighting went on for a week. The republicans surrendered on April 29. The British army fired heavy guns at the building, and it caught fire.

▶ This picture shows the remains of a motor car used as a barricade in the streets of Dublin during the 1916 Easter Rising. On one side of the barricades were the republicans, and on the other were the British forces. Many civilians died in the shooting.

Many Irish people wanted Home Rule, and a Home Rule Bill was approved by the British Parliament in 1912. This would have become law, giving Ireland its own parliament to deal with domestic affairs, but it was suspended when World War I broke out in 1914.

In the north, Protestants opposed Home Rule because it would make them a minority in a Catholic country. Some of the Irish (known as republicans) wanted Ireland to be an independent republic. Many supported a political party called Sinn Féin ('We alone'). Some belonged to the Irish Volunteers, the Irish Republican Brotherhood or the Irish Citizen Army.

On Easter Monday 1916, members of the Irish Volunteers and the Irish Citizen Army, led by Padraic Pearse and James Connolly, took control of public buildings in Dublin in an event that became known as the Easter Rising. From headquarters in the General Post Office, Pearse and Connolly declared a republic, but were soon defeated by the British army. In the 1918 election, Sinn Féin won 73 of the 105 Irish seats in the British parliament.

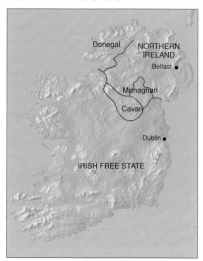

The Anglo–Irish Treaty of 1921 made southern Ireland into a self-governing country. In 1949, it became a republic, completely independent of Britain.

Sinn Féin set up their own parliament, Dáil Eireann, and declared Ireland to be an independent republic in 1919. This led to war between the Irish Republican Army (IRA) and the Royal Irish Constabulary (RIC). Armed police, the Black-and-Tans, were sent to support the RIC. The fighting continued until 1921.

◀ Michael Collins (1890–1922), centre, took part in the 1916 Easter Rising, and was arrested and imprisoned by the British. He became leader of Sinn Féin and head of intelligence in the Irish Volunteers. He was elected to the Irish parliament in 1918 and negotiated the peace treaty with Britain in 1921, becoming head of the provisional government in 1922. He was killed in an ambush in August 1922.

▲ Éamon de Valera (1882-1975) was born in the USA. He was arrested and imprisoned by the British for his part in the 1916 Easter Rising and in 1926 founded the Fianna Fáil Party. Between 1937 and 1959 he served as prime minister of Ireland three times. He then became president until 1973.

THE ANGLO–IRISH TREATY

The British government wanted to divide Ireland into two, with six of the counties of Ulster in the north separate from the rest. Under the 1920 Government of Ireland Act, each of the two parts of Ireland would have some self-government. The six Ulster counties had a Protestant majority who did not want to be ruled from Dublin. They agreed to the act and formed the new state of Northern Ireland. Dáil Eireann, led by Éamon de Valera, opposed the act because they wanted complete independence for all Ireland.

In an attempt to bring peace to the country, the Anglo–Irish Treaty of 1921 made southern Ireland into a dominion of Great Britain. Called the Irish Free State, it was established in 1922. But this action led to civil war. On one side were the Free Staters who agreed to the treaty's terms. On the other side were the republicans.

The civil war lasted until 1923 when de Valera ordered the republicans to stop fighting. In 1926, he founded a new political party, called Fianna Fáil. In the general election of 1932, he defeated the Free Staters. The new constitution of 1937 renamed southern Ireland, Eire, but it stayed within the British Commonwealth. It became independent from Britain in 1949, and left the Commonwealth.

KEY DATES	
1916	Easter Rising in Dublin is put down by the British after a week
1918	In elections, Sinn Féin win 73 of the 105 Irish seats in the British Parliament
1919	Sinn Féin declares Ireland independent – this leads to civil war
1922	Southern Ireland, known as the Irish Free State, becomes a self-governing dominion of Britain
1923	Civil war ends
1926	Fianna Fáil Party founded
1937	New constitution renames southern Ireland Eire

▼ Both the Free Staters and the republicans were well supplied with weapons during the civil war. This field gun belonged to the Free Staters and was used in County Limerick.

RUSSIA 1917–1924

After years of rule by a corrupt and inept government, the people of Russia rose against the tsar and his advisors and seized power in November 1917.

Tsar Nicholas II (1868-1918) was forced to abdicate in 1917. He and his family were then imprisoned and killed by the Bolsheviks in 1918.

During the March 1917 riots in Petrograd, many soldiers refused to obey orders and attached the Red Flag to their bayonets as a sign of support for the rioters.

Following the defeat of Russia by Japan in 1904 there were workers' strikes and revolts throughout Russia. The new tsar, Nicholas II, issued a declaration promising civil rights and a national government, called the Duma. The Duma did not keep its promises. Elections were rigged so that reformers were kept out of government. Opponents of the government were arrested, and the leaders fled. But the Russian people thought that the tsar was out of touch with the population and that his advisers were corrupt. The government, which had not been very efficient in peacetime, was even less effective during World War I. Soldiers who thought they would be sent to fight in the war began to question their loyalty to their country.

Food and fuel were in short supply, and many people in the cities began to starve. The economy was on the way to collapse. In March 1917, riots broke out in the capital, St Petersburg, which had been renamed Petrograd at the start of World War I. Rioting crowds were usually broken up by troops, but they refused to disperse when told to. When the troops joined the rioters, the tsar abdicated and his advisers resigned. A temporary government was set up, led by Prince George Lvov.

Grigori Rasputin (1871–1916) was advisor to Tsar Nicholas II and his wife Alexandra. They thought he was a holy man who could make their sick son better. But he was hated by the people of Russia.

Armed workers and Bolshevik-led soldiers and sailors attacked the Winter Palace in Petrograd on November 6, 1917. Although it was the headquarters of the tsar's government, it was not well defended and was soon in Bolshevik hands.

◄ Vladimir Lenin (1870–1924) became a Marxist in 1887 after his brother was executed for trying to assassinate the tsar.

Leon Trotsky (1879–1940) was the most influential person after Lenin in the revolution. In the Russian Civil War he directed the Red Army to victory. He hoped to become president after Lenin's death, but lost to Stalin.

THE BOLSHEVIKS SEIZE POWER

The government found it difficult to continue with the war. Alexander Kerensky succeeded Prince Lvov as chief minister. After the March revolution, the Bolshevik Party was still determined to seize power. In April, their leader, Vladimir Lenin, returned from exile in Germany.

The Bolsheviks in Petrograd wanted Russia to become a communist state. After struggling with the government, the Bolsheviks, led by Lenin, seized power in November 1917. In March 1918, the new government signed the Treaty of Brest-Litovsk which made peace with Germany. It moved the capital from Petrograd to Moscow and broke up the large estates, giving the farmland to the peasants. Control of factories was given to workers. Banks were taken into state control, and Church property was seized.

The White Russians (anti-communists) opposed these moves, and later in 1918, the Russian Civil War broke out. The White Russians were finally defeated by the Bolshevik Red Army in 1922. Around 100,000 people had been killed and two million had emigrated. In the same year, the country's name was changed to the Union of Soviet Socialist Republics (USSR) or Soviet Union. Lenin led the USSR until his death in 1924, when a new power struggle began between Leon Trotsky and Josef Stalin. Stalin won and went on to dominate Soviet politics until 1953.

Josef Stalin (1879–1953) joined the Bolshevik Party in 1903. In 1922, Stalin became general secretary of the Communist Party and in 1924 leader of the USSR.

▶ When Josef Stalin became leader of the USSR in 1924 he carried out the Great Purge in which millions of people were arrested and murdered. He set out to strip farmers of their land in order to reorganize farming into larger state-owned units called collectives. His orders were brutally carried out by the army and secret police. Villages were burned and the villagers killed or evicted.

WORLD WAR I: THE AFTERMATH 1918–1923

Germany, free of Russia, launched an assault on the Western Front in 1918. Newly arrived American troops helped stop the attack and Germany asked for peace.

World War I involved whole populations. Women went to work to produce armaments and keep industries going while the men were at war.

The arrival of American troops in Europe in 1917 meant that the Allies could launch fresh attacks on the Western Front. In 1918, Russia withdrew from the war, so German soldiers were no longer needed on the Eastern Front. By 1918, more than 3.5 million German soldiers were fighting on the Western Front. In March, they broke through the trenches and advanced towards Paris. The French counterattacked in July and in August, British tanks broke through the German line at Amiens. As the USA poured troops into France, the Germans retreated.

The fighting in World War I left many areas of Belgium and northeast France devastated. Cities such as Ypres in northwest Belgium were left in ruins.

By October, the fighting was nearing the German border and a naval blockade was causing starvation in Germany. Early in the morning of November 11, Germany signed an armistice. Kaiser Wilhelm II abdicated, and at 11 o'clock, fighting in World War I ended. Almost 10 million people had been killed and more than 20 million wounded. Most were young men and their loss changed the social structure of several countries. As a result, many women gained more equality and freedom than they had before the war. In many places they also gained the right to vote.

▶ German submarines, or U-boats, attacked surface shipping by firing torpedoes at them from under the water. They were so successful in attacking Allied shipping that Britain came close to defeat in 1917.

▶ On January 31, 1917, the Germans announced to the world that they would begin unrestricted submarine warfare. This threatened US ships. In February, U-boats sank a US ship and this led to President Wilson's declaration of war on Germany in April 1917. The arrival of American troops in Europe tipped the balance in 1918 when the Germans launched a massive, and final, attack on the Western Front.

THE TREATY OF VERSAILLES

World War I was formally ended at the Paris Peace Conference which was discussed between 1919 and 1923. All the nations that had been involved in the war (except Germany) met to draw up a peace agreement, but the United States, Britain, France, and Italy were dominant. Five separate treaties were drawn up.

The most important was the Treaty of Versailles, which punished Germany for its part in World War I. Vast amounts of reparations (compensation) were to be given to the Allies. The size of Germany was reduced and seven million people were removed from German rule. Germany had to surrender all her overseas colonies and reduce her army to 100,000 men. The German economy collapsed which led to hyperinflation. Other nations also suffered as they tried to pay back money they had borrowed during the war. This led to political and economic upheaval.

Further strife was caused by the redrawing of international boundaries in Europe following the collapse of the German, Austro–Hungarian, Russian, and Ottoman (Turkish) empires.

The Treaty of Versailles, signed on June 28, 1919, settled the fate of Germany because it contained a declaration that Germany's rulers were solely responsible for the outbreak of war.

THE LEAGUE OF NATIONS

The Paris Peace Conference also set up the League of Nations. This aimed to help keep world peace by settling disputes by discussion and agreement, but it failed. The problem was that it had little power because the US refused to join and there were still rivalries between some of the 53 members. These weakened the League and reduced its power, so by the late 1930s, few countries took any notice of it.

HYPERINFLATION

German industry was totally destroyed in the war and the country was unable to repay the reparations demanded by the Allies in the Treaty of Versailles. The Germans regarded the Treaty as unjust and indefensible. One outcome was that the German economy was hit by hyperinflation in the 1920s. Hyperinflation is very fast inflation which causes the value of money to drop quickly. People needed enormous amounts of money just to buy a loaf of bread.

After the Paris Peace Conference of 1919, Germany gave back lands to France and Belgium. The Habsburg monarchy was ended and Poland, Czechoslovakia, Hungary and Yugoslavia all became new states.

Because of hyperinflation, this million mark note, issued in Germany during the 1920, was worth virtually nothing.

THE RISE OF FASCISM 1922–1939

The political belief known as fascism became popular in many countries throughout Europe during the 1930s. To many it offered a way out of economic decline.

Benito Mussolini (1883–1945) became the fascist dictator of Italy in 1922.

▼ Young Italian fascists march past Mussolini during a March of Triumph in Rome in October 1935.

Fascist ideas gained support after World War I with the first fascist government appearing in Italy in the 1920s. The term 'fascism' comes from *fasces*, a bundle of rods with an axe that was a symbol of power in Ancient Rome. Fascism was based on the idea that a nation would only succeed through disciplined, ruthless action and a determined will. To many people, it offered a way out of economic decline.

Fascists believed that achieving a worthwhile aim made any action they took acceptable. Schools, religion, newspapers, the arts and sciences were expected to serve the nation. Military power and a secret police organization supported the fascist governments. Fascists believed that their race was superior to others. They opposed communism, encouraged national pride and racism (prejudice against other races). In Germany, this hatred was directed particularly at Jews and gypsies.

ITALY AND BENITO MUSSOLINI

In Italy, the Fascist Party was founded by Benito Mussolini in 1919, when economic depression and the threat posed by the communists helped its rise to power. His followers were officially called *Fasci de Combattimento*, but were known as 'Blackshirts' because of the colour of their uniform. In 1922, Mussolini took advantage of growing unrest and a general strike to seize power. Using the title *Il Duce* (leader), he became prime minister, and in 1928–29, imposed one-party rule.

To avenge a humiliating defeat in 1896, Mussolini's army invaded Abyssinia (Ethiopia) in 1935–36 and then formed an Axis pact with Germany. In May 1939, Mussolini and the German fascist dictator, Adolf Hitler, agreed a military treaty called the Pact of Steel. Mussolini's leadership led Italy to defeat in World War II and he was dismissed and imprisoned by King Victor Emmanuel in 1943. He was later released by German soldiers and set up fascist rule in the north of the country. In April 1945, he was captured and executed by Italian partisans.

GERMANY AND ADOLF HITLER

The terms of the Versailles Treaty were harsh on Germany, and the economic recession of the early 1930s saw large-scale unemployment in the country. The fragile Weimar Republic was under threat from the communists and Adolf Hitler's National Socialist German Workers' Party (known as Nazis). Hitler promised to end unemployment and poverty, and to build the country into a great state after its humiliation in World War I. Amid political turmoil and violence, President Hindenburg appointed Hitler as chancellor in January 1933. As Führer (leader), Hitler crushed all opposition, and ordered the murder of millions of Jews, gypsies and others. In 1939, he led Germany into World War II, but killed himself when faced with defeat.

THE SPREAD OF FASCISM

In other countries, economic difficulties and threat of communism in the postwar period led to the establishment of many fascist governments. In Spain, the army leader General Miguel Primo de Rivera took power in 1923 and ruled until 1930. In 1933 his son, José Antonio Primo de Rivera, formed the fascist Falange Party.

To avenge Italy's humiliating defeat in 1896, Mussolini sent his army to invade Abyssinia. In 1936, Italian troops under General Badoglio victoriously entered the capital, Addis Ababa. The invasion led to a worldwide outcry and Italy's withdrawal from the League of Nations.

The Falangists supported General Francisco Franco's nationalist forces during the Spanish Civil War (1936–39). With the support of fascist Germany and Italy, Franco took power in 1939. He ruled as a dictator until his death in 1975.

Fascism also won support in Portugal, Austria, the Balkan states and South America in the years before World War II. Juan Perón ruled Argentina with his wife Eva in the 1940s and 1950s. Antonio Salazar was dictator of Portugal from 1932 to 1968. In England, former Cabinet minister Sir Oswald Mosley founded the fascist New Party in 1931, during a period of economic depression and mass unemployment. His public meetings were famous for the violence between his supporters and his opponents.

KEY DATES

1919	Italian Fascist Party founded by Mussolini
1922	Mussolini becomes prime minister of Italy
1923	Primo de Rivera takes power in Spain
1928	Mussolini becomes dictator of Italy
1933	José Antonio Primo de Rivera forms Spanish Falange Party. Hitler appointed chancellor of Germany
1936	Italian troops invade Abyssinia
1939	General Franco becomes dictator of Spain. World War II begins

◀ Sir Oswald Mosley (1896–1980) resigned from Ramsay MacDonald's Labour government in 1931 to form the British Union of Fascists. Its followers stirred up anti-semitism (anti-Jewish feeling), especially in the East End of London.

This anti-fascist poster was issued by the Socialist Party of Catalonia in Spain.

José Antonio Primo de Rivera (1903–36) founded the Spanish Falange nationalist movement in 1933.

Adolf Hitler rose from obscurity to found the National Socialist German Workers' Party. During political unrest in 1933, he was appointed chancellor.

THE GREAT DEPRESSION 1929–1939

After World War I, the economy of the USA saw rapid growth. The Wall Street Crash of 1929 brought an abrupt end to this and led to worldwide depression.

During the Depression of the 1930s, thousands of poverty-stricken American families fled the east coast and rural farming areas to search for work in the west, in California.

In October 1936, 200 men from Jarrow in northeast England marched to London with a petition, drawing attention to the unemployment caused by the closure of the Jarrow shipyard.

The causes of the Great Depression can be traced back to the end of World War I. In 1919, the Treaty of Versailles forced Germany to pay huge compensation to the victorious Allies. Many Germans lost all their savings as the value of money collapsed. In Britain, France and the United States, industry struggled to adjust to peacetime trade. Millions of soldiers came home and looked for jobs. Trade unions called workers to strike against employers who demanded wage cuts. The first ever General Strike in Britain happened in 1926. Food prices fell so low that many farmers were ruined and gave up their land.

During the 1920s, the rapid growth of the American economy was partly due to the repayment of several billion dollars of war loans made by London to New York. The growth was also encouraged by the economic policies of presidents Harding and Coolidge. The price of shares in the USA had been forced up beyond their real value by reckless speculators.

The Wall Street Crash caused panic on the streets of New York in October 1929. Share prices dropped so rapidly that many people lost all their money.

THE WALL STREET CRASH

In October 1929, people began to panic and sell their shares rapidly. On a single day, 13 million shares were sold on the New York Stock Exchange. This started an economic crisis known as the Wall Street Crash (named after New York's financial district) which soon affected the whole world.

Many people lost all their money. Banks and businesses closed and unemployment began to increase. By 1933, the worst year of the Depression, there were 12 million people unemployed in the USA alone. Those who were still in work saw their salaries halved and more than 85,000 businesses failed.

The situation in the United States was made worse by a drought in the agricultural centre of the country. The soil turned to dust in many places and blew away in the wind, leading to crop failure. Thousands of farmers and their families were forced to leave their land to start a new life on the west coast.

THE DUST BOWL

Because of a long drought in the 1930s, the soil in the southern Great Plains of the United States became very dry. A series of terrible dust storms swept across the area which became known as the Dust Bowl. By 1933, hundreds of millions of tonnes of topsoil had been carried off by the winds, destroying the land. Faced with ruin, thousands of poverty-stricken families fled the Dust Bowl looking for work in California and elsewhere.

Franklin D. Roosevelt (1882–1945) was elected governor of New York in 1928. In 1932, he was elected president and in 1933 introduced the New Deal to combat poverty.

ROOSEVELT'S NEW DEAL

For the first two years of the Depression, the United States government and President Hoover took little direct action, believing that the economy would recover naturally. Franklin D. Roosevelt was elected president in 1932 and in 1933 he introduced the New Deal to combat the problems caused by the Depression. This was a set of laws designed mainly to ease the worst of the poverty, provide support for the banks and protect people's savings. Farm prices were supported, a minimum wage was introduced and a huge programme of construction was begun to create employment. The New Deal helped considerably, but it was not until 1939, when the outbreak of World War II gave an enormous boost to heavy industry, that the Depression came to an end.

▶ Although the USSR escaped the worst effects of the Depression, Stalin's five-year plan caused other problems. Announced in 1928, the plan included a programme to introduce collective farms. To put this into action, the richest peasant farmers were either executed or banished to Siberia and the rest of the peasants were forced to work on collective farms. This action severely disrupted agriculture and led to a famine in 1933.

WORLDWIDE DEPRESSION

The Wall Street Crash led to the collapse of the system of international loans which had been set up to handle war reparations. This affected Europe and North America directly. Other parts of the world were also badly hit as much of their trade and business relied on selling food and raw materials to Europe and North America. As these markets collapsed, many people around the world lost their jobs. As a result, unrest increased, and nationalism grew in many countries.

▲ Under Roosevelt's New Deal many unemployed people were given work in state-funded projects in the 1930s. Here, young members of the Civilian Conservation Corps lift seedlings from the ground in Oregon for the US Forest Service.

WEIMAR AND HITLER 1919–1939

Adolf Hitler took advantage of the economic and social turmoil in the Germany of the 1920s to promote fascism. He seized power in 1933.

Field Marshal von Hindenburg (1847–1934) became president of the German Republic in 1925. On his death, Adolf Hitler became Führer (leader).

Following Germany's defeat in 1918, Kaiser Wilhelm II abdicated and fled to the Netherlands. Germany became a republic and its new government ruled from Weimar, instead of Berlin. From 1919 to 1933, Germany was known as the Weimar Republic. Following elections in January 1919, Friedrich Ebert, a socialist, became its first president. Under his leadership, the Weimar Republic accepted the harsh terms of the Treaty of Versailles. In 1922–23, the Republic survived several attempts to bring it down, first by the Bolsheviks, then by financial pressure and finally through an attempted political revolution led by a hitherto unknown Austrian fascist called Adolf Hitler.

Ebert died in 1925 and was succeeded by Field Marshal Paul von Hindenburg who was by then 78 years old. Germany joined the League of Nations in 1926. However, the worldwide Depression of the early 1930s led to massive social and financial problems in Germany.

THE NUREMBERG RALLIES

German soldiers parade with the 'Standards of Victory' at a Nazi party rally at Nuremberg in 1933. The Nazi propaganda techniques of the 1930s were successfully used to conjure up enormous public support for Hitler. His policies were popular because they promised to make Germany powerful.

Adolf Hitler (1889–1945) was born in Austria. In World War I, he served in the German army and won the Iron Cross. Hitler became leader of the Nazi Party in 1920.

THE RISE OF ADOLF HITLER

The next presidential election was in 1932, when Germany was in economic crisis, with massive inflation and high unemployment. Hindenburg was elected as president again, with Adolf Hitler, by then the leader of the National Socialist German Workers' (Nazi) Party, in second place. Amid much intimidation and violence instigated by the followers of Hitler, the Nazi Party won the most seats in the Reichstag (German parliament), and Hindenburg reluctantly appointed Hitler as chancellor in January 1933.

When the Reichstag was burned down in February, Hitler brought in emergency powers and called new elections. By April 1933, he had gained absolute power in Germany, and established one-party rule. As a result, Germany withdrew from the League of Nations.

On the 'Night of the Long Knives' in June 1934, Hitler had many of his rivals killed. When Hindenburg died in August, Hitler was appointed Führer (leader) of the Third Reich (German empire). He set out to avenge the humiliation forced on Germany by the Versailles Peace Settlement and make Germany a powerful empire.

THE RISE OF ANTI-SEMITISM

Blaming the Jews and the labour unions for Germany's problems, Hitler and his Nazis began persecuting them. The Nuremberg Laws of 1935 deprived Jews of their German citizenship and banned them from marrying non-Jews. Many Jews were forced to live in ghettos and wear a yellow star to show that they were Jews.

On *Kristallnacht* ('night of broken glass') in November 1938, Nazi mobs attacked Jewish property and synagogues all over Germany. Some 30,000 Jews were arrested, the start of a full-scale massacre of Jews in Germany. Over the following seven years, six million Jews, gypsies, homosexuals and coloured people were sent to concentration camps.

▲ In the wake of German soldiers entering the Sudetenland, Adolf Hitler received a hero's welcome as he entered the town of Wildenau in 1938.

The deliberate burning of the Reichstag building in Berlin on February 27, 1933 was an excuse for Adolf Hitler to bring in emergency powers and call new elections.

GERMAN MILITARY EXPANSION

In 1935 Germany abolished its agreement to the armament restrictions imposed by the 1919 Versailles treaty. In 1936, its forces entered the Rhineland, an area of Germany that had been demilitarized at the end of World War I, and entered into alliances with fascist Italy and the military rulers of Japan. German forces also became involved in the Spanish Civil War, where they supported the fascist side led by General Francisco Franco.

▲ In Hitler's Germany, most Jews were forced to wear a yellow star to show that they were Jews.

KEY DATES

1919	Friedrich Ebert becomes first president of German Republic
1921	Adolf Hitler becomes leader of Nazi Party
1925	Ebert dies; Hindenberg becomes president
1933	Hitler is appointed chancellor
1934	Hindenberg dies and Hitler becomes Führer. Night of the Long Knives takes place
1935	Jews deprived of German citizenship
1936	German forces enter demilitarized Rhineland. Germany forms alliances with Italy and Japan
1938	Germany annexes Austria and the Sudetenland
1939	Germany annexes Czechoslovakia and invades Poland. World War II starts

▶ When Hitler came to power, he sought to destroy all opposition. This included the imposition of state censorship of newspapers, books and radio. In support of this, students and members of the Nazi party threw banned literature into a bonfire in Berlin in May 1933.

THE SPANISH CIVIL WAR 1936–1939

The Spanish Civil War was a battle between two opposing ideologies – fascism and socialism. Fascism won, and was followed by 36 years of rule by dictator.

Francisco Franco (1892–1975) led the rebellion against the republican government in 1936. From 1939 until his death, he ruled Spain as dictator.

Before World War I, Spain sent military expeditions to strengthen its position in Morocco in northern Africa. In 1921, the Spanish forces were defeated by the Berber leader, Abd el-Krim, and it was not until 1927 that Spain was able to subdue the Berbers. In 1923, a military defeat in Morocco led to a fascist military dictatorship in Spain headed by General Primo de Rivera.

Primo de Rivera ruled Spain until he fell from power in 1930. In the following year, King Alfonso XIII gave in to the demand for elections. The Republican Party won and the monarchy was overthrown. The government survived revolts in Asturias and Catalonia, and a new Popular Front government was elected in February 1936.

The new government under the presidency of Manuel Azana included members of the Socialist Workers Party and the Communist Party. With their support, it opposed the power of the Roman Catholic Church in Spanish affairs. The Church was supported by the army and by the fascists.

Both men and women took part in the civil war. These republican militiawomen are defending a barricade on a Barcelona street in 1936. The USSR and the International Brigade of foreign volunteers helped the republicans.

FASCISM VERSUS SOCIALISM

On July 17, 1936, Spanish army generals in Spanish Morocco began a rebellion. Led by General Francisco Franco, and supported by the nationalists or Falange Party, they invaded mainland Spain. They also had the support of the fascist governments of Italy and Germany. The rebellion led to a bitter civil war. By the end of 1936, the nationalists controlled most of western and southern Spain.

FRIENDS OF THE SPANISH REPUBLIC DONATIONS TO HAMPSTEAD

▲ During the Spanish Civil War people from many countries volunteered to fight in support of their political ideals. This British poster was designed by the artist Roland Penrose to aid fund-raising for the republican side.

▶ The nationalists were supported by the fascist governments of Italy and Germany. This photograph by the famous war photographer Robert Capa, shows nationalist militia in action against republicans on the Cordoba Front in September 1936.

BATTLEGROUND OF BELIEFS

The republicans, supported by the Soviet Union, held the urban areas to the north and east, including the cities of Barcelona, Bilbao, Madrid and Valencia. The nationalists captured Bilbao in 1937. In support of the nationalists, German dive-bombers attacked the Basque town of Guernica on April 27 of that year and killed hundreds of civilians. This was the first time that unrestricted aerial bombardment was used in wartime against civilians and marked a turning-point in modern warfare.

The Civil War was a battleground between the beliefs of fascism and socialism. People from many countries, supporting one side or the other, volunteered to travel to Spain to fight because of their political ideals.

Some 750,000 people were killed in the war before government forces surrendered, Barcelona in January 1939 and Madrid in March, to the nationalists. General Franco was declared 'Caudillo of the Realm and Head of State'.

Franco banned any opposition to the Falange Party, restored power to the Roman Catholic Church and took Spain out of the League of Nations. Although sympathetic to Hitler, he kept Spain neutral during World War II. Franco ruled Spain until his death in 1975, when the monarchy and democracy were restored.

▲ General Franco's troops are shown in battle with the republicans in the streets of Madrid during 1936. The surrender of Madrid by the republicans in March 1939 marked the end of the civil war.

▼ A turning-point in modern warfare was the unrestricted aerial bombing of civilians in the town of Guernica by German aircraft in 1937. The event is recorded in one of Pablo Picasso's most famous paintings.

GERMAN EXPANSION 1938–1939

In an attempt to keep peace in Europe, Britain and France tolerated Hitler's expanionist policies, allowing Germany to annex Austria and Czechoslovakia.

After the signing of the Munich Agreement in September 1938, Britain's prime minister, Neville Chamberlain, declared, 'I believe it is peace for our time.'

▲ Artur von Seyss-Inquart (1892–1946), the leader of the Austrian Nazis, was a member of the government. He invited the Germans to occupy his country and become part of the Third Reich. The annnexation of Austria in March 1938 brought little criticism from Britain or France.

▶ German troops entered Prague in April 1939. To appease the Nazis, Czechoslovakia was forced to return the Sudetenland to Germany in 1938. However, this was not enough for Hitler, and German forces invaded Czechoslovakia on March 15, 1939.

One of Adolf Hitler's ambitions was to unite Germany and Austria. This union had been forbidden by the Treaty of Versailles in 1919 because France and other countries thought it would make Germany too powerful. By the early 1930s, however, many people in Germany and Austria wanted their countries to unite, but in 1934, an attempted Nazi coup in Austria failed. In 1938, Hitler met with the Austrian chancellor, Kurt von Schuschnigg, and made new demands. With chaos and German troops threatening his country, Schuschnigg resigned in favour of Artur von Seyss-Inquart, leader of the Austrian Nazis. He invited German troops to occupy Austria, and the union, or *Anschluss*, of the two countries was formally announced on March 13, 1938.

Hitler also wanted to reclaim the areas of Europe given to other states by the Treaty of Versailles and which contained many people of German descent. One of these areas was the Sudetenland of Czechoslovakia. In an attempt to keep peace in Europe, the Munich Agreement was signed in September 1938.

German troops marching into Vienna in 1938. Hitler wanted to unite all German-speaking peoples into a 'Greater Germany', an important part of his vision of the third German empire (Third Reich).

The agreement gave the Sudetenland to Germany. This was part of what were seen as reasonable concessions to Hitler, and it was called 'appeasement'. But it was not enough for Hitler, and in March 1939, German troops took over Czechoslovakia. There were many protests at this, but no action was taken.

THE BEGINNING OF WORLD WAR II 1939

Hitler's confidence grew after years of appeasement, but his invasion of Poland led to a declaration of war on Germany by Britain and France.

Winston Churchill (1874–1965) became British prime minister in 1940 and led Britain during World War II.

Messerschmitt Me 109

Supermarine Spitfire

The three Axis Powers, German, Italy and Japan, all wanted more territory. After his invasion of Czechoslovakia, Hitler did not expect any international military action against his plans to expand further. To counter any military threat from the east, he signed a non-aggression pact, the Molotov–Ribbentrop Pact, with the Soviet Union in August 1939. The two countries secretly agreed to divide eastern Europe. Despite appeals from Neville Chamberlain, President Roosevelt and the pope, and feeling secure from any military threat, Hitler invaded Poland on September 1, 1939. Britain and France declared war on Germany two days later.

Troops from the Soviet Union, which had signed the non-aggression pact with Germany, then invaded Poland from the east. Poland was divided between Germany and the USSR. In April 1940, German troops invaded Denmark and Norway, and in May, they invaded Belgium, the Netherlands and France.

German forces attack the poorly equipped Polish army near the Vistula River in September 1939. Much of western Poland was taken into the Third Reich and many of its people were deported to Germany as forced labour.

In June, Italy declared war on the Allies. British forces sent to France were forced to retreat to Dunkirk, from where hundreds of thousands of them were evacuated to Britain. With most of Europe under fascist control, Hitler planned to invade Britain, while the United States stayed in isolation. In July 1940, the Luftwaffe (German air force) started to attack targets in Britain.

▲ Between July and October 1940, the German air force (Luftwaffe) bombed British cities and attacked the British air force (RAF). During these bombings, the RAF destroyed 1,733 Luftwaffe planes and lost only 915. By October 31, the British had won the Battle of Britain.

▶ On May 10, 1940, German forces invaded Holland and Belgium. British troops were sent to France in an unsuccessful attempt to halt the German advance. They were forced to retreat to the French port of Dunkirk. Between May 29 and June 4, 335,000 British and Allied troops were evacuated safely to England from the beaches around Dunkirk.

WAR IN THE WEST 1939–1945

After German successes in Europe and northern Africa, Allied victories at El Alamein and Stalingrad were a turning-point in the war, and led to Germany's defeat.

Erwin Rommel (1891–1944) was leader of the German armoured units. In northern Africa, his tanks showed their superiority over ageing British machines.

Bernard Montgomery (1887–1976) led the British forces in northern Africa and Europe. The victory of his Eighth Army at El Alamein was a major turning-point in the war.

Georgy Zhukov (1896–1974) commanded the Soviet Red Army in its struggle against the German invaders.

Dwight D. Eisenhower (1890–1969) was Supreme Allied Commander in the war and became president of the USA in 1952.

The Battle of Britain lasted until October 31, 1940, and forced Hitler to abandon his plan to invade Britain. Instead, he turned his attention to night-time bombing of Britain's industry, cities and shipyards. This lasted until May 1941, but failed to break the morale of Britain which was receiving substantial supplies and equipment from the United States.

GERMAN ADVANCES

Meanwhile, the Italians had invaded Greece and northern Africa. British forces pushed back the Italians in northern Africa, but in April 1941, Hitler's troops occupied Greece and Yugoslavia to assist Mussolini's troops. The Germans drove the British out of Greece and sent a large force, under General Rommel, to northern Africa. His superior forces succeeded in driving the British back to Egypt.

In June 1941, encouraged by military successes in the West and to gain supplies of oil, Hitler's armies launched a massive attack on Russia. The Germans drove the Russian army back as far as Leningrad, Moscow and Kiev. However, during the harsh Soviet winter, they lost a large part of their recently gained territory.

British air force (RAF) pilots rest beside a Spitfire fighter plane during a lull in the Battle of Britain. Completely outnumbered but with superior aircraft, the British pilots halted the German air force's bombing of Britain.

THE TIDE TURNS AGAINST GERMANY

In August 1941, the British prime minister, Winston Churchill, and the US president, Franklin D. Roosevelt, signed the Atlantic Charter – a declaration of freedom for all people. In December, the United States entered the war after a Japanese attack on Pearl Harbor. Meanwhile, Allied troops had been sent to northern Africa to stop Rommel's advance on Egypt. In November 1942, the Allies won the decisive battle of El Alamein in Egypt against the Germans and the Italians. To the east, the Russians launched a counterattack against German forces at Stalingrad and forced them to retreat. These two Allied victories marked the turning-point of the war in the West.

A German mortar detachment moves off in support of the infantry during the battle of Stalingrad. In November 1942, the Russians launched a surprise counterattack on the German forces attacking the city and forced them to retreat.

By 1941, Germany had conquered most of Europe apart from Britain, and was expanding into North Africa. From June 1940, Vichy France was ruled from the town of Vichy by Marshal Pétain as a stooge of the Germans.

A British Halifax bomber flies over the target during a daylight bombing raid on the oil plant at Wanne-Eickel in the Ruhr in 1944. The heavy bombing of German industry and cities by Allied air forces was a significant factor in the final defeat of Germany.

Throughout 1942 and 1943, German U-boats attacked ships carrying supplies and equipment to Britain. This threat was countered by protection from naval ships and aircraft. In 1943, Britain and the USA started bombing German industry and cities. In July, British and US forces landed in Sicily, and by September, had landed in Italy. This brought about the downfall of Mussolini and the surrender of Italy.

When France fell in 1940, General Charles de Gaulle became the leader of the Free French. He served as president of France in 1945 and 1959.

FINAL DEFEAT OF GERMANY

On the Eastern front, Russian troops were slowly driving the Germans back to their homeland. A second front was opened on D-Day, June 6, 1944, with the Allied invasion of Normandy, France. The Germans launched a counter-offensive but had to retreat in January 1945. The Soviet army began to march toward Berlin. The Allies reached the German border by December. By March, the Allies had crossed the Rhine and the Soviets had reached Berlin. Hitler killed himself on April 30. On May 7, Germany surrendered unconditionally.

THE HOLOCAUST

The Allies soon discovered the most extreme example of genocide in history – twelve million Jews, gypsies, homosexuals and other victims of Hitler's persecution exterminated, mostly in concentration camps. Around half were Jewish and the survivors settled in many countries.

On D-Day, June 6, 1944, Allied forces landed on the coast of Normandy. 1,200 warships and 4,100 landing craft put 132,500 men ashore, while 10,000 aircraft attacked German positions. The D-Day landings allowed Allied troops to drive the Germans out of France.

WAR IN THE PACIFIC 1941–1945

The Japanese attack on Pearl Harbor catapulted the United States into World War II. After initial successes, the Japanese were slowly driven back to their homeland.

Admiral Yamamoto Isoroku (1884-1943) planned Japan's attack on Pearl Harbor. In April 1943, while flying to inspect Japanese forces in the Solomon Islands, his route was located by Allied code-breakers listening to Japanese radio signals. He was killed when American fighters shot his plane down.

Since September 1940, Japan had allied itself with Germany and Italy, but had not been involved in the fighting. After Japan's invasion of China in 1937, it had come under increasing pressure from the United States to withdraw its forces from that country. The war in the Pacific began on December 7, 1941, when Japanese aircraft from six aircraft carriers carried out an unprovoked attack on the US naval base at Pearl Harbor, Hawaii. More than 2,400 American soldiers and sailors were killed, and 18 major naval ships were destroyed or severely damaged. The Japanese lost fewer than 100 men. Japanese forces invaded Thailand on the same day. On the following day, the US Congress declared war on Japan. Germany and Italy then declared war on the USA.

The US battleships *Tennessee* and *West Virginia* on fire after the Japanese attack on Pearl Harbor on December 7, 1941. In the attack, 18 major US ships, including eight battleships, were destroyed or severely damaged.

JAPANESE KAMIKAZE PILOTS

Kamikaze means 'divine wind', a reference to a heaven-sent gale which scattered the ships of a Mongol invasion fleet in 1281. Towards the end of the war in the Pacific, there was no shortage of Japanese pilots who volunteered to die for their emperor by diving their aircraft, laden with bombs, straight into an Allied ship. More than half the total number of 2,900 Kamikaze sorties were flown during the defence of the island of Okinawa. The most common Kamikaze plane used was the *Zero* fighter.

▼ Kamikaze attacks were first mounted by the Japanese Imperial Navy on October 25, 1944, during the battle of Leyte Gulf. During the war, around 300 Allied ships were hit by Kamikaze attacks.

▲ Kamikaze pilots often performed rituals before takeoff, and wore a special scarf.

On December 10, 1941, the British battleship *Prince of Wales* and the battle-cruiser *Repulse* were sunk in the Gulf of Siam by Japanese aircraft. With the US and British fleets severely damaged, the Japanese now thought that they had complete control of the Pacific. Within five months, their forces had overrun Burma, Hong Kong, Singapore, Malaya, the Dutch East Indies (Indonesia), Thailand and the Philippines. They also invaded New Guinea and threatened the north coast of Australia. With most of its own troops and equipment helping the Allies in Europe, Australia had to look to the United States for defence.

JAPANESE LOSSES AT SEA

However, not all of the US fleet had been sunk at Pearl Harbor. Three US aircraft carriers were at sea at the time of the attack, and they were soon joined by two new carriers. Japanese hopes of further expansion were stopped in 1942 by two major sea battles.

The battle of the Coral Sea (May 4–8) was the first in naval history in which enemy ships were out of sight of each other during the fighting. It was fought by aircraft launched from aircraft carriers. There was no clear winner, but the battle did halt Japanese plans to invade Australia. In June, the Japanese planned to invade the small but strategic island of Midway and the Aleutian Islands. But first they had to destroy US aircraft based on Midway. However, the US had cracked Japanese radio codes and were prepared for the attack.

In the battle of Midway (June 4–6) the Japanese navy was so severely damaged by US carrier-borne aircraft that it retreated. Midway was a decisive victory for the US forces and a turning-point in the war. With the Japanese advance halted, the task of recapturing territory began.

Over the following three years, the US regained the Gilbert, Marshall, Caroline and Mariana islands. From there, they could bomb Japanese cities and industry. In September 1944, US forces began to retake the Philippines, while the British Fourth Army began to reconquer Burma. After fierce fighting, US forces took the Japanese islands of Okinawa and Iwo Jima in early 1945.

▲ Following their victory at Midway, the Americans took the island of Guadalcanal in August 1942. Following in their footsteps, New Zealand troops come ashore at Guadalcanal Bay in November 1943.

▼ Dislodging the Japanese from the jungles of Burma was a difficult task. In the early stages of the war a small British force under General Wingate, known as the Chindits, operated many kilometres behind Japanese lines.

KEY DATES

1941 December 7 – Japan attacks US Pacific Fleet in Pearl Harbor, Hawaii. United States declares war on Japan. Japanese sink British warships in Gulf of Siam

1942 Japanese overrun Hong Kong, Burma, Thailand, Singapore, Malaya, Dutch East Indies and the Philippines. Battles of Coral Sea, Midway and Guadalcanal

1944 Battle of Leyte Gulf. US forces recapture the Philippines

1945 US forces take islands of Okinawa and Iwo Jima. US air force drops atomic bombs on Hiroshima and Nagasaki. Japan surrenders on August 14

PEACE IN THE PACIFIC 1945–1948

With the US forces on their doorstep, the Japanese were prepared to fight to the last man. The dropping of two atomic bombs forced them into surrender.

Japanese representatives wait to sign the formal statement of surrender with General Douglas MacArthur on board the US battleship *Missouri* on September 2, 1945.

When the island of Okinawa was taken, more than 100,000 Japanese and 12,000 American soldiers were killed. After these enormous losses, Allied commanders were fearful of the deaths that would be incurred if they invaded the Japanese mainland. They knew that the Japanese would fight to their last drop of blood to defend their country, and estimated that up to a million Allied soldiers would die in the invasion.

In the United States, Roosevelt had been elected to his third term of office as president in 1944. Meanwhile, amid great secrecy, American scientists had been developing a new and terrible weapon – the atomic bomb. Roosevelt died on April 12, 1945 and his successor Harry Truman made the major decision to drop the new atomic bomb on Japan.

JAPANESE SURRENDER

Truman argued that the use of atomic bombs would quickly end the war and possibly save millions of Allied soldiers' lives. At the end of July 1945, the Allies gave Japan an ultimatum threatening complete destruction if Japan did not surrender. No Japanese surrender was forthcoming, so an atomic bomb was dropped on Hiroshima on August 6, 1945. It killed about 130,000 people. Three days later a second atomic bomb was dropped on the city of Nagasaki and caused up to 750,000 deaths. Thousands more died later from injuries and radiation sickness. The use of these bombs finally persuaded the Japanese to surrender on August 14.

World War II ended when the Japanese formally surrendered on September 2, 1945. More than two million Japanese had been killed in World War II, 100 of their cities were destroyed by bombing and industrial production had practically ceased. It took ten years for Japanese industry to regain its pre-war levels.

THE BOMBING OF HIROSHIMA

The development of the atomic bomb by US scientists had been kept secret. There were only two atomic bombs used in war. The five-tonne 'Little Boy' was dropped on Hiroshima (below) by an American B-29 Superfortress *Enola Gay* on August 6, 1945. Three days later, a second atomic bomb, 'Fat Man' was dropped from another Superfortress *Bockstar* to destroy the city of Nagasaki.

The Boeing B-29 Superfortress bomber was the largest bomber used in World War II.

THE UNITED NATIONS 1945–1948

At the end of World War II, the victorious Allied powers divided Germany into four zones. The United Nations was established to keep international peace.

At the Yalta Conference in February 1945, the 'Big Three' Allied powers, represented by their leaders Churchill, Roosevelt and Stalin, decided to divide Germany into four zones after the war.

Following the Yalta Conference, the division of Germany was confirmed by the 'Big Three' Allied powers at the Potsdam Conference. By this time, Roosevelt had died and been replaced by Harry S. Truman as the new US president. Britain was represented by their prime minister, Clement Attlee. Germany also lost some of its territory to Poland and the USSR. Countries conquered by Germany and Japan regained their former status. But the influence of the Soviet Union increased when Bulgaria, Hungary, Poland, Romania, Czechoslovakia, Yugoslavia and eastern Germany became communist states. The US promised to help all free peoples who felt threatened (the Truman Doctrine) and provided the Marshall Plan for economic recovery.

On April 25, 1945, the UN organization was set up formally at a conference in San Francisco. It aimed to keep international peace and solve problems by international co-operation.

THE UNITED NATIONS

The term 'United Nations' (UN) was first used in January 1942 when the Atlantic Charter was signed by the Allies. In the Charter, they agreed to fight the Axis countries and not to make any separate peace agreements. The UN planned to be stronger than the League of Nations had been. It had a powerful Security Council which would decide what should be done if disputes broke out. Members were to contribute arms and personnel to peacekeeping missions organized by the UN. In 1948, the UN isssued a Universal Déclaration of Human Rights which was not binding.

▲ The Potsdam Declaration of 1945 made it possible to bring Nazi war criminals to justice in war trials held first in Berlin, and then in Nuremburg. Here, former Nazi leaders, Hermann Goering, Rudolf Hess and Joachim von Ribbentrop await cross-examination at the trials. All three were found guilty. Goering committed suicide just hours before his execution; Hess received a life sentence and died in 1987 in Spandau prison; von Ribbentrop was hung, along with nine other high-ranking Nazis on October 16, 1946.

▶ On June 25, 1948, the Soviet Union set up a blockade around Berlin to try and force France, Britain and the USA to give up their rights to the western part of Berlin. To feed the population, Britain and the USA flew supplies into the city for 15 months until the blockade was lifted.

ISRAEL 1948–1949

Growing demands for a separate Jewish state and the flood of refugees from Europe forced the British to withdraw from Palestine. Israel became a reality.

David Ben-Gurion (1886–1973) was born in Poland. As a young man he went to live in Palestine and in 1930 became leader of the Mapai Party. In 1948, he announced the state of Israel and became its first prime minister.

Until the end of World War I, Palestine was part of the Ottoman empire. It was inhabited by Arabs and a growing number of Jews who wanted to settle in a Jewish homeland. When the Ottoman empire collapsed, Palestine was ruled by Britain under a League of Nations' mandate. In 1917, Britain had promised its support to establish a Jewish homeland in Palestine. However, more Jews began arriving during the 1930s as problems grew in Europe.

Between 1922 and 1939, the Jewish poulation in Palestine had risen from 83,000 to 445,000 and Tel Aviv had become a Jewish city with a population of 150,000. The Arabs resented this and fighting often broke out between the two groups. After World War II, more Jewish people wanted to move to Palestine. Under pressure from the Arabs, Britain restricted the number of new settlers allowed. This led Jewish terrorists to attack both the Arabs and the British.

The new state of Israel was surrounded by Arab states. On May 14, 1948, the Arab League of Lebanon, Syria, Iraq, Jordan and Egypt declared war on Israel and attacked it. They were defeated and Israel increased its territory.

A secret Jewish army called Haganah (self-defence) was formed in 1920. More extremist groups were later formed, notably Irgun and the Stern Gang. Both groups thought that Britain had betrayed the Zionist cause – to establish a Jewish state in Palestine – and took part in a violent terrorist campaign against the Arabs and the British. Jewish leaders such as Chaim Weizmann and David Ben-Gurion took a more peaceful approach.

▲ One result of the hostility between the Arabs and Jews in 1948 was the migration of nearly one million Arabs from Palestine. They left their homes and became refugees because they were afraid of the action Israel might take after the war with the Arab League.

▶ After World War II, the number of Jewish refugees from Europe trying to enter Palestine became a problem for the British. In October 1947, the ship *Jewish State* arrived at the port of Haifa with 2,000 illegal Jewish immigrants aboard.

By June 1945, an enormous number of Jewish refugees, displaced by the war in Europe, were clamouring to live in Palestine. Despite British efforts to stop them, the number of refugees entering the country continued to increase. Pressure was brought to bear on Britain by the United States to allow the admission of 100,000 refugees, but Britain refused. It soon found itself involved in a full-scale war with Jewish terrorist organizations.

THE NEW STATE OF ISRAEL

Unwilling to be caught up in another bloody and costly war, Britain took the matter to the United Nations. In 1947, the UN voted to divide Palestine into two states. One would be Jewish and the other one Arab. Jerusalem, which was sacred to Jews, Muslims and Christians, would be international. The Jews agreed to this, but the Arabs did not.

On May 14, 1948, Britain gave up its mandate to rule Palestine and withdrew its troops. On the same day the Jews, led by Mapai Party leader David Ben-Gurion, proclaimed the state of Israel, and its legitimacy was immediately recognized by the governments of the United States and the Soviet Union.

Israel was attacked by the surrounding Arab League states of Lebanon, Syria, Iraq, Jordan and Egypt. Israel defeated them and increased its territory by a quarter. Nearly one million Palestinian refugees, afraid of Jewish rule, fled to neighbouring Arab countries. The United Nations negotiated a ceasefire in 1949, but conflicts between Israel and its Arab neighbours continue to this day.

During the War of Independence, Jewish Haganah militiamen watch over the road to Jaffa. This important position was captured by them on April 17, 1948 after stiff Arab resistance.

Members of Haganah, the Jewish defence force, keep a sharp lookout for possible Arab looters in the destroyed Jewish border city quarter between Jaffa and Tel Aviv, the scene of constant disorder.

▲ The Israeli flag was raised at Eilat on the Gulf of Aqaba in 1949. It is Israel's most southerly point and its only port on the Red Sea.

BRITISH COMMONWEALTH 1914–1949

In 1931, the countries that formed the British empire joined together to form the Commonwealth. Over the next 60 years, they were given their independence.

During both World Wars, soldiers from all corners of the British empire and Commonwealth fought on the side of Britain. Here, members of the Rhodesian Air Askari Corps practise square drill in 1943.

The relationship between Britain and parts of its empire had begun to change by the beginning of the 20th century. Some of the larger countries became independent as British dominions. They were self-governing, but they kept strong links with Britain. Dominions retained the British Crown (king or queen) as the symbolic head of state. Each dominion had a lieutenant governor, a native resident of that country. He or she represented the Crown.

In the 1920s, the dominions asked for a clear definition of their relationship with Britain. This was given in 1931 in the Statute of Westminster when dominions were defined as 'autonomous (self-ruling) communities within the British empire, equal in status ... united by a common allegiance to the Crown and freely associated as members of the British Commonwealth of Nations'. After this statute, the name British Commonwealth of Nations was used instead of British empire, and many colonies started to clamour for independence.

▼ Commonwealth premiers pose with King George VI at Buckingham Palace while in London attending the Conference of Commonwealth Prime Ministers in April 1949.

INDEPENDENT MEMBERS OF THE COMMONWEALTH

Antigua and Barbuda 1981	Nauru 1968
Australia 1901	New Zealand 1907
Bahamas 1973	Nigeria 1960
Bangladesh 1972	Pakistan 1947
Barbados 1966	Papua New Guinea 1975
Belize 1981	St Kitts-Nevis 1983
Botswana 1966	St Lucia 1979
Brunei 1984	St Vincent & the Grenadines
Canada 1931	1979
Cyprus 1960	Seychelles 1976
Dominica 1978	Sierra Leone 1961
Gambia 1965	Singapore 1965
Ghana 1957	Solomon Islands 1978
Grenada 1974	South Africa 1994
Guyana 1966	Sri Lanka (Ceylon) 1948
India 1947	Swaziland 1968
Jamaica 1962	Tanzania 1961
Kenya 1963	Tonga 1970
Kiribati 1979	Trinidad and Tobago 1962
Lesotho 1966	Tuvalu 1978
Malawi 1964	Uganda 1962
Malaysia 1957	United Kingdom 1931
Maldives 1965	Vanuatu 1980
Malta 1964	Western Samoa 1962
Mauritius 1968	Zambia 1964
Namibia 1990	Zimbabwe 1980

In 1932, the dominions received better terms for trading with Britain than countries outside the Commonwealth. Canada, Australia, New Zealand and South Africa had all become dominions before World War I. The Irish Free State also became a dominion in 1921. The first three to gain their independence after World War II were India (1947), Ceylon (1948) and Burma (1948). India and Ceylon (Sri Lanka) stayed in the Commonwealth, but Burma did not join, and the Republic of Ireland left in 1949.

COMMUNIST CHINA 1945–1949

**After the defeat of Japan in 1945, the Chinese
nationalists and communists resumed their civil war.
In 1949, the People's Republic of China was declared.**

The communists introduced a system of collective farming to China. This meant that all the land, buildings and machinery belonged to the community. Committees in each village decided what to grow. One improvement was they replaced their oxen with tractors, which they called 'Iron Oxen'.

In 1936, the Chinese nationalist leader, Chiang Kai-shek, was forced to make an alliance with the Communist Party to fight against the Japanese in Manchuria. This alliance lasted until 1945 and brought China into World War II on the Allies' side. While the Chinese were fighting the Japanese, Britain and the USA provided them with aid. After the defeat of Japan in 1945, the alliance collapsed and civil war broke out in 1946. The nationalists were weak and divided, but Mao Zedong's communists had the support of the people. The communists also had a large army, and by January 1949, they had taken Tianjin and Beijing (Peking). From there they moved southwards, where they defeated Chiang Kai-shek and the nationalists and took control of the whole country. The People's Republic of China was declared on October 1, 1949, but many countries refused to recognize it.

The People's Republic of China came into being on October 1, 1949. In the following years, the Chinese communist leader Mao Zedong introduced reforms in the countryside in order to gain the support of the people. This 1949 poster for the Chinese Communist Party shows farmers and soldiers working together.

Large posters of Communist Party leaders formed the backdrop to speeches at a meeting of the Communist Party in Shanghai. When they took power in 1949, the communists soon moved to control the press and nationalized industries.

THE MODERN WORLD

1950 – 2000

The years between 1950 and the present day are recent history. Some of the events may have occurred during our lifetime, or we may have seen reports of them on television. The latter half of the 20th century has seen social, technological and environmental changes on a scale never witnessed before. Politicians and policy-makers, as well as historians, have identified several important trends which will continue to transform our world: environmental pollution, ever-increasing populations, changing family structures, and a growing gap between rich and poor, people and countries.

▲ Aircraft carriers from Britain and the USA played an important peace-keeping role in the 1990s in various world trouble spots, such as the Middle East and Yugoslavia.

◄ The Space Shuttle *Discovery* blasts off from the Kennedy Space Centre at the beginning of its 21st spaceflight in July 1995.

THE WORLD AT A GLANCE 1950–2000

This period was dominated by the Cold War between communist nations and the capitalist West. The United States and the USSR played leading parts. These two were also involved in the space race. The USSR was the first to send a man into space, and the USA the first to put a man on the Moon. Changes in the USSR led to the end of the Cold War but created uncertainty about the future as nationalists demanded independence.

In western Europe, the European Union encouraged economic growth and worked towards political union. In Africa, many nations became independent, but faced severe economic problems as well as droughts and famines. In southeast Asia, technology and industry developed, and Japanese business became the most successful in the world. China experienced a cultural revolution and Indochina was devastated by a whole series of wars.

NORTH AMERICA

This half-century was the high point of development of the USA, which led the way materially and culturally. By now, the US west coast was as much a centre for the film and aircraft industries as the east coast, and home to many futuristic ideas. The USA led the way in the nuclear arms race and was equal to the USSR in the space race. The 1950s saw growing prosperity, though this led to troubles in the 1960s over civil rights and social issues. American culture reached its high point in music, films, inventions and new ideas in the 1970s, though rocked by war in Vietnam and the exposure of government corruption. In the 1980s, computer technology and free-market economics brought economic boom, the space shuttle and the end of the Cold War. In the 1990s, Asia made great strides catching up, and USA became more multi-cultural. The USA acted as a global policeman in a complex world, and its internal politics have never been settled. Yet this was its greatest time in history. The American culture of Coca-Cola, Disney and Boeings spread to every corner of the world.

NORTH AMERICA

CENTRAL AND SOUTH AMERICA

CENTRAL AND SOUTH AMERICA

Until the 1970s, there was a battle between right-wing dictators and left-wing revolutionaries in Latin America. Poverty, power and guerrilla wars were the big issues. As the continent grew richer and more liberal governments came to power, these pressures eased. The Catholic Church also lost ground, and rainforest destruction, government corruption, human rights and the drugs trade grew as new issues. Civil wars in countries like Peru and Nicaragua were resolved, and in the 1990s Latin America, now industrialized, played an increasing role in global affairs.

EUROPE

Ruined by World War II and overshadowed by the Cold War, Europe made a dramatic recovery in the 1950s–1970s, beginning a long process of co-operation through the founding of the European Community. Europe worked with a 'social market' model of economics, with ample welfare and social systems which, by the 1990s, became a burden. Despite crises, such as the Hungarian uprising of 1956 and the 'Prague Spring' of 1968, Europe remained in peace. The greatest breakthrough was the ending of the Cold War, which reunited Germany and brought reconciliation between east and west, though ugly scenes such as the Yugoslavian civil wars of the 1990s hindered progress. Environmental and social concerns were important, especially after the Russian nuclear disaster at Chernobyl in 1986. Europe began to play a more equal role in the world community than in previous centuries.

ASIA

During this period, the fortunes of Asia rose again. The Maoist era in China brought mixed results, some impressive, some disastrous. They led to reforms in the 1980s and to China's re-entry into the world's market economy. Japan became the economic and technological powerhouse of Asia, and fuelled great economic growth in southeast Asia from the early 1970s. India modernized in the 1970s, though conflicts continued with Pakistan. The withdrawal of colonial powers, the Vietnam War, the rise of Islamic and Confucian values, the fall of the USSR in Central Asia and the globalization of the world economy have all had a great effect on Asia.

EUROPE

ASIA

MIDDLE EAST

AFRICA

AUSTRALASIA

Australia and New Zealand became leading countries, although they had to get used to being neighbours to Asia. Australia became one of the world's wealthiest countries. Polynesia became a tourist destination, but also a place for atomic bomb testing.

AUSTRALASIA

AFRICA

After a promising start in the 1960s, when most states gained independence, Africa was troubled with wars, corruption, famine and social crises. Foreign interference and over-exploitation were common. In South Africa, torn by apartheid, reform came in 1990 and brought the dawn of a new multi-racial society.t Africa remains troubled but lessons learned may lead to great future improvements.

MIDDLE EAST

Oil-rich, the Middle East witnessed great extremes of wealth and suffering during this period. Rising Islamic fundamentalism had mixed outcomes, disturbing peace, yet helping the poor and downtrodden. Caught between different world powers, war and interference by foreign powers were common.

THE COLD WAR 1945–1989

After the end of World War II, tensions between East and West and the build-up of nuclear weapons almost brought the world to the brink of a third world war.

A 1962 cartoon, produced at the time of the Cuba missile crisis, shows the two superpower leaders arm-wrestling for power. The USSR's Nikita Khrushchev (1894–1971), on the left, faces the US president John F. Kennedy (1917–63). They are both sitting on their own nuclear weapons.

The USSR and the USA fought together as allies against Germany and Japan in World War II, but in 1945, these two great countries, known as superpowers, became rivals and then enemies. This division became known as the Cold War, a war conducted in the main without fighting. The USA and USSR 'fought' by making threats and by strengthening their armed forces.

Both countries built up an enormous stockpile of nuclear weapons. Peaceful, friendly contacts between their peoples ceased. The USSR became completely shut off from the rest of the world by Soviet troops. The British statesman Sir Winston Churchill memorably described the frontier between East and West as an 'iron curtain' in a speech that he gave in Missouri, USA, on March 5, 1946.

The Cold War dominated world politics for many years. On one side, the United States became the leader of NATO, a military alliance of Western nations ranged against the communist powers. On the other side, the USSR dominated the Warsaw Pact, a military alliance of East European states that backed communism.

Because of the serious threat of nuclear war between East and West during the 1960s, many Americans built fall-out shelters in their back gardens.

BERLIN: THE DIVIDED CITY

In 1945, the USA, France and Britain took control of West Germany and the USSR controlled East Germany. The capital, Berlin, inside East Germany, was also divided, and in 1948, the Soviets closed all access to west Berlin. The Western powers brought in essential supplies by air until the Russians lifted the blockade in May 1949. From 1949 to 1958, three million people escaped from east to west Berlin. In 1961, East Germany closed off this escape route by building the Berlin Wall through the centre of the city. It crossed tramlines and roads, and created an area on either side known as no man's land.

▲ The Berlin Wall, built in 1961 to divide east and west Berlin, finally fell in November 1989.

▶ By 1949, most European states had joined rival alliances. Warsaw pact countries supported the USSR. Members of NATO backed the USA.

NATO countries in Europe

Warsaw Pact

NORWAY — FINLAND — SWEDEN — NETHERLANDS — IRELAND — DENMARK — USSR — GREAT BRITAIN — EAST GERMANY — BELGIUM — WEST GERMANY — POLAND — LUXEMBOURG — CZECHOSLOVAKIA — SWITZERLAND — FRANCE — AUSTRIA — HUNGARY — PORTUGAL — SPAIN — ITALY — YUGOSLAVIA — ROMANIA — BULGARIA — ALBANIA — TURKEY — GREECE

CUBAN MISSILE CRISIS

Although the USA and the USSR never actually fought, they came close to it. The world held its breath for a whole week in October 1962 when the US president, John F. Kennedy, received air force photographs showing that the USSR was building missile launch sites in Cuba. From there, the nuclear missiles could reach and destroy many US cities. On October 22, the president ordered a naval blockade of Cuba. The United States made plans to invade Cuba, and the world braced itself for nuclear war. Finally, on October 28, Nikita Khrushchev, the Soviet leader, backed down and agreed to remove the missiles and destroy the Cuban launch sites. The crisis was over.

THE END OF THE COLD WAR

In the 1980s, the friendly relationship between US president Ronald Reagan and the Soviet leader Mikhail Gorbachev helped to reduce Cold War tensions, and by 1987, they had agreed to abolish medium-range nuclear missiles. In 1989, Gorbachev allowed the communist countries of eastern Europe to elect democratic governments, and in 1991, the USSR broke up into 15 republics. The Cold War was over. On March 12, 1999, Hungary, Poland and the Czech Republic joined NATO. The joining ceremony was held at the Harry S. Truman memorial library in Independence, Missouri, in the United States.

◀ Francis Gary Powers was the pilot of an American U-2 spy plane which was shot down over Soviet territory in 1960. He was released in exchange for the imprisoned Soviet spymaster Rudolf Abel.

▼ Czech students tried to stop Soviet tanks in Prague, in August 1968. The USSR feared that independent actions by Warsaw Pact members might weaken its power, so the Russians moved into Czechoslovakia.

▶ During the Cold War, many groups of people, such as the Peace Pledge Union, were formed to try and influence governments and stop the spread of nuclear weapons.

◀ Supporters of the Campaign for Nuclear Disarmament (CND) marched through London in 1983 to demonstrate against the deployment of Cruise and Trident nuclear missiles on British soil.

IN SPACE 1957–2000

Space exploration began in 1957 when the USSR launched Sputnik I, the first artificial satellite to orbit the Earth. In 1969, the first man walked on the Moon.

The development of technology during World War II helped scientists to realize that one day it might be possible for people to travel in space. Cold War rivalry between the USA and the USSR triggered a space race. Both sides felt that being the first nation in space would increase their prestige. They also hoped that space science would help them develop new, more powerful weapons.

The Soviets achieved the first 'space first' when they sent a satellite into orbit around the Earth in 1957. Soon, both sides were investing enormous amounts of time and money in space science. The Soviets achieved another space first in 1961 when Yuri Gagarin became the first man in space. Other notable achievements by both countries included probes being sent to the Moon and past Venus, further manned flights, spacewalks and the launch of communications satellites.

The Apollo programme of space flights enabled the USA to land men on the Moon. Between July 1969 and December 1972, the USA successfully carried out six of these missions, the last three involving the use of a Lunar Roving Vehicle.

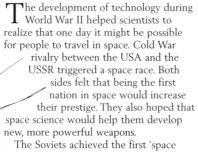

Sputnik 1 was launched by Russia on October 4, 1957. The satellite was used to broadcast scientific data and orbited the Earth for six months.

Russian cosmonaut Yuri Gagarin in the cabin of Vostok 1, the spacecraft in which he became the first person to orbit the Earth on April 12, 1961.

In the run-up to the Apollo flights, the American Gemini programme was designed to teach astronauts how to cope with space travel. In November 1966 'Buzz' Aldrin carried out three spacewalks high over the Earth.

The ending of the Cold War and the economic crisis of the 1970s led the two superpowers to scale down their space programme. However, the Soviets gained valuable experience with long-endurance flights on permanent space stations. Co-operation between the two countries is important for the future construction of an international space station.

MAN ON THE MOON

In 1961, the United States president, John F. Kennedy, said that his scientists would send a man to the Moon by 1970. In fact, the first manned Moon landing took place on July 20, 1969 with the American *Apollo 11* mission. The crew consisted of Neil Armstrong, the first man to set foot on the Moon, Edwin 'Buzz' Aldrin, who was the second man to walk on the Moon, and Michael Collins who remained in lunar orbit in the command and service module. Armstrong described walking on the Moon as "one small step for a man, one giant leap for mankind".

◀ *Apollo 11* was launched from Cape Canaveral, Florida, on July 16, 1969 and made the first manned landing on the Moon just four days later.

SPACE SHUTTLES

In the USA, the National Aeronautics & Space Administration (NASA) required a reusable space vehicle to construct and serve planned space stations. The space shuttle could take off like a rocket – with a large payload – and return to Earth like a plane. The launch of the first shuttle in 1981 marked a new phase in space exploration. Since that first flight, space shuttles have carried a variety of payloads and retrieved and repaired satellites. In 1995, the space shuttle *Atlantis* docked with the Russian space station *Mir*, marking an important step forward in international co-operation.

▲ This picture of the dusty, rock-strewn surface of Mars, was taken by one of the two US Viking landers in 1975. Part of the spacecraft is visible in the foreground.

The Soviet space station *Mir* was launched in 1986. It was designed to stay in orbit for long periods, so that complicated scientific experiments could be carried out on board. It has now far exceeded its planned life. Although it requires fairly constant repair and maintenance, the station is still manned after 13 years' service.

EXPLORING DEEP SPACE

Unmanned space probes have flown by, or landed on, every planet in the solar system except Pluto. Soviet probes succeeded in landing on Venus in 1975 and sent back pictures. In 1976, two US Viking craft landed on Mars and began observations that lasted for six years. In 1977, the US launched the two Voyager missions which travelled round the solar system using the 'slingshot' technique – the spacecraft being flung from planet to planet by their gravitational fields. Before they disappeared into deep space, they transmitted valuable data and colour photographs of Jupiter, Saturn, Uranus and Neptune.

The Hubble space telescope, launched by the US in 1990, enabled scientists to produce high-resolution images of objects billions of light years way, and provided valuable information about the Universe.

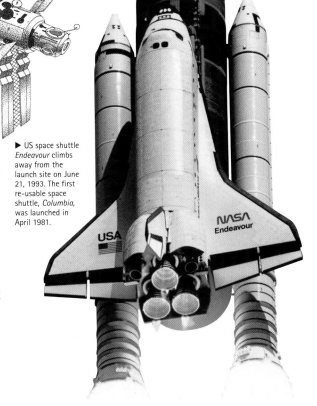

▶ US space shuttle *Endeavour* climbs away from the launch site on June 21, 1993. The first re-usable space shuttle, *Columbia*, was launched in April 1981.

WORLD ECONOMY 1950 – 2000

The industrialized countries of the world had improved their standard of living since 1950, but many poorer countries saw little or no improvement.

The flag of the European Union, the successor to the European Economic Community first formed after the two Treaties of Rome in March 1957. The EU currently includes 15 member states.

▼ There was panic trading on the floor of the New York Stock Exchange in October 1987. In that year, stockmarkets around the world suffered a dramatic downward revaluation in the value of shares.

After the end of World War II, the USA and many countries in western Europe enjoyed a rapid growth in their economies. After the war, there was an enormous amount of re-building to be done, particularly in Europe. There was full employment and the amount people were paid, compared to what things cost to buy, steadily climbed. This rise in 'standard of living' also applied to a slightly lesser extent to countries such as Australia and New Zealand, as well as southeast Asian states such as Hong Kong, Singapore and Taiwan.

This prosperity came to a sudden halt in 1973 when the price of crude oil started to increase. The Organization of Petroleum Exporting Countries (OPEC) was founded in 1960 to get the best price on world markets for its member states' oil. OPEC members include many Middle Eastern Arab states as well as Venezuela, Algeria, Indonesia, Nigeria and the Gabon. Between 1973 and 1974, OPEC

The OECD (Organization for Economic Co-operation and Development) was created to protect weak nations from powerful market forces and aid economic development.

quadrupled the price of oil, and this led to a worldwide energy crisis. Poorer nations were badly hit by the rise in oil prices. By 1981, this had increased almost twenty times and their economies had to be supported by loans from the West. In the advanced nations, the energy crisis caused inflation, because the rise in oil prices was passed on in the form of raised prices for goods, and unemployment everywhere rose as less goods were exported.

COMMON MARKETS

Throughout the world, neighbouring states, or states with shared economic interests, have joined together to form powerful international associations. Some groups of states have also set up economic communities known as 'common markets'. Within these markets, members buy and sell at favourable rates. They agree to protect one another from economic competition from the outside.

In Asia, there are the Asia-Pacific Economic Co-operation Group (APEC) and the Association of Southeast Asian Nations (ASEAN). The North American Free Trade Agreement (NAFTA), originally the US and Canada, now includes Mexico. The Group of Seven, or G-7, is a group of major countries that meets to monitor the world economic situation. The European Community (EU) is the successor of the European Economic Community (EEC) of the 1950s. It has 15 members and forms a significant world trading-block. There are currently plans for a single European currency, as well as taxation and legal systems.

The collapse of the Soviet Union in the early 1990s meant that the former communist countries had to compete with other third world countries. While the richer Western nations provided aid to poorer countries in the past, they remained reluctant to share a substantial part of their wealth or expertise.

By the 1990s, it was estimated that the world's oil reserves amounted to around 700 billion barrels, of which 360 billion barrels were to be found in the Middle East.

▲ The European Currency Unit (ECU) is the proposed currency that will be used by members of the European Union instead of their own individual currencies.

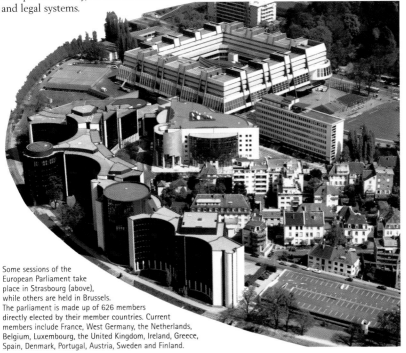

Some sessions of the European Parliament take place in Strasbourg (above), while others are held in Brussels. The parliament is made up of 626 members directly elected by their member countries. Current members include France, West Germany, the Netherlands, Belgium, Luxembourg, the United Kingdom, Ireland, Greece, Spain, Denmark, Portugal, Austria, Sweden and Finland.

WARS IN ASIA 1950–1988

Japan's defeat and the collapse of colonial rule led to fighting between political rivals throughout Asia. The superpowers took sides and began to join in.

In 1950, many countries in the East had still not recovered from Japanese invasions during World War II. People needed peace and stability, but many nations were at war. These wars caused further damage to people, cities and the land. Eastern countries no longer wished to be colonies of distant European powers. And the old colonial masters (France, Britain and the Netherlands) wanted to hold on to these potentially rich lands.

Australian soldiers were part of the United Nations forces that by the end of 1950 had pushed the North Koreans back as far as the border with China.

Fighting broke out in Vietnam and its neighbours Laos, Thailand and Cambodia, as well as in Indonesia, Malaysia, Burma and the Philippines. These wars were often complicated by political differences between rival groups seeking independence. The situation became more dangerous still when the Soviet, Chinese and American superpowers joined in with offers of money, weapons or technical advice for one side or the other.

▼ Fighting between rival political groups flared up in many parts of Asia between 1946 and 1988 following Japan's defeat in World War II and the collapse of European colonial power.

In 1945, French colonial rule was restored to Vietnam. French Foreign Legion troops were sent to North Vietnam in 1953 to try to suppress a communist uprising.

THE KOREAN WAR

The Korean War began when communist North Korea attacked South Korea in June 1950. The United Nations quickly authorized its members to aid South Korea. The United States, together with 16 other countries, began sending in troops. Within two months, North Korean troops had captured most of South Korea. In September 1950, UN forces mounted a massive land, sea and air assault at Inchon, near Seoul. The UN troops recaptured most of South Korea and advanced into the North. By November, they had reached the North Korean border with China. Chinese troops then entered the fighting and forced the UN forces to retreat south. A ceasefire ended the war in July 1953.

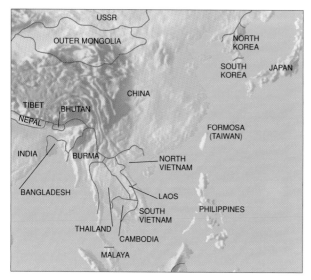

USSR

OUTER MONGOLIA

NORTH KOREA

SOUTH KOREA   JAPAN

CHINA

TIBET   BHUTAN

NEPAL

FORMOSA (TAIWAN)

INDIA   BURMA

NORTH VIETNAM

BANGLADESH

LAOS

SOUTH VIETNAM   PHILIPPINES

THAILAND

CAMBODIA

MALAYA

▲ Between 1948 and 1960, British troops were sent to Malaya to fight the communist guerrilla offensive. Here, soldiers of a jungle patrol rest under a temporary shelter.

During the Vietnam War (1964–75), many parts of the country were devastated. Thousands of civilians were killed, and others were made homeless and fled as refugees to neighbouring countries. Peace finally came in 1976 when Vietnam was united.

Ho-Chi Minh (1892–1969) was a founder member of the French Communist Party and a revolutionary Vietnamese leader. He led the struggle against the French colonial rule of Vietnam and American-supported South Vietnam.

WAR IN VIETNAM

After the French were defeated by Vietnamese communists in 1954, the country was temporarily divided into two – north and south. Planned elections for the country did not take place and the communists in the north started giving aid to South Vietnamese communists, the Viet Cong, to help them overthrow the government of Ngo Dinh Diem.

In 1965, the United States sent the first troops to help the south and by 1969 there were more than half a million US troops in Vietnam. After Richard Nixon became US president in 1969, he began to withdraw troops. A ceasefire was signed in 1973, and the remainder of American soldiers went home. During the war, more than 57,000 Americans were killed or went missing in action.

CIVIL WAR IN CAMBODIA

In Cambodia, a guerrilla army, the Khmer Rouge, was led by Pol Pot, and they sought to overthrow the government of Lon Nol. The Khmer Rouge took over Cambodia in 1975 and Pol Pot became prime minister. His terror regime ended in 1979 when he was overthrown by Vietnamese troops.

▲ After Richard Nixon (1913–94) became president in 1969, he began to withdraw US troops from Vietnam. In 1973, a ceasefire was signed and the US troops were withdrawn.

◄ In Cambodia, Pol Pot (1926–98) was the leader of the Khmer Rouge guerrillas. They fought a long civil war beginning in 1963, and finally took over the country in 1975. Over the following three years, it is estimated that between two and four million people were executed or died of famine and disease.

KEY DATES	
1950	North Korean forces invade South Korea
1953	Ceasefire in Korea
1954	Vietminh communists defeat the French and Vietnam is divided
1963	Civil war starts in Cambodia
1965	First US troops land in Vietnam
1969	Richard Nixon becomes US president
1973	All US troops withdrawn from Vietnam
1975	Pol Pot takes over Cambodia
1979	Pol Pot deposed by Vietnamese forces
1993	First free elections in Cambodia for 20 years

TERRORISM 1952–2000

During the latter half of the 20th century, many people used violence to promote particular political causes, often aimed at overthrowing the established order.

During 1981, some members of the Irish Republican Army (IRA) who were serving prison sentences in Northern Ireland for terrorist offences went on hunger strike. When one of them died, there was rioting.

▼ In 1988, an American jumbo jet was blown up by a bomb in mid-air over the Scottish town of Lockerbie, killing 270 people. Terrorists were suspected of being responsible for this act.

Some groups of people use violence (terrorism) to gain publicity and win support for a political cause. They are often called freedom fighters by their supporters. Terrorists murder and kidnap people, set off bombs and hijack aircraft. The reasons behind terrorism are not always the same. Some people want to spread their own political beliefs while others (nationalists or liberationists) want to establish a separate state for peoples who do not have a country of their own. For example, in the Middle East, terrorists have kidnapped people and carried out bombing campaigns to draw attention to the cause of the Palestinian people who do not have a homeland.

In Spain, an extreme group, *Euzkada Ta Askatasuna* (ETA) began a terrorist campaign in the 1960s to pressurize the government into creating a separate state for the Basque people. Similarly, in Northern Ireland, Nationalist groups such as the Irish Republican Army (IRA) escalated their terrorist campaign in the 1970s against British rule in the province.

In April 1995, a bomb exploded and destroyed the Federal Office building in Oklahoma City, USA. This was one of very few terrorist attacks on the North American mainland.

During the 1970s, the Red Army Faction were involved in acts of violence in West Germany. They robbed banks, and in 1977, kidnapped and murdered a businessman, Hans-Martin Schleyer. They were also involved in acts of terrorism carried out by Palestinians, including the murder of Israeli athletes at the 1972 Olympic Games in Munich. In Italy, in 1978, terrorists called the Red Brigade kidnapped and murdered the former prime minister of Italy, Aldo Moro.

Most governments around the world reject terrorist demands because they fear that to give in would only encourage other terrorists to commit violence.

FAMINE IN AFRICA 1967–2000

Africa has suffered periodic drought and famine since ancient times. More recently, civil war in newly independent states has only added to the misery.

In 1985, the pop musician Bob Geldof organized the Live Aid music concerts. These raised £50 million to help the victims of the famine in Ethiopia.

Widespread famines have occurred periodically in most parts of sub-Saharan Africa since ancient times. Factors such as a failure of the annual rains, poor soil conditions and negligible food reserves have all played a part in these tragedies. Following independence, in the latter half of the 20th century, civil wars have added to the misery.

CIVIL UNREST AND FAMINE

Most of the worst famines during this period happened in countries that suffered civil unrest. In Nigeria, the people who lived in the east of the country were the Christian Ibo tribe. They were oppressed by the majority Islamic Hausa and Fulani peoples. When tens of thousands of Ibos were massacred, the Eastern Region declared its independence as the state of Biafra in May 1967. War continued between the two sides until January 1970. It is believed that more than a million Biafrans died because the Nigerians stopped emergency food getting through.

▼ Zaire has had periods of military uprising and civil strife which has made life dangerous for foreign aid workers. In 1994, the arrival of hundreds of thousands of refugees from neighbouring Rwanda prompted massive aid from international relief agencies.

Civil strife in Mozambique in the 1980s led to the almost total collapse of health care, education and food production. By the beginning of the 1990s, nearly a million people had died and another million and a half had fled and were refugees in neighbouring countries.

During the 1991–93 civil war in Somalia, it is thought that about 300,000 people starved to death because the war made it too dangerous to deliver food aid.

Ethiopia suffered from drought and famine for many years. Between 1977 and 1991, the combination of civil war and famine killed millions of Ethiopians.

In Ethiopia, the combination of the withdrawal of aid from the USSR, drought and a civil war in the 1970s and 1980s led to millions of people dying from famine. Through the Western media, people all round the world became aware of the catastrophe. International relief charities, such as the Red Cross and Oxfam, the Live Aid pop concerts of 1985 and various governments all provided vast amounts of aid for the victims.

▲ Foreign aid is not only used to provide food for the starving people of Africa. This project provided clean water for a community in Kenya. Projects like this help to improve the health of the local people.

WARS IN THE MIDDLE EAST 1956–2000

Following the formation of the state of Israel in 1948 there have been many tensions in the Middle East that have led to bitter disputes and even war.

The Six Day War took place June 5–10, 1967. In a surprise attack, Israeli bombers destroyed Egyptian planes, and then sent in troops to capture the Egyptian soldiers left in Sinai.

▼ The Yom Kippur War began in 1973 when Egypt and Syria launched a surprise attack on Israel after it refused to give up land captured during the Six Day War.

The lands around Jerusalem have been believed for centuries by Jews to be the traditional home of the Jewish people. After World War II, many Jewish refugees settled in Palestine although the area was occupied by Arab peoples. The state of Israel was formed in 1948 and fighting broke out with neighbouring Arab countries and continued on and off for many years. In 1956, Egypt took over the control of the Suez Canal which was owned by Britain and France. Because it felt threatened, Israel invaded Egyptian territory in Sinai, and Britain and France attacked the canal area. There was international disapproval, and the USA and the USSR both called for a ceasefire. UN troops moved in to keep the peace after the withdrawal of Israeli, British and French troops.

There have been many conflicts in the Middle East between Israeli, Palestinian and Arab peoples, particularly since 1948. Some areas of territory are still in dispute.

Tensions continued to grow in the 1960s between Israel and the Arab countries of Egypt, Jordan and Syria. They were aided by several other Arab countries including Iraq, Kuwait, Saudi Arabia, Algeria and Sudan. Both sides were hostile and unwilling to negotiate differences. Both sides were also occupied with preparing their troops for a possible armed conflict. In May 1967, Egypt closed the Gulf of Aqaba to Israeli shipping.

In 1980, Iraq invaded Iran. The two countries fought a long and bitter war which was not to end until August 1988 and which cost the lives of over a million of their soldiers, with nearly two million wounded.

THE SIX DAY WAR

In June 1967, the Israeli air-force launched a surprise air attack on the Arab forces' air bases which put them completely out of action. Over a period of six days, the Israelis moved their army to occupy the Gaza Strip and parts of the Sinai. They also pushed back the border with Jordan and captured the Golan Heights from Syria.

IRAQI AGRESSION

In 1979, the Shah of Iran was deposed and replaced by Islamic fundamentalist Shiite Muslims led by the Ayatollah Khomeini. Tensions between Iran and Iraq finally resulted in Iraq invading the oil-rich Iranian territory of Khuzistan in 1980. Iraq feared the power of the new Iranian government set up by Ayatollah Khomeini. When the war ended in 1988, neither country had made any gains, but the cost to two nations was over a million dead with nearly two million injured.

Rivalries within the Arab world have often been caused by the region's oil deposits. In 1990, Iraq invaded Kuwait in order to improve its sea access. The UN Security Council passed several resolutions that demanded that Iraq immediately withdraw its troops. When Saddam Hussein refused, a multinational force led by the Americans forced him to withdraw. Kuwait City was liberated within the first five days and thousands of Iraqi soldiers were captured. Retreating Iraqi forces caused huge ecological damage because they set fire to most of Kuwait's oil wells.

Other tensions in the region are caused by religious differences. There are two main forms of Islam, Sunni and Shiite. Sunnis follow 'the practice of the Prophet'. Shiites follow the teachings of the Prophet Muhammad's son-in-law, Ali.

Saddam Hussein (b.1937) is the leader of Iraq. He fought a costly war against Iran (1980–88) and invaded Kuwait in August 1990. US, British and other Middle East forces drove him out in February 1991.

▼ The US forces mounted a massive international military campaign to liberate their ally Kuwait when Iraq invaded in 1990. Preparation for the war was extensive but the actual fighting was fairly short-lived.

KEY DATES

1948	Independent state of Israel declared; fighting with Arab neighbours erupts
1956	Suez crisis
1964	Palestinian Liberation Organization (PLO) founded in Lebanon
1967	Six Day War between Israel and Egypt
1973	Yom Kippur War in Israel
1979	Saddam Hussein rules Iraq
1979	Shah of Iran deposed
1980	Iraq invades Iran
1988	Iran–Iraq war ends
1990	Iraq invades Kuwait
1991	Iraq forced out of Kuwait

THE SCIENTIFIC REVOLUTION 1950–2000

The second half of the 20th century was a period of rapid development in science and technology. The age of the computer revolutionized people's lives.

Scientists and business people were able to develop discoveries made earlier in the century and put them to practical use. Business and industry realized that there were enormous financial benefits to be gained from working with universities and other academic institutions and important research was done through partnership between the two.

ELECTRONICS

One of the most breakthroughs invention was the silicon chip, a tiny component which could be cheaply mass-produced. It replaced old, bulky and fragile pieces of equipment, and enabled much smaller but more powerful electronic machines to be built. Microprocessors, complex circuits fitted onto a single chip, were widely used in electrical devices ranging from computers to space rockets and robots to telephones. The silicon chip influenced most people's lives in the late 20th century.

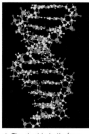

Since lasers were invented in the early 1960s, they have been used for a wide range of purposes that include eye surgery, construction work, mapping and weapons guidance systems.

▲ The double helix (two intertwined strands) of DNA was discovered by Francis Crick and James Watson in 1953. This structure carries the blueprint for life. The discovery is helping scientists understand the causes of many diseases.

▶ By 1990, many repetitive tasks, such as the assembly-line manufacture of cars, were being carried out by computer-controlled robots. This meant that industry operated more efficiently, but it also resulted in the reduction of the human workforce.

The silicon chip microprocessor was developed in the USA in 1971 and brought about a technological revolution. The chips were 'printed' with tiny electrical circuits that enabled computers to process and store information.

THE COMPUTER AGE

The developments in electronics also generated a revolution in communications. Photocopiers and fax machines, meant that office workers could handle vast amounts of information more quickly than before. They could also communicate rapidly with other offices around the world. As electronic communications spread throughout the world, information became more freely available. By the end of the 20th century, anyone with a personal computer and a phone line could contact millions of other people around the world in an instant using the Internet.

In industry, electronics also brought about a new industrial revolution. By the 1990s, most aspects of the manufacturing process in a wide range of industries were computer controlled. Repetitive tasks on assembly lines were carried out by electronic machines known as robots. Stock control, distribution and administrative systems also came under the control of computer technology.

MEDICAL BREAKTHROUGHS

First developed in the 1960s, lasers were used in surgery to clear diseased tissue and carry out delicate eye operations.

In the 1950s, British and American scientists discovered the structure of DNA, the basic building blocks from which living cells are made. This led to the production by genetic engineering of new drugs which helped cure serious diseases. The discovery of DNA means that it will one day be possible to cure many genetic illnesses, passed down through families.

Genetic engineering also meant that the new or improved strains of plants and animals, resistant to disease, could be created in the laboratory. This technology is already helping to feed people in poorer countries. There are concerns, however, that genetically modified (GM) foods may affect human health. All GM foods must be thoroughly tested.

◀ The Hubble Space Telescope was launched into orbit by the US space shuttle *Discovery* in April 1990. It enabled scientists to produce images of objects billions of light years away in space.

▲ The first communication satellite was launched in 1960. The introduction, in 1964, of geosynchronous satellites, which remain over the same place on Earth, meant that any two places on Earth could be linked almost instantly.

THE WORLD WIDE WEB

The World Wide Web (www) was invented in 1990 so that users could 'surf the net' quickly. By clicking on hot-spots on the screen with the mouse, the user jumps to pages of information consisting of words and pictures located on various computers around the world. Each of these has its own hot-spots which led to further pages.

▼ Search engines greatly speed up the process of finding Web pages and specific pieces of information on the Web.

▼ People are able to view live video clips of a current US space mission from NASA.

▲ Many goods and services can be ordered and paid for over the Internet.

▶ Using email, people can send letters and pictures to one another across the world within minutes.

◀ Information on shows, films, zoos, circuses and many other forms of entertainment can be found on the Internet.

THE ENVIRONMENT 1950–2000

Unlike any other species on Earth, humans have the power to destroy the whole world. Only recently did people realize that the environment was threatened.

In the latter half of the 20th century, people began to realize that the Earth was in danger, threatened with pollution and over-exploitation as a result of ignorance and greed. At first only a few naturalists, such as Rachel Carson, dared to speak up. Her book *Silent Spring* caused a sensation when it was published in the 1950s. It showed how widespread the damage caused by pesticides was, and led to the banning of DDT in the USA in 1973, as well as in many other countries. Then pressure groups such as Friends of the Earth and Greenpeace also began to campaign. It slowly became clear that the environment had been seriously damaged.

The oceans in many parts of the world had been over-fished, and in many cases, scientists believed that for stocks to return to their previous levels, fishing would have to stop completely for between five and ten years. Car exhausts and factories pumped fumes into the air. Some of these gases mixed with clouds to form acid rain which kills plants. In many of the world's larger cities, like Los Angeles in California, the air quality was so polluted that a smog formed over them. Continual exposure to smog causes serious breathing problems and premature death.

On the night of March 24, 1989, the *Exxon Valdez*, a 300-metre long oil tanker, ran aground in Prince William Sound, Alaska. The ship leaked more than 35,000 tonnes of toxic petroleum over the next two days and was the biggest oil spill in American history, destroying wildlife and causing a major clean-up operation.

▼ Cities such as Sao Paulo in Brazil suffered from dangerous levels of air pollution from motor vehicles and industry.

Hundreds of oil-well fires were lit when retreating Iraqi troops left Kuwait in 1991 causing widespread pollution to the desert. It took a whole year to extinguish them all.

PROTECTING THE ENVIRONMENT

In the 1970s, British scientists working in Antarctica discovered that the ozone layer above them was becoming thinner. The ozone layer is vital to all life on Earth because it blocks much of the Sun's harmful ultraviolet radiation. It was soon learned that this protective barrier was being seriously damaged by the release of chemicals called CFCs, which were used in refrigeration and for aerosols. These chemicals have now been banned in the many countries.

By the 1980s, some governments passed laws to protect the environment, but some scientists believed that these attempts to protect our planet were too little and too late. Change was slow to take effect because at first people did not believe that the Earth was really in danger. New information was collected by scientists which proved that the threat was real. Clean (non-polluting) products started to appear but they proved expensive to buy and less profitable to produce.

It took environmental disasters such as accidents at nuclear reactors in the USA and the USSR, explosions at chemical plants in Italy and India, and oil spillage at sea, to show people that new technology could be deadly.

▲ Huge tracts of the tropical rainforests in South America are being destroyed so that local farmers can graze cattle.

Public opinion gradually forced many governments to take action and to reduce pollution. Laws were passed to protect the environment and encourage conservation and recycling.

However, in poorer countries of the world, people's only income still comes from farming or forestry which often damages the land. Their governments do not like being told by the developed world to slow growth and reduce pollution.

▲ In 1900, the world's population was around one billion. By 1990, it had risen to almost six billion. In the year 2050, almost 10 billion people will be living on the Earth.

RENEWABLE ENERGY

Most of the world's electricity is produced in power stations by burning coal, oil or gas. These fuels are known as fossil fuels and there is a limited supply of them to be taken from the Earth. Electricity made by using the force of energy from rivers (hydroelectric power), the energy from the Sun (solar energy) and from the wind (wind power), are non-polluting and are all renewable because they will not run out.

▼ Wind turbines are built on exposed sites where wind power is used to generate electricity.

▶ Solar power uses the Sun's heat to provide a clean, non-polluting source of energy.

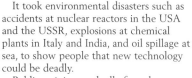

ASIAN ECONOMIES 1970–2000

With the help of Western aid, monetary growth in the 'tiger' economies of southeast Asia was very rapid. It soon outstripped that of the Europe and the USA.

Manufacturing was the single most important economic activity in Japan. Japanese factories used the most advanced equipment and processes available, producing high-quality goods for export to the rest of the world.

In Japan, government and business had to rebuild their economy after their defeat in World War II. They followed a different approach to China and planned a complete industrial redevelopment of their country, and rapid capitalist growth. America had occupied the Japanese islands and encouraged them to move to a democracy. They also helped Japan financially and after the war the Americans provided money at the rate of more than ten million dollars a week. The Japanese brought in industrial and land reforms and greatly improved the education system for their children. Free elections were held and women were not only allowed to vote for the first time, but some were elected to the Japanese parliament. In the 1970s and 1980s, Japan's economic growth was one of the most rapid in the world.

Along with other stock markets around the world, the Tokyo Stock Market saw panic selling in October 1987. In one day, it traded over one billion shares.

OTHER ECONOMIES

Although it took longer to get started, by the late 1970s and 1980s, South Korea's industrialization was growing at nearly ten percent every year, far more than Western countries. Again, the USA supplied aid and Japan helped as well. Hong Kong also became a major southeast Asian financial trading centre, attracting a large quantity of outside investment.

Malaysia became a major exporter of both raw materials and metals such as tin, oil and natural gas, rubber, palm oil and timber, as well as manufactured goods such as electrical machinery and semiconductors.

Singapore soon became one of the countries with a high standard of living when, in the 1960s, it began to build up its industry. Shipping took a growing part in the economy along with the establishment of extensive oil refineries. Singapore became a major exporter of petroleum products, rubber and electrical goods.

By the beginning of the 1990s, these economies gradually suffered from the downturn in world markets. Japan's export-led economy, worth more than half the region's total, had been in poor shape since 1989, and over the next ten years, its stockmarket value fell by two-thirds. This inevitably had a knock-on effect on the other countries in the region and slowed their growth dramatically.

Built as a symbol of Malaysia's once-booming economy, the twin Petronas Towers in Kuala Lumpur are the world's tallest office buildings at a height of 452 metres.

PEACEKEEPING 1950–2000

In 1945, the international community formed the United Nations to guarantee civil liberties and to work for peace and stability on a global scale.

Fifty countries formed the United Nations after the end of World War II. At the end of the century, the membership had increased to over 180.

The United Nations was formed after World War II with the intention of trying to ensure that such a war could not happen again. It was established to maintain international peace and security, to develop friendly relations among nations, to achieve international co-operation in solving economic, social and cultural problems and to encourage respect for human rights and for fundamental freedoms. Delegates from 50 nations attended what was known as the United Nations Conference on International Organization in San Francisco in April 1945. The United Nations charter was approved in June, and the organization's headquarters were located in New York.

▲ The civil war in Lebanon between Christians and a Muslim–PLO alliance in 1975–76 caused much destruction and bloodshed. United Nations forces were sent in as a peacekeeping force.

THE SECURITY COUNCIL

Keeping international peace is the job of the UN Security Council. The permanent members are China, France, Britain, the USA and Russia; there are ten other members who are elected for two-year terms.

▶ During conflicts in the former Yugoslavia in the 1990s, UN peacekeeping troops were fired upon by more than one side. Here, French UN troops keep a watchful eye out for snipers in Sarajevo's notorious sniper alley.

During the 1990s, Britain used its significant naval presence to support UN peacekeeping and humanitarian missions in many parts of the world.

WORLD PEACEKEEPING

A United Nations peacekeeping force was used for the first time during the Korean War in 1950, and they remained there until 1953, when an armistice was signed. Further deployment occurred in Egypt during the Suez Crisis in 1956 when UN forces supervized the withdrawal of invading British, French and Israeli forces.

The first large-scale UN operation in Africa went into action in 1960. Belgium had granted independence to the Republic of the Congo, now known as Zaire, but civil unrest threatened the new country. UN troops were able to provide aid as well as security. In the following years, UN peacekeeping forces were involved in many troubled areas of the world including Cyprus, Lebanon, Somalia and Rwanda.

SOUTH AFRICA 1990–2000

South Africa was the last bastion of imperialist, white minority rule in Africa. The release of Nelson Mandela from prison in 1990 signalled the end of apartheid.

Frederick W. de Klerk (b.1936) became president of South Africa in 1989 after P. W. Botha resigned through ill health. De Klerk worked towards ending apartheid.

▲ Nelson Rolihlahla Mandela (b.1918) shared the Nobel Peace Prize with F. W. de Klerk in 1993 for their work in ending apartheid. Following free elections in 1994, he became the first black president of South Africa.

▶ Under apartheid, many black South Africans were moved out of cities and forced to live in slum conditions in shanty towns on the outskirts.

Apartheid, the separation of people according to their colour or race, was begun by the Boers in South Africa at the beginning of the 20th century. It separated the people of South Africa into whites, black Africans and 'coloureds', people of mixed race. Asians were later added as a fourth group. The African National Congress (ANC) was formed in 1912 to fight these repressive laws.

The South African, white-dominated, government brought in a series of harsh laws to try to suppress opposition. In 1960, it made all black political parties illegal after the violent anti-apartheid riots at Sharpeville. In the mid-1970s, the government relaxed its controls a little and started to allow some unions. In the mid-1980s, the government allowed coloureds into Parliament but not black people.

The ANC and other black political parties wanted a true democracy where everyone had a vote irrespective of their colour or race. P. W. Botha, president of South Africa from 1978, was the first white leader to want reform.

As the Archbishop of Cape Town and head of the Anglican church, Desmond Tutu (b.1931) won the Nobel Peace Prize in 1984 for his fight against apartheid.

THE REFORMER

Although Botha had brought in some changes to make life fairer for blacks these had not made a radical difference. His health failed him and he resigned in 1989. A reformer, F. W. de Klerk, then became president, and in 1990, ended the ban on black people's political parties, including the ANC. In order to show he really intended change, he also had many black political prisoners released from prison. One of these was Nelson Mandela, who had been in prison since 1964. De Klerk had regular meetings with him, both while he was in prison and after his release.

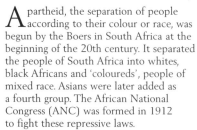

THE END OF APARTHEID

Nelson Mandela became the leader of the ANC. He campaigned for the civil rights of his people, but he also argued strongly for a peaceful settlement. By working closely with de Klerk, it was possible for both white and black people to work for change. In 1992, de Klerk organized a whites-only referendum that asked whether they would like to end apartheid. Two-thirds of the votes were in favour of ending apartheid.

After a great deal of negotiation, the first free election, in which black people could also vote, was held in South Africa in April 1994. The ANC won a decisive victory and Nelson Mandela became the first black president of South Africa when de Klerk handed over power to him in May. Although the ANC now formed a government, de Klerk stayed on as one of two vice-presidents.

Although a great victory for equality had been won, the new democracy still faced enormous problems. By the end of the century there were two million children who were receiving no schooling at all. Over half of the people still lived in homes without electricity. Twelve million people had no access to a steady supply of clean drinking water. A third of the adult population was unemployed. And the great gap between the rich and the poor created a major rise in street crime.

▲ The modern city of Johannesburg is the financial centre of South Africa and lies in the area known as Witwatersrand, at the heart of the gold mining area.

▲ Supporters of Nelson Mandela celebrate the triumph of the African National Congress after the first free elections in South Africa in 1994. The ANC were clear winners and Nelson Mandela became president.

◀ Following the end of apartheid, some South African white farmers were concerned that the huge farms that they lived on would be taken away from them by the government and given to black farmers in land redistribution.

YEAR 2000 AND BEYOND

The 20th century ended with a technological revolution yet our world is still threatened by war, poverty and human rights abuses. What does the future hold for us?

Racial harmony, tolerance, equal opportunity and individual freedom will be important factors taught to young people for achieving world peace and prosperity in the future.

The 20th century saw more change in the world than any previous century. Most of the household objects that we now use every day and take for granted did not exist a hundred years ago. The motor car was in its infancy and telephone and radio were still in the early stages of development. The televison, video recorder, credit card, computer and jet aeroplane had not yet been thought of.

At the end of the 20th century, the ability to communicate with people all over the world, thanks to the Internet and modern satellite telecommunications, brought about an explosion of information exchange. It also made it difficult for some governments to keep people in ignorance of what was happening elsewhere.

PREDICTIONS AND CONCERNS

It would have been very hard for someone living in 1900 to foretell these changes and we can only guess at our future during the coming century.

There are some things that seem likely – for example, that doctors and scientists will invent new ways of preventing and curing more diseases. Other predictions are more speculative. We would like to think that major wars will be a thing of the past, but there is no guarantee of this.

The growing population of the world is a major concern for the future. Although as a planet we grow enough food to feed everyone, millions go without because it is not distributed evenly. Most of the children in poorer countries still receive little or no education, which makes self-improvement impossible.

The environmental concerns of the latter half of the 20th century will continue to perplex governments and scientists. The Earth has finite resources that need to be carefully looked after and shared among all of its peoples.

International co-operation will be an important factor in the exploration of our resource-rich solar system. This artist's impression of a manned base on Mars shows what many people believe will be the next great space adventure. It will take an enormous amount of money and resources to accomplish, but there is good reason to believe it may happen in the first half of the 21st century.

INDEX

ACKNOWLEDGEMENTS

The publishers wish to thank the following for their contributions to this book:

Photographs

(*t* = top; *b* = bottom; *m* = middle; *l* = left; *r* = right)
Page 1 *bl* ET Archive, *ml* Bridgeman Art Library; 2 *mtl* Werner Forman Archive, *m* ET Archive; 6–7 Gavin Hellier/Robert Harding Picture Library; 8 Robert Harding Picture Library; 16 ET Archive; 17 Ancient Art & Architecture Collection Ltd; 18 AKG; 19 *t* ET Archive, *ml* AKG; 20 ET Archive; 21 ET Archive; 22 *tl* ET Archive, *bl* ET Archive, *br* ET Archive; 23 ET Archive; 27 Ancient Art & Architecture Collection Ltd; 28 ET Archive; 30 ET Archive; 32 AKG; 33 ET Archive; 34 ET Archive; 36 *t* ET Archive, *b* ET Archive; 38 Roy Rainford/Robert Harding Picture Library; 47 *t* Ronald Sheridan/Ancient Art & Architecture Collection Ltd, *b* Ronald Sheridan/Ancient Art & Architecture Collection Ltd; 57 Robert Harding Picture Library; 58 Richard Ashworth/Robert Harding Picture Library; 59 Richard Ashworth/Robert Harding Picture Library; 61 ET Archive; 63 *t* ET Archive, *b* ET Archive; 65 Ancient Art & Architecture Collection Ltd; 68 Robert Frerck/Robert Harding Picture Library; 69 Bridgeman Art Library; 72 Bridgeman Art Library; 73 *t* ET Archive, *b* ET Archive; 77 ET Archive; 78 *tl* Ancient Art & Architecture Collection, *tr* Bridgeman Art Library, *b* Bridgeman Art Library; 80 ET Archive; 81 The Bridgeman Art Library; 87 AKG; 89 *t* Robert Harding Picture Library, *b* Robert Harding Picture Library; 92 Bridgeman Art Library; 95 *t* R. Sheridan/Ancient Art & Architecture Collection, *m* Ancient Art & Architecture Collection; 96 *t* ET Archive, *b* ET Archive; 97 *tl* ET Archive, *tr* ET Archive; 98 ET Archive; 104 ET Archive; 106 ET Archive; 107 ET Archive; 112 ET Archive; 113 ET Archive; 115 Robert Harding Picture Library/Geoff Renner; 120 ET Archive; 124 ET Archive; 125 *m* ET Archive, *b* ET Archive; 126 Robert Harding Picture Library; 127 A. Barrington/Ancient Art & Architecture Collection; 128 ET Archive; 137 *tl* ET Archive, *tr* ET Archive, *b* ET Archive; 138 Bridgeman Art Library; 139 ET Archive; 144 *tl* Werner Forman Archive, *tr* Werner Forman Archive, *bl* Werner Forman Archive; 145 Bridgeman Art Library; 147 ET Archive; 150 Bridgeman Art Library; 155 *t* Ancient Art & Architecture Collection Ltd, *b* Bridgeman Art Library; 156 Bridgeman Art Library; 157 *t* AKG, *b* AKG; 160 Margaret Collier/Robert Harding Picture Library; 163 *mr* ET Archive, *br* ET Archive; 164 Werner Forman Archive; 165 Werner Forman Archive; 167 Bridgeman Art Library; 168 *tl* ET Archive, *ml* AKG; 169 *t* AKG, *m* AKG, *b* AKG; 171 *t* ET Archive, *b* Ancient Art & Architecture Collection Ltd; 173 Bridgeman Art Library; 175 ET Archive; 176 Bridgeman Art Library; 177 *t* Bridgeman Art Library, *m* Werner Forman Archive; 178 *t* ET Archive, *b* ET Archive; 179 *t* ET Archive, *b* ET Archive; 182 Bridgeman Art Library; 183 *t* AKG, *m* ET Archive; 184 *t* Bridgeman Art Library, *b* Bridgeman Art Library; 185 Bridgeman Art Library; 186 *tl* ET Archive, *ml* Bridgeman Art Library; 190 ET Archive; 194 ET Archive; 195 ET Archive; 196 *l* Bridgeman Art Library, *b* Bridgeman Art Library; 197 *t* ET Archive, *m* ET Archive; 198 ET Archive; 199 ET Archive; 201 ET Archive; 203 *t* Bridgeman Art Library, *b* Bridgeman Art Library; 205 ET Archive, *b* ET Archive; 206 *tl* ET Archive, *tr* ET Archive; 207 ET Archive; 208 *tl* ET Archive, *ml* ET Archive; 209 ET Archive; 217 Peter Newark's American Pictures; 218 ET Archive; 219 ET Archive; 220 ET Archive; 223 ET Archive; 226 *tl* ET Archive, *b* ET Archive; 227 *t* ET Archive, *b* ET Archive; 228 ET Archive; 229 *t* ET Archive, *b* ET Archive; 230 ET Archive; 231 *t* ET Archive, *b* ET Archive; 233 Hulton Getty Picture Library; 234 Hulton Getty Picture Library; 235 AKG; 236 ET Archive; 237 ET Archive; 238 ET Archive; 239 ET Archive; 241 ET Archive; 242 *tr* Hulton Getty Picture Library, *ml* Hulton Getty Picture Library, *b* ET Archive; 243 ET Archive; 244 *t* Hulton Getty Picture Library, *b* ET Archive; 245 ET Archive; 246 ET Archive; 247 ET Archive; 248 *ml* Peter Newark's American Pictures, *bl* Peter Newark's American Pictures; 249 Mary Evans Picture Library; 250 ET Archive; 251 ET Archive; 252 ET Archive; 254 ET Archive; 255 Imperial War Museum; 256 ILN; 257 *t* Hulton Deutsch Collection, *b* Hulton Getty Picture Library; 258 ET Archive; 259 *b* ET Archive; 260 Hulton Getty Picture Library; 261 Hulton Getty Picture Library; 262 *tl* ILN, *ml* ILN, *tr* ILN; 263 *tl* ET Archive, *tr* ILN, *mr* ILN; 264 *tl* Imperial War Musem, *tr* ET Archive, *b* ET Archive; 265 *tr* ET Archive, *mr* ILN; 266 *tl* ILN, *b* Hulton Deutsch Collection; 267 *t* Hulton Getty Picture Library, *mr* ET Archive, *br* ILN, *bl* ET Archive;

268 *tl* Hulton Getty Picture Library, *tr* Hulton Getty Picture Library, *bl* Hulton Getty Picture Library; 269 *mr* Corbis, *b* Novosti; 270 *tl* AKG, *ml* ILN, *b* ET Archive; 271 *t* ILN, *tr* AKG, *br* AKG; 272 *tl* ILN, *ml* ET Archive, *tr* Magnum Photos, *b* Magnum Photos; 273 *tr* ET Archive, *b* ET Archive; 274 *tl* AKG, *ml* AKG, *tr* ET Archive, *b* AKG; 275 *tl* ILN, *tr* ET Archive, *b* ET Archive; 276 *tr* ILN, *b* ET Archive; 277 *tr* Imperial War Museum, *m* ILN; 278 ET Archive; 279 *tr* Imperial War Museum, *b* ET Archive; 280 *tl* ET Archive, *b* ET Archive; 281 *tl* ET Archive, *tr* ET Archive, *ml* ILN, *br* Hulton Getty Picture Library; 282 Hulton Deutsch Collection; 283 *tr* Hulton Getty Picture Library, *bl* Hulton Getty Picture Library; 284 *tl* Imperial War Museum, *b* Hulton Getty Picture Library; 285 ET Archive; 286 Science & Society Picture Library; 288 Bridgeman Art Library, *br* Stuart Franklin/Magnum Photos, *bl* G.Mendel/Magnum Photos; 290 *tr* Popperfoto, *bl* Rex Features; 291 *t* Hulton Getty Picture Library, *m* Magnum Photos, *br* ET Archive, *bl* Hulton Getty Picture Library; 292 *ml* Novosti/Science Photo Library, *bl* NASA/Science Photo Library, *tr* NASA/Science Photo Library; 293 *t* NASA/Science Photo Library, *b* NASA/Science Photo Library; 294 *tr* OECD, *b* Elliot Erwitt/Magnum Photos; 295 *t* Abbas/Magnum Photos, *mr* Popperfoto/Reuters, *b* European Parliament/Airdiasol; 296 *tl* Hulton Getty Picture Library, *tr* Roger-Viollet, *bl* Corbis; 297 *t* Magnum Photos, *b* Griffiths/Magnum Photos; 298 *tl* James Natchwey/Magnum Photos, *tr* Rex Features, *b* Rex Features; 299 *tr* F. Scianna/Magnum Photos, *bl* Liba Taylor/Robert Harding Picture Library, *br* Robert Harding Picture Library; 300 *tl* Burt Glinn/Magnum Photos, *b* Jones-Griffiths/Magnum Photos; 301 *t* Jean Gaumy/Magnum Photos, *mr* Stuart Franklin/Magnum, *br* Steve McCurry/Magnum Photos; 302 *tl* Hank Morgan/University of Massachusetts at Amherst/Science Photo Library, *ml* Alfred Pasieka/Science Photo Library, *b* Brian Brake/Science Photo Library, *t* Tim Davis/Science Photo Library, *tr* Dr Jeremy Burgess/Science Photo Library; 303 *t* NASA/Science Photo Library, *mr* NASA/Science Photo Library; 304 *tr* Steve McCurry/Magnum Photos, *b* Bruno Barbey/Magnum Photos; 305 *tl* G.Peress/Magnum Photos, *tr* Thomas Hopker/Magnum Photos, *bl* Russell D. Curtis/Science Photo Library, *br* Martin Bond/Science Photo Library; 306 *tl* Robert Harding Picture Library, *bl* Rob Francis/Robert Harding Picture Library, *tr* Rene Burri/Magnum Photos; 307 *ml* Micha Bar-Am/Magnum Photos, *br* Paul Lowe/Magnum Photos; 308 *tl* G.Mendel/Magnum Photos, *ml* G.Mendel/Magnum Photos, *b* Frank Spooner Pictures/Gamma, *tr* Gideon Mendel/Magnum Photos; 309 *t* Frank Spooner Pictures/Gamma, *m* Frank Spooner Pictures/Gamma, *b* Frank Spooner Pictures/Gamma; 310 *tl* Eli Reed/Magnum Photos, *b* Detlev Van Ravenwaay/Science Photo Library.

Artwork archivists Wendy Allison, Steve Robinson

Editorial and design Aimee Johnson, Sheila Clewley, Julie Ferris, Emma Wild, Dileri Johnston, Giles Sparrow, Joanne Brown

Artists Jonathan Adams, Hemesh Alles, Marion Appleton, Sue Barclay, R. Barnett, Noel Bateman, Simon Bishop, Richard Bonson, Nick Cannan, Vanessa Card, Tony Chance, Harry Clow, Stephen Conlin, Peter Dennis, Dave Etchell, Jeff Farrow, James Field, Ian Fish, Michael Fisher, Eugene Fleury, Chris Forsey, Dewey Franklin, Terry Gabbey, Fred Gambino, John Gillatt, Matthew Gore, Jeremy Gower, Neil Gower, Ray Grinaway, Allan Hardcastle, Nick Harris, Nicholas Hewetson, Bruce Hogarth, Christian Hook, Richard Hook, Simon Huson, John James, Peter Jarvis, John Kelly, Deborah Kindred, Adrian Lascombe, Chris Lenthall, Jason Lewis, Chris Lyon, Kevin Maddison, Shirley Mallinson, Shane Marsh, David MacAllister, Angus McBride, Stefan Morris, Jackie Moore, Teresa Morris, Frank Nichols, Chris D. Orr, Sharon Pallent, R. Payne, R. Philips, Jayne Pickering, Melvyn Pickering, Malcolm Porter, Mike Posen, Mike Roffe, Chris Rothero, David Salarya, Mike Saunders, Rodney Shackell, Rob Shone, Mark Stacey, Paul Stangroom, Branca Surla, Smiljka Surla, Stephen Sweet, Mike Taylor, George Thompson, Martin Wilson, David Wright, Paul Wright